ON WAR AND LEADERSHIP

ON WAR AND LEADERSHIP

THE WORDS OF COMBAT COMMANDERS
FROM FREDERICK THE GREAT TO
NORMAN SCHWARZKOPF

Owen Connelly

PRINCETON UNIVERSITY PRESS   PRINCETON AND OXFORD

Library of Congress Cataloging-in-Publication Data
Connelly, Owen, 1929–
On war and leadership : the words of combat commanders from Frederick the Great to
Norman Schwarzkopf / by Owen Connelly.
p. cm.
Includes bibliographical references and index.
ISBN 0-691-03186-X
1. Leadership.   2. Command of troops.   3. Military history.   4. Decision making.
UB210 .C67 2002
355.3'3041—dc21   2002016914

This book has been composed in Berkeley Oldstyle Typeface

Printed on acid-free paper. ∞

www.pupress.princeton.edu

Printed in the United States of America

10 9 8 7 6 5 4 3

Contents

Acknowledgments ───────────────────

First, I thank my editor, Brigitta van Rheinberg, who "kept me in the game"; without her support, this book might never have appeared. My gratitude extends also to her coworkers, notably Carol Hagan, Bill Laznovsky, Elise Bajo, and Jodi Beder.

General Hal Moore was wonderfully helpful and generous, as was Joe Galloway; they are *exceptional* men. General Nick Vaux, Royal Marine Commandos, gave me support with a dash of wry British humor. Major Dik Daso, USAF (fighter pilot–historian), put me in touch with General Chuck Horner, Air Force commander in the Gulf War, who briefed me on his style of leadership.

Among others who gave me guidance were my friends Dennis Showalter (Colorado College), Dr. Hal Winton (School of Advanced Airpower Studies), and S. Paul MacKenzie (University of South Carolina). At the Institute for Advanced Study, Princeton, I am grateful to Director Phillip A. Griffiths, who allowed me extra time at that renowned place, and Peter Paret, who invited me to join his "Levée-en-masse Seminar" (1995–97), whose members, especially Alan Forrest (York University) and Dan Moran (Naval Postgraduate School), extended me sage counsel. And I acknowledge the favor of the Directors of the *Consortium on Revolutionary Europe*, who allowed me to use its meetings as a sounding board for many of the concepts and quotations used in this book. I must also thank my department chairs at U.S.C., successively Peter Becker and Pat Maney, for allowing me free time and travel funds.

Finally, I extend my heartfelt appreciation to assistants who facilitated my work over the years: Robert Alderson (now Ph.D.), James Elkins, Mark Mayer, Scott Hileman, and Bart Brodowski.

Chapter VII: Excerpts from The Rommel Papers *copyright © 1953 by B. H. Liddell-Hart and renewed 1981 by Lady Kathleen Liddell-Hart, Fritz Bayerlein-Dittmar, and Manfred Rommel. Reprinted by permission of Harcourt, Inc., and David Higham Associates, Ltd.*

Chapter VIII: Excerpts from The Patton Papers, *2 vols., edited by Martin Blumenson. Copyright © 1974 by Martin Blumenson. Reprinted by permission of Houghton Mifflin Company. All rights reserved.*

Chapter X: Excerpts reprinted with permission from Lost Victories *by Erich von Manstein, ca. 1958. Published in the United States in 1982 by Presidio Press, 505B San Marin Drive, ste. 160, Novato, CA 94945.*

Chapter XII: Excerpts from Defeat into Victory *by Field Marshall Sir William Slim. 2d ed. London: Cassell & Co, 1956. Copyright holder unknown.*

Chapter XIV: Excerpts from Soldier: The Memoirs of Matthew B. Ridgway *by General Matthew B. Ridgway. Copyright © 1956 by Matthew B. Ridgway and Harold H. Martin. Copyright © 1956 by Curtis Publishing Company. Copyright renewed 1984. Reprinted by permission of HarperCollins Publishers, Inc.*

Chapter XVII: Excerpts from We Were Soldiers Once . . . and Young *by Lt. Gen. H. G. Moore and Joseph L. Galloway. Copyright © 1992 by Lt. Gen. H. G. Moore and Joseph L. Galloway. Used by permission of Random House, Inc.*

Chapter XVIII: Excerpts from Take That Hill! Royal Marines in the Falklands War *by Maj. Gen. Nick Vaux. McLean, VA: Brassey's (US), 1990.*

Chapter XIX: Excerpts from It Doesn't Take a Hero *by General H. Norman Schwarzkopf and Peter Petre. Copyright © 1992 by H. Norman Schwarzkopf. Used by permission of Bantam Books, a division of Random House, Inc.*

ON WAR *AND* LEADERSHIP

Introduction _____

THIS IS an anthology of the thoughts on leadership of combat commanders—twenty in all—over the past 250 years. Their written (or spoken) words are quoted from primary sources—translated where necessary. They are Western leaders, save Vo Nguyen Giap (a North Vietnamese general) and perhaps Moshe Dayan (an Israeli commander but European in culture and training). The views of warriors may help balance the scale of military thought, which, since the fall of Napoleon, has been tipped heavily toward theory by a surfeit of books, beginning with Carl von Clausewitz's *Vom Kriege* (1832)[1] and Antoine de Jomini's *Précis de l'art de la guerre* (1838).[2]

This collection should allow historians in general to try to discern (or divine) the commanders' ontological, epistemological, and teleological views (their hermeneutics are traditional), and surely be useful to military historians and their readers. It should also be of interest to people in all walks of life who make executive decisions, civil or military; they can compare their management and leadership ideas with those of military masters.

The leaders I have chosen all belong to what has been termed the "muddy boots" school of leadership.[3] This, of course, reflects my personal predilection. Among my choices, personalities vary from charismatic to enigmatic to stern to outwardly hateful (e.g., Joseph Stilwell, called "Vinegar Joe"). *But these men all led from the front.* This was true of Frederick the Great, Napoleon, and the others, whether (at the time their leadership is examined) they were at the head of armies (Sherman, Rommel, Patton, Ridgway); brigades or corps (Stonewall Jackson), battalions (Harold Moore, Nick Vaux), or guerrilla bands (Lawrence of Arabia, John Mosby), or had experience at both lower and higher command (DeGaulle, Manstein, Slim, Montgomery, Moshe Dayan, Giap, and Schwarzkopf). They were all also improvisors, believers in single command, and mildly or flagrantly eccentric.

Naturally, not all worthy commanders are quoted herein. Another writer might have chosen differently, and surely many of the best left no records because they were killed or lacked the talent, inclination, or personality to write or dictate their ideas.[4] The Elder Helmuth von Moltke does not figure in this collection because his chief work was perfecting the Prussian general staff. Ulysses S. Grant and Robert E. Lee of the American Civil War are passed over because neither addressed leadership issues in a forthright way; Sherman did and is included; he also represents what has been called the "American way of war."[5]

Soviet Marshal Georgii Konstantinovich Zhukov, of World War II, is also omitted, because he attributes his successes to Josef Stalin and the Communist
Party and his own leadership techniques are obscure. Vo Nguyen Giap shows
the same tendencies as Zhukov, but is quoted, since he was both a Communist Party leader and North Vietnam's generalissimo—and also because of
continuing American and Western interest in the Vietnam War. Other selec-
tions or exclusions were made on similar bases, or represent personal choices,
or, in part, the urge to give voice to reviled commanders (e.g., Wavell and
Stilwell), who did well, considering their circumstances, missions, and limited
resources.

Some of our commanders (e.g., Stonewall Jackson, Erwin Rommel) fought in
wars that were lost because their countries lacked effective political leadership,
or economic resources, or industry, or manpower, or allies, or all of these.
Others led their troops well, but lost because their societies were defeatist or
defensive-minded (e.g., DeGaulle in France in 1940),[6] or divided over support
of a war (e.g., Schwarzkopf—among hundreds of other dedicated officers and
NCOs—as a battalion commander in Vietnam).

All were effective *in their time*, in their war, with the troops they led. I have
put the commanders in chronological order because it seemed better to attach
commanders to particular wars, of which readers would have some knowledge,
rather than put them in categories. For example, a guerrilla category would
include Mosby and Lawrence; there were similarities in their operations, but
their wars and the societies and cultures that produced the commanders and
their troops were radically different. Mosby and his rangers and rebel sympathizers are presented in the context of the American Civil War, and Lawrence
and his Bedouins that of the First World War in the Middle East. In all cases,
the sociocultural milieu of troops—especially in mass warfare—has had a
marked effect on national or coalition power.

Of course *there have been dramatic changes in war* over more than two centu-
ries, which must be taken into account. As governments and societies changed,
so did war. Populations increased worldwide—44 to 100% in European nations
during the eighteenth century—and the trend continued, agriculture became
more technical, enabling ever fewer farmers to feed nations; labor was available
for industry, and opportunity bred entrepreneurs. Ever larger armies could be
fed and equipped. The same developments spawned democratic revolutions.[7]
With the spread of democracy, governments, whether authoritarian or representative, felt justified to draft citizens to fight and to demand universal support of
war efforts. As scientific and technical knowledge and industrial skill and capacity increased, armed forces took advantage of new "tools of war." Wars have
accelerated discovery and innovation when nations have put their resources
behind research. For example, the development of nuclear power, space explo-
ration, and satellite communication since 1945 has been based on advances in
nuclear science, electronics, and rocketry during World War II.[8]

The Changing Nature of War

The major changes in warfare since 1740 have derived from or been necessitated by the ever burgeoning *size* of armed forces through World War II (1939–45), followed by the reduction since 1945 of forces *actually deployed*; improvements in weaponry, communications and transportation; and the escalating need for armies to cooperate closely with navies and air forces. The trend through 1945 was toward total war; since 1945, toward limited war. We shall treat these changes chronologically.

Frederick the Great never commanded over 90,000 men in the field, and won his greatest victories with forces of 25–35,000. Napoleon's battlefield forces seldom numbered more than 70,000—though his total forces were much larger. (For example, the *Grande Armée* that invaded Russia [1812] was 611,000 strong, but Napoleon fought the greatest battle, Borodino, with 130,000 men.) Mass armies were raised first in revolutionary France by the *levée en masse* (1793), linked to the dictum that male citizens had a duty to fight for their country. (In 1794, French forces peaked at 800,000 [1,000,000 on paper], then declined.)[9] Conscription was continued by Napoleon, who liked to identify with the Revolution: "The Imperial Guard always marched to the *Marseillaise*."[10]

Neither the generals of the Revolution nor Napoleon could maneuver great masses of troops, however, given the primitive state of communications; nor could their economies support them. Neither could the generals of France's enemies who matched her field armies in size largely by traditional means.[11]

Weapons of this period were short-range: infantry muskets had a maximum range of 200–300 yards,[12] field artillery, 1,000 yards.[13] Horses pulled the cannon and supply wagons, and were mounts for officers, cavalry, and men of the horse artillery.[14] Commanders could *see* the whole battlefield—from one high hill or with a little galloping about. Communication was by messenger or visual or sound signal.[15]

In the American Civil War (1861–65), the Union fielded 2,300,000 men and the Confederacy 1,000,000—both using the draft.[16] The Spencer and Sharps carbines (.56) were used by the Union cavalry. A few Union infantry units had the Sharps rifle (.52), and some the Springfield rifled musket (.58), but the infantry on both sides fought mostly with smooth-bore muskets. The officers and cavalry had Colt and Remington six-shot pistols (.44 revolvers). Confederate officers' favorite was the nonissue .40 Lemat revolver, nine shot, with a shotgun barrel in the center. The Union army had a crude machine gun, the Gatling gun, with six rotating barrels. Rifled artillery was available, some breech-loading, as well as smooth-bore "Napoleons";[17] but all fire was still direct, at visible targets, and remained so until end of the century, so that often guns were judged by power, not range. Infantry used hand grenades, mines, and booby traps. Both sides transported troops by rail and communicated via electric telegraph. Generals (with exceptions) learned to stay out of artillery range.

In the nineteenth century, most western nations adopted conscription (the British not until 1916). During this time the Prussians devised a means to command mass armies—the *Grosse Generalstab* (Great General Staff), "perfected" by General (later Field Marshal) Helmuth von Moltke while chief of staff (1857–88). He used it to plan and win seemingly effortless victories over Austria in 1866 and France in 1870–71.[18] Moltke's triumphs convinced other powers to adopt the staff system, modified according to national inclinations.[19]

In *World War I (1914–18)* conscription produced the largest armies the world had yet seen. The British Empire mustered 8.9 million troops; France 8.4 million; the United States 4.4 million; Russia 12 million; and Germany 11 million. For the first time in large numbers, women had an official role, chiefly as nurses.

World War I saw the advent of the tank—clumsy and undependable, but able to roll over barbed wire and trenches. (On 20 November 1917, at Cambrai, 324 tanks led a British attack; by day's end over 300 were out of action—most of them broken down.) Horse cavalry was deployed, but was effective only in the Middle East and occasionally on the Russian front. The infantry had long-range magazine-fed rifles and belt-fed machine guns.[20] Field artillery and high-trajectory howitzers fired millions of high-explosive rounds on and behind enemy lines before attacks.[21] Both sides came to use poison gas. Airplanes and dirigibles were employed for observation, then as fighters and bombers. The aircraft were fragile but inspired hope in proponents of airpower. Glory went to fighter pilots,[22] but aircraft also supported ground action.[23]

Communication was by messenger (horse or motorcycle), telegraph, semaphore, and primitive radio. Horse- or oxen-drawn wagons, motorized trucks, and railroads carried supplies and troops.

Generals on both sides—down to division level—made few or no trips to the front lines, and commanded through staffs. Leadership was the most impersonal in history. Casualties were enormous.[24]

In *World War II (1939–45)* more men (and women) were mobilized than in the Great War. The United States mustered 14.9 million men and women; the British Empire raised 6.2 million; the USSR 25 million; Germany 12.5 million; Japan 7.5 million. Battle casualties were light for the western allies, but more civilians were killed than during World War I.[25] Many women entered the armed forces to fill noncombat positions. The U.S. Army Air Force had hundreds of women pilots, some of whom had such hazardous duty as flying aircraft from the United States to the war zones. The USSR had women in combat roles; their fighter pilots made an astonishing record.[26]

Tanks dominated the battlefield where terrain and weather allowed.[27] The German "Tiger" tank (88mm gun) was arguably the best, but came late and in small numbers. Infantry had improved magazine-fed rifles, carbines, grenades, mortars, the United States a 2.36 inch "bazooka" (shoulder-fired anti-tank rocket), and flamethrowers. German infantry had effective anti-tank guns. Heavy artillery could hit targets far behind enemy lines, light artillery in the opponent's rear.[28] The Germans had heavy *nebelwerfer* (rocket artillery).[29] Late in the war, U.S. and British four-engine bombers—1,000 or more, day and night—struck deep into Europe; larger U.S. B-29 bombers hit Japan. Allied fighters escorted bombers, tangled with German and Japanese aircraft, and supported ground troops. For the invasion of Normandy, the Allies put up over 5,000 bombers and 3,500 fighters. The Germans, with 1,424 aircraft of all types, were overwhelmed, although since late 1944 they had sent up 500 mph jet fighters, superior to anything flying. Their V-1 and V-2 rockets with heavy explosive warheads terrorized London in 1944. Naval aircraft carriers played a key role in the war against Japan, and helped elsewhere.

British and American cryptanalysts broke the German and Japanese military codes, which gave Allied commanders—ground, air, and naval—advance knowledge of enemy moves.[30] British technicians had invented radar to detect incoming aircraft and sonar to detect submarines before the war. The United States developed the atomic bomb; two, dropped on Japan in 1945, ended the war in Asia.[31]

The general and lower staffs were still standard, and had become even larger, but had less authority in operations, and more in logistical and personnel matters. The high commanders had been young officers in the Great War, and knew the hazards of the system. With vastly improved vehicles, tanks, aircraft, and weapons, strategists introduced maneuver back into the war. Generals had to handle both ground and air forces, make use of airborne troops, and cooperate with the navies. Command of the air and often the sea became mandatory for victory, although the war was still won by infantry, greatly aided by tanks, artillery, and fighter planes. There were superb commanders at army level who led personally, did their own reconnaissance, and trusted their intuition. (See chapters VII [Rommel] and VIII [Patton].)

Hardly had World War II ended when the *"Cold War"* *(1949–89)* began. It evolved into a standoff between the two major nuclear powers, the United States and the Soviet Union. Neither power was willing to risk war involving atomic weapons—even small "tactical" ones. Giant steps were made in technology; both nations developed rockets and guided missiles and put satellites into orbit—for general use and intelligence—and sent men into space. Both developed nuclear-powered naval vessels, including submarines capable of launching intercontinental ballistic missiles (ICBMs).

The real wars were either conventional and small-scale (e.g., the Arab-Israeli conflicts; the Falklands War) or ultimately fought for limited objectives (the Korean and Vietnam wars, both terminated by negotiation and without victory). Forces were reduced accordingly.

The *Korean War (1950–53)* pitted the forces of the Republic of (South) Korea, aided by United Nations (mainly U.S.) forces, against those of the People's Republic of (North) Korea, reinforced by Chinese units. The maximum strength of UN forces was about 500,000—two-thirds ground forces, eventually well equipped and supported by USAF and USN fighters and bombers and occasionally naval fire.

American infantry went in with World War II weapons, which sufficed, with some additions.[32] Helicopters were used for medical evacuation. New USAF jet aircraft took control of the skies, but were too fast to give the infantry accurate support; slower World War II fighters did the job. The U.S. Navy controlled the seas from the start. Transport included aircraft, railroad, trucks, and jeeps. It was a war of fronts until 1952, when lines of trenches and emplacements were built on both sides of a frequently violated DMZ (demilitarized zone) at the 38th parallel, during "peace talks." African-Americans, assigned to segregated units in previous wars, were integrated into formations of the U.S. Army, Navy, and Air Force for the first time.

After a very rocky start, leadership was personal, selfless, and inventive. Allies fielded elite units, notably British Commonwealth, French, and Turkish forces.

The war ended with the restoration of the (South) Korean Republic; an armistice was signed in July 1953, but no peace treaty. American and ROK troops remain in the DMZ today (2002).

The *Vietnam War (1964–73)* began after a decade of U.S. assistance to the anti-Communist (South) Vietnamese Republic and army (ARVN). U.S. forces were drawn into the ARVN antiguerrilla campaign, and in 1965 into war with the Peoples' Republic of (North) Vietnam.

At peak U.S. forces in this war numbered about 500,000. In nine years of fighting, some 3,000,000, many draftees, served tours of one year or less in Vietnam, mostly in ground forces.[33] Women and African-Americans were prominently represented. Conscription was abolished in the United States after this war.

American forces were well equipped throughout. Helicopters came into their own as gunships and cargo and troop carriers.[34] The infantry had improved rifles and machine guns, grenades, and the monster M-79 grenade launcher. They were backed by artillery, Army gunships, and USAF and USN planes.[35] The latter took control of the air, and at times heavy bombers struck at targets in North Vietnam and Cambodia. Tanks were of little use in the jungle. It was an infantry war; men moved in by air and on foot, and by truck in rear areas. Actions ranged from patrols to company and battalion "sweeps" to brief larger engagements. There were no fronts.

Generals normally visited by helicopter, or flew overhead and talked to lower commanders by radio. The more effective brigade and division commanders landed most often in battle zones. Leadership was good throughout at the fighting level, but became increasingly difficult as American society turned against the war. (See chapters XVII [Moore] and XIX [Schwarzkopf].) US forces never lost a major battle.

Washington opted to end the war by negotiation, and technically succeeded. All U.S. forces withdrew (late 1972), leaving the Army of the Republic of (South) Vietnam armed to defend the country. But the ARVN was demolished by the Peoples' Army of (North) Vietnam (PAVN), which attacked and unified Vietnam in 1975.

In the *Persian Gulf War (1991)*, U.S. and allied forces totalled 500,000 men and women—roughly 250,000 army, 80,000 air force, and 170,000 navy and marines, including U.S. reserve and National Guard units. Iraq had almost 600,000 men, virtually all ground troops. The U.S. infantry had improved versions of Vietnam-era weapons, plus new tank-killing guided missiles,[36] and moved in armored personnel carriers or infantry fighting vehicles (APCs or IFVs).[37] U.S. tanks mounted 105 and 120mm guns (plus machine guns). Artillery had heavy guns,[38] plus 12-barrel multiple rocket launchers, with computer fire control, launching projectiles of up to 334 pounds. Attack helicopters could launch up to 70 rockets. Ground forces were backed by USAF, USN, and allied fighters with advanced computer targeted and guided projectiles.[39]

Iraq was defeated in "100 hours"—24–27 February 1991—by the forces of the United States and her allies, after a lengthy air campaign. Allied armament overwhelmed the enemy. Leadership was professional, by the book, heavily dependent on staffs, and undramatic but effective. American officers took pains to see that the United States did not get into another "Vietnam situation."[40]

In the Gulf War the Allied force, although considered small, numbered more than the maximum Napoleon had on any battlefield (190,000, at Wagram, 1809).[41] Practically speaking, there was no limit to the range of weapons—taken all together. Every part of the enemy's homeland could be hit by artillery or aircraft rockets. The generals in command could view any given part of the battle via television; USAF commander General Charles Horner had such a good view and good radio connections with his aircraft that he could have micromanaged the air war, but declined to do so.[42] A U.S. infantry battalion in the Gulf had more than the firepower of Napoleon's entire *Grande Armée* of 1812. Napoleon had foot soldiers, horse-drawn artillery, and cavalry on horses that had to be rested frequently to be effective. In the Gulf, infantry went forward in tracked vehicles, the First Cavalry Division in helicopters. Tanks and self-propelled artillery kept pace. Aircraft, on instant call by radio, prepared the way and supported the ground forces. General Norman Schwarzkopf's task was far from simple, all the same. He had to know the capabilities and limitations of all his troops and their weapons, including Allied contingents. He had to execute on a front of over 600 miles what would have been a tactical envelopment for Napoleon on a front of perhaps five miles—holding on his right while delivering a massive left hook that penetrated the enemy rear.

About This Book

This book reveals much about the mind of the warrior, a player in every nation's life—his views on life, death, loyalty, duty, honor, patriotism, religion, sending men into battle; the degrees of cruelty and kindness to troops necessary for discipline while building trust, loyalty, and camaraderie; the proper regard due troops' families, and related matters. The commanders discuss problems of supply, the effectiveness of new weapons as they appear, when numbers count, the importance of airpower and sea power, and other matters.

The commanders quoted *in extenso* led troops who risked their lives in battle.

Such leaders are essential to victory—no matter how inspired the plans spun out at higher levels. Wars decide the fate of nations and the power balance in the world. That is a reality, however unpleasant. War has always been part of human history, and promises to continue to be; thus it should be fruitful to examine what successful military leaders have said, over the past 250 years, about how to lead men to victory.

The first chapter of this anthology gives, briskly, via aphorisms, the views of both Frederick the Great and Napoleon, to whom most of the our commanders express a debt.[43] Subsequent chapters are devoted to each of the other eighteen commanders. Each includes a short biographical sketch followed by passages quoted from their works (for which, in the cases of Jackson, Rommel, and Patton, their wives are greatly responsible) and for some, the writings of reliable associates.

Frederick, Napoleon, Montgomery, and some others left commentary or instructions intended to educate future leaders. Their thoughts have been organized under various headings. Some, like George Patton and Erich von Manstein, left a few disquisitions which can be so organized, but other parts of their *oeuvres* do not fit into neat categories, and have been left as written (except for editorial notations in *italics*). Others left only narrative accounts of their actions, interspersed with jottings in diaries or letters; Lawrence of Arabia, Erwin Rommel (for the most part), Moshe Dayan, Nick Vaux, and Norman Schwarzkopf are in this category. In such cases, a few headings have been added, but the narrative has been left undisturbed except when it was felt necessary to shorten certain sections; then summaries of intervening events have been supplied.

There are brief conclusions at the end of each chapter, but none make comparisons among commanders. The general conclusions at the end of the book discuss points of leadership on which all or most of them seem to agree, despite changes in the nature of war.

It is hoped that this book will find a readership. Perhaps it will also have a modest effect on how the "art of War" is taught, which would please a current resident of Valhalla, General George S. Patton, Jr., who wrote after World War II:

> The horrid thought obtrudes itself that, in spite of my efforts . . . the tactics of the next war will be written by someone who never fought and who acquired his knowledge by a . . . study of the regulations of this and the last World War, none of which were ever put into practice in battle.[44]

Bitter Root, Montana
1 April 2001

I

The Modern Originals

FREDERICK THE GREAT (1713–1786) AND

NAPOLEON (1769–1821)

This chapter differs from those that follow in that it largely comprises aphorisms. The intent was to make it short, but still give the major ideas of Frederick and Napoleon, to whom the commanders in the chapters that follow owe a debt.

Backgrounds

Among purveyors of wisdom on the art of war, Frederick the Great and Napoleon have surely had the most influence over the past 200 years. For whatever reasons, their pronouncements are strikingly similar on many subjects. Thus it seems reasonable to devote a single chapter to them and their thoughts.

The future Frederick II of Prussia had a miserable boyhood because his soldier-father, Frederick-William I (1688–1740), was enraged by his intellectual interests and flute-playing. Napoleon, future emperor of the French, grew up in Italian-speaking Corsica in a normal, happy home—if subject to his mother's stern discipline and religiosity. Frederick was "born to the purple," and Napoleon not, but both were trained to be officers—Frederick almost from birth, Napoleon from age 9 in royal French military schools.

Frederick acceded to the throne in 1740, and almost immediately began using his army to enlarge his kingdom. He left the field in the middle of his first battle, Mollwitz (1741), because one of his father's old generals, in command, predicted defeat; the battle was later won nevertheless. Angry with himself, he thereafter led in person with almost insane bravery. Stories tell of spent musket balls falling from his coat when he stopped at soldiers' campfires. He fought two wars (1741–45) with Austria, and the Seven Years War (1757–63) (aided only by Great Britain, largely with money) against Austria, her German Empire, France, and Russia. His forte was tactical misdirection of the enemy, preceded by strategic surprise, by which he defeated armies much larger than his own.

Napoleon was commissioned at 16, and at 24 was a general—thanks to his talent and the chaotic conditions of the French Revolutionary era. In 1796, at 26, he was given command of an army, and for 20 years he was the most feared general in Europe, fighting first for the French Republic, then his own Consulate and Empire. His forte was *improvision*, by which (until *all* his enemies finally allied against him) he steadily won over armies larger than his own.

Despite the differences in the early lives of Napoleon and Frederick, there were similarities in their habits and personalities. For example, they were both avid readers. "At the age of puberty," Napoleon said at St. Helena, " . . . reading became a passion pushed to the edge of rage." He had a specially bound library of almost 1,000 books that he carried on campaign.[1] Frederick, during one period of his life, lived on books and coffee, day and night, until he collapsed. Both were hypersensitive, nearly paranoid—which was useful on campaign, where both rode herd on their subordinates relentlessly, and let their minds run on how to counter every possible move the enemy might make.[2] Both were men whose lives were their work. Both seemed perpetually awake in the field; and in their palaces, they kept schedules night and day, sleeping for a few hours around midnight, rising to work, returning to bed before dawn, rising before the normal business day began.

Both believed in the heavy use of artillery. Frederick, whenever possible, had *seven* guns per 1,000 men.[3] Napoleon, whose guns were more maneuverable and (on average) of heavier caliber, had only two to three per 1,000 men.[4] But their purposes were the same—to spare the infantry—to open avenues for attack. Both were steadfast (or stubborn) to the extreme; *neither would ever quit.*

Both fought where possible to annihilate enemy armies, though both wanted a "profit" from ultimate victory—territorial or otherwise. Ritter says Frederick fought battles of annihilation but wanted to defeat the Habsburgs only to acquire Silesia.[5] Frederick wrote: "Our wars should be short and quickly fought. . . . A long war destroys . . . our [army's] discipline; depopulates the country, and exhausts our resources."[6] Napoleon tried to shorten his wars (and end his campaigns) with a crushing victory, as at Austerlitz, which campaign was fought in three months and netted him two new Napoleonic kingdoms, Naples and Holland.

Like Frederick, Napoleon convinced his troops that he was fearless, even unkillable, and that *success* made him "worth 40,000 men" on the battlefield. Delbrück writes of Frederick: "Why did [opposing commanders] not take advantage of the favorable opportunities that he offered them frequently enough? They did not dare. They believed him capable of everything."[7] Napoleon preferred that the troops see him as the man of destiny—simultaneously the personification of French grandeur and glory and the "Little Corporal," unafraid (as at Lodi, 1796) to get dirty while aiming the cannon himself. His appearances left unforgettable images that were the stuff of tales of veterans and their descendants for generations.

Like Frederick, Napoleon was a patron and friend to his troops, but demanding, severe, and downright nasty with the officers. He got generals and marshals to obey in knee-jerk fashion with violent abuse for any mistakes (including some that were really his), balanced by generous gifts of money, lands, titles, and medals. Drill sergeants and horse trainers also use this method.

Did Napoleon emulate Frederick, or were the two just similar in thought and habit? No one will ever know. That Napoleon admired the Prussian king is certain. In 1788, as a lieutenant, he made notes on books on Frederick and Prussia.[8] They list events, battles, dates, names, and (a lifetime fascination) figures—poor evidence that he learned any of Frederick's secrets. All the same, he always held that Frederick was the greatest modern general; he visited the king's tomb in Potsdam after defeating the Prussian army (1806). During his final exile on St. Helena (1815–21), he analyzed Frederick's campaigns and dismissed his critics:

> They reproach the great captain [for a variety of mistakes] . . . But his faults are eclipsed by great actions, beautiful maneuvers, fearless decisions which allowed him to walk away victorious from struggles where the odds were against him. *He was greatest in the most critical moments*, which is the highest tribute one can make to his character.[9]

Napoleon agreed with Frederick on many basic tenets, the major exception being the king's tactical *oblique order*, which Napoleon thought was a drillfield maneuver that Frederick never used in battle; he found it amusing that foreign observers of his maneuvers recommended their armies adopt it.[10]

Both were intellectuals as well as soldiers; Napoleon was elected to the French *Institut* while a general of the Republic, wrote essays and novellas in his youth, dictated voluminous memoirs in exile on St. Helena, and left behind hundreds of edicts and orders amid thousands of letters. Frederick left 30 volumes of *Oeuvres*, mostly in French, including his *Principes généraux de la guerre* and instructions to his generals, and much more.[11]

———————

Paired below are the opinions of Frederick and Napoleon on various subjects. Translations are largely from Frederick's *Principes* and Napoleon's *Correspondance*,[12] with a few additions from the compilations of Picard, Palluel, and Dansette.[13]

———————

Great Commanders Are Born

FREDERICK:
  What is called the *coup d'oeil* [sweep of the eye] . . . consists of two things, of which one is the talent to instantly judge the number of [the enemy]. That can be acquired by practice. . . . The other talent, which is altogether superior, is [the ability] to instantly judge all the advantages that can be drawn from the terrain; one can acquire and perfect that talent provided *one was* born with a genius for war.[14]

NAPOLEON:
  The art of war . . . can be learned neither from books nor from practice [experience]: it is a touch for command that constitutes a genius for war.[15]

My presence was indispensable anywhere I wanted to win a victory. It was a flaw in my armor: None of my generals had the [personal] force for a large independent command.[16]

Attitude While on Campaign

FREDERICK:

One should constantly analyze the situation in which one finds oneself: What plan would I form if I were the enemy? After imagining several, one should think about what means to use to counter the plans, and immediately correct anything that is defective in one's position.[17]

NAPOLEON:

A great captain ought to say to himself several times a day: If the enemy army should appear on my front, or my right or on my left, what will I do? If he is embarrassed by the question, he is badly posted, he is not in proper order, he must remedy that.[18]

Unity of Command

FREDERICK:

[A commander] should act on his own [*doit agir par lui-même*][19]

The secret of war is never found in councils of war.[20]

The general [should] talk of war from time to time with the most enlightened generals of his army . . . and if, in free conversation, they offer good advice, he should profit by it *without remarking who has found a good thing*; but once it is executed with success, he should say, in the presence of a big group of officers: It is to so-and-so that I owe the success in this affair. You flatter the egos [*amour-propre*] of others . . . you win friends.[21]

NAPOLEON:

In military operations, I consulted no one but myself.[22]

One bad general . . . is worth more than two good ones.[23]

Unity of command is the first necessity of war. It is vital . . . to concentrate the greatest possible forces on the field of battle, to profit by all opportunities, for fortune is a woman; if you lose her today, don't expect to get her back tomorrow.[24]

Keeping Forces Together

FREDERICK:

It is an ancient rule of war . . . if you separate your forces, you will be beaten in detail; if you want to give battle, assemble as many troops as you can; no better way is known to put them to better use.[25]

_____

NAPOLEON:

The art of war does not consist of dividing the troops.[26]

General rule: When you want to fight a battle, assemble all your forces, do not neglect any; one battalion can sometimes decide the day.[27]

Generals

FREDERICK:

A general considered audacious in another country is only ordinary in [Prussia]; [our general] is able to dare and undertake anything it is possible for men to execute [do].[28]

How many contradictory virtues enter into the makeup of a general! I suppose, he should be a gentleman and good citizen, qualities without which skills [in] the art of war are more pernicious than useful. One also asks that he should be devious [and] straightforward, gentle and severe, defiant without ceasing and always tranquil, sensitive about humanity and sometimes free with the blood of soldiers, intellectual, personally active, discreet, profound, educated in everything, not forgetting one thing to do another, and not neglecting the little details that are so critical to the support of great things.[29]

NAPOLEON:

Military genius is a gift from God, but the most essential quality of a general-in-chief is the strength of character and resolution to win at all costs.[30]

In war, men are nothing; it is one man [the commander] who is everything.[31]

The tactics, . . . the science of the engineer and artilleryman can be learned from books . . . like geometry; but knowledge of the higher elements of war can be acquired only through the study of the history of the wars . . . of the great commanders and through experience. There are no precise, determined rules; everything depends on the character that nature has given the general: . . . the nature of the troops, the arms available, the season, and a thousand other circumstances that may never have arisen before.[32]

[The Romans] had fixed attack and defensive formations [*ordres de bataille constant*]; but, since the invention of firearms, the manner of occupying a position . . . or giving battle depend on many different factors—and vary with circumstances . . . the *coup d'oeil militaire*—the decision according to the experience or genius of the general-in chief—that is the main thing.[33]

_____

[*Comment on Jomini's works:*] Generals are beaten who . . . follow the principles which they have been taught [*principes qu'on leur a inculqués*]. There are too many diverse elements in war.[34]

Offense and Defense

FREDERICK:
If I disapprove [and I do] of a totally defensive campaign, it is not because I think you can always fight a completely offensive war; but I ask that a general not feel badly about going on defense, and that he instead turn it into a ruse, excite the ego of his enemies, and induce them to make mistakes from which he can profit.[35]

NAPOLEON:
The art of war consists of a well reasoned, extremely circumspect defense, and an audacious and rapid offense.[36]

A defensive war does not exclude the attack, just as the offensive does not exclude the defense.[37]

The Art of War

FREDERICK:
In war, one dons alternately the skin of the lion and the skin of the fox.[38]

Pretend feebleness or timidity. Tempt the enemy with an ostensibly stupid maneuver. Excite his vanity [*amour propre*].[39]

The discipline of our troops is the foundation of the glory and preservation of [our] country.[40]

[Sometimes] the full details of the situation ought to oblige the general to yield [decide according] to his means and to prefer a practicable project to a brilliant one.[41]

NAPOLEON:
Always remember three things: unity of forces, positive action, and firm resolution to perish [if need be] with glory. These are the grand principles of the military art that always gave me good fortune in all my operations. Death is nothing; to live defeated and without glory is to die every day.[42]

War can only be fought with force, decision, and . . . determination; there can be no uncertainty or hesitation.[43]

The art of war is a simple art and all in execution . . . it is all common sense; nothing about it is theoretical.[44]

A good general, good cadres, a good organization, good instruction, good discipline make good troops, independent of the cause for which they fight; however, it is true that fanaticism, love of country, national glory, can inspire young troops to advantage.[45]

The musket is the best war machine ever invented by man.[46]

In war, morale and opinion are the better part of reality. The art of the great captains has always been to publish and make appear to the enemy that their troops are more numerous, and to their own army that the enemy is quite inferior [in strength].[47]

In war, three quarters [is] morale; the balance of real forces make up the other quarter.[48]

Planning and Improvision

FREDERICK:

In general, campaign projects have to be adjusted to conditions [time, weather], the number of the enemy. . . . The more one foresees obstacles to his plans, the less one will find of them later in the execution. In a word, everything must be foreseen; find the problems and resolve them.[49]

The principal work of a general is in his office, devising projects, combining ideas . . . to foresee the designs of the enemy, anticipate them, and keep the enemy disturbed. But that is not enough; he must also be active, and see that what he orders is executed, that he sees everything himself. He must observe [the enemy] camps [and] their guards, and walk the battle line frequently to get familiar with it; then if he is attacked by an improvisor, nothing will be new to him.[50]

NAPOLEON:

Campaign plans are to be modified *à l'infini*, according to the circumstances, the talent of the general, the nature of his troops, and the topography.[51]

I have the habit of thinking about what I ought to do four or five months in advance.[52]

[The first quality of a great general] is the courage of the *improviste*. . . . War is composed altogether of accidents. . . . A [great] commander never loses sight of what he can do to profit by these accidents. . . . The outcome of a battle . . . is the result of one instant, one thought . . . you mix it up [*on s'mêle*], you fight for a time, the decisive moment arrives, a mental spark [*une étincelle morale*] tells you so; the smallest of reserves [wins the battle].[53]

Among the accidents of terrain, some [are] favorable and some unfavorable; the art of positions consists in using the favorable accidents to fortify his battle formations, and leaving the unfavorable accidents in front or to his flanks, where they weaken the battle order of the aggressor. . . . One does not pre-scribe a constant disposition of troops.[54]

Rapport with the Troops

FREDERICK:

If you want to gain the affection of the soldier, do not wear him out or expose him [to fire, danger] unless it is necessary. Be his father, and not his executioner.[55]

Kindness and severity work alternately with the soldier; a general should [make himself] popular: talk with the soldiers, both when you pass their tents or when they are on the march. Sample often to see if the cookpots have some-thing good; find out their small needs and do what you can to satisfy them; spare them unnecessary exertion. But let fall the full vigor of the law on the mutinous soldier, the backbiter, the pillager, when necessary order the severest punishment for deserters.[56]

NAPOLEON:

My soldiers were very much at ease and very free with me; they often ad-dressed me in familiar terms (*me tutoyer*). I remember that at Jena, I believe . . . on the eve of battle, visiting certain posts almost alone, a sentinel stopped me . . . and said that even if I was the "little corporal," he could not let me pass. When he found that I was indeed the *le petit caporal*, he was not disconcerted. He knew he had done his duty. . . . I passed for *un homme terrible* . . . among the officers and even the generals, but never among the soldiers; they instinc-tively felt . . . [my] sympathy; they knew me as their protector and if need be, their avenger.[57]

Always, when you are in the presence of the enemy, bivouac with your troops. I've done that for a long time, and have found it a good thing. It sets the right example for everybody.[58]

Feeding the Troops

FREDERICK:

Hunger will defeat a man more surely than the courage of his adversary, but, as the loss of a convoy or a depot will not lose a war, winning battles must come first; it is necessary to consider both factors in deciding how to win.[59]

———

Whatever beautiful plan you have dreamed up, you will not be able to execute it if your soldiers have not been well fed.[60]

Before beginning an expedition the commissariat must brew plenty of brandy [*eau-de-vie*] and beer. . . . I must add that our soldiers receive two pounds of bread and two pounds of meat per week, free. We take along herds of cattle . . . with the escorts of the convoys.[61]

[Part of controlling mercenaries] is being constantly certain that the troops lack for nothing, not bread, or meat . . . or wine, etc.; in studying the reasons for desertion . . . [one should find out] if the soldier regularly receives his pay and all the small comforts due him, or if his captain is guilty of misappropriation.[62]

NAPOLEON:
[You must] feed your army, and draw on the country where you have re-sources . . . that is a great part of the art of war.[63] [*There is an obvious difference here; unlike Frederick's, Napoleon's men lived off the land.*]

Winning Over a "Superior" Enemy

FREDERICK:
The most difficult campaigns are those in which one is opposed by many strong enemies. . . . Militarily, it is necessary to know how to lose [ground] to advantage (*he who tries to defend everything defends nothing*), sacrifice a province to one enemy, and march . . . with all your forces against the others, make them fight a battle, make your best effort to destroy them, then march away and hit the others.[64]

I prefer . . . the audacity of a general who risks a battle . . . for he has everything to gain [*il a tout à espérer*] and, even if he loses, there is always the option of the defensive.[65]

NAPOLEON:
With an inferior [smaller] army, the art of war consists of always having more forces than the enemy at the point where you attack or at the point where you are attacked.[66]

On Reconnaissance

FREDERICK:
[Marching into battle] it is mandatory that the general boldly ride ahead, that *he reconnoiter the terrain himself* . . . from one end to the other, so that he will have several possible [plans and] positions in mind . . . in case he encounters the enemy.[67]

Knowledge and choice of terrain are the most essential things; but, knowing them, you must know how to profit by placing the troops where they can be most effective.[68]

Most modern battle orders are ineffective [*vicieux*] in that they always follow the same plan, without regard to the terrain.[69]

In choosing a position, profit from every swamp, stream, inundation, or obstacle that will narrow the front [fill gaps between units] . . . because it is not your entrenchments that stop the enemy, but the troops that [you concentrate] to oppose him.[70]

NAPOLEON:

The basic [*primitif*] battle formation should always be matched to the terrain, in such a way as to turn all accidents to the profit of an attack or defense. . . . [Today] the terrain alone does not decide the battle order, which must be determined by all the circumstances together.[71]

Most often one should have an advance guard, [and] the general-in-chief ought to be with it, to direct the movements of his army.[72]

Discipline ties the troops to their flags; it is not harangues . . . that makes them brave: old soldiers are irritated [by speeches]; the young ones forget them at the first cannon shot. . . . The gesture of a general who is liked—held in esteem by his troops—is better than the most beautiful speech.[73]

Looting and Pillaging

FREDERICK:

One maintains a severe discipline to crack pillaging and marauding [and] punishes it severely, as one would enemies with the most sinister intentions.[74]

NAPOLEON:

My great reputation in Italy is in part due to the fact that I did not [allow] pillaging. . . . It is a very important function of a general-in-chief. The least fault can cost the lives of thousands of men.[75]

Respect for History and Generals of the Past

FREDERICK:

It is not . . . the great examples and great models that form [great generals]; and if heroes like Eugene, Condé, Turenne, or Caesar demand our admiration, how much more would we be moved by a combination of the strong points of all of them.[76]

NAPOLEON:

Make offensive war like Alexander, Hannibal, Caesar, Gustavus-Adolphus, Turenne, Prince Eugene and *Frederick*; read, re-read the history of their eighty-three campaigns, model yourself after them.[77]

The principles of Caesar were the same as those of Alexander and Hannibal: keep your forces united, be vulnerable at no point; move rapidly to important points, bear in mind maintaining morale, the reputation of your arms, the fear that it inspires; . . . give yourself every possible chance of victory . . . unite all your troops.[78]

Conclusions

Any summing up here would seem superfluous. The maxims of Napoleon, often echoing the *principes* of Frederick, have been at the core of military doctrine for the past 200 years. The reader will note that the commanders whose writings appear *in extenso* herein usually quote Napoleon or Frederick, and if not, echo their ideas, or cite one of Napoleon's interpreters, usually Carl von Clausewitz.

II

William Tecumseh Sherman

(1820–1891)

UNION GENERALS William T. Sherman and Ulysses S. Grant set patterns for the mass warfare of the twentieth century. Moreover, their campaigns, combining the destruction of the enemy homeland and mass assault into it, are still at the heart of what Weigley calls "the American Way of War."[1] In 1864–65, Sherman burned Atlanta and marched to the sea at Savannah, then north through the Carolinas, destroying the material base of the Southern armies and the morale of Southern troops and civilians. Grant, in the East, and Sherman in the West and South, forced the Rebels to build fortifications and use trenches and barbed wire to offset Yankee numbers and firepower. Union troops, in turn, took to trenches as well. Grant and Sherman left a legacy of trench warfare. That, conscription, and the Prussian general staff system[2] would all be used by both sides in the Great War (1914–18), and account for its horrors. Sherman especially, assailing the South with masses of men and superior weapons, did what bombing and the Soviet and Western invasions of Germany would do for the Allies in World War II—and for the United States in lesser wars since.

Sherman is included here because he was the more intellectual of the leading Northern commanders, and had more to say about generalship in his *Memoirs* (cited below). He is remembered for his "War is Hell," which he meant in all senses. But for him, although it is rarely mentioned, it was Hell because his heart was with the South, while his head was against destroying the Union. His devastation of the South was meant to end the war quickly—and did. Nonetheless, his name meant "burner and killer" to generations of southerners.

Born in Ohio to a well-off and influential family, he graduated from West Point in 1840 (Sixth in his class) and was commissioned in the artillery. He married the daughter of the secretary of the interior and served mostly in southern posts. During the Mexican War, he was a disgruntled staff officer, angry at not seeing action. After the war he got more desk assignments. He resigned in 1853, went into business and failed, but found his niche as president of (what became) Louisiana State University. In 1861, he entered Union service as a colonel; he fought at Bull Run, and then was posted to the western theater of war, where he served under Ulysses S. Grant, who became his friend and admirer. When President Lincoln called Grant to command in the East, Sherman succeeded him in the West.

In constant telegraph communication, Grant and Sherman decided that the way to victory was for Sherman to strike deep into the South and destroy the already shaky economic base of the Confederacy, while Grant defeated Robert E. Lee's army in Virginia. Both mercilessly used the superior numbers, weaponry, and supplies of the Union to accomplish their purposes. In 1864, Sherman led three armies from Chattanooga to Atlanta, took and burned the city, and marched on Savannah (November and December 1864), burning warehouses and crops, killing livestock, destroying railways and roads he did not need himself, and sometimes setting towns and cities ablaze. He then marched north through South Carolina into North Carolina, doing the same. Southern general J. E. Johnston could not stop him, and surrendered on 13 April 1865 near Durham, North Carolina—only days after Lee's surrender to Grant on 9 April at Appomattox, Virginia.

After Grant was elected president of the United States (1868), Sherman became General-of-the-Army, a post he held until 1883, and in a grade not granted any officer again until World War II. During his term, he founded the Infantry and Cavalry School at Fort Leavenworth, Kansas, which became the Army General Service and Staff College (1901) and is today the Army Command and General Staff College.[3] Sherman refused the Republican nomination for president in 1884, and died in New York City in 1891.

———————

The passages below are from Sherman's *Memoirs*. They are chosen over excerpts from Grant's more voluminous *Memoirs* because, although Grant had very similar ideas, he did not sum up his thinking about the Civil War or about the art of war in general; Sherman did.[4]

———————

Single Command

From "The Military Lessons of the War." No army can be efficient unless it be a unit for action; and the power must come from above, not from below: the President usually delegates his power to the commander-in-chief, and he to the next, and so on down to the lowest actual commander of troops, however small the detachment. No matter how troops come together, when once united, the highest officer in rank is held responsible, and should be . . . armed with the fullest power of the Executive, subject only to law and existing orders. The more simple the principle, the greater the likelihood of determined action; and the less a commanding officer is circumscribed by bounds or by precedent, the greater is the probability that he will make the best use of his command and achieve the best results.[5]

The Staff. Chief-of-Staff.

In like manner as to the staff. The more intimately it comes into contact with the troops, the more useful and valuable it becomes. The almost entire separation of the staff from the line, as now practised by us, and hitherto by the French, has proved mischievous, and the great retinues of staff-officers with which some of our earlier generals began the war were simply ridiculous. I don't believe in a chief of staff at all, and any general commanding an army, corps, or division, that has a staff-officer who professes to know more than his chief, is to be pitied. Each regiment should have a competent adjutant, quartermaster, and commissary, with two or three medical officers. Each brigade commander should have the same staff, with the addition of a couple of young aides-de-camp, habitually selected from the subalterns of the brigade, who should be good riders, and intelligent enough to give and explain the orders of their general.

The same staff will answer for a division. The general in command of a separate army, and of a *corps d'armée*, should have the same professional assistance, with two or more good engineers, and his adjutant-general should exercise all the functions usually ascribed to a chief of staff, viz., he should possess the ability to comprehend the scope of operations, and to make verbally and in writing all the orders and details necessary to carry into effect the views of his general, as well as to keep the returns and records of events for the information of the next higher authority, and for history.

A bulky staff implies a division of responsibility, slowness of action, and indecision, whereas a small staff implies activity and concentration of purpose. The smallness of General Grant's staff throughout the civil war forms the best model for future imitation. So of tents, officers' furniture, etc., etc. In real war these should all be discarded, and an army is efficient for action and motion exactly in the inverse ratio of its *impedimenta*. Tents should be omitted altogether, save one to a regiment for an office, and a few for the division hospital. Officers should be content with a tent fly, improvising poles and shelter out of bushes. The *tente d'abri*, or shelter-tent, carried by the soldier himself, is all-sufficient. Officers should never seek for houses, but share the condition of their men.[6]

Post-War Red Tape

With us, to-day, the law and regulations are that, no matter what may be the emergency, the commanding general in Texas, New Mexico, and the remote frontiers, cannot draw from the arsenals a pistol-cartridge, or any sort of ordnance-stores, without first procuring an order of the Secretary of War in Washington. The commanding general—though intrusted with the lives of his soldiers and with the safety of a frontier in a condition of chronic war—cannot touch or be trusted with ordnance-stores or property, and that is declared to be the law. *Every officer of the old army remembers how, in 1861, we were hampered with the old blue army-regulations, which tied our hands, and that to do any thing positive and necessary we had to tear it all to pieces*—cut the red-tape, as it was called—a dangerous thing for an army to do, for it was calculated to bring the law and authority into contempt; but war was upon us.

Chain of Command

In this country . . . Congress controls the great questions of war and peace, makes all laws for the creation and government of armies, and votes the necessary supplies, leaving to the President to execute and apply these laws. . . . The executive power is further subdivided into the seven great departments, and to the Secretary of War is confided the general care of the military establishment, and his powers are further subdivided into ten distinct and separate bureaus.

The chiefs of these bureaus are under the immediate orders of the Secretary of War, who, through them, in fact commands the army from "his office," but cannot do so "in the field"—an absurdity in military if not civil law.

The subordinates of these staff-corps and departments are selected and chosen from the army . . . or fresh from West Point, and too commonly construe themselves into the *élite*, as made of better clay than the common soldier. Thus they separate themselves more and more from their comrades of the line, and in process of time realize the condition of that old officer of artillery who thought the army would be a delightful place for a gentleman if it were not for the d----d soldier; or, better still, the conclusion of the young lord in "Henry IV," who told Harry Percy (Hotspur) that "but for these vile guns he would himself have been a soldier." This is all wrong; utterly at variance with our democratic form of government and of universal experience; and now that the French, from whom we had copied the system, have utterly "proscribed" it, I hope that our Congress will follow suit. I admit, in its fullest force, the strength of the maxim that the civil law should be superior to the military in time of peace; that the army should be at all times subject to the direct control of Congress; and I assert that, from the formation of our Government to the present day, the Regular Army has set the highest example of obedience to law and authority; but, for the very reason that our army is comparatively so very small, I hold that it should be the best possible, organized and governed on true military principles, and that in time of peace we should preserve the "habits and usages of war," so that, when war does come, we may not again be compelled to suffer the disgrace, confusion, and disorder of 1861.

The commanding officers of divisions, departments, and posts, should have the amplest powers, not only to command their troops, but all the stores designed for their use, and the officers of the staff necessary to administer them, within the area of their command; and then with fairness they could be held to [total] responsibility. The President and Secretary of War can command the army quite as well through these generals as through the subordinate staff-officers. Of course, the Secretary would, as now, distribute the funds according to the appropriation bills, and reserve to himself the absolute control and supervision of the larger arsenals and depots of supply. The error lies in the law, or in the judicial interpretation thereof, and no code of army regulations can be made that meets the case, until Congress, like the French *Corps Législatif*, utterly annihilates and "proscribes" the old law and the system which has grown up under it.[7]

Taking Care of the Troops

The feeling of the soldier should be that, in every event, the sympathy and preference of his government is for him who fights, rather than for him who is on provost or guard duty to the rear, and, like most men, he measures this by the amount of pay. Of course, the soldier must be trained to obedience, and should be "content with his wages"; but whoever has commanded an army in the field knows the difference between a willing, contented mass of men, and one that feels a cause of grievance. There is a soul to an army as well as to the individual man, and no general can accomplish the full work of his army unless he commands the soul of his men, as well as their bodies and legs.[8]

Food and Forage

The "feeding" of an army is a matter of the most vital importance, and demands the earliest attention of the general intrusted with a campaign. To be strong, healthy, and capable of largest measure of physical effort, the soldier needs about three pounds gross of food per day, and the horse or mule about twenty pounds. When a general first estimates the quantity of food and forage needed for an army of fifty or one hundred thousand men, he is apt to be dismayed, and here a good staff is indispensable, though the general cannot throw off on them the responsibility. He must give the subject his personal attention, the army reposes in him alone, and should never doubt the fact that their existence overrides in importance all other considerations. Once satisfied . . . that all has been done that can be, the soldiers are always willing to bear the largest measure of privation. Probably no army ever had a more varied experience in this regard than the one I commanded in 1864–65.

Supply by Rail, River, and Wagon

Our base of supply was at Nashville, supplied by railways and the Cumberland River, thence by rail to Chattanooga, a "secondary base," and thence forward a single-track railroad. The stores came forward daily, but I endeavored to have on hand a full supply for twenty days in advance. These stores were habitually in the wagon-trains, distributed to corps, divisions, and regiments, in charge of experienced quartermasters and commissaries, and became subject to the orders of the generals commanding these bodies. They were generally issued on provision returns, but these had to be closely scrutinized, for too often the colonels would make requisitions for provisions for more men than they reported for battle. Of course, there are always a good many non-combatants with an army, but, after careful study, I limited their amount to twenty-five per cent. of the "effective strength," and that was found to be liberal. An ordinary army-wagon drawn by six mules may be counted on to carry three thousand pounds net, equal to the food of a full regiment for one day, but, by driving along beef-cattle, a commissary may safely count the contents of one wagon as sufficient for two days' food for a regiment of a thousand men; and as a corps should have food on hand for twenty days ready for detachment, it should have three hundred such wagons, as a provision-train; and for forage, ammunition, clothing, and other necessary stores, it was found necessary to have three hundred more wagons, or six hundred wagons in all, for a *Corps d'armée.*

The Commander's Responsibility

These should be absolutely under the immediate control of the corps commander, who will, however, find it economical to distribute them in due proportion to his divisions, brigades, and even regiments. Each regiment ought usually to have at least one wagon for convenience to distribute stores, and each company two pack-mules, so that the regiment may always be certain of a meal on reaching camp without waiting for the larger trains.[9]

Equip and Arm the Men; Don't Overload Them

Each soldier should, if not actually "sick or wounded," carry his musket and equipments containing from forty to sixty rounds of ammunition, his shelter-tent, a blanket or overcoat, and an extra pair of pants, socks, and drawers, in the form of a scarf, worn from the left shoulder to the right side in lieu of knapsack, and in his haversack he should carry some bread, cooked meat, salt, and coffee. I do not believe a soldier should be loaded down too much, but, including his clothing, arms, and equipment, he can carry about fifty pounds without impairing his health. . . . A simple calculation will show that by such a distribution a corps will thus carry the equivalent of five hundred wagon-loads—an immense relief to the trains.

Beef, Salt, Bacon, Bread, and Coffee

Where an army is near one of our many large navigable rivers, or has the safe use of a railway, it can usually be supplied with the full army ration, which is by far the best furnished to any army in America or Europe; but when it is compelled to operate away from such a base, and is dependent on its own train of wagons, the commanding officer must exercise a wise discretion in the selection of his stores. In my opinion there is no better food for man than beef-cattle driven on the hoof, issued liberally, with salt, bacon, and bread. Coffee also has become almost indispensable, though many substitutes were found for it, such as Indian-corn, roasted, ground, and boiled as coffee; the sweet-potato, and the seed of the okra-plant. . . .

————————

Therefore I would always advise that the coffee and sugar ration be carried along, even at the expense of bread, for which there are many substitutes. Of these, Indian-corn is the best and most abundant. Parched in a frying-pan, it is excellent food, or if ground, or pounded and boiled with meat of any sort, it makes a most nutritious meal. The potato, both Irish and sweet, forms an excellent substitute for bread, and at Savannah we found the rice also suitable, both for men and animals. . . . During the Atlanta campaign we were supplied by our regular commissaries with all sorts of patent compounds, such as desiccated vegetables, and concentrated milk, meat-biscuit, and sausages, but somehow the men preferred the simpler and more familiar forms of food, and usually styled these "desecrated vegetables and consecrated milk." We were also supplied liberally with lime-juice, sauerkraut, and pickles, as an antidote to scurvy.[10]

Care of the Sick and Wounded

The sick, wounded, and dead of an army are the subject of the greatest possible anxiety, and add an immense amount of labor to the well men. Each regiment in an active campaign should have a surgeon and two assistants always close at hand, each brigade and division should have an experienced surgeon as medical director. The great majority of wounds and sickness should be treated by the regimental surgeon, on the ground, under the eye of the colonel. As few should be sent to the brigade or division hospital as possible, for the men always receive better care with their own regiment than with strangers, and as a rule the cure is more certain; but when men receive disabling wounds, or have sickness likely to become permanent, the sooner they go far to the rear the better for all. The tent or the shelter of a tree is a better hospital than a house, whose walls absorb fetid and poisonous emanations, and then give them to the atmosphere. To men accustomed to the open air, who live on the plainest food, wounds seem to give less pain, are attended with less danger to life than to ordinary soldiers in barracks.[11]

The Necessity of Improvising in Combat

Very few of the battles in which I have participated were fought as described in European text-books, viz., in great masses, in perfect order, maneuvering by corps, divisions, and brigades. We were generally in a wooded country, and, though our lines were deployed according to tactics, the men generally fought in strong skirmish lines, taking advantage of the shape of ground, and of every cover. We were generally the assailants, and in wooded and broken countries the "defensive" had a positive advantage over us, for they were always ready, had cover, and always knew the ground to their immediate front; whereas we, their assailants, had to grope our way over unknown ground, and generally found a cleared field or prepared entanglements that held us for a time under a close and withering fire. Rarely did the opposing lines in compact order come into actual contact, but when, as at Peach-Tree Creek and Atlanta, the lines did become commingled, the men fought individually in every possible style, more frequently with the musket clubbed than with the bayonet, and in some instances the men clinched like wrestlers, and went to the ground together. Europeans frequently criticized our war, because we did not always take full advantage of a victory; the true reason was, that habitually the woods served as a screen, and we often did not realize the fact that our enemy had retreated till he was already miles away and was again intrenched, having left a mere skirmish-line to cover the movement, in turn to fall back to the new position.

Outposts and Outriders

In relation to guards, pickets, and vedettes, I doubt if any discoveries or improvements were made during our war, or in any of the modern wars in Europe. These precautions vary with the nature of the country and the situation of each army. When advancing or retreating in line of battle, the usual skirmish-line constitutes the picket-line, and may have "reserves," but usually the main line of battle constitutes the reserve.[12]

New Weapons and Their Future Use

Our war was fought with the muzzle-loading rifle. Toward the close I had one brigade . . . armed with breech-loading "Spencer's"; the cavalry generally had breech-loading carbines, "Spencer's" and "Sharp's" [sic], both of which were good arms.

The only change that breech-loading arms will probably make in the art and practice of war will be to increase the amount of ammunition to be expended, and necessarily to be carried along; to still further "thin out" the lines of attack, and to reduce battles to short, quick, decisive conflicts. It does not in the least affect the grand strategy, or the necessity for perfect organization, drill, and discipline. The companies and battalions will be more dispersed, and the men will be less under the immediate eye of their officers, and therefore a higher order of intelligence and courage on the part of the individual soldier will be an element of strength.

Discipline and Intelligence

When a regiment is deployed as skirmishers, and crosses an open field or woods, under heavy fire, if each man runs forward from tree to tree, or stump to stump, and yet preserves a good general alignment, it gives great confidence to the men themselves, for they always keep their eyes well to the right and left, and watch their comrades; but when some few hold back, stick too close or too long to a comfortable log, it often stops the line and defeats the whole object. Therefore, the more we improve the fire arm the more will be the necessity for good organization, good discipline and intelligence on the part of the individual soldier and officer. There is, of course, such a thing as individual courage, which has a value in war, but familiarity with danger, experience in war and its common attendants, and personal habit, are equally valuable traits, and these are the qualities with which we usually have to deal in war. All men naturally shrink from pain and danger, and only incur their risk from some higher motive, or from habit, so that I would define true courage to be a perfect sensibility of the measure of danger, and a mental willingness to incur it, rather than that insensibility to danger of which I have heard far more than I have seen. The most courageous men are generally unconscious of possessing the quality; therefore, when one professes it too openly, by words or bearing, there is reason to mistrust it. I would further illustrate my meaning by describing a man of true courage to be one who possesses all his faculties and senses perfectly when serious danger is actually present.

The Fighting Arms and Fortifications

Modern wars have not materially changed the relative values or proportions of the several arms of service: infantry, artillery, cavalry, and engineers. If any thing, the infantry has been increased in value. The danger of cavalry attempting to charge infantry armed with breech-loading rifles was fully illustrated at Sedan, and with us very frequently. So improbable has such a thing become that we have omitted the infantry-square from our recent tactics. Still, cavalry against cavalry, and as auxiliary to infantry, will always be valuable, while all great wars will, as heretofore, depend chiefly on the infantry. Artillery is more valuable with new and inexperienced troops than with veterans. In the early stages of the war the field-guns often bore the proportion of six to a thousand men; but toward the close of the war one gun, or at most two, to a thousand men, was deemed enough. Sieges, such as characterized the wars of the last century, are too slow for this period of the world, and the Prussians recently almost ignored them altogether, penetrated France between the forts, and left a superior force "in observation," to watch the garrison and accept its surrender when the greater events of the war ahead made further resistance useless; but earth-forts, and especially field-works, will hereafter play an important part in wars, because they enable a minor force to hold a superior one in check for a *time*, and time is a most valuable element in all wars. It was one of Prof. Mahan's maxims that the spade was as useful in war as the musket, and to this I will add the axe. The habit of intrenching certainly does have the effect of making new troops timid. When a line of battle is once covered by a good parapet, made by the engineers or by the labor of the men themselves, it does require an effort to make them leave it in the face of danger; but when the enemy is intrenched, it becomes absolutely necessary to permit each brigade and division of the troops immediately opposed to throw up a corresponding trench for their own protection in case of a sudden sally. We invariably did this in all our recent campaigns, and it had no ill effect, though sometimes our troops were a little too slow in leaving their well-covered lines to assail the enemy in position or on retreat. Even our skirmishers were in the habit of rolling logs together, or of making a lunette of rails, with dirt in front, to cover their bodies; and, though it revealed their position, I cannot say that it worked a bad effect; so that, as a rule, it may safely be left to the men themselves. On the "defensive," there is no doubt of the propriety of fortifying; but in the assailing army the general must watch closely to see that his men do not neglect an opportunity to drop [leave] . . . defenses, and act promptly on the "offensive" at every chance.

Personal Reconnaissance and Leadership

I have many a time crept forward to the skirmish-line to avail myself of the cover of the pickets' "little fort," to observe more closely some expected result; and always talked familiarly with the men, and was astonished to see how well they comprehended the general object, and how accurately they were informed of the state of facts existing miles away from their particular corps.

Soldiers are very quick to catch the general drift and purpose of a campaign, and are always sensible when they are well commanded or well cared for. Once impressed with this fact, and that they are making progress, they bear cheerfully any amount of labor and privation. . . . [I]n the presence of an active enemy, it is much easier to maintain discipline than in barracks in time of peace.[13]

Leadership "From the Front"

It is related of Napoleon that his last words were, *Tête d'armée!* Doubtless . . . the last thought that remained for speech was of some event when he was directing an important "head of column." I believe that every general who has handled armies in battle must recall from his own experience the intensity of thought on some similar occasion, when by a single command he had given the finishing stroke to some complicated action; but to me recurs another thought that is worthy of record, and may encourage others who are to follow us in our profession. I never saw the rear of an army engaged in battle but I feared that some calamity had happened at the front—the apparent confusion, broken wagons, crippled horses, men lying about dead and maimed, parties hastening to and fro in seeming disorder, and a general apprehension of something dreadful about to ensue; all these signs, however, lessened as I neared the front, and there the contrast was complete—perfect order, men and horses full of confidence, and it was not unusual [to see] general hilarity, laughing, and cheering. Although cannon might be firing, the musketry clattering, and the enemy's shot hitting close, there reigned a general feeling of strength and security that bore a marked contrast to the bloody signs that had drifted rapidly to the rear; therefore, for comfort and safety, I surely would rather be at the front than the rear line of battle. So also on the march, the head of a column moves on steadily, while the rear is alternately halting and then rushing forward to close up the gap; and all sorts of rumors, especially the worst, float back to the rear. Old troops invariably deem it a special privilege to be in the front—to be at the "head of column"—because experience has taught them that it is the easiest and most comfortable place, and danger only adds zest and stimulus to this fact.

The hardest task in war is to lie in support of some position or battery, under fire without the privilege of returning it; or to guard some train left in the rear, within hearing but out of danger, or to provide for the wounded and dead of some corps which is too busy ahead to care for its own.

To be at the head of a strong column of troops, in the execution of some task that requires brain, is the highest pleasure of war—a grim one and terrible, but which leaves on the mind and memory the strongest mark; to detect the weak point of an enemy's line; to break through with vehemence and thus lead to victory; or to discover some key-point and hold it with tenacity; or to do some other distinct act which is afterward recognized as the real cause of success. These all become matters that are never forgotten. Other great difficulties, experienced by every general, are to measure truly the thousand-and-one reports that come to him in the midst of conflict; to preserve a clear and well-defined purpose at every instant of time, and to cause all efforts to converge to that end.

To do these things he must know perfectly the strength and quality of each part of his own army, as well as that of his opponent, and must be where he can personally see and observe with his own eyes, and judge with his own mind. No man can properly command an army from the rear, he must be "at its front;" and when a detachment is made, the commander thereof should be informed of the object to be accomplished, and left as free as possible to execute it in his own way; and when an army is divided up into several parts, the superior should always attend that one which he regards as most important. Some men think that modern armies may be so regulated that a general can sit in an office and play on his several columns as on the keys of a piano; this is a fearful mistake. The directing mind must be at the very head of the army—must be seen there, and the effect of his mind and personal energy must be felt by every officer and man present with it, to secure the best results. Every attempt to make war easy and safe will result in humiliation and disaster.

The Telegraph and Railroad

For the rapid transmission of orders in an army covering a large space of ground, the magnetic telegraph is by far the best, though habitually the paper and pencil, with good mounted orderlies, answer every purpose. I have little faith in the signal-service by flags and torches. . . . There was one notable instance in my experience, when the signal-flags carried a message of vital importance over the heads of Hood's army, which had interposed between me and Allatoona, and had broken the telegraph-wires . . . but the value of the magnetic telegraph in war cannot be exaggerated, as was illustrated by the perfect concert of action between the armies in Virginia and Georgia during 1864. Hardly a day intervened when General Grant did not know the exact state of facts with me, more than fifteen hundred miles away as the wires ran. So on the field a thin insulated wire may be run on improvised stakes or from tree to tree for six or more miles in a couple of hours, and I have seen operators so skillful, that by cutting the wire they would receive a message with their tongues from a distant station. As a matter of course, the ordinary commercial wires along the railways form the usual telegraph-lines for an army, and these are easily repaired and extended as the army advances, but each army and wing should have a small party of skilled men to put up the field-wire, and take it down when done. . . . Our commercial telegraph-lines will always supply for war enough skillful operators.

The value of railways is also fully recognized in war quite as much as, if not more so than, in peace. The Atlanta campaign would simply have been impossible without the use of the railroads from Louisville to Nashville—one hundred and eighty-five miles—from Nashville to Chattanooga—one hundred and fifty-one miles—and from Chattanooga to Atlanta—one hundred and thirty-seven miles. Every mile of this "single track" was so delicate, that one man could in a minute have broken or moved a rail, but our trains usually carried along the tools and means to repair such a break. We had, however, to maintain strong guards and garrisons at each important bridge or trestle—the destruction of which would have necessitated time for rebuilding. For the protection of a bridge, one or two log block-houses, two stories high, with a piece of ordnance and a small infantry guard, usually sufficed. . . . These points could usually be reached only by a dash of the enemy's cavalry, and many of these block-houses successfully resisted serious attacks by both cavalry and artillery. . . .

Our trains from Nashville forward were operated under military rules, and ran about ten miles an hour in gangs of four trains of ten cars each. Four such groups of trains daily made one hundred and sixty cars, of ten tons each, carrying sixteen hundred tons, which exceeded the absolute necessity of the army, and allowed for the accidents that were common and inevitable. But, as I have recorded, that single stem of railroad, four hundred and seventy-three miles long, supplied an army of one hundred thousand men and thirty-five thousand animals for the period of one hundred and ninety-six days, viz., from May 1 to

November 12, 1864. To have delivered regularly that amount of food and forage by ordinary wagons would have required thirty six thousand eight hundred wagons of six mules each, allowing each wagon to have hauled two tons twenty miles each day, a simple impossibility in roads such as then existed in that region of country. Therefore, I reiterate that the Atlanta campaign was an impossibility without these railroads . . . because we had the men and means to maintain and defend them, in addition to what were necessary to overcome the enemy.[14]

The Press

Newspaper correspondents with an army, as a rule, are mischievous. They are the world's gossips, pick up and retail the camp scandal, and gradually drift to the headquarters of some general, who finds it easier to make reputation at home than with his own corps or division. They are also tempted to prophesy events and state facts which, to an enemy, reveal a purpose in time to guard against it. Moreover, they are always bound to see facts colored by the partisan or political character of their own patrons, and thus bring army officers into the political controversies of the day, which are always mischievous and wrong. Yet, so greedy are the people at large for war news, that it is doubtful whether any army commander can exclude all reporters, without bringing down on himself a clamor that may imperil his own safety. Time and moderation must bring a just solution to this modern difficulty.[15]

Conclusions

Sherman defends using fortifications, but with qualifications. He advocates centralized command, personal leadership "from the front," and offensive war. He distrusts doctrine or "books" on war, and opposes large staffs. Repeatedly, he discusses taking care of the troops as a primary duty and practical necessity if they are expected to fight. He makes clear that the telegraph and railroads facilitated victory, and speculates about the effects of repeating weapons. As to the future roles of the various arms, he is dead right about the infantry, and perceptive, for his time, about artillery, cavalry, and the engineers. On matters relating to command, he is in general agreement with Frederick and Napoleon. His major importance is that he was a pioneer of the "American way of war."

III

Stonewall Jackson

(1824–1863)

THOMAS JONATHAN JACKSON was referred to by contemporaries as the "Napoleon of our War" (the American Civil War). His Shenandoah Valley Campaign was "extra-Napoleonic," according to Colonel Claude Crozet, who had served under Napoleon.[1] Jackson belongs in this anthology because his unorthodox leadership and repeated victories won him the blind devotion of his troops, and his operations are especially instructive for "small wars" such as those fought since 1945.

Jackson won the sobriquet "Stonewall" at the Battle of Bull Run or First Manassas (1861), where his brigade was first immovable and then led the assault that won the battle. Born in what is now West Virginia to a family of early Scots-Irish settlers, he was reared by a horseman uncle, who failed to see to his education. He made it through the United States Military Academy (West Point) by "all work and no play." Commissioned in the artillery (1846), he almost immediately saw action in the Mexican War, where his heroism (see eyewitness account below) won him promotion to brevet major. He had once stopped 1,500 Mexican cavalry with two 6 pound cannons: "I opened up on them and with every fire we cut lanes through them. . . . It was splendid."[2] The peacetime army frustrated him, however; he resigned to teach at the Virginia Military Institute.

When the Civil War began in 1861, he volunteered to serve in the Confederate Army to "protect God-fearing people of the South." To him, the war was a religious crusade.[3]

He was made a colonel, then a brigadier general, CSA. At Bull Run he became the South's first great hero, but wanted to follow up the victory: "Let me take my brigade and I'll be in Washington tonight. We'll take the White House. We'll end it all."[4] Men vied to serve under "Old Jack," despite his harsh discipline and eccentricities (wearing his battered Mexican War uniform, continually eating lemons, refusing to tell his subordinate generals his plans).[5] He gained even greater fame for his Shenandoah Valley Campaign (March–June 1862), where he drove his "foot cavalry" relentlessly, day and night, but was always with them, through rain, mud, and darkness. With fewer than 16,000 Confederates he defeated some 70,000 Union troops under John C. Frémont, Nathaniel Banks, and Irvin McDowell.[6]

He then joined Lee's Army of Northern Virginia and became a corps commander. Weary and perhaps reluctant to take orders after his triumphs, he was ineffective in the Seven Days Battles. But he quickly revived to "star" again at Second Manassas, Fredericksburg, and Chancellorsville (May 1863). In the latter, he took his corps from the extreme right to the left to crush Hooker's flank and win the battle. But he was mortally wounded by his own troops while reconnoitering after the battle, and died a week later. Early on, he had said: "My religious belief teaches me to feel as safe in battle as in bed. God has fixed the time for my death. I do not concern myself about that."[7] His faith sustained him to the end.

Jackson had been Lee's right arm. To quote J.F.C. Fuller: "Jackson possessed that brutality essential in war; Lee did not."[8] Still, for his reputation, it may be good that Jackson died when he did. The war of maneuver at which he excelled was giving way to mass warfare—a bludgeoning match in which the South could not compete in either masses of men or resources.

––––––––

The passages below are from Jackson's letters to his wife, Anna, the memoirs of Henry Kyd Douglas, a young staff officer constantly at Stonewall's side,[9] and other sources.

Determination

[*Entry c. 1845, in Jackson's West Point Notebook.*]
You can be whatever you resolve to be.[10]

––––––––

The Art of War

LIEUTENANT HENRY KYD DOUGLAS:
"Audacity, audacity, always audacity." This quality Danton thought was the key to success. General Jackson said: "Mystery—mystery is the secret of success." His was not the mystery of speech; it was the mystery of action. General Jackson came and went; his enemies knew not whence he came, nor his friends whither he was gone. He moved, but gave no reason for his movement. He never looked to his subordinates for advice and it was seldom volunteered. His plans were his own and he took the responsibility.[11]

Always mystify. Mislead and surprise the enemy if possible. And when you strike and overcome him, never let up in pursuit so long as your men have strength to follow, for an army routed, if hotly pursued, becomes panic stricken, and can then be destroyed by half their number.

Another rule—never fight against heavy odds, if by any possible maneuvering you can hurl your own forces on only a part, and that the weakest part, of your enemy and crush it. Such tactics will win every time, and a small army may thus destroy a large one in detail, and repeated victory will make it invincible.[12]

Up-Front Leadership

[Chapultepec, 12–13 September 1847.]

A FELLOW OFFICER:

Lieutenant Jackson's section of Magruder's [artillery] battery was subjected to . . . fire from the Castle of Chapultepec. The little six-pounders could effect nothing against the guns of the Mexicans, of much heavier calibre, firing from an elevation. The horses were killed or disabled, and the men became so demoralized that they deserted the guns and sought shelter behind wall or embankment. Lieutenant Jackson remained at the guns, walking back and forth, and kept saying, "See, there is no danger; l am not hit!" While standing with his legs wide apart, a cannon-ball passed between them; and this fact probably prevented him from having any confidence in what the soldiers playfully called being "stung by a bomb."

When the castle was captured, many of the stormers dispersed in search of plunder and liquor. A few pursued promptly the retreating column of Mexicans. Lieutenants D. H. Hill and Barnard Bee [sic] followed down the causeway towards the Garita of San Cosme. . . . After the chase had been continued over a mile, Lieutenant Jackson came up with two pieces of artillery, and joined with the two young officers. They now pressed on vigorously. Captain Magruder himself soon appeared with caissons and men, but no additional guns. He expressed a fear of losing the two guns, as the division of General Worth was far in the rear, but he yielded to the solicitations of the young men, and continued the march. Shortly after the arrival of Captain Magruder a column of two thousand cavalry, under General Arripudia, made a demonstration of charging upon the guns. They were unlimbered, and a rapid fire was opened upon the Mexicans, who retreated without attacking the artillery. It was not judged prudent to proceed farther, and the command halted until General Worth came up. The part played later in the day by the battery at the Garita of San Cosme is mentioned in the official reports. For gallantry in the battles of Contreras and Cherubusco, on the 20th of August, Lieutenant Jackson had been brevetted a captain; and now this storming of Chapultepec, on the 13th of September won him the brevet of major.[13]

A Touch of Camaraderie: The "Rebel Yell"

[*First Manassas (Bull Run), where Jackson won the sobriquet "Stonewall"; 21 July 1861. Jackson was at the top of Henry House Hill; his brigade was behind him on the reverse slope.*]

Steady, men, steady. Reserve your fire, reserve your fire! Wait . . . until they come within fifty yards, then fire into them and give them the bayonet. . . . When you charge, yell like furies![14]

Modesty and Religiosity

[*Jackson to his wife, Anna, after First Manassas (Bull Run, 21 July 1861).*] I received only one wound, the breaking of the longest finger of my left hand; but the doctor says the finger can be saved. It was broken about midway between the hand and knuckle, the ball passing on the side next the forefinger. Had it struck the centre, I should have lost the finger. My horse was wounded, but not killed. [My] coat got an ugly wound near the hip but my servant, who is very handy, has so far repaired it that it doesn't show very much. My preservation was entirely due, as was the glorious victory, to our God, to whom be all the honor, praise, and glory. The battle was the hardest that I have ever been in, but not so hot in its fire. I commanded in the centre more particularly, though one of my regiments extended the right for some distance. There were other commanders on my right and left. Whilst great credit is due to other parts of our gallant army, God made my brigade more instrumental than any other in repulsing the main attack. This is for your information only—say nothing about it. Let others speak praise, not myself.[15]

Regard for Troop Morale

[*Jackson to Anna, 17 August 1861.*] You want to know whether I could get a furlough. My darling, I can't be absent from my command, as my attention is necessary in preparing my troops for hard fighting should it be required, and as my officers and soldiers are not permitted to go and see their wives and families, I ought not to see my *esposita*, as it might make the troops feel that they were badly treated, and that I consult my own pleasure and comfort regardless of theirs: so you had better stay at Cottage Home for the present, as I do not know how long I shall remain here.[16]

The Shenandoah Valley Campaign

The Shenandoah Valley Campaign (First Phase) against Union Generals John C. Frémont and Nathaniel P. Banks, 30 April–27 May 1862: Frémont was advancing from the west; Banks from the north, confidently, having defeated Jackson at Kernstown (with 38,000 troops against Jackson's 6,000). Jackson left General Richard S. Ewell, who had just joined him with 8,500 men, at Conrad's Store to block Banks if necessary (but without telling him his plan). Jackson went west and defeated Frémont's advance force (division of Robert H. Milroy) at the village of McDowell, then joined with Ewell and turned on Banks, driving the Federals from Front Royal and north along the Shenandoah through Winchester and across the Potomac. Jackson's peculiar handling of Ewell is mentioned first in the passages below.

Secrecy and Personal Leadership

LIEUTENANT HENRY KYD DOUGLAS:
The dispatch I carried that night was an order from General Jackson to General [Richard S.] Ewell to put his division in readiness to move toward Swift Run Gap and unite with the Army of the Valley west of the Blue Ridge. That was the initial move in that great game of war now known as Stonewall Jackson's Valley Campaign.

General Ewell moved toward Jackson as ordered and encamped near Stanardsville, east of the Blue Ridge. On the 30th of April, General Jackson sent to him the following order . . . : "General. Please let your command come on this side of the Blue Ridge at once." . . . On that day Ewell crossed the Blue Ridge and moved to Conrad's Store: but *Jackson was gone* and he occupied the camps in which the dying fires still smouldered. Ewell was surprised and somewhat indignant, for *Jackson had not left him an order or an intimation of his future movements—an eccentricity that rumors had partially prepared him for.* . . . Thus entered General Ewell into the Army of the Valley, to whose . . . brilliant success he so largely contributed.[17]

[*Ewell camped near Conrad's Store until after Jackson's next move.*]

Setting an Example

On the afternoon of April 30th General Jackson started with his division [*the "Stonewall Brigade" plus some local militia, about 6,000 men, total*] on that terrible march along the east side of the Shenandoah River to Port Republic. It was only about sixteen miles, but it took him two days and a half to do it . . . over soft and bottomless roads into which horses and wagons and artillery sank, at times almost out of sight, dragged along by main force of horses and men, the General himself on foot, lifting and pushing among the struggling mass, wet, covered with mud from cap to boots, encouraging soldiers and teamsters by word and example, at the risk any moment of ruinous attacks from the Federal guns from opposite bluffs.

Improvising to Respond to the Unexpected

Near Port Republic we turned eastward up into the Blue Ridge and over it through Brown's Gap, and on Saturday evening [3 May] went into camp at White Hall. It was the intention of the General to remain quiet in camp over Sunday, but during the night word came to him from Staunton that the enemy was marching rapidly on that place. Early on Sunday the troops were off via Mechum's River Station, where the General and his staff took the train at once for Staunton. His troops followed. At Staunton the General found that the report was unfounded. [*Jackson was joined at Staunton by a small force under General Edward Johnson,*] "Old Alleghany," "Club Johnson," "Old Blucher," as he was variously and affectionately called by his troops. . . . [Also] At Staunton the army was joined by two hundred cadets from the Virginia Military Institute at Lexington, under command of General F. H. Smith. The natty appearance of these youthful soldiers afforded a striking contrast to the seedy . . . veterans, but before they returned from McDowell much of the gloss was gone.

[*Jackson now had about 7,000 men; Frémont's force numbered 20,000.*]

Defeating the Enemy: Advance Against Frémont

After a day of getting ready we started westward, and . . . came up with General Johnson, who then marched in advance [6 May]. There was some skirmishing but the enemy retired until the afternoon of Thursday, the 8th of May, when they made a stand on a spur of Bull Pasture Mountain, looking down upon a little village called McDowell. The Federal troops [*vanguard of the army of Gen. John C. Frémont*] were commanded by Generals R. H. Milroy and Robert C. Schenck. [After] some preliminary skirmishing, battle began in earnest about half-past four in the afternoon. . . . It was an obstinately contested little battle of about four hours, when the enemy was routed. The loss on both sides was heavy for the numbers engaged. . . .

Jackson's laconic dispatch announcing the result [read]: "God blessed our arms with victory at McDowell yesterday. The Federal troops made a stiff fight, such as they might well be proud of."[18]

[*Frémont retreated; his plan to cooperate with Gen. Nathaniel P. Banks against Jackson in the valley was ruined.*]

Defeating the Enemy: Jackson Turns on Banks

General Jackson followed the enemy with occasional skirmishing for several days as far as Franklin. He then retraced his steps by way of McDowell, Lebanon Springs, off to Bridgewater where he quietly spent Sunday the 18th [*of May*] and then on to Harrisonburg. Thence with no delay he moved down the Valley pike to New Market, crossed to the eastern side of the Massanutten Mountain and united with General Ewell who had moved down from near Conrad's Store. There they proceeded to act jointly and to carry out their plans "in Stonewall Jackson's way."[19]

[*Banks retreated north in confusion—"down" the valley. The Union war secretary urgently called for more troops to defend Washington.*]

Improvision: Jackson Marches on Front Royal

When General Jackson and General Ewell united, their combined force was about 17,000.[20] [*Banks had 40,000.*] The General knew both from information from Generals Lee and [Joseph E.] Johnston and from his own intuition that it was important that the Federal Government [not be able to] send heavy reinforcements from Banks . . . to help [Gen. George B.] McClellan in his siege of Richmond. It was his duty . . . to prevent this if possible with his little army, and he determined to try it without delay.

On the 22nd of May he began his march, with Ewell in front, down [*north*] through the Luray Valley to Front Royal, taking precaution through [cavalry General Turner] Ashby to keep his movements veiled from the enemy. This he succeeded in doing with rare success.[21]

Tip from a Beautiful "Spy"

In the early afternoon of the next day Ewell struck the pickets of the enemy within sight of and negligently near to Front Royal. They were driven in and the small body of infantry supporting them easily routed. We stopped to form on a hill overlooking the small town of Front Royal and the hurried movement of blue coats and the galloping of horsemen here and there told of the confusion in the enemy's camp. General Jackson, not knowing the force of the enemy there was so small or so unprepared by reinforcements for his approach, was endeavoring to take in the situation before ordering an advance.

I observed, almost immediately, the figure of a woman in white glide swiftly out of town on our right and, after making a little circuit, run rapidly up a ravine in our direction and then disappear from sight. She seemed, when I saw her, to heed neither weeds nor fences, but waved a bonnet as she came on, trying, it was evident, to keep the hill between herself and the village. I called

General Jackson's attention to [her] . . . and at General Ewell's suggestion, he sent me to meet her and ascertain what she wanted. . . . I saw that the visitor was the well-known Belle Boyd whom I had known from her earliest girlhood. She was just the girl to dare to do this thing.

Nearly exhausted, and with her hand pressed against her heart, she said in gasps, "I knew it must be Stonewall, when I heard the first gun. Go back quick and tell him that the Yankee force is very small—one regiment of . . . infantry, several pieces of artillery and several companies of cavalry. . . . Tell him to charge right down and he will catch them all. I must hurry back. Good-by. My love to all the dear boys—and remember if you meet me in town you haven't seen me today."

I raised my cap, she kissed her hand and was gone. I delivered her message speedily. . . .

Very soon the First Maryland Infantry [CSA] and Major Roberdeau Wheat's Louisiana battalion were rushing down the hill and into the town. General Jackson with a semi-smile suggested that I had better go with them and see if I could get any more information from that young lady. [*He did, but got only a red rose.*] It took very little time to get into Front Royal and clean it out. The pursuit of the retreating Federals was kept up, with cavalry, the infantry following as quickly as possible.[22]

Pursuit of Banks: Personal Leadership

The pursuit begun was kept up vigorously. There was much handsome work done by Flournoy's cavalry, with good results. Another brilliant charge was made by a squadron of Ashby's cavalry in which two of the best captains in his command, George F. Sheetz and John Fletcher, were killed. . . . The result of the day's work was about 750 prisoners . . . and about 150 killed and wounded Union soldiers. A great quantity of valuable stores and material of war was taken. The loss of the Confederates was small.

The next day General Jackson moved on toward Middletown. It was soon evident that Banks either was late in getting information of the result at Front Royal or did not appreciate its meaning. He hesitated, delayed, and seemed unwilling to leave Strasburg until convinced that he must do it. His column was struck and cut in two before it had passed Middletown, although General Banks himself and the bulk of his infantry had gone. With the cavalry and the artillery left behind and some little infantry, all sorts of a mixed-up fight ensued. Middletown is five miles from Strasburg and thirteen miles from Winchester. Colonel Oliver R. Funsten of Ashby's cavalry was sent to the right, accompanied by a section of W. T. Poague's [*artillery*] battery, to intercept the retreating enemy in the direction of Newtown. The road was literally lined with wagons of all kinds, miles of them. Funsten's and Poague's attack soon created a stampede and the train of quartermaster and commissary stores fell into our hands.

Jackson Directs the Artillery

A regiment of Federal cavalry, coming from Strasburg . . . saw that the way was stopped. [But] the commander decided promptly to go on to Winchester in spite of obstacles. . . . General Jackson had gone off to direct Poague in person. . . . [With the staff were] about one hundred infantry—which General Dick Taylor had considerately sent forward with General Jackson . . . with orders to follow and keep up with the General when he moved off to the front so far from his troops—I directed the officer to take these men to a stone fence along the road and [stop] the enemy's cavalry. I didn't want them to get past Middletown, for if they did . . . they might do serious damage to Funsten, Poague, and perhaps to the General. [*The cavalry was stopped.*][23]

Jackson Presses Forward

With all possible promptness we moved on toward Winchester by the pike. The road was encumbered with evidence of the hurry of flight. Wagons broken down, overturned, some with their contents scattered, some sound and untouched, some with good teams, some horseless . . . a general wreck of military matter.

I was riding with the General and a small party of staff and couriers along the road. He was in good spirits but silent and thoughtful. Once [*Jackson*] dismounted and took from an overturned wagon a cracker, hard and not too clean, and attempted to eat it, for he had eaten nothing since early morning.[24]

Cavalry Fails to Crush Banks

It was after dark when we passed through Newtown, over which a small artillery duel had been fought for several hours. Ashby's cavalry, having given themselves up, in their hunger, to plundering wagons, were so reduced in numbers that they were virtually inefficient. That the defeat of Banks was not his destruction is due to the failure of the cavalry . . . and General Jackson never ceased to lament and condemn that costly want of discipline.

Determination: Jackson Drives His Weary Men

The General had no thought of going into camp. True, the army had been marching almost daily for weeks, had been up nearly all the night before, had been living for some time on much excitement and very small rations; it was exhausted, broken down, and apparently unfit for battle; but the General was determined to push on that night. Of course no one was surprised for that was already Stonewall's way. The soldiers were tired and weary and grumbled a bit as usual, but they had faith and plodded on, not cheerfully but resignedly. By the sweat of their brow, he was saving their blood.

For some miles from Newtown we rode by the light of burning wagons, to which the enemy set fire when they abandoned them. This bonfire was expensive, but grateful, for it announced to the people of Winchester that Jackson was coming. After passing these, night enveloped us in impenetrable darkness. Footsore and weary, the column moved, Jackson, Ashby, and our staff at its head, and all nodding with hopeless drowsiness—all except Ashby. . . . There was Pendleton, whose intense sleepiness took the expression of anger, Lieutenant Colonel S. Crutchfield (descendant of the man who invented sleep) muttering in disgust, "This is uncivilized," Dr. McGuire, meditative as becomes a surgeon, thinking of his home and people in Winchester.

Jackson Leads From the Front

Suddenly a sharp volley of musketry, flashing almost in our faces, sounded an alarum on the night and awakened us. We were ambuscaded by a party of the enemy's rear guard, perhaps a score, who had let our cavalry scouts pass and had hidden themselves behind a stone fence. They fired and fled. They must have been terribly scared for not a man [on the Confederate side] was hit. Such an escape was miraculous.

One would suppose that little incident was enough to satisfy the General that he, his chief of cavalry, and his staff, all asleep, were not [a proper] advance guard. The staff had reached that conclusion on previous occasions, but their opinion lacked weight in convincing the General. We moved on as before [but after another ambush, Jackson halted and sent infantry ahead; they ambushed the ambushers.] . . . Then the enemy deployed some skirmishers . . . which served to delay our march until we reached Kernstown.

Whenever the column stopped for a minute, the sleepy officers and men would throw themselves on the ground. And thus, skirmishing and halting, marching while sleeping, the night wore away, and within a few hours of daylight we halted within two miles of Winchester. Jackson, Ashby, and the staff halted and fastened their horses to the fences. The little cavalcade was greatly reduced. Several of the staff had fallen asleep and had been left by the wayside; couriers, sent off, had not returned. The General and Ashby to keep awake were walking, separately, up and down the pike, passing each other like silent sentinels, absorbed in their own thought.[25]

[At dawn, at Winchester, Banks seemed ready to fight.]

Jackson Storms Winchester

Jackson and Ashby mounted their horses, and orders were sent along the line to close up and get ready for attack. . . . The Stonewall Brigade opened the engagement, and . . . drove the enemy from their first position. While arrangements were being made for still further advance, I conducted the General, at his request, to General Dick Taylor's brigade. The soldiers we passed . . . ordered to observe silence, took off their hats in silent salute; he did the same. But they watched him carefully and earnestly, looked up into his face, scanned his features, his expression, as if they were trying to read, "what the signs of promise are."

Riding up to General Taylor, [Jackson] said: "General, can your brigade charge a battery?"

"It can try."

"Very good; it must do it then. Move it forward."

Only this and nothing more. Jackson rode back; Taylor, a worthy son of General Zack Taylor, followed with his command. But as the General was returning, the troops could not stand . . . that unnatural silence any longer. . . they let forth in one of their deafening yells. Old Jack smiled and passed on.

Calmness under Fire

But soon the enemy's artillery sent a shower of shells in acknowledgment of the salute. While under that fire, the General rode along quietly, with his chin thrown out as usual and his cap close over his eyes, in apparent unconcern. I was wondering if this unconsciousness of the "deadly imminent" shot flying through the air was simply indifference to danger, or the action of nerve and will-power; and this may have caused me, involuntarily, to imitate his bearing. The situation seemed to strike a little Irishman of the ranks as amusing, for he cried out, "Be jabers, have your eye on Auld Jack. I'll wager you he thinks them blatherin' bangs are singin' birds." And, with a chuckle, "look at yon officer behint him, imitatin' the Ginril and tryin' to look as bauld as himself." I dodged the next shell.

General Taylor threw his brigade into line where directed, and it moved forward in gallant style. I have rarely seen a more beautiful charge. . . . The battery was not taken, because it did not wait. It departed and its infantry support was quickly driven after it.

General Ewell on the Front Royal road with equal success had driven the enemy before him toward the town.[26]

Camaraderie: Now Let's Holler!

Shortly afterwards followed some sharp fighting but no general engagement. General Jackson and a few of his staff were sitting mounted on the crest of a hill overlooking Winchester. He paid little attention to the line of skirmishers advancing against us, but was watching the movement of troops and artillery in and about town. He was evidently surprised, as if he was expecting something else, and turning to me quickly he said, "Order forward the whole line, the battle's won." Soon the men of Taylor and of Winder came sweeping past and as they did the General cried out, "Very good! Now let's holler!" That is the very language the Professor used. He raised his old grey cap, his staff took up the cheer, and soon from the advancing line rose and swelled a deafening roar. . . . A panic seized the enemy and the retreat became a rout.

Galloping down the hill, the General and staff went into town with the skirmishers. . . . [Winchester was taken.][27]

It was Sunday—was Jackson always to fight on Sunday?—but church bells were silent. The streets were lined with people, but not on their way to the sanctuaries; they had come to meet their own troops.

Jackson Dodges the Limelight

The reception of General Jackson cannot be described. There were tears and smiles, like rain and sunshine; lips that spoke blessings, and quivering lips that could not speak at all; men, women, and children all joining in the strange welcome. . . .

But he could not stop. He was not a man of words, and such devotion was enough to overwhelm him. Breaking away as quickly as he could, he pushed forward with his troops. The only order he seemed to give was, "Push on to the Potomac." He kept up the chase with his infantry for five miles and then was forced to rest his troops—even their energy and endurance had a limit. Again the cavalry failed him. Banks' army, defeated, scattered, only needed some command to push it and demand surrender. That was the duty of the cavalry, and they were not there. Had they done their duty as well as the infantry, Banks' army would have ceased to exist that day. He might have escaped, but he would not have sent that comic message to Washington that his army had "retired in good order across the Potomac." . . . General Jackson and his army entered Winchester Sunday morning, May the 25th. The next day the army rested, and by order of the General the chaplains held services in their regiments at 4:00 P.M. It was Sunday, *nunc pro tunc*.[28]

Phase Two of the Valley Campaign

[*Jackson chased Banks across the Potomac, but his rear was threatened by Federal forces—Frémont from the west and General Irvin McDowell's forces from the northeast. On 31 May, Jackson had to retreat south, with the enemy closing in from the west, north and east. There were tense moments and some happy ones.*]

[*At Strasburg*] During the day a small skirmish and artillery duel took place between some of General Ewell's troops and the advance of General Frémont. It was soon over, and the day passed quietly but slowly and anxiously away. Night came at length and General Jackson moved out of Strasburg and [south] up the Valley pike unmolested and unpursued.

About midnight the staff regaled themselves at Woodstock with a hetero-geneous supper, furnished by the different sutler stores of General Banks. There were probably too many delicacies of inconsistent qualities to suit the taste of a *bon vivant*, but we had no one with us to make objections. It was indeed a sumptuous table: cake and pickled lobsters, cheese, canned peaches, piccolo-mini and candy, coffee, ale, and condensed milk. It was a feast the like of which was seldom vouchsafed to Confederate soldiers, and with inexpressible thanks we drank the health of General Banks. Not knowing from the dark situation of affairs how soon we and our possessions might fall into the hands of the enemy, we determined to place a great portion of these viands beyond the possibility of recapture.[29]

Jackson's Brand of Discipline

[*The march was not without confusion.*] One brigade divided another, and gen-erals and colonels were wandering through the mass in search of their com-mands. The clouded brow and closed lips of General Jackson were ominous: he was becoming impatient at the delay. Quickly and sharply he hurried his staff in every direction while, stern and watchful, he rode along the tangled line. . . .

The General rode up to an officer whose brigade had been divided into two or three parts. "Colonel, why do you not get your brigade together, keep it together and move on?"

"It's impossible, General; I can't do it."

"Don't say it's impossible. Turn your command over to the next officer. If he can't do it, I'll find someone who can, if I have to take him from the ranks."

Soon a different state of things showed the effect of the indomitable will of this man.[30]

[*Jackson paused to regroup at Port Republic; he put Ewell to the west to block Fré-mont. But McDowell's forces had taken Front Royal, and the vanguard, 20,000 men under Brig. Gen. James Shields, was closing on Port Republic from the north faster than Jackson had expected.*]

Calmness under Pressure

[*On 8 June 1862, a Sunday, Cavalryman Henry Kerfoot (16) galloped up to Jackson, who was sitting on a porch, to report Union Horsemen were on the outskirts of Port Republic.*]

Jackson accepted the report "without excitement or change of countenance" and said . . . : "Well, sir, go back and fight them." [*Jackson galloped out of Port Repub-lic past Union cavalry, who might have captured him if they had recognized him. Still, he made one stop—to reprimand Dr. Hunter McGuire, who was evacuating patients from Port Royal Church, which had come under Union artillery fire.]*

Religiosity—To Extremes

McGuire wrote, "I . . . was riding up and down the line of ambulances threatening to shoot the first man who left [and] in order to enforce my commands was using some profane language. I felt somebody touch me on the shoulder, and looking around, found it was Gen. Jackson, who had . . . ridden on down the main street of the village until he came to the church. The general asked mildly, "Doctor, don't you think you can manage these men without swearing?" "I told him I would try."[31]

[Jackson rode furiously across the North River bridge and joined his troops.]

When Frémont heard what he supposed was Shields' attack upon our position at Port Republic, he advanced against Ewell, and very soon the battle was in earnest. Ewell's position was a good one, and he did not hesitate because of Frémont's superior force. He fought his battle well and with his small division defeated Frémont with heavy loss to him.

Risk Taking

General Frémont repulsed, General Shields checked and not in sight, it was believed General Jackson would take advantage of the night and slip out of the trap with his prisoners and stores. But the General seemed to like traps and, at any rate, was not yet satisfied with the risks he had run and the blows he had inflicted. He directed his quartermaster, Major Harman, to bring up all the wagons, over the river, that the troops might cook rations. . . . The staff [was] confounded. Pendleton, McGuire, Crutchfield, Boswell, and all present exchanged looks and smiles, as Pendleton said "crazy again." We were getting used to this kind of aberration, but this did seem rather an extra piece of temerity. Nevertheless, the wagons came up. Frémont and Shields must have seen the campfires and been confused accordingly. The night was beautiful, after the eventful day, and we retired taking much thought for the morrow.

Jackson Had a Plan

General Jackson's intention was very soon made plain. Before the sun had risen [9 June], or Frémont either, our army had crossed into Port Republic and from there upon a temporary bridge of wagons over the South Branch on its way to measure strength with Shields' unwhipped army. . . . About two miles below Port Republic, the skirmishers . . . became engaged, and . . . the lines went at each other. The result was a hot fight continued for several hours with great vigor and varying success, as was announced by alternate "Rebel yells" and "Yankee cheers." For the only time in my life I saw a regiment, from Ohio I believe, change front to rear on first company, under fire, and with admirable precision. I knew then, that it would be no easy matter to defeat an army of such troops. The fighting of both armies was obstinate, the gallantry of officers conspicuous, and the loss among them unusually heavy. Finally the Federals began to retire, then to retreat, and then the rout was complete; the pursuit of them was continued for about five miles and prisoners and guns were captured.[32] [With the defeat of Shields, the Confederates "owned" the Valley for the time being. Jackson's most famous campaign was over. He had kept McDowell from reinforcing Gen. George McClellan, who was moving on Richmond; and he could now reinforce Lee, who was defending the Confederate capital.]

Order of Major General Jackson, 13 June 1862

The fortitude of the troops under fatigue and their valor in action have again, under blessing of Divine Providence, placed it in the power of the commanding general to congratulate upon the victories of June 8th and 9th. Beset on both flanks by two boastful armies, you have escaped their toils, inflicting successively crushing blows on each of your pursuers. Let a few more such efforts be made, and you may confidently hope that our beautiful valley will be cleansed from the pollution of the invader's presence. *The major-general commanding invites you to observe tomorrow, June 14th, from three o'clock P.M., as a season of thanksgiving, by a suspension of all military exercises, and by holding divine service* in the several regiments.[33]

Jackson's Views on Fighting the War

[A conversation with his brother-in-law, Captain Rufus Barringer of the 1st North Carolina Cavalry, serving with Jeb Stuart (as reported by Barringer), 14 July 1862.]

Jackson Favors Offensive War

JACKSON [recalling an earlier talk]:
   Neither of us had any special concern for slavery, but both agreed that if the sword was once drawn, the South would have no alternative but to defend her homes and firesides, slavery and all. . . . I always thought we ought to meet the Federal invaders on the outer verge of just right and defence and [the outer limits of the Confederacy] raise at once the black flag, viz. No quarter to the violators of our homes and firesides! [To wage offensive war] would in the end have proved true humanity and mercy. The Bible is full of such wars, and it . . . would bring the North to its senses.

The Nature of War Has Changed

I have . . . accepted the policy of our leaders. They are great and good men.
Possibly . . . [only a defensive] policy was left open to us. . . . But all this is
now suddenly changed by the cruel and . . . barbarous orders of [Union] General [John] Pope, who is . . . subsisting his army on the people of [Virginia],
. . . levying contributions . . . [and] has laid communities under the . . . penal-
ties of death or banishment; and in certain cases directed that houses shall be
razed . . . and citizens shot without waiting [for] civil process.

This new phase of the struggle is full upon us, and General Lee is in great
perplexity how to meet it. . . . But I gave him . . . outlines of my own plan of
waging the contest, which he considered favorably, and which he promised to
lay before Mr. [Jefferson] Davis [President of the Confederate States].

Jackson's Grand Strategy for the CSA

[*Jackson first inquired about the volunteer 1st North Carolina Cavalry, adding: "I
have some prejudices against the narrow ideas of the (regular) army officers."*]

BARRINGER:

I then gave him the full details of our organization, camp methods, and the
esprit de corps of both men and officers. He beamed with delight, and answered:
"You are fortunate to have such men to command, and the Confederacy fortunate to have such officers to lead them. With such troops I would not hesitate
to risk a march even to New York or to Chicago." . . .

JACKSON:

As to a general policy, I think it unwise to attempt to defend the whole of our
extended lines, especially our extended coast and water line. The enemy largely
exceed us in men and material of war, especially in naval appliances, and our
limited supply of both troops and munitions of war would ultimately be exhausted in a prolonged, gigantic struggle. To offset [the Union's] palpable advantage in this respect, I would seek to utilize the special points in which the
South clearly leads the North, and I would risk the whole issue on the development of these special characteristics, and the war policy based thereon. As I
always said, my own first policy would have been the black flag to all comers
against the safety of our Southern homes. Next to that, I would give up, as
circumstances might seem to require, exposed points and all untenable positions, and gradually concentrate our choicest fighting men and valuable material at a few strong interior camps, thoroughly fortified, and so located as best,
at and the same time, to protect our communications, defend our people and
territory against invasions of the enemy, and also keep up ceaseless aggressions
upon them. These counter-invasions would be main feature of my policy. I
would organize our whole available fighting force, so selected and located, into
two, four, or more light movable columns, specially armed and trained and
equipped for sudden moves and for long and rapid marches. These light mov-

able columns I would hurl against the enemy as they entered our borders, but only when sure of victory, and when the loss of an army was impossible. But better, I would hurl these thunderbolts of war against the rich cities and teeming regions of our Federal friends. I would seek to avoid all regular battles. I would subsist my troops, as far as possible, on the Northern people. I would lay heavy contributions in money on their cities. I would encumber my marches with no prisoners, except notable leaders, held mainly as hostages for ransom or for retaliation. *All the rank and file I would parole, but only at the risk of life if the parole was violated.* [Barringer's italics] All this just as Pope is doing in Northern Virginia. I would train and practise the troops with special reference to the tactics of "Attack and Retreat." But before turning my back to the foe or the enemy country, I would see that some other one or more of these "movable columns" was on the march, and striking at some other vital point—possibly hundreds of miles away. And so I would make it hot for our friends at *their* homes and firesides, all the way to Kansas . . . and doubly so for Ohio and Pennsylvania.

This programme would, of course, involve giving up much of our territory, and some large cities also, merely taking the chance of crossing the Mississippi and other navigable streams. But it would save the risk of losing whole armies by capture, disease, or death in battle. My whole policy would aim to husband our resources of men, money, and material. At first, this policy might not have been so easily appreciated, but now our people begin to learn something of war. . . . Ben Butler, Fremont, and Pope are fast opening their eyes. The garrison and fortification policy has lost us whole armies at Donaldson and elsewhere, while the malaria of the ordinary camp and the coast will soon decimate our ranks, and possibly break the spirit of our people. We have just gained great victories here at Richmond, and our troops would now rejoice at the hope of an aggressive movement. That mode of war best suits the temper of our people and the dash and daring of the Southern soldier, and I would right now seize the golden moment to show the North what they may expect.

In a war thus waged, the cavalry and horse artillery would play a most important part. In fact, in certain operations I would depend almost entirely on mounted troops. The one vital advantage of the South lies in the horsemanship of the Southern boy, and the personal courage of the Southern freeman. And now is just the time to bring it to bear. See what Stuart has done in sweeping clear around McClellan's army.

But I well know that General Lee is not at liberty to choose his own policy now. In three hours I may be on the march—possibly to flank McClellan, but more likely to fight Pope. . . . But if the two main Federal armies remain stationary, and we get a few days to turn around in, General Lee has assented to [my] policy, so far as to promise me the organization of at least one of these "light movable columns," and with it I am to make the invasion, of course only at such point as may then seem open.[34]

BARRINGER:

I next met him . . . on the night of the terrible slaughter at Sharpsburg, September 17th, 1862. He was withdrawing part of his lines, for a little repose. . . . I said, with some concern: General, isn't our army pretty badly worsted to-night? He answered: Yes, but oh! how I'd like to see the Yankee camp right now! And then added, with a twinkle in his eye, If I only had my movable column![35]

Possibly greater disasters . . . would have befallen our unfortunate people had [Jackson's] vigorous war policy been actually adopted. But . . . when the supreme moment came for President Davis and General Lee to decide on the last . . . chance left for . . . ultimate success, they both accepted . . . this "movable column policy" of . . . Jackson, as laid down by him on July 14th, 1862, nearly three years before the catastrophe came. When General Lee gave up Richmond and Petersburg, he frankly avowed his purpose to retire to the strongholds of our long mountain ranges, and there maintain the contest; while Mr. Davis, in his last proclamation, at Danville, uttered these words: "Relieved from the necessity of guarding particular points, our army will be free to move from point to point, to strike the enemy in detail," and "no longer forego opportunities for promising enterprises."[36]

Determination

[*13 December 1862 at Fredericksburg.*]

DR. HUNTER McGUIRE:

"What shall we do, General, with such vast numbers against us?"

JACKSON:

"Kill them, Kill them all, sir! Kill every man!"[37]

Chancellorsville: Jackson as Improvisor

[*On 2 May 1863 Jackson marched his corps across the rear of the Confederate Army while General Lee held the enemy at bay, and smashed the flank of General Joseph Hooker's Union Army. He had won the battle, though fighting continued until 6 May, when Hooker retreated across the Rappahannock River. As night fell on 2 May, Jackson went forward on reconnaissance, was mistaken for an enemy, and wounded by his own men. He was at first expected to live, and one day after the battle, discussed his part in it.*]

Our movement yesterday was a great success; I think the most successful military movement of my life. But I expect to receive far more credit for it than I deserve. Most men will think that I had planned it all from the first but it was not so. I simply took advantage of circumstances as they were presented to me in the providence of God. I feel that His hand led me—let us give Him all the glory.[38]

[*Jackson died on 10 May 1863, with his beloved Anna at his side. Lucid almost to the end, he asked to be buried in Lexington, and, calling on all present to have faith in God, tried to minimize the grief of his wife and many friends and admirers.*]

Conclusions

Jackson's leadership was unrelentingly from the front. His courage and ability to endure hardship set an example for his men. He concentrated on the mission; only religious "duties" could distract him from it. He was a strict disciplinarian, with no tolerance for officers or men he decided were shirkers or cowards; with him, it was obey or die. But he was a winner, which seemed to compensate for his harshness and eccentricities. The troops worshipped him. Henry Kyd Douglas wrote of the men during the retreat up the Valley in June 1862—continually on alert, with Union armies on either side of them, marching for days "without sleep, rest or food," but not worried:

> The opinion of all may be inferred from the expression of one I overheard, "Old Jack got us into this fix, and with the blessing of God he will get us out." Many who have wondered at General Jackson's success might have learned one of the secrets of it if they had been with him at Strasburg. His army was brave, well-disciplined; *that was not it.* They had unbounded confidence in their leader and he in them; *that was it.*
>
> "Stonewall Jackson's men will follow him to the devil and he knows it," said a Federal officer who had been taken prisoner. General Lee was the great Chieftain of the army; they were proud of him . . . but they loved "Old Jack." He was as a father to them, sometimes stern and exacting; they were his children, sometimes sullen but always obedient.[39]

He demanded the best from his troops, but he took care of them. Frugal "Old Jack" distribued captured Yankee stores to his men with special glee, together with the best he could requisition.

The plan he gave Barringer might not have won the war, but it was infinitely more rational than that followed by the Confederacy.

IV

John Singleton Mosby

(1833–1916)

COLONEL JOHN SINGLETON MOSBY, CSA, was the consummate guerrilla. Excerpts from his writings are included here for the lessons they may give in guerrilla, counter-guerrilla and counterterrorist warfare, all of importance today. He is among the few historical figures in the Hall of Fame of the United States Army Ranger Association.[1] Mosby used the friendly Virginia population as what Mao Zedong later called "a vast sea in which to drown the enemy."[2] While Mosby's "sea" extended only to the Potomac, it allowed him and his "Children of the Mist"[3] to strike at the enemy and disappear.

Mosby became a storied Southern hero at the head of "Mosby's Rangers" (officially, the 43rd Battalion, Virginia Cavalry). The Federals called him "Scarlet Cloak" and "the Gray Ghost." Some of them also called him cutthroat and guerrilla, and accused him of sending men in Union uniforms or civilian clothes to murder Yankee pickets.[4] He was a guerrilla, alright; the rest is unproven.[5] Mosby himself always wore Confederate gray on raids. He was described as "ordinary" in appearance, an asset when under scrutiny by his enemies; he was about 5′7″ tall (average for his time) and weighed 130 pounds; his face was strong, but not handsome; his eyes blue and hair brown.

Of an old Virginia family, but hardly "tidewater aristocracy," Mosby was educated in rural schools and the University of Virginia, where his third year ended abruptly after he shot the town bully, almost killing him. Convicted of "unlawful shooting" and given a light sentence, he later "read law" with his prosecutor, and in 1861 was a practicing lawyer.

Mosby opposed secession, but when war came, he enlisted in the 1st Virginia Cavalry and fought under J.E.B. "Jeb" Stuart at Bull Run. In 1862 he was made a lieutenant, but he resigned when Fitzhugh Lee took over the regiment, and became a civilian scout for Stuart, whom Robert E. Lee had given command of a division (later of the cavalry of the Army of Northern Virginia). It was Mosby's report that prompted Stuart to make his famous ride around McClellan's army

(June 1862).[6] After the Battle of Fredericksburg (December 1862), with Jeb's assent, Mosby left "temporarily" to lead "partisan" attacks on Union occupation troops in Northern Virginia. It proved a permanent assignment.

When the Confederate Congress outlawed partisans, Robert E. Lee had Mosby commissioned a captain.[7] At war's end, he was a colonel.

After Appomattox, Mosby disbanded his men rather than surrender, but most of them soon swore allegiance to the United States and went home. Mosby hid out until he was sure he would not be arrested, then went in and signed the parole, and returned to his law practice. In time he joined the Republican Party, became a friend of U. S. Grant, and was successively consul in Hong Kong, an official in the General Land Office and, an assistant attorney general. His "turn-coat" politics alienated many southerners, but his war legend was perpetuated by both friend and enemy. He died in poverty at age 82, before his *Memoirs* were published.

The passages below are from Mosby's *Reminiscences* (transcripts of his lectures, mostly to northern audiences) and his *Memoirs*, written just before his death.[8] He wrote plainly and well, and demonstrated a wide knowledge of history and literature.

Purposes and Techniques

My purpose was to weaken the armies invading Virginia, by harassing their rear. As a line is only as strong as its weakest point, it was necessary for it to be stronger than I was at every point, in order to resist my attacks. It is easy, therefore, to see the great results that may be accomplished by a small body of cavalry moving rapidly from point to point on the communications of an army. To destroy supply trains, to break up the means of conveying intelligence, and thus isolating an army from its base, as well as its different corps from each other, to confuse their plans by capturing despatches, are the objects of partisan war. It is just as legitimate to fight an enemy in the rear as in front. The only difference is in the danger. Now, to prevent all these things from being done, heavy detachments must be made to guard against them. The military value of a partisan's work is not measured by the amount of property destroyed, or the number of men killed or captured, but by the number he keeps watching. Every soldier withdrawn from the front to guard the rear of an army is so much taken from its fighting strength.

I endeavored, as far as I was able, to diminish this aggressive power of the army of the Potomac, by compelling it to keep a large force on the defensive.[9]

Strike and Vanish

My men had no camps. If they had gone into camp, they would soon have all been captured. They would scatter for safety, and gather at my call, *like the Children of the Mist*. A blow would be struck at a weak or unguarded point, and then a quick retreat. The alarm would spread through the sleeping camp, the long roll would be beaten or the bugles would sound to horse; there would be mounting in hot haste and a rapid pursuit. But the partisans generally got off with their prey. Their pursuers were striking at an invisible foe. I often sent small squads at night to attack and run in the pickets along a line of several miles. Of course, these alarms were very annoying, for no human being knows how sweet sleep is but a soldier. I wanted to use and consume the Northern cavalry in hard work. I have often thought that their fierce hostility to me was more on account of the sleep I made them lose than the number we killed and captured. It has always been a wonder with people how I managed to collect my men after dispersing them. The true secret was that it was a fascinating life, and its attractions far more than counterbalanced its hardships and dangers. They had no camp duty to do, which, however necessary, is disgusting to soldiers of high spirit. To put them to such routine work is pretty much like hitching a race-horse to a plow.

Objectives and Tactics

I had promised [J.E.B.] Stuart, as an inducement to let me have some men, either to compel the enemy to contract their lines in Fairfax County or to reinforce them heavily. Having no fixed lines to guard or defined territory to hold, it was always my policy to elude the enemy when they came in search of me, and carry the war into their . . . camps.

This was the best way to keep them at home. To have fought my own command daily, on equal terms and in open combats against the thousands that could have been brought against it by the North, would soon have resulted in its entire annihilation. I endeavored to compensate for my limited resources by stratagems, surprises, and night attacks, in which the advantage was generally on my side, notwithstanding the superior numbers we assailed. For this reason, the complaint has often been made against me that I would not fight fair. So an old Austrian general complained that Bonaparte violated all military maxims and traditions by flying about from post to post in Italy, breaking up his cantonments and fighting battles in the winter time. The accusations that have been made against my mode of warfare are about as reasonable.[10]

General View of War

In one sense the charge that I did not fight fair is true. I fought for success and not for display. There was no man in the Confederate army who had less of the spirit of knight-errantry in him, or took a more practical view of war than I did. The combat between Richard and Saladin by the Diamond of the Desert is a beautiful picture for the imagination to dwell on, but it isn't war, and was no model for me. I never admired . . . the example of the commander who declined the advantage of the first fire. But, while I conducted war on the theory that the end of it is to secure peace by the destruction of the resources of the enemy, with as small a loss as possible to my own side, there is no . . . act of mine which is not perfectly in accordance with approved military usage. Grant, Sheridan, and Stonewall Jackson had about the same ideas that I had on the subject of war.[11]

Preference for the Revolver

I had no faith in the sabre as a weapon. I only made the men draw their sabres to prevent them from wasting their fire before they got to closer quarters. I knew that when they got among [the enemy] the pistol would be used.[12]

Testing a Deserter-Recruit: Raid on Fairfax

I now determined to give [James F. "Big Yankee"] Ames [a deserter from the Union Cavalry] one more trial and so took him with me on a raid to Fairfax. But he went as a combatant without arms. I had found out that there was a picket post at a certain crossroads and went to attack it in a rain on a dark night, when there was snow on the ground. As only a raccoon could be supposed to travel on such a night, I knew the pickets would feel safe and would be sound asleep, so that a single shot would create a panic. We stopped to inquire of a farmer the location of the post. He had been there during the day and said that there were 100 men who slept in a schoolhouse. He asked me how many men I had, and I replied, "Seventeen, but they will think there are a hundred." They could not count in the dark. We made no attempt to flank the picket to prevent his giving the alarm, but we went straight down the road. One of the men, Joe Nelson, was sent ahead to catch the vidette [mounted sentry]. When the vidette saw Joe, he fired at him and started at full speed to the reserve; but we were on his heels and got there almost as soon as he did. The yells of my men resounded through the pines, and the Yankees all fled and left their horses hitched to the trees. As it was very dark, we could not catch many of the men, but we got all their horses. . . . We were soon back on the pike and trotting the Blue Ridge with the prisoners and horses. When it was daylight, [Col. Percy] Wyndham mounted his squadrons and started full speed after us.[13] After going twenty miles, he returned to camp with half of his men leading broken-down horses. He was soon afterwards relieved, but not before we had raided his headquarters and carried off his staff, his horses, and his uniform.[14]

Risk-Taking: The Stoughton Raid

[8 March 1863.] I now determined to execute my scheme to capture both General [Edwin H.] Stoughton [Vermont Brigade commander] and Wyndham. . . . Ames, about whose fidelity there was no longer any question, knew where their head-quarters were, and the place was familiar to me as I had been in camp there. I also knew, both from Ames and the prisoners, where the gaps in the lines were at night. The safety of the enterprise lay in its novelty; nothing of the kind had been done before. On the evening of March 8, 1863, in obedience to orders, twenty-nine men met me at Dover, in Loudoun County. None knew my objective point, but I told Ames after we started. I remember that I got dinner that day with Colonel Chancellor, who lived near Dover. Just as I was about to mount my horse, as I was leaving, I said . . . "I shall mount the stars to-night or sink lower than plummet ever sounded." I did not rise as high as the stars, but I did not sink. . . .

The weather conditions favored my success. There was a melting snow on the ground, a mist, and, about dark, a drizzling rain. Our point was about twenty-five miles from Fairfax Court House. It was pitch dark when we got near the cavalry pickets at Chantilly—five or six miles from the Court House. At Centreville, three miles away on the Warrenton pike and seven miles from the Court House, were several thousand troops. Our problem was to pass between them and Wyndham's cavalry without giving the alarm. Ames knew where there was a break in the picket lines between Chantilly and Centreville, and he led us through this without a vidette seeing us. After passing the outpost the chief point in the game was won. I think no man with me, except Ames, realized that we were inside the enemy's lines. But the enemy felt secure and was as ignorant as my men. The plan had been to reach the Court House by midnight so as to get out of the lines before daybreak, but the column got broken in the dark and the two parts travelled around in a circle for an hour looking for each other. After we closed up, we started off and struck the pike between Centreville and the Court House. But we turned off into the woods when we got within two or three miles of the village, as Wyndham's cavalry camps were on the pike. We entered the village from the direction of the railroad station. There were a few sentinels about the town, but it was so dark that they could not distinguish us from their own people. Squads were detailed to go around to the officers' quarters and to the stables for the horses. The court-house yard was the rendezvous where all were to report. *[Wyndham was in Washington.]* But Ames got [Wyndham's] two staff officers, his horses, and his uniform. One of the officers, Captain Barker, had been Ames's captain. Ames brought him to me and seemed to take great pride in introducing him to me as his former captain.[15]

Capture of Stoughton

When the squads were starting around to gather prisoners and horses, Joe Nelson brought me a soldier who said he was a guard at General Stoughton's headquarters. Joe had also pulled the telegraph operator out of his tent; the wires had been cut. With five or six men I rode to the house, now the Episcopal rectory, where the commanding general was. We dismounted and knocked loudly at the door. Soon a window above us was opened, and some one asked who was there. I answered, "Fifth New York Cavalry with a dispatch for General Stoughton." The door was opened and a staff officer, Lieutenant Prentiss, was before me. I took hold of his nightshirt, whispered my name in his ear, and told him to take me to General Stoughton's room. Resistance was useless, and he obeyed. A light was quickly struck, and on the bed we saw the general sleeping as soundly as the Turk when Marco Bozzaris woke him up. There was no time for ceremony, so [with my saber] I drew up the bedclothes, pulled up the general's shirt, and gave him a spank on his bare back[side] and told him to get up. As his staff officer was standing by me, Stoughton did not realize the situation and thought that somebody was taking a rude familiarity with him. He asked in an indignant tone what all this meant. I told him that he was a prisoner, and that he must get up quickly and dress.

I asked him if he had ever heard of "Mosby," and he said he had.

"I am Mosby," I said. "Stuart's cavalry has possession of the Court House; be quick and dress." He then asked whether Fitz Lee was there. [*Fitzhugh Lee, who commanded a cavalry brigade under Stuart.*] I said he was, and he asked me to take him to Fitz Lee—they had been together at West Point. Two days afterwards I did deliver him to Fitz Lee at Culpeper Court House. My motive in trying to deceive Stoughton was to deprive him of all hope of escape and to induce him to dress quickly. We were in a critical situation, surrounded by the camps of several thousand with several hundred in the town. If there had been any concert between them, they could easily have driven us out; but not a shot was fired although we stayed there over an hour. . . . Stoughton had the reputation of being a brave soldier, but a fop. He dressed before a looking-glass as carefully as Sardanapalus did when he went into battle. He forgot his watch and left it on the bureau, but one of my men, Frank Williams, took it and gave it to him. Two men had been left to guard our horses when we went into the house. There were several tents for couriers in the yard, and Stoughton's horses and couriers were ready to go with us, when we came out with the general and his staff.

When we reached the rendezvous at the courtyard, I found all the squads waiting for us with their prisoners and horses. There were three times as many prisoners as my men, and each was mounted and leading a horse. To deceive the enemy and baffle pursuit, the cavalcade started off in one direction and, soon after it got out of town, turned in another. We flanked the cavalry camps, and were soon on the pike between them and Centreville. As there were several thousand troops in that town, it was not thought possible that we would go that way to get out of the lines, so the [Federal] cavalry, when it started in pursuit, went in an opposite direction. Lieutenant Prentiss and a good many prisoners who started with us escaped in the dark, and we lost a great many of the horses.

A ludicrous incident occurred when we were leaving Fairfax. A window was raised, and a voice inquired, in an authoritative tone, what cavalry was doing in the street. He was answered by a loud laugh from my men, which was notice to him that we were not his friends. I ordered several men to dismount and capture him. They burst through the front door, but the man's wife met them in the hall and held her ground like a lioness to give her husband time to escape. He was Colonel Johnstone, who was in command of the cavalry brigade during Wyndham's absence. He got out through the back door in his night clothes and barefooted, and hid in garden. He [probably] spent some time there, as he did not know when we left.[16]

Escape and Escorting the Prisoner to Fitz Lee

Our safety depended on our getting out of the Union lines before daybreak. We struck the pike about four miles from Centreville; the danger I then apprehended was pursuit by the cavalry, which was in camp behind us. When we got near the pike, I halted the column to close up. Some of my men were riding in the rear, and some on the flanks to prevent the prisoners from escaping. I left a sergeant, Hunter, in command and rode forward to reconnoitre. As no enemy was in front, I called to Hunter to come on and directed him to go forward at a trot and to hold Stoughton's bridle reins under all circumstances. Stoughton no doubt appreciated my interest in him.

With Joe Nelson I remained some distance behind. We stopped frequently to listen for the hoofbeats of cavalry in pursuit, but no sounds could be heard save the hooting of owls. My heart beat higher with hope every minute; it was the crisis of my fortunes.

Soon the camp fires on the heights around Centreville were in sight; my plan was to flank the position and pass between that place and the camps at Chantilly. But we soon saw that Hunter had halted, and I galloped forward to find out the cause. I saw a fire on the road about a hundred yards ahead of us—evidently a picket post. So I rode forward to reconnoitre, but nobody was by the fire, and the picket was gone. We were now half a mile from Centreville, and the dawn was just breaking. It had been the practice to place a picket on our road every evening and withdraw it early in the morning. The Officer in charge concluded that, as it was near daylight, there was no danger in the air, and he had returned to camp and left the fire burning. That was the very thing I wanted him to do. I called Hunter to come on, and passed the picket fire and then turned off to go around the forts at Centreville. I rode some distance ahead of the column. The camps were quiet; there was no sign of alarm; the telegraph had been cut, and no news had come about our exploit at the Court House. We could see the cannon bristling through the redoubts and hear the sentinel on the parapet call to us to halt. But no attention was paid to him, and he did not fire to give the alarm. No doubt he thought that we were a body of their own cavalry. . . .

After we had passed the forts and reached Cub Run, a new danger was before us. The stream was swift and booming from the melting snow, and our choice was to swim, or to turn back. In full view behind us were the white tents of the enemy and the forts, and we were within cannon range. Without halting a moment, I plunged into the stream, and my horse swam to the other bank. Stoughton followed . . . next to me. As he came up the bank, shivering from his cold morning bath, he said, "Captain, this is the first rough treatment I have to complain of."

Fortunately not a man or a horse was lost. When all were over, I knew there was no danger behind us, and that we were as safe as Tam O'Shanter thought he would be if he crossed the bridge of Doon ahead of the witches. I now left Hunter in charge of the column, and with one of my men, George Slater, galloped on to see what was ahead of us. I thought a force might have been sent to intercept us on the pike we had left that runs through Centreville. I did not know that Johnstone, with his cavalry, had gone in the opposite direction.

We crossed Bull Run at Sudley Ford and were soon on the historic battlefield. From the heights of Groveton we could see that the road was clear to Centreville, and that there was no pursuit. Hunter soon appeared in sight. The sun had risen, and in the rapture of the moment I said to Slater, "George, that is the sun of Austerlitz!"[17]

I could not but feel deep pity for Stoughton when he looked back at Centreville and saw that there was no chance of his rescue. Without any fault of his own, Stoughton's career as a soldier was blasted.

There is an anecdote told of Mr. Lincoln that, when it was reported to him that Stoughton had been captured, he remarked . . . that he did not mind so much the loss of a general—for he could make another in five minutes—but he hated to lose the horses.

Slater and I remained for some time behind as a rear guard and overtook Hunter, who had gone on in command, at Warrenton. We found that population had turned out and were giving my men an ovation. Stoughton and the officers had breakfast. . . .[18]

[*Mosby turned Stoughton over to Fitz Lee, who greeted the general warmly, but seemed to ignore Mosby.*]

[Stoughton's capture] created a sensation in both armies, but the reception I received [from Fitz Lee] convinced me that I was not a welcome person at those headquarters. So, bidding the prisoners good-by and bowing to Fitz Lee, Hunter and I rode off in the rain to the telegraph office to send a report to Stuart. . . .

Stuart published a general order announcing the capture of Stoughton and had it printed, giving me fifty copies. That satisfied me, and I soon returned to my field of operations and again began war on the Potomac.

[*General Robert E. Lee also commended Mosby in a letter to CSA President Jefferson Davis. Stoughton was repatriated, but did not return to the United States Army.*][19]

A Message to Mr. Lincoln

What were called my depredations had caused another brigade of cavalry to be sent into Fairfax to protect Washington. The frequent incursions we had made down there created great alarm and an apprehension that they might be extended across the Potomac. The deliberations of the Senate were frequently disturbed by the cry that the Gauls were at the gate. One day I rode down on a scout in sight of the dome of the Capitol, when a wagon came along, going to Washington, which was driven by the wife of a Union man who had left his home in Virginia and taken refuge there. I stopped it, and, after some conversation with the driver, told her who I was. With a pair of scissors she had I cut off a lock of my hair and sent it to Mr. Lincoln, with a message that I was coming to get one of his soon. A few days after this, I saw in the *Star* that it had been delivered to him, and that the President enjoyed the joke.[20]

Recruits

I had about that time received another recruit, who became famous in the annals of my command. His home was in Loudoun, and his name was William Hibbs. He was always called the "Major," although he never held a commission. He was a blacksmith by trade, over fifty years old, and had already fully discharged the duty he owed to the Southern Confederacy by sending his two sons into the army. But for my appearance in the vicinity, he would probably have lived and died unheard.

The fame of the exploits of my men, and the rich prizes they won, aroused his martial ambition; and he determined to quit the forge and become a warrior bold. The country soon echoed the notes of his fame, as the anvil had once rung with the strokes of his hammer. Around the triumvirate—Dick Moran, John Underwood, and Major Hibbs—recruits now gathered as iron filings cluster around a magnet. They were the germs from which my command grew and spread like a banyan tree. Beattie, who was always my faithful Achates, had been captured, but was soon afterward exchanged.[21]

The Chantilly Raid

No Initial Surprise

[23 March 1863] [John] Underwood, on his return from his scout, reported a body of about 100 cavalry at Chantilly, which was in supporting distance of several other bodies of about equal numbers. An attack on the post there would be extremely hazardous, on account of the proximity of the others. The chance of success was a poor one; but, as about fifty men had assembled to go with me, I did not like to disappoint them. Each man wanted a horse, as well as a leader to show him how to get one. They were all willing to risk a good deal, and so was I. We started off for Chantilly, down the Little River Turnpike, as the mud prevented our travelling any other route. The advantage of attacking at Chantilly was not only that we had a good road to travel on, but I knew it was the very last place they expected I would attack. They did not look for my approach in broad daylight along the pike, but thought I would come by some crooked path after dark through the pines.

On the Chantilly raid I was accompanied by Captain Hoskins, an English officer, who had just reported to me with a letter from Stuart. He had been a captain in the English army and had won the Crimean medal. After the conclusion of peace he had returned home, but disliking the monotonous life of the barracks, had sold his commission and joined Garibaldi in his Sicilian expedition. He was a thorough soldier of fortune, devoted to the profession of arms, and loved the excitement of danger and the joy of battle. He had been attracted to our shores by the great American war, which offered a field for the display of his courage and the gratification of his military tastes. He was a noble gentleman and a splendid soldier, but his career with me was short. A few weeks after that he fell fighting by my side.

I mounted Hoskins and his companion, Captain Kennon, on captured horses, and they went to try their luck with me. The post at Chantilly was only two miles from the camp of a division of cavalry, and flanked by strong supporting parties on each side. When I got within two or three miles of it, I turned obliquely off to the right, in order to penetrate, if possible, between them and Centreville, and gain their rear. But they were looking out for me, and I found there was no chance for a surprise. I despaired almost of doing anything; but [finally] ordered a few men to chase in the pickets, in hopes that this would draw their main body out for some distance. They did so, and several were killed and captured. From a high position I saw the reserve mount, form, and move up the pike.[22]

Improvision . . . Offense . . . and Surprise

I regained the pike also, so as not to be cut off. I got ready to charge as soon as they were near, although I did not have half their number, when I discovered another large body of cavalry, that had heard the firing, coming rapidly from the direction of Fryingpan to reinforce them. These were more than I had bargained to fight in the open, so I ordered a retreat at a trot up the turnpike. I was certain that they would pursue rapidly, thinking I was running away, and, getting strung out along the pike, would lose their advantage in numbers, and give me a chance to turn and strike back. My calculation was right. I kept my men well closed up, with two some distance behind, to give me notice when they got near. I had just passed over a hill, and was descending on the other side, when one of my men dashed up and said the enemy was right upon me. I looked back, but they were not in sight. I could distinctly hear their loud cheers and the hoof strokes of their horses on the hard pike. I had either to suffer a stampede or make a fight. . . . If I had gone a step further my retreat would have degenerated into a rout.

The Charge

My horses were jaded by a long day's march, while the enemies' were fresh. I promptly ordered the men to halt, right about wheel, and draw sabres. It was all done in the twinkling of an eye. Fortunately, just at the place where I halted was an abattis, formed of fallen trees, which had been made by the army the year before. The men formed behind these, as I knew that when they darted out it would create the impression on my pursuers that I had drawn them into an ambuscade. [My troopers] stood there, calmly waiting for me to give the word [to charge].

We had hardly got into position before the head of the pursuing column appeared over the hill, less than 100 yards off. They had expected to see our backs, and not our faces. It was a rule from which, during the war, I never departed, not to stand still and receive a charge, but always to act on the offensive. This was the maxim of Frederick the Great, and the key to the wonderful successes he won with his cavalry. At the order to charge, my men dashed forward with a yell that startled and stunned those who were foremost in pursuit. I saw them halt, and I knew then that they had lost heart and were beaten. Before they could wheel, my men were among them. Those who were coming up behind them, seeing those in front turn their backs, did the same thing. They had no idea they were running away from the same number of men they had been chasing. My men had returned their sabres to their scabbards, and the death-dealing revolver was now doing its work.

The Pursuit

I never witnessed a more complete rout, or one with less cause for it. The chase continued two or three miles. It was almost dark when we stopped. . . . We left the killed and wounded on the field, brought off thirty-six prisoners and about fifty horses. By strategy and hard fighting, four times our numbers had been defeated. The only casualty in my command happened to Major Hibbs, who had his boot-heel shot off. He had been one of the foremost leaders in the charge, and like Byron's corsair, everywhere in the thickest of the fight "shone his mailed breast and flashed his sabre's ray." When the "Major" rode up to me, after the fight was over, he was almost a maniac, he was so wild with delight. And when, in the presence of all the men, I praised his valor, he could no longer contain himself; he laughed and wept by turns. All that he could say in reply was: "Well, Captain, I knew the work had to be done, and that was the way to do it." One thing is certain, the Major got a good horse as a reward. The regiment we had fought happened to be the very one to which [James F."Big Yankee"] Ames had belonged, and from which he had deserted a few weeks before to join me. He had gone through their ranks like an avenging angel, shooting right and left. . . . It was Hoskins's first fight with me. He said it was better than a fox chase. I recall his image now as it rises above the flood of years, as he hewed his path through the broken ranks. It was a point of honor . . . with him to use his sword and not his pistol. In this way he [later] lost his life. I reported to Stuart the result of the engagement and [got back congratulations quoting Gen. Robert E. Lee: "Hurrah for Mosby! I wish I had a hundred like him."][23]

The Value of a Reputation

My success had been so uninterrupted that the men thought that victory was chained to my standard. Men who go into a fight under the influence of such feelings are next to invincible, and are generally victors before it begins.[24]

Recruiting and Retaining Men

[The men on the next raid] were better dressed, but almost as motley a crowd as Falstaff's regiment. There were representatives of nearly all the cavalry regiments in the army, with a sprinkling of men from the infantry, who had determined to try their luck on horseback. A good many of this latter class had been disabled for performing infantry duty by wounds; there were others who had been absent from their regiments without leave ever since the first battle of Bull Run. There were a number of the wounded men who carried their crutches along tied to their saddle bows. As soon as their commanders heard that I had reclaimed and converted them . . . into good soldiers they not only [demanded] to have them returned to their regiments, but actually complained to General Lee of their being with me.

Now I took a practical and not a technical view of the question, and when a man volunteered to go into a fight with me I did not consider it to be any more a duty of mine to investigate his military record than his pedigree. Although [the CSA was] a revolutionary government, none was ever so much under the domination of red tape as the one at Richmond. The martinets who controlled it were a good deal like the hero of Molière's comedy, who complained that his antagonist had wounded him by thrusting in *carte*, when, according to the rule, it should have been in *tierce*. I cared nothing for the form of a thrust if it brought blood. I did not play with foils. . . . When I received these complaints, which were sent through, but did not emanate from headquarters, I notified the men that they were forbidden any longer to assist me in destroying the enemy. They would sorrowfully return to their homes. It was no part of my contract to spend my time in the ignoble duty of catching deserters. I left that to those whose taste was gratified in doing the work. Several of these men, who had been very efficient with me, were, on my application, transferred to me by the Secretary of War. I always had a Confederate fire in my rear as well as that of the public enemy in my front. I will add that I never appealed in vain for justice either to General R. E. Lee, General Stuart, or the Secretary of War, Mr. Seddon.[25]

The Rangers Fall into a Trap

[*At Miskel's Farm, at the junction of Goose Creek and the Potomac, 31 March–1 April 1863, Mosby set out to attack 300 Vermont cavalry isolated from the Union Army. He got more than he had bargained for.*]

The enterprise looked hazardous, but I calculated on being able to surprise the camp, and trusted a good deal to my usual good luck. Ames, Dick Moran, Major Hibbs, and John Underwood, who never failed to be on time, went with me. I thought I would vary my tactics a little this time, and attack about dusk. They would hardly look for me at vespers; heretofore I had always appeared either in the daytime or late at night. I got to Herndon Station, where I had had the encounter two weeks before with the Vermont cavalry, about sundown, and learned there that the camp at Dranesville, which was about three miles off, had been broken up on the day before, and the cavalry had been withdrawn beyond Difficult Run, several miles below. This stream has its proper name, as there are few places where it can be crossed, and I knew that these would be strongly guarded. So it was hopeless to attempt anything in that direction. As I was so near, I concluded to go on to Dranesville that night, in hopes that by chance I might pick up some game. After spending an hour or so there, we started up the Leesburg pike to find a good place with forage for camping that night. I expected that our presence would be reported to the cavalry camps below, which would probably draw out a force which I could venture to meet. As all the forage had been consumed for several miles around, we had to march five or six miles to find any. About midnight we stopped at Miskel's farm, which is about a mile from the turnpike and just in the forks of Goose Creek and the Potomac.[26]

[*Uncharacteristically, Mosby posted no pickets on the Leesburg Pike.*] About sunrise the next morning, I had just risen and put on my boots when one of the men came in and said that the enemy on the hill over the river was making signals. I immediately went out into the back yard to look at them. I had hardly done so, when I saw Dick Moran coming at full speed across the field, waving his hat, and calling out, "The Yankees are coming!"

He had stopped about two miles below, near the pike, and spent the night with a friend; and just as he woke up, about daylight, he had seen the column of Union cavalry going up the pike on our trail. By taking a short cut across the fields, he managed to get to us ahead of them. The barnyard was not a hundred yards from the house; and we all rushed to it. But not more than one-third of our horses were then bridled and saddled. I had buckled on my arms as I came out of the house. By the time we got to the inclosure where our horses were, I saw the enemy coming through a gate just on the edge of a clump of woods about two hundred yards off. The first thing I said to the men was that they must fight. The enemy was upon us so quick that I had no time to bridle or saddle my horse, as I was busy giving orders. I directed the men not to fire, but to saddle and mount quickly. The Union cavalry were so sure of their prey that they shut the gates after passing through, in order to prevent any of us from escaping. As Capt. Flint dashed forward at the head of his squadron, their sabres flashing in the rays of the morning sun, I felt like my final hour had come. Another squadron, after getting into the open field, was at the same time moving around to our rear. In every sense, things looked rather blue for us. We were in the angle of two impassable streams and surrounded by at least four times our number, with more than half of my men unprepared for a fight.[27]

The "Efficacy of a Charge"

But I did not despair. I had great faith in the efficacy of a charge; and in the affair at Chantilly had learned the superiority of the revolver over the sabre. I was confident that we could at least cut our way through them. The Potomac resounded with the cheers of the troops on the northern bank, who were anxious spectators, but could not participate in the conflict. When I saw Capt. Flint divide his command, I knew that my chances had improved at least fifty per cent. When he got to within fifty yards of the gate of the barnyard, I opened the gate and advanced, pistol in hand, on foot to meet him, and at the same time called to the men that had already got mounted to follow me. They responded with one of those demoniac yells which those who once heard never forgot, and dashed forward to the conflict "as reapers descend to the harvest of death." Just as I passed through the gate, at the head of the men, one of them, Harry Hatcher, the bravest of the brave, seeing me on foot, dismounted, and gave me his horse. Our assailants were confounded by the tactics adopted, and were now in turn as much surprised as we had been. They had thought that we would remain on the defensive, and were not prepared to receive an attack. I mounted Harry Hatcher's horse, and led the charge. In a few seconds Harry was mounted on a captured one whose rider had been killed. When the enemy saw us coming to meet them they halted, and were lost.

The powerful moral effect of our assuming the offensive, when nothing but surrender had been expected, seemed to bewilder them. Before they could recover from the shock of their surprise Captain Flint, the leader, had fallen dead in their sight. Before the impetuous onset of my men they now broke and fled. No time was given them to re-form and rally. The remorseless revolver was doing its work of death in their ranks, while their swords were as harmless as the wooden sword of harlequin. Unlike my adversaries, I was trammelled with no tradition that required me to use an obsolete weapon. The combat was short, sharp and decisive. In the first moment of collision, they wheeled and made for the gate which they had already closed against themselves. The other squadron that had gone around us, when they saw their companions turn and fly, were panic-stricken and forgot what they had been sent to do. Their thoughts were now how to save themselves. Our capture was now out of the question. They now started pell-mell for the gate in order to reach it ahead of us. But by this time our men had all mounted, and like so many furies were riding and shooting among their scattered ranks. The gate was at last broken through by the pressure, but they became so packed and jammed in the narrow passage that they could only offer a feeble resistance, and at this point many fell under the deadly fire that was poured in from behind. Everywhere above the storm of battle could be heard the voices and seen the forms of the Dioscuri—"Major" Hibbs and Dick Moran—cheering on the men as they rode headlong in the fight. Dick Moran got into a hand-to-hand conflict in the woods with a party, and the issue was doubtful, when Harry Hatcher came up and decided it. There was with me that day a young artillery officer—Samuel F. Chapman—who at the first call of his State to arms had quit the study of divinity and become, like Stonewall Jackson, a sort of military Calvin, singing the psalms of David as he marched into battle. I must confess that his character as a soldier was more on the model of the Hebrew prophets than the Evangelist or the Baptist in whom he was so devout a believer. Before he got to the gate Sam had already exhausted every barrel of his two pistols and drawn his sabre. As the fiery Covenanter rode on his predestined course the enemy's ranks withered wherever he went. He was just in front of me—he was generally in front of everybody in a fight—at the gate. It was no fault of the Union cavalry that they did not get through faster than they did, but Sam seemed to think that it was. Even at that supreme moment in my life, when I had just stood on the brink of ruin and had barely escaped, I could not restrain a propensity to laugh.

Sam, to give more vigor to his blows, was standing straight up in his stirrups, dealing them right and left with all the theological fervor of Burly of Balfour. I doubt whether he prayed that day for the souls of those he sent over the Stygian river. I made him a captain for it. The chase was kept up for several miles down the pike.[28]

Pursuit of the Foe

The reverend Sam was not satisfied with the amount of execution he had done at the gate, but continued his slaughter until, getting separated in the woods from the other men, he dashed into a squad of the Vermont men, who were doing their best to get away, and received a cut with a sabre. But one of my men, Hunter, came to his rescue, and the matter in dispute was quickly settled. Down the pike the Vermont cavalry sped, with my men close at their heels. Lieutenant Woodbury had got three miles away, when a shot from Ames laid him low. They never drew rein or looked back to see how many were behind them. I got pretty close to one, who, seeing that he was bound to be shot or caught, jumped off his horse and sat down on the roadside. As I passed him he called out to me, "You have played us a nice April fool, boys!" This reminded me that it was the first day of April. Some of the men kept up the pursuit beyond Dranesville, but I stopped there. The [Union] dead and wounded were strewn from where the fight began, at Miskel's, for several miles along the road. I had one man killed and three slightly wounded. I knew that as soon as the news reached the camps in Fairfax a heavy force would be sent against me, so I started off immediately, carrying eighty-three prisoners and ninety-five horses, with all their equipments.

At Dranesville were two sutlers' stores that had not been removed by their owners when the camps were broken up. These were, of course, appropriated, and helped to swell the joy of the partisans. A more hilarious party never went to war or a wedding than my men. . . . Danger . . . gives a keener relish for the joys of life.[29]

[*Mosby had other successes, but there were inevitable failures, and his command suffered increasing casualties—in the course of the war probably 40 percent. Some 80 rangers were killed or died from wounds; seven were executed by General George Armstrong Custer, part of Philip Sheridan's force sent by Grant to desolate the Shenandoah Valley. Over 700 spent time in Union jails. In December 1864, Mosby was betrayed and trapped in a friend's house while having dinner by men of the 13th New York Cavalry; a trooper shot him through a window. The Union major in charge did not recognize Mosby, however, and was sure he was dying anyway. He took captive Mosby's ranger companion, Tom Love, but left Mosby with his hostess. Mosby recovered, after weeks of being shuttled from house to house by staunch friends and Confederates and finally to his father's house in Lynchburg. He left to resume command of his battalion on 24 February 1865, but it was the Reverend Chapman (then a lieutenant colonel) and others who conducted raids. Before Mosby was fully recovered, the war ended on 9 April 1865.*]

Conclusions

The "Gray Ghost" depended on surprise, including sudden attack when the enemy expected defense; he knew the value of foul weather and dark of night for the raider; he believed in speed, violence, and force, using the most practical weapons (the pistol over the saber). He did not train his men, but enforced discipline; he established a reputation for winning, which drew recruits. He led personally (until gravely wounded) and displayed determination, courage, coolness under stress, and the ability to improvise on every raid.

Mosby loved his work, and picked men who, like himself, gloried in taking risks—calculated risks, normally, but improvised, spur-of-the-moment actions as well—which demanded men who were both steady and daring. He knew that success bred success, and that high morale was vital. There was never any doubt, however, that Mosby was in command. There was great camaraderie among his rangers, but it came from success, not any courting of the men by their leader. He did take care of his men, of course, with rewards of booty. That he was religious is evident. Speaking of Stuart and Lee, he wrote: "With both of these two great Christian soldiers. . . [my] military conduct received from them not only approbation, but many encomiums."

He disdained the usual customs of war, obedience to which would have made his forays impossible—but extended gentlemanly courtesies when he could. He knew Napoleon's and Frederick's maxims and something of conventional war; he quickly took advantage when his enemies violated accepted principles—as when the unfortunate Captain Flint divided his forces at Miskel's Farm.

If Mosby's operations had little effect on the outcome of the war, they made victory more difficult for the Union. A handful of rangers tied up hundreds—even thousands—of Federal troops, and destroyed tons of enemy weapons, ammunition, and stores.

Of more importance for today, Mosby left a legacy for the special operations forces that are important today for antiterrorist and peacekeeping missions, and for very limited wars, such as those of the United States in Grenada (1983) and Panama (1989). In 2002 almost every country has special forces: the United States has Army Rangers and Special Forces, and Navy SEALs; the United Kingdom, Commandos, and the Special Air Service (SAS); Australia, the SAS Regiment (SASR); France, the COS (*Commandement des Operations Speciales*), a naval group, and the parachute regiment of the *Legion Étrangère* (Foreign Legion); Germany, *Grenzschutzgruppe 9* (GSG-9) and *Kommando Spezialkräfte* (KSK); Russia, *Spetsnaz* troops and naval units; Israel, *Zahal, Sayeret Matkal*, and naval and air force units. Special forces have also been organized by Argentina, Brazil, Chile, Canada, Denmark, Egypt, Hungary, India, Ireland, Italy, both Koreas, Mexico, the Netherlands, Norway, Pakistan, Portugal, Spain, Sweden, Turkey, and elsewhere.[30]

V

Thomas Edward Lawrence

(1888–1935)

"LAWRENCE OF ARABIA"

LAWRENCE is included here because of his mastery of guerrilla warfare. His operations and accounts of them have been praised by military writers, beginning with B. H. Liddell Hart in the 1920s. He is admired by such as General Vo Nguyen Giap, who was a guerrilla before organizing the Army of the People's Republic of (North) Vietnam,[1] and by many in special operations worldwide. Though only a temporary British colonel, he looms important today in an era of limited or small wars and antiterrorist operations.

Though not for the reasons cited above, "Lawrence of Arabia" was and is the most celebrated figure of the "Great War," rivalled only by the German Flying Ace, Manfred von Richthofen, the "Red Baron."[2] An eccentric genius and a quintessential British intellectual, Lawrence led Arab Bedouin guerrillas against the Turks for less than two years, but became their hero, greeted by shouts of "Orens! Orens!" [Lawrence! Lawrence!] when he appeared. In the name of his king (in good faith), he promised the Arab leaders, Grand Sherif Hussein of Mecca and his son Emir Feisal, that in return for their support of the British campaign against the Turks (allied with the Germans) in the Middle East, they would have an Arab state after the war—covering most of the Middle East, at the time populated principally by Arabs. The Arab chieftains understood, but not their followers. They were nomadic people who identified with their tribes—as Billi, Juheina, Ateiba, Howeitat, or Ageyl—not as "Arabs." Lawrence could only unite them by preaching a "crusade" against their common enemy, the Turks, but clung to the dream of an Arab nation. When no such nation was created after the war, Lawrence took it personally, as a betrayal of himself and the Arabs by his government.

Lawrence's background made him an improbable leader of Bedouin guerrillas, except that he knew Arabic. Son of a British aristocrat,[3] educated at exclusive schools and Oxford, he had spent most of the years 1909–14 in the Middle East at archeological digs. When the war began (August 1914), he volunteered, was rejected, then posted to Egypt as an Army Intelligence lieutenant. Until late 1916, he manned a desk in Cairo.

Meanwhile, the British had encouraged Sherif Hussein of the Hejaz to revolt against the Turks, allies of the Germans and a threat to the Suez Canal. Hussein ruled much of western Arabia, held the Muslim Holy City of Mecca, and was a descendant of Mohammed, which gave him royal status with Muslim Arabs.[4] In July 1916 he finally launched an Arab revolt, led by his son, Sherif Feisal, who took the coastal cities of Rabegh and Yenbo with help from the British Royal Navy in the Red Sea. The Turks began a campaign to take Mecca. In October 1916, Lieutenant Lawrence was sent to report on the situation, made friends with Feisal, and was sent back "permanently."

By that time the Arab revolt had strong support from the British in Egypt; Sir Reginald Wingate was British high commissioner at Cairo, and General (later Field Marshal) Edmund H. H. Allenby was in command of British forces. Money and weapons got to the fighting tribes (past embezzling sheikhs) thanks to Lawrence and Feisal.

Lawrence (5′5″ tall) reported to the giant Allenby in July 1917. The general, Lawrence later wrote, was unprepared "for anything so odd as myself—a little bare-footed silk-skirted man offering to hobble the enemy . . . if given stores and arms and . . . two hundred thousand sovereigns [pounds sterling]."[5] Actually, Lawrence was wearing the robe of an Arab sheikh, a mark of Feisal's respect. Lawrence and the Arabs had just captured Akaba, a feat thought impossible for them. Thus Allenby gave him an attentive hearing. The general knew that Lawrence was eccentric and often insubordinate, *but*, Allenby reasoned, he had worked a sort of miracle—uniting Arab tribes, often at war with each other—to fight the Turks.

Lawrence's secret lay in influencing the actions of Sheikh Feisal. He had won over Feisal—and the wild Bedouin (desert nomads)—by becoming one of them. He spoke Arabic, showed the Arabs that he could match them in going long distances by camel with little or no food and water, and became an Arab in dress and diet.

Lawrence persuaded Feisal to take Wejh, where he could be supplied from the sea. Meanwhile, they concentrated on attacking the Hejaz railway, the lifeline of the Turks in Medina—hitting trains in isolated, unguarded spots. Lawrence brought in British explosives experts, who taught the Arabs to demolish railroad bridges and tracks, and in January 1917, began leading raids in person. Feisal's forces swelled, partly because of the rich booty from the trains.

As more tribes joined the fight, Lawrence, with the likable old thief and fabled warrior, Sheikh Auda abu Tayi, took Akaba, a key Red Sea port, handing it to the British. When Allenby's army attacked into Syria in 1917, Lawrence and Feisal pinned down some 27,000 Turks in the Hejaz who otherwise might have attacked the flank of the British army. In 1918, Allenby put Lawrence's Arabs on his flank for his final drive for Damascus. Victory made them more ruthless; on one day they killed 5,000 Turks, including prisoners and wounded, which sickened Lawrence. Then shortly Allenby told him there would be no single Arab state. Lawrence wrote later: "My will had gone and I feared to be alone, lest the winds of circumstance, or power, or lust, blow my empty soul away."[6]

1919, Lawrence joined Feisal at the Paris Peace Conference to press, in vain, for an Arab state. Disillusioned, Lawrence refused proffered government employment, and lived under aliases until his death in a motorcycle accident in 1935.

Lawrence's exploits were glamorized during the war by Lowell Thomas, a leading American radio personality and adventure writer. He has since been the subject of scores of books, none of which, as history or literature, match his own *Seven Pillars of Wisdom* (1935).[7]

The passages below are from *Seven Pillars of Wisdom*, (1935) with a few from *Revolt in the Desert* (1927), an abridgement of an early version of the book.[8]

Feisal

[*Lawrence's first visit, October 1916.*]

[Feisal] was a man of moods, flickering between glory and despair, and just now dead-tired. He looked years older than thirty-one; and his dark . . . eyes, set a little sloping in his face, were bloodshot, and his hollow cheeks deeply lined and puckered with reflection. His nature grudged thinking, for it crippled his speed in action. . . . In appearance he was tall, graceful and vigorous . . . [with] a royal dignity of head and shoulders. Of course he knew it, and a great part of his public expression was by sign and gesture. . . .

His [service with Turkish officials] had made him past-master in diplomacy. His military service with the Turks had given him a working knowledge of tactics. His life in Constantinople and in the Turkish Parliament had made him familiar with European questions and manners. He was a careful judge of men. If he had the strength to realize his dreams he would go very far, for he was wrapped up in his work and lived for nothing else; but the fear was that he would wear himself out . . . or . . . die of too much action. His men told me after a long spell of fighting, in which he had to . . . lead the charges . . . he had collapsed physically and was carried away . . . unconscious, with the foam flecking his lips.[9]

Later I saw Feisal again, and promised to do my best for him. My chiefs would arrange a base at Yenbo, where the stores and supplies he needed would be put ashore for his exclusive use. . . . We would form gun crews and machine-gun crews . . . and provide them with such mountain guns and light machine-guns as were obtainable in Egypt. Lastly, I would advise that British Army officers . . . be sent down to act as advisers and liaison officers with him in the field.[10]

Arab Views of an Arab Nation

[*Lawrence is back to stay.*]

The Semites idea of nationality was the independence of clans and villages. . . . Constructive policies, an organized state, an extended empire, were not so much beyond their sight as hateful in it. They were fighting to get rid of the [Turkish] Empire, not to win it.[11]

The Arab "Troops"

The men received me cheerfully. Beneath every great rock or bush they sprawled like lazy scorpions, resting from the heat, and refreshing their brown limbs with the early coolness of the shaded stone. Because of my khaki they took me for a Turk-trained officer who had deserted to them, and were profuse in good-humoured but ghastly suggestions of how they should treat me. Most of them were young, though the term "fighting man" in the Hejaz meant anyone between twelve and sixty sane enough to shoot. They were a tough-looking crowd, dark-coloured, some negroid. They were physically thin, but exquisitely made, moving with an oiled activity. . . . It did not seem possible that men could be hardier or harder. They would ride immense distances day after day, run through sand and over rocks bare-foot in the heat for hours without pain, and climb their hills like goats. Their clothing was mainly a loose shirt . . . and a head-shawl usually of red cloth, which acted towel or handkerchief or sack as required. They were corrugated with bandoliers, and fired joy-shots when they could.

The Power of British Money

They were in wild spirits, shouting that the war might last ten years. It was the fattest time the hills had ever known. The Sherif was feeding not only the fighting men, but their families, and paying two pounds a month for a man, four for a camel. Nothing else would have performed the miracle of keeping a tribal army in the field for five months on end. . . . The Turks cut the throats of their prisoners with knives, as though they were butchering sheep. Feisal offered a reward of a pound a head for prisoners, and had many carried in to him unhurt. He also paid for captured mules or rifles.

The actual contingents were continually shifting, in obedience to the rule of flesh. A family would own a rifle, and the sons serve in turn for a few days each. Married men alternated between camp and wife, and sometimes a whole clan would become bored and take a rest. Consequently the paid men were more than those mobilized, and policy often gave to great sheikhs, as wages, money that was a polite bribe for friendly countenance. Feisal's eight thousand men were one in ten camel-corps and the rest hill-men. They served only under their tribal sheikhs, and near home, arranging their own food and transport. Nominally each sheikh had a hundred followers. Sherifs acted as group leaders, in virtue of their privileged position, which raised them above the jealousies which shackled tribesmen.

Blood feuds were nominally healed, and really suspended in the Sheriflan area: Billi and Juheina, Ateiba and Ageyl [tribes] living and fighting side by side in Feisal's army. All the same, the members of one tribe were shy of those of another. . . . Each might be . . . against the Turk, but perhaps not quite to the point of failing to work off a . . . grudge upon a family enemy in the field. Consequently they could not attack. One company of Turks firmly entrenched in open country could have defied the entire army of them; and a pitched defeat, with its casualties, would have ended the war by sheer horror.

The Use of Bedouins and Others

I concluded that the tribesmen were good for defence only. Their acquisitive recklessness made them keen on booty, and whetted them [sic] to tear up railways, plunder caravans, and steal camels; but they were too free-minded to endure command, or to fight in team. A man who could fight well by himself made generally a bad soldier and these champions seemed to me no material for our drilling; but if we strengthened them by light automatic guns of the Lewis type, to be handled by themselves, they might be capable of holding their hills and serving as an efficient screen behind which we could build up, perhaps at Rabegh, an Arab regular mobile column, capable of meeting a Turkish force (distracted by guerilla warfare) . . . and of defeating it piecemeal. For such a body of real soldiers no recruits would be forthcoming from Hejaz. It would have to be formed of . . . Syrian and Mesopotamian towns-folk already in our hands, and officered by Arabic-speaking officers trained in the Turkish army.[12]

Artillery Problem

The sole disquieting feature was the very real success of the Turks in frightening the Arabs by artillery. . . . [T]he sound of a fired cannon sent every man within earshot behind cover. They thought weapons destructive in proportion to their noise. They were not afraid of bullets, not indeed overmuch of dying: just . . . death by shell-fire as unendurable. It seemed to me that their moral confidence was to be restored only by having guns, useful or useless, but noisy, on their side. . . .

When I told them of the landing of the five-inch howitzers at Rabegh they rejoiced. . . . The guns would be of no real use to them: . . . it seemed to me that they would do the Arabs positive harm; for their virtues lay in mobility and intelligence, and by giving them guns we hampered their movements and efficiency. Only if we did not give them guns they would quit.[13]

Picking Up Arab Allies

[To the north] lay various tribes owning obedience to Nuri Shaalan, the great Emir of the Ruwalla, who, after the Sherif [Hussein] and ibn Saud and ibn Rasind, was the fourth figure among the precarious princes of the desert. . . . His favour would open to us the Sirhan, a famous roadway, camping ground, and chain of water-holes, which . . . extended from Jauf . . . in the south-east, northwards to Azrak, near Jebel Druse, in Syria. It was the freedom of the Sirhan we needed to reach the tents of the Eastern Howeitat, those famous abu Tayi, of whom Auda, the greatest fighting man in northern Arabia, was chief. Only by means of *Auda abu Tayi* could we swing the tribes from Maan to Akaba so violently in our favour that they would help us take Akaba and its hills from their Turkish garrisons.[14]

Lawrence Works Out a "Doctrine"

[*Thoughts while lying ill in a hot tent on an extended raid.*]

War Aim

I began to drum out the aim in war. The books gave it pat—the destruction of the armed forces of the enemy by the one process—battle. Victory could be purchased only by blood. This was a hard saying for us. . . . The Arabs would not endure casualties. How would . . . Clausewitz [win this war]? Von der Goltz had [said it] . . . was necessary not to annihilate the enemy, but to break his courage. Only we showed no prospect of ever breaking anybody's courage.

However [I concluded] these wise men must be talking in metaphors; for we were indubitably winning our war; and as I pondered slowly, it dawned on me that we had won the Hejaz war. Out of every thousand square miles of Hejaz nine hundred and ninety-nine were now free. . . . If we held [most of the Hejaz] the Turks were welcome to the tiny fraction on which they stood, till peace or Doomsday showed them the futility of clinging to our window-pane.

Strategy and Tactics

When it grew too hot for dreamless dozing, I [began] considering now the whole house of war in its structural aspect, which was strategy, in its arrangements, which were tactics, and in the sentiment of its inhabitants, which was psychology; for my personal duty was command, and the commander, like the master architect, was responsible for all.

The first confusion was the false antithesis between strategy, the aim in war . . . and tactics, the means towards a strategic end. . . . They seemed only points of view from which to ponder the elements of war, the Algebraical element of things, a Biological element of lives, and the Psychological element of ideas.

The algebraical element looked to me a pure science, subject to mathematical law, inhuman. . . . My wits, hostile to the abstract, took refuge in Arabia again. Translated into Arabic, the algebraic factor would first take practical account of the area we wished to deliver, and I began idly to calculate how many square miles: sixty: eighty: one hundred: perhaps one hundred and forty thousand square miles. And how would the Turks defend all that? No doubt by a trench line across the bottom, if we came like an army with banners; but suppose we were . . . an influence, an idea, a thing intangible, invulnerable, without front or back, drifting about like a gas?. . . We might be a vapour, blowing where we listed.

Then I figured out how many men they would need to sit on all this ground. . . . I knew the Turkish Army exactly, and even allowing for their recent [greater use of] aeroplanes and guns and armoured trains . . . still it seemed they would have need of a fortified post every four square miles [with not fewer] than twenty men. If so, they would need six hundred thousand men to meet the illwills of all the Arab peoples, combined with the active hostility of a few zealots.

Advantages of the Arab Side

How many zealots could we have? At present we had nearly fifty thousand: sufficient for the day. It seemed the assets in this element of war were ours. If we [used them properly], then climate, railway, desert, and technical weapons could also be attached to our interests. The Turks were stupid, the Germans behind them dogmatical. They would believe that rebellion was absolute like war, and deal with it on the analogy of war. Analogy in human things was fudge, anyhow; and war upon rebellion was messy and slow, like eating soup with a knife.

This was enough of the concrete; so I . . . plunged into the nature of the biological factor in command. . . . The war-philosophers had properly made an art of it, and had elevated one item, "effusion of blood," to . . . an essential. . . . A line of variability, Man, persisted like leaven through its estimates, making them irregular. The components were sensitive and illogical.

Intuition in Commanders—Improvision

The "felt" element in troops, not expressible in figures, had to be guessed at . . . and the greatest commander of men was he whose intuitions most nearly happened. Nine-tenths of tactics were . . . teachable in schools; but the irrational tenth was like the kingfisher flashing across the pool, and in it lay the test of generals. It could be ensued only by Instinct (sharpened by thought practising the stroke) until at the crisis it came naturally, a reflex. There had been men whose [intuition] so nearly approached perfection that by its road they reached certainty.

Men vs. Material

My mind seesawed back to apply this to ourselves, and at once knew that . . . it applied also to materials. In Turkey things were scarce and precious, men less esteemed than equipment. Our cue was to destroy, not the Turk's army, but his minerals [sic]. The death of a Turkish bridge or rail, machine or gun or charge of high explosive, was more profitable to us than the death of a Turk. In the Arab Army at the moment we were chary both of materials and of men. Governments saw men only in mass; but our men, being irregulars, were not formations, but Individuals. An individual death, like a pebble dropped in water, might make but a brief hole; yet rings of sorrow widened out therefrom. We could not afford casualties.

Materials were easier to replace. . . . Orthodoxy had laid down the maxim, applied to men, of being superior at the critical point and moment of attack. We might be superior in equipment in one dominant moment or respect; and for both things and men we might give the doctrine a twisted negative side, for cheapness' sake, and be weaker than the enemy everywhere except in that one point or matter. The decision of what was critical would always be ours. Most wars were wars of contact. . . . Ours should be a war of detachment. We were to contain the enemy by the silent threat of a vast unknown desert, not disclosing ourselves till we attacked. The attack [should be] directed not against him, but against his stuff . . . his most accessible material. In railway-cutting it would be usually an empty stretch of rail; and the more empty, the greater the tactical success. We might . . . develop a habit of never engaging the enemy. This would chime with the [rule of] never affording a target. . . . We were never on the defensive except by accident and in error.

Intelligence and Propaganda

The corollary of such a rule was perfect "intelligence", so that we could plan in certainty. . . . When we knew all about the enemy we should be comfortable. We must take more pains in the service of news than any regular staff.

I was getting through my subject. . . . There remained the psychological element to build up into an apt shape. I went to Xenophon and stole, to name it, his word *diathetics* which had been the art of Cyrus before he struck.

Of this our "propaganda" was the stained and ignoble offspring. It was the pathic [sic], almost the ethical, in war. Some of it concerned the crowd, an adjustment of its spirit to the point where it became useful to exploit in action. . . . Some of it concerned the individual, and then it became a rare art . . .

transcending, by purposed emotion, the gradual logical sequence of the mind. It was more subtle than tactics . . . better worth doing, because it dealt with uncontrollables, with subjects incapable of direct command. It considered the capacity for mood of our men, their complexities and mutability, and the cultivation of whatever in them promised to profit our intention. We had to arrange their minds in order of battle just as carefully and as formally as other officers would arrange their bodies. And not only our own men's minds. . . . We must also arrange the minds of the enemy, so far as we could reach them, then those other minds of the nation supporting us behind the firing line, since more than half the battle passed there in the back; then the minds of the enemy nation waiting the verdict; and of the neutrals looking on; circle beyond circle.

The Power of Confidence and an Aggressive Attitude

As we had seldom to concern ourselves with what our men did, had they thought, the diathetic for us would be more than half the command. In Europe it was . . . entrusted to men outside the General Staff. In Asia the regular elements were so weak that irregulars could not let the metaphysical weapon rust unused. Battles in Arabia were a mistake, since we [gained] only by the ammunition the enemy fired off. Napoleon had said it was rare to find generals willing to fight battles; but the curse of this war was that so few would do anything else.

Speed and Time, Not Power

We had nothing material to lose, so our best line was to defend nothing and to shoot nothing. Our cards were speed and time, not hitting power. The invention of bully beef . . . gave us strategical . . . strength, since in Arabia range was more than force, space greater than the power of armies.

Summary of Principles

I had now been eight days lying in this remote tent. . . . The fever passed: my dysentery ceased; and with restored strength the present again became actual to me. . . . So I [listed] my shadowy principles, to have them. . . . precise before my power to evoke them faded.

It seemed to me proven that our rebellion had an unassailable base, guarded not only from attack, but from the fear of attack. It had [an] . . . alien enemy, disposed as an army of occupation in an area greater than could be dominated effectively from fortified posts. It had a friendly population, of which some two in the hundred were active, and the rest quietly sympathetic. . . . The active rebels had the virtues of secrecy and self-control, and the qualities of speed, endurance and independence of arteries of supply. They had technical equipment enough to paralyse the enemy's communications. . . . Final victory seemed certain.[15]

[*Lawrence had formulated classic rules for guerrilla fighting. He tried to persuade the regulars[16] that they should not take Medina, but let the Turks keep it, and the Hejaz railway, which he could keep cutting, forcing the Turks to fritter away their strength. He lost the argument to the British regulars. However, since the Arabs (as he had predicted) could not get organized enough to take Medina, he was allowed to keep raiding in 1917, but in 1918, when the British invaded Syria, his Arabs became the right wing of Allenby's army—if in swarms of semi-independent semi-mobs rather than disciplined ranks.*]

————

[In 1917,] Our ideal was to keep [the Turks'] railway just working, but only just, with the maximum of loss and discomfort. The factor of food would confine him to the railways, but he was welcome to the Hejaz Railway, and the Trans-Jordan railway, and the Palestine and Syrian railways . . . so long as he gave us the nine hundred and ninety-nine thousandths of the Arab world.[17]

Raid on a Railway Junction

[*In the Turkish camp.*] We could see about three hundred men in all. We had heard that the Turks patrolled . . . actively at night. A bad habit this: so we sent off two men to lie by each blockhouse, and fire a few shots after dark. The enemy, thinking it a prelude to attack, stood-to in their trenches all night, while we were comfortably sleeping; but the cold woke us early with restless dawn wind blowing across the Jurf [*sic*], and singing in the great trees round our camp. As we climbed to our observation point the sun conquered the clouds and an hour later it grew very hot.

We lay like lizards in the long grass round the stones of the foremost cairn upon the hill-top, and saw the [Turkish] garrison parade. There were a hundred and ninety-nine infantry, little toy men, [who] ran about when the bugle sounded, and formed up in stiff lines below the black building till there was more bugling: then they scattered, and after a few minutes the smoke of cooking fires went up. A herd of sheep and goats in charge of a little ragged boy issued out toward us. Before he reached the foot of the hills there came a loud whistling down the valley from the north, and a tiny, picture-book train rolled slowly into view across the hollow sounding bridge and halted just outside the station, panting out white puffs of steam.

The shepherd lad held on steadily. . . . We sent two Juheina down behind a ridge beyond sight of the enemy, and they ran from each side and caught him. [*The shepherd had to be held captive while the raid proceeded. Most of the details are omitted, as well as a long, poetic aside by Lawrence on the lives of shepherds and a description of the countryside.*]

At dusk we climbed down again with the goat-herd prisoner, and what we could gather of his flock. Our main body would come this night; so that [Sherif] Fauzan and I wandered out across the darkling plain till we found a pleasant gun-position in some low ridges not two thousand yards from the station. On our return, very tired, fires were burning among the trees. Shakir [Hussein's youngest son] had just arrived, and his men and ours were roasting goat-flesh contentedly.[18] The shepherd was tied up . . . because he had gone frantic when [they killed his goats]. [*He was eventually set free.*]

After supper [Sherif] Shakir told me that he had brought only three hundred men instead of the agreed eight or nine hundred. However, it was his war . . . so we hastily modified the plans. We would not take the station; we would frighten it by a frontal artillery attack, while we mined the railway to the north and south in the hope of trapping that halted train. Accordingly we chose a party of Garland-trained dynamiters[19] who should blow up something north of the bridge at dawn, to seal that direction; while I went off with high explosive and a machine-gun with its crew to lay a mine to the south of the station, the probable direction from which the Turks would seek or send help, in their emergency.

Mohammed el Khadi guided us to a deserted bit of line just before midnight. I dismounted and fingered its thrilling rails. . . . Then, in an hour's busy work, we laid the mine, which was a trigger action to fire into twenty pounds of blasting gelatine when the weight of the locomotive overhead deflected the metals. Afterwards we posted the machine-gunners in a little bush-screened watercourse, four hundred yards from and fully commanding the spot where we hoped the train would be derailed. They were to hide there; while we went on to cut the telegraph, that isolation might persuade [the station at] Aba el Naam to send the train for reinforcements, as our main attack developed.

So we rode another half-hour, and then turned in to the line, again were fortunate to strike an unoccupied place. Unhappily four remaining Juheina [tribesmen] proved unable to climb a telegraph pole and I had to struggle up it myself. It was all I could do, after my illness; and when the third wire was cut the flimsy pole shook so that I lost grip, and came slipping down the sixteen feet upon the stout shoulders of Mohammed who ran in to break my fall. . . . We took a few minutes to breathe, but . . . were able to regain our camels. Eventually we arrived in camp just as the others had saddled up to go forward.

Our mine-laying had taken four hours longer than we had planned and the delay put us in the dilemma either of getting no rest, or of letting the main body march without us. Finally by Shakir's will we let them go, and fell down under our trees for an hour's sleep, without which I felt I should collapse utterly. The time was just before daybreak, an hour when the uneasiness of the air affected trees and animals, and made even men-sleepers turn over sighingly. Mohammed, who wanted to see the fight, awoke. To get me up he came over and cried the morning prayer-call in my ear, the raucous voice sounding battle, murder, and sudden death across my dreams. I sat up and rubbed the sand out of red-rimmed aching eyes, as we disputed vehemently of prayer and sleep. He pleaded that there was not a battle every day, and showed the cuts and bruises sustained during the night in helping me. By my blackness and blueness I could feel for him, and we rode off to catch the army. . . .

A band of trodden untidiness in a sweep of gleaming water-rounded sand showed us the way, and we arrived just as the guns opened fire. They did excellently, and crashed in all the top of one building, damaged the second, hit the pump-room, and holed the water-tank. One lucky shell caught the front waggon of the train in the siding, and it took fire furiously. This alarmed the locomotive, which uncoupled and went off southward. We watched her hungrily as she approached our mine, and when she was on it there came a soft cloud of dust and a report and she stood still. The damage was to the front part . . . [and] while the drivers got out, and jacked up the front wheels and tinkered at them, we waited and waited in vain for the machine-gun to open fire. Later we learned that the gunners, afraid of their loneliness, had packed up and marched to join us when we began shooting. Half an hour after, the repaired engine went away towards Jebel Antar, going at a foot pace and clanking loudly; but going none the less.

Our Arabs worked in towards the station, under cover of the bombardment. . . . Smoke clouds from the fire trucks screened the Arab advance which wiped out one enemy outpost, and captured another. The Turks withdrew their surviving detachments to the main position, and waited rigorously in their trenches for the assault. . . . With our advantages . . . the place would have been a gift to us, if only we had had some of Feisal's men to charge home.

Meanwhile the wood, tents and trucks in the station were burning, and the smoke was too thick for us to shoot, so we broke off the action. We had taken thirty prisoners, a mare, two camels and some more sheep, and had killed and wounded seventy of the garrison, at a cost to ourselves of one man slightly hurt. Traffic was held up for three days. . . . So we did not wholly fail.

We left two parties in the neighbourhood to damage the line . . . while we rode to [Feisal's brother] Abdullah's camp on April the first. Shakir, splendid in habit, held a grand parade on entry, and had thousands of joy-shots fired in honour of his partial victory.[20]

Auda Abu Tayi

[British weapons instructors had arrived; all was going well] and I was about to take my leave [of Feisal at Wejh] when Suleiman, the guest-master, hurried in and whispered to Feisal, who turned to me with shining eyes, trying to be calm, and said, "Auda is here". I shouted, "Auda abu Tayi", and at that moment the tent-flap was drawn back, before a deep voice which boomed salutations to Our Lord, the Commander of the Faithful. There entered a tall, strong figure, with a haggard face, passionate and tragic. This was Auda, and after him followed Mohammed, his son, a child in looks, and only eleven years old in truth.

Feisal had sprung to his feet. Auda caught his hand and kissed it, and they

. . . looked at each other—a splendidly unlike pair, typical of much that was best in Arabia, Feisal the prophet, and Auda the warrior, each filling his part to perfection, and immediately understanding and liking the other. They sat down. Feisal introduced us one by one, and Auda with a measured word seemed to register each person.

We had heard much of Auda, and were banking to open Akaba with his help; and after a moment I knew, from the force and directness of the man, that we would attain our end. He had come down to us like a knight-errant, chafing at our delay in Wejh, anxious only to be acquiring merit for Arab freedom in his own lands. If his performance was one-half his desire, we should be prosperous and fortunate. The weight was off all minds before we went to supper.[21]

The Great Prize: Taking Akaba

Fortunately the poor handling of the enemy gave us an unearned advantage. They slept on, in the valley, while we crowned the hills in wide circle about them unobserved. We began to snipe them steadily in their positions under the slopes and rock-faces by the water, hoping to provoke them out and up the hill in a charge against us. Meanwhile, [Sheikh] Zaal rode away with our horsemen and cut the Mann telegraph and telephone in the plain.

This went on all day. It was terribly hot—hotter than before I had felt it in Arabia—and the anxiety and constant moving made it hard for us. Some even of the tough tribesmen broke down under the cruelty of the sun, and crawled or had to be thrown under rocks to recover in their shade. We ran up and down to supply our lack of numbers by mobility, ever looking over the long ranges of hill for a new spot from which to counter this or that Turkish effort. The hillsides were steep, and exhausted our breath, and the grasses twined like little hands about our ankles as we ran, and plucked us back. The sharp reefs of limestone which cropped out over the ridges tore our feet, and long before evening the more energetic men were leaving a rusty print upon the ground with every stride.

Our rifles grew so hot with sun and shooting that they seared our hands; and we had to be grudging of our rounds, considering every shot, and spending great pains to make it sure. The rocks on which we flung ourselves for aim were burning, so that they scorched our breasts and arms, from which later the skin drew off in ragged sheets. The present smart [sic] made us thirst. Yet even water was rare with us; we could not afford men to fetch enough from Batra, and if all could not drink, it was better that none should.

We consoled ourselves with knowledge that the enemy's closed valley would be hotter than our open hills: also that they were Turks . . . little apt for warm weather. So we clung to them, and did not let them move or mass or sortie out against us cheaply. They could do nothing valid in return. We were no targets for their rifles, since we moved with speed, eccentrically. Also, we were able to laugh at the little mountain guns which they fired up at us. The shells passed over our heads to burst behind us in the air. . . .

Just after noon I had a heat-stroke, or so pretended, for I was dead weary of it all, and cared no longer how it went. So I crept into a hollow where there was a trickle of thick water in a muddy cup of the hills, to suck some moisture off its dirt through the filter of my sleeve. Nasir [Sherif of Medina] joined me, panting like a winded animal, with his cracked and bleeding lips shrunk apart in his distress: and old Auda appeared, striding powerfully, his eyes bloodshot and staring, his knotty face working with excitement.

Lawrence Leads by Wounding Pride and Enraging Auda

[Auda] grinned with malice when he saw us lying there, spread out to find coolness under the bank, and croaked at me harshly, "Well, how is it with the Howeitat? All talk and no work?" "By God, indeed," spat I back again, for I was angry with every one and with myself, "they shoot a lot and hit a little." Auda almost pale with rage, and trembling, tore his headcloth off and threw it on the ground beside me. Then he ran back up the hill like a madman, shouting to the men in his dreadful strained and rustling voice.

They came together to him, and after a moment scattered away down hill. I feared things were going wrong, and struggled to where he stood alone on the hill-top, glaring at the enemy: but all he would say to me was, "Get your camel if you want to see the old man's work." Nasir called for his camel and we mounted.

The Arabs passed before us into a little sunken place, which rose to a low crest; and we knew that the hill beyond went down in a facile slope to the main valley of Aba el Lissan, somewhat below the spring. All our four hundred camel men were here tightly collected, just out of sight of the enemy. We rode to their head, and asked the Shimt what it was and where the horsemen had gone.

He pointed over the ridge to the next valley above us, and said, "With Auda there": and as he spoke yells and shots poured up in a sudden torrent from beyond the crest. We kicked our camels furiously to the edge, to see our fifty horsemen coming down the last slope into the main valley like a run-away, at full gallop, shooting from the saddle. As we watched, two or three went down, but the rest thundered forward at marvellous speed, and the Turkish infantry, huddled together under the cliff ready to cut their desperate way out towards Maan in the first dusk, began to sway in and out, and finally broke before the rush, adding their flight to Auda's charge.

Nasir screamed at me, "Come on," with his bloody mouth; and we plunged our camels madly over the hill, and down towards the head of the fleeing enemy. The slope was not too steep for a camel-gallop, but steep enough to make their pace terrific, and their course uncontrollable: yet the Arabs were able to extend to right and left and to shoot into the Turkish brown [sic]. The Turks had been too bound up in the terror of Auda's furious charge against their rear to notice us as we came over the eastward slope: so we also took them by surprise and in the flank; and a charge of ridden camels going nearly thirty miles an hour was irresistible.

The Howeitat were very fierce, for the slaughter of their women [by Turks] on the day before had been a new and horrible side of warfare suddenly revealed to them. So there were only a hundred and sixty prisoners, many of them wounded; and three hundred dead and dying were scattered over the open valleys.

A few of the enemy got away, the gunners on their teams, and some mounted men and officers with their Jazi guides. Mohammed el Dheilan chased them for three miles into Mreigha, hurling insults as he rode, that they might know him and keep out of his way.

Auda the Warrior Redeemed

Auda came swinging up on foot, his eyes glazed over with the rapture of battle, and the words bubbling with incoherent speed from his mouth. "Work, work, where are words, work, bullets, Abu Tayi" . . . and he held up his shattered field-glasses, his pierced pistol-holster, and his leather sword-scabbard cut to ribbons. He had been the target of a volley which had killed his mare under him, but the six bullets through his clothes had left him scathless.

He told me later, in strict confidence, that thirteen years before he had bought an amulet Koran for one hundred and twenty pounds and had not since been wounded. . . . The book was a Glasgow reproduction, costing eighteen pence, but Auda's deadliness did not let people laugh at his superstition.

He was wildly pleased with the fight, most of all because he confounded me and shown what his tribe could do. Mohammed's wroth with us for a pair of fools, calling me worse than Auda, since I had insulted him by words like flung stones to provoke folly which had nearly killed us all: though it had killed only two of us, one Rueili and one Sherari.

It was, of course, a pity to lose any one of our men, but time [was of] importance to us, and so imperative was the need of dominating Maan, to shock the little Turkish garrisons between us and the sea into surrender, that I would willingly have lost much more than the two. On occasions like this Death justified himself and was cheap.

Auda Goads the "Army" Forward

Meanwhile our Arabs had plundered the Turks, their baggage train, and their camp; and soon after moonrise, Auda came and said that we must move. It angered Nasir and myself. To-night there was a dewy west wind blowing, and at Aba el Lissan's four thousand feet, after the heat and burning passion of the day, its damp chill struck very sharply on our wounds and bruises. The spring itself

was a thread of silvery water in a runnel of pebbles across delightful turf, green
and soft, on which we lay, wrapped in our cloaks, wondering if something to
eat were worth preparing: for we were subject at the moment to the physical
shame of success, a reaction of victory, when it became clear that nothing was
worth doing, and that nothing worthy had been done.

Auda insisted. Partly it was superstition—he feared the newly-dead around
us; partly lest the Turks return in force; partly lest other clans of the Howeitat
take us, lying there broken and asleep. Some were his blood enemies: others
might say they came to help our battle, and in the darkness thought we were
Turks and fired blindly. So we roused ourselves, and jogged the sorry prisoners
into line.

Most had to walk. Some twenty camels were dead or dying from wounds
which they had got in the charge, and others were over weak to take a double
burden. The rest were loaded with an Arab and a Turk; but some of the Turkish
wounded were too hurt to hold themselves on pillion. In the end we had to
lead about twenty on the thick grass beside the rivulet, where at least they
would not die of thirst, though there was little hope of life or rescue for them.

Nasir set himself to beg blankets for these abandoned men, who were half-
naked; and while the Arabs packed, I went down the valley where the fight had
been, to see if the dead had any clothing they could spare. But the Beduin had
been beforehand with me, and had stripped them to the skin. Such was their
point of honour.

Bedouin Spoils of Victory

To an Arab an essential part of the triumph of victory was to wear the clothes of
an enemy: and next day we saw our force transformed (as to the upper half)
into a Turkish force, each man in a soldier's tunic: for this was a battalion
straight from home . . . and dressed in new uniforms.

In the end our little army was ready, and wound slowly to the height and
beyond into a hollow sheltered from the wind and there, while the tired men
slept, we dictated letters to the Sheikhs of the coastal Howeitat, telling them of
the victory, that they might invest their nearest Turks, and hold them till we
came. We had been kind to one of the captured officers, a policeman despised
by his regular colleagues, and him we persuaded to be our Turkish scribe to the
commandants of Guweira, Kethei and Hadra, the three posts between us and
Akaba, telling them that if our blood was not hot we took prisoners, and that
prompt surrender would ensure their good treatment and safe delivery to Egypt.

Approach March

This lasted till dawn, and then Auda marshalled us for the road, and led us up
the last mile of soft heath-clad valley between the rounded hills. It was intimate

and home-like till the last green bank; when suddenly we realized it was the last, and beyond lay nothing but clear air. The lovely change this time checked me with amazement; and afterwards, however often we came there was always a catch of eagerness in the mind, a pricking forward of the camel and straightening up to see again over the crest into openness.

Shtar hill-side swooped away below us for hundreds and hundreds of feet. . . .

After days of travel on the plateau in prison valleys, to meet this brink of freedom was a rewarding vision, like a window in the wall of life. We walked down the whole zigzag pass of Shtar, to feel its excellence, for on our camels we rocked too much with sleep to dare see anything. At the bottom the animals found a matted thorn which gave their jaws pleasure; we in front made a halt, rolled on to sand soft as a couch, and incontinently slept.

Auda came. We pleaded that it was for mercy upon our broken prisoners. He replied that they alone would die of exhaustion if we rode, but if we dallied, both parties might die: for truly there was now little water and no food. However, we could not help it, and stopped that night short of Guweira, after only fifteen miles. At Guweira lay Sheikh ibn Jad, balancing his policy to come down with the stronger: and to-day we were the stronger, and the old fox was ours. He met us with honeyed speeches. The hundred and twenty Turks of the garrison were his prisoners: we agreed with him to carry them at his leisure and their ease to Akaba.

Final Palavers and Attacks

To-day was the fourth of July. Time pressed us, for we were hungry, and Akaba was still far ahead behind two defences. The nearer post, Kethira, stubbornly refused parley. . . . Their cliff commanded the valley—a strong place which it might be costly to take. We assigned the honour, in irony, to ibn Jad and his unwearied men, advising him to try it after dark. He shrank, made difficulties, pleaded the full moon: but we cut hardly into this excuse, promising that to-night for awhile there should be no moon. By my diary there was an eclipse. Duly it came, and the Arabs forced the post without loss, while the superstitious soldiers were firing rifles and clanging copper pots to rescue their threatened satellite. Reassured we set out across the strand-like plain. Niazi Bey, the Turkish battalion commander, was Nasir's guest, to spare him the humiliation of Beduin contempt.

The narrows of Wadi Itm increased in intricate ruggedness as we penetrated deeper. Below Kethira we found Turkish post after Turkish post, empty. Their men had been drawn in to Khadra, the entrenched position (at the mouth of Itm), which covered Akaba so well against a landing from the sea. Unfortunately for them the enemy had never imagined attack from the interior, and of all their great works not one trench or post faced inland. Our advance from so new a direction threw them into panic.

In the afternoon we were in contact with this main position, and heard from the local Arabs that the subsidiary posts about Akaba had been called in or reduced, so that only a last three hundred men barred us from the sea. We dismounted for a council, to hear that the enemy were resisting firmly, in bomb-proof trench with a new artesian well. Only it was rumoured that they had little food.

No more had we. It was a deadlock. Our council swayed this way and that. Arguments bickered between the prudent and bold. Tempers were short and bodies restless in the incandescent gorge whose granite peaks radiated the sun. . . .

Our numbers had swollen double. So thickly did the men crowd in the narrow space, and press about us, that we broke up our council twice or thrice, partly because it was not good they should overhear us wrangling, partly because in the sweltering confinement our unwashed smells offended us. . . .

We sent the Turks summonses, first by white flag, and then by Turkish prisoners, but they shot at both. This inflamed our Beduin, and while we were yet deliberating a sudden wave of them burst up on to the rocks and sent a hail of bullets spattering against the enemy. Nasir ran out barefoot, to stop them, but after ten steps on the burning ground screeched for sandals; while I crouched in my atom of shadow, too wearied of these men (whose minds all wore my livery) to care who regulated their febrile impulses.

We had a third try to communicate with the Turks, by means of a little conscript, who said that he understood how to do it. We walked down close to the trenches with him, and sent in for an officer to speak with us. After some hesitation this was achieved, and we explained the situation on the road behind us; our growing forces; and our short control over their tempers. The upshot was that they promised to surrender at daylight. So we had another sleep (an event rare enough to chronicle) in spite of our thirst.

Next day at dawn fighting broke out on all sides, for hundreds more hill-men, again doubling our number, had come in the night; and, not knowing the arrangement, began shooting at the Turks, who defended themselves. Nasir went out, with ibn Dgheithir and his Ageyl marching in fours, down the open bed of the valley. Our men ceased fire. The Turks then stopped, for their rank and file had no more fight in them and no more food, and thought we were well supplied. So the surrender went off quietly after all.

Akaba Falls—The Aftermath

As the Arabs rushed in to plunder I noticed an engineer in grey uniform, with red beard and puzzled blue eyes; and spoke to him in German. He was the well-borer, and knew no Turkish. Recent doings had amazed him, and he begged me to explain what we meant. I said that we were a rebellion of the Arabs against the Turks. This, it took him time to appreciate. He wanted to know who was our leader. I said the Sherif of Mecca. He supposed he would be sent to Mecca. I said rather to Egypt. He inquired the price of sugar, and when I replied, "cheap and plentiful," he was glad. The loss of his belongings he took philosophically, but was sorry for the well, which a little work would have finished as his monument. He showed me where it was, with the pump only half-built. By pulling on the sludge bucket we drew enough delicious clear water to quench our thirsts. Then we raced through a driving sandstorm down to Akaba, four miles further, and splashed into the sea on July the sixth [1917], just two months after our setting out from Wejh.

We sat down to watch our men streaming past as lines of flushed vacant faces without message for us. For months Akaba had been the horizon of our minds, the goal: we had had no thought, we had refused thought, of anything beside.

Now, in achievement, we were a little despising the entities which had spent their extremest effort on an object whose attainment changed nothing radical either in mind or body.

Decision to Travel to Cairo

Hunger called us out of our trance. We had now seven hundred prisoners in addition to our own five hundred men and two thousand expectant allies. We had not any money [or anyplace to spend money]; and the last meal had been two days ago. In our riding camels we possessed meat enough for six weeks, but it was poor diet . . . indulgence in which would bring future immobility upon us.

Supper taught us the urgent need to send news over the one hundred and fifty desert miles to the British at Suez for a relief-ship. I decided to go across myself with a party of eight, mostly Howeitat, on the best camels in the force.[22]

Interview with General Allenby

[Lawrence rode 49 hours in the desert, then made his way across to Suez and Cairo, where he first met General Edmund Allenby, later Field Marshal Viscount Allenby.]

Before I was clothed the Commander-in-Chief sent for me, curiously. In my report, thinking of Saladin and Abu Obeida, I had stressed the strategic importance of the eastern tribes of Syria, and their proper use as a threat to the communications of Jerusalem. This jumped [sic] with his ambitions, and he wanted to weigh me.

It was a comic interview, for Allenby was physically large and confident . . . [and] the comprehension of our littleness came slow to him. He sat in his chair looking at me—not straight, as his custom was, but sideways, puzzled. He was newly from France, where for years he had been a tooth of the great machine grinding the enemy. He was full of Western [front] ideas . . . but, as a cavalryman, was already half persuaded to throw up the new school, in this different world of Asia, and [adopt a strategy] of manoeuvre and movement. . . .

Allenby could not make out how much [of me] was genuine performer and how much charlatan. The problem was working behind his eyes, and I left him unhelped to solve it. He did not ask many questions, nor talk much, but studied the map and listened to my unfolding of Eastern Syria and its inhabitants. At the end he put up his chin and said quite directly, "Well, I will do for you what I can", and that ended it. I was not sure how far I had caught him; but we learned gradually that he meant exactly what he said; and that what General Allenby could do was enough for his very greediest servant.[23]

Conclusions

Lawrence was a self-taught master of guerrilla warfare, though he knew the military exemplars and theorists from Xenophon through Napoleon to Clausewitz and Von der Goltz. His guerrilla methods are described in his "principles," given above: Victory for his "army" required an unassailable base (he had most of northern Arabia, since the Turks could only control strong points); a friendly population, which would help his fighters or not hinder them (the Bedouin); a hated enemy (the Turks); sufficient men (the Sheikhs with British money assured that); a source of weapons (in this case the British); men who could keep secrets, and knew their weapons well enough to strike with confidence, speed, and violence.

Beyond question, his Bedouins contributed to the British victory in the Middle East—for all their studied leisureliness, disorganization, odd apprehensions, and greed for loot. As noted above, Lawrence felt they should have been awarded an Arab state. The British government, of course, had to consider the interests of the French, Arab chieftains other than Hussein, and the Jews of Palestine and the Zionist organization. Arabia proper went to him who then controlled Mecca, Ibn Saud (Saudi Arabia). France took Syria (including Lebanon) under mandate. The British assumed mandates over Trans-Jordan, Mesopotamia, and Palestine. In time, the first two became the kingdoms of Jordan and Iraq, under sons of Hussein. The British ruled Palestine and attempted, without unduly disturbing the Arab majority, to create a Jewish "homeland" there, as promised to the Zionist leaders.[24]

Winston Churchill, who admired Lawrence, employed him at the Colonial Office, but Lawrence was against British policy toward the Arabs and French, although he approved of Zionist (Jewish) aspirations. In 1917, he had written the diplomat Mark Sykes (negotiating with the French) to tell him what the Jews wanted, and that he would persuade Feisal not to oppose them. The Sherif had already assured the Arab-speaking Palestinian Jews that he would not move east of the Jordan River.[25]

Lawrence felt that his personal honor was soiled because he had kept the Arabs fighting on promise of an Arab state (although at all stages he had known there was doubt about it). He renounced all honors and medals, and spent the remainder of his life, under assumed names, as an enlisted man in the Royal Air Force or Army.[26] On 13 May 1935, riding his motorcycle at high speed (a rare enjoyment), he suddenly came on two boys in a dip on a narrow road. He swerved to avoid them, crashed, suffered a concussion, and died six days later.

VI

Archibald Percival Wavell

(1883–1950)

FOR THOSE who know General Wavell only from World War II in North Africa, he may seem an odd choice to cite on the art of war. He routed the Italians, but retreated under the blows of Rommel's Afrika Korps. Winston Churchill, always ready with a *bon mot*, dispatched him to India "to sit under a Pagoda tree."[1] Before World War II, however, he was highly respected as a military theorist and historian—and one who (unlike most senior officers) did not laud the General Staff system. Field Marshal Rommel carried a German translation of Wavell's *Generals and Generalship* in the desert;[2] he beat his "mentor," but the odds were already in Rommel's favor when he encountered Wavell in 1941.

Wavell was educated at "public" school and Sandhurst, joined his father's regiment, the Black Watch (42nd Highlanders), and at age 18, saw the end of the Boer War (1902). In 1915–16, he fought in France, was wounded, and was assigned as liaison officer with the Russian Army of the Caucusus. When the Russian Revolution began he was recalled and sent with General Allenby to the Middle East (1917–18), where he saw every major battle. He rose rapidly between the world wars, commanded in Palestine and Jordan in 1937–38, and was made Supreme Commander of British forces in the Middle East in 1939.

Wavell's forces, under General Richard O'Connor, demolished the Italian army in Libya in 1940–41, taking thousands of prisoners. He had to suspend operations, however, to send units to Greece to oppose the German conquest.[3] They were too late, but at the same time, his troops seized Italian East Africa, saved Iraq from pro-German forces, and took Syria from the Vichy French (allied with the Germans). When Rommel arrived in North Africa, Wavell's counteroffensive (June 1941) with depleted forces could not stop him.

Churchill sent Wavell to command in India (July 1941). In January 1942 Wavell took command of Allied forces in the Far East—American, British, Dutch, and Australian—and attempted to limit the Japanese conquest of Southeast Asia and the Pacific islands. Wavell organized forces in India to recapture Burma in 1942–43. His efforts failed, but laid groundwork for later Allied victory. He was promoted to field marshal and made viceroy of India (1943–47), where he prepared India and Pakistan for independence. He died in London in 1950.

In World War II, Wavell was always given tasks too great for his resources. He was a better general than his win-loss record indicates. His writings include *Allenby, A Study in Greatness: The Biography of Field-Marshal Viscount Allenby* (1940), *Generals and Generalship* (1941), *Soldiers and Soldiering* (1941), and several volumes of poetry.

———

The passages below are from Wavell's *Generals and Generalship* and *Soldiers and Soldiering.*[4]

———

Essential Qualifications for High Command

While I was [reading expositions of] the essential qualifications of a higher commander . . . I found . . . one that seemed to me to go to the . . . root of the matter; it is attributed to . . . *Socrates*. It reads . . .:

> The general must know how to get his men their rations and every other kind of stores needed for war. He must have imagination to originate plans, practical sense and energy to carry them through. He must be observant, untiring, shrewd; kindly and cruel; simple and crafty; a watchman and a robber; lavish and miserly; generous and stingy; rash and conservative. All these and many other qualities, natural and acquired, he must have. He should also, as a matter of course, know his tactics; for a disorderly mob is no more an army than a heap of building materials is a house.

Now the first point that attracts me about that definition is the order in which it is arranged. It begins with . . . administration, which is the real crux of generalship, to my mind; and places tactics, the handling of troops in battle, at the end of his qualifications instead of at the beginning. . . . Also it insists on practical sense and energy as two of the most important qualifications; while the list of the many and contrasted qualities . . . rightly gives an impression of the great field of activity that generalship covers and the variety of the situations with which it has to deal, and the need for adaptability in the make-up of a general.

The First Essential: Robustness

But even this definition of Socrates does not . . . emphasize sufficiently what I hold to be the first essential of a general, the quality of robustness, the ability to stand the shocks of war.

Now the mind of the general in war is buried . . . for days and weeks, in the mud and sand of unreliable information and uncertain factors, and may at any time receive, from an unsuspected move of the enemy, an unforeseen accident, or a treacherous turn in the weather, a bump equivalent to a drop of at least a hundred feet on to something hard. Delicate mechanism is of little use in war; and this applies to the mind of the commander as well as to his body; to the spirit of an army as well as to the weapons and instruments with which it is equipped. All material of war, including the general, must have a certain solidity, a high margin over the normal breaking strain.[5]

The civil comparison to war must be that of . . . a very rough and dirty game, for which a robust body and mind are essential. The general is dealing with men's lives, and must have a certain mental robustness to stand the strain of this responsibility. How great that strain is you may judge by the sudden deaths of many of the commanders of [World War I]. When you read military history take note of the failures due to lack of this quality of robustness.

Physical Requirements

I propose to say a few words about the physical attributes of a general: courage, health, and youth. Personal appearance we need not worry about: an imposing presence can be a . . . useful asset; but good generals [, like] good race-horses, "run in all shapes." Physical courage is not so essential . . . in reaching high rank as it was in the old days of close-range fighting, but it still is of . . . importance . . . in determining the degree of risk a commander will take to see for himself what is going on; and in mechanized warfare we may again see the general leading his troops almost in the front of the fighting, or . . . reconnoitering and commanding from the air.[6]

Calm Courage and Determination

Courage, physical and moral, a general undoubtedly must have. Voltaire praises in Marlborough "that calm courage in the midst of tumult, that serenity of soul in danger, which is the greatest gift of nature for command." A later military writer, [with little] admiration for Joffre, was compelled to admit that his stolid calm and obstinate determination in the darkest days . . . offset many of the grave strategical blunders . . . he committed. Health in a general is, of course, most important, but it is a relative quality. . . . We would . . . I imagine, sooner have Napoleon sick on our side than many of his opponents whole. A great spirit can rule in a frail body, as Wolfe and others have shown us. Marlborough during his great campaigns would have been [rejected] by most modern medical boards.

The Question of Age

Next comes the vexed question of age. . . . But at exactly what age a general ceases to be dangerous to the enemy . . . is not easy to determine. Hannibal, Alexander, Napoleon, Wellington, Wolfe, and others may be [cited] as proof that the highest prizes of war are for the young men. On the other hand, Julius Caesar and Cromwell began their . . . soldiering when well over . . . 40; Marlborough was 61 at the time of his most admired manoeuvre, when he forced the Ne Plus Ultra lines; Turenne's last campaign at . . . 63 is said to have been his boldest and best. Moltke, the most competent of the moderns, made his name at . . . 66 and confirmed his reputation at 70. Roberts was 67 when he went out to South Africa. . . and restored the situation. . . . Foch at 67 still possessed energy and vitality and great originality.[7]

Character, Humanity, and the Will to Win

I don't think I need [dwell] on the moral qualities of a leader. No amount of study or learning will make a man a leader unless he has the natural qualities of one. The qualities of a leader are well known. . . . Here I will mention only the barest essentials.

He must have "character," which simply means that he knows what he wants and has the courage and determination to get it. He should have a genuine interest in, and a real knowledge of, humanity, the raw material of his trade; and, most vital . . . he must have . . . fighting spirit, the will to win. You all know and recognize it in sport, the man who plays his best when things are going badly, who has the power to come back at you when apparently beaten, and who refuses to acknowledge defeat.

Zest for the Game

There is one other moral quality I would stress as the mark of the really great commander. . . . He must have a spirit of adventure, a touch of the gambler in him. As Napoleon said: "If the art of war consisted merely in not taking risks glory would be at the mercy of very mediocre talent." Napoleon always asked if a general was "lucky." . . . He [meant], "Was he bold?" . . . No general can be lucky unless he is bold. The general who allows himself to be . . . hampered by regulations is unlikely to win a battle.[8]

Common Sense and Knowledge

So [much for] the general's physical and moral make-up. Now for his mental qualities. The most important is what the French call *le sens du praticable*, and we call common sense, knowledge of what is and what is not possible. It must be based on a . . . sound knowledge of the "mechanism of war," i.e., topography, movement, and supply. These are the real foundations of military knowledge, not strategy and tactics. . . . It is the lack of . . . knowledge of the principles and practice of military movement and administration—the "logistics" of war . . .—[that misleads] amateur strategists . . . not the principles of strategy . . . which can be [mastered quickly] by any reasonable intelligence.[9]

Administrative Factors

Unfortunately, in most military books strategy and tactics are emphasized at the expense of the administrative factors. . . . There are 10 military students who can tell you how Blenheim was won for one who [knows anything] of the . . . preparations that made the march to Blenheim possible. There were months of . . . planning to make Allenby's manoeuvre at . . . Gaza practicable. . . . I should like you always to bear in mind when you study military history . . . the importance of this administrative factor, because it is where most critics and many generals go wrong.

The Complexities of Modern Command

I wonder if you realize what a very complicated business this modern soldiering is. A commander to-day has now to learn to handle air forces, armoured mechanical vehicles, anti-aircraft artillery; he has to consider the use of gas and smoke, offensively and defensively; to know enough of wireless to make proper use of it for communication; to understand something of the art of camouflage, of the business of propaganda; to keep himself up to date in the developments of military engineering: all this in addition to the more normal requirements of his trade. On the battlefield, of course, conditions are completely different. Marlborough at Blenheim, after placing the batteries himself and riding along his whole front, lunches on the battlefield under cannon fire waiting for his colleague Eugene on the right flank. . . . Napoleon at Austerlitz can . . . see the enemy expose himself . . . irretrievably to the prepared counter-stroke, and can judge the exact moment . . . to launch it. Wellington at Salamanca, seeing his opponent make a false move, has only to issue a few verbal orders, and can then turn . . . to the Spanish representative [and] remark: "*Mon cher Alava, Marmont est perdu.*" Even at Sedan, 60 years later, Moltke . . . can watch practically the whole agony of the French army from a small hill. . . . In the late war [*World War I*] no battalion commander . . . had anything like such a clear picture of the situation as any of these, while the Commander-in-Chief was not on the battlefield . . . but . . . in an office many miles back or . . . pacing the garden of a château waiting for news . . . [*which*] when it came was usually misleading.

Command of Ground and Air Forces

So much for the past, now for the future. There are new forces to handle, both on the ground and in the air, with potentialities that are largely unexplored. . . . The commander with the imagination—the genius, in fact—to use the new forces may have his name written among the "great captains." But he will not win that title . . . easily; consider for a moment the qualifications he will require. On the ground he will have to handle forces moving at a speed and ranging at a distance far exceeding that of the most mobile cavalry of the past; a study of naval strategy and tactics as well as those of cavalry will be essential to him. Some ideas on his position in battle and the speed at which he must make his decisions may be derived from the battle of Jutland; not much from [land battles]. Needless to say, he must be able to handle air forces [as well as] forces on land.

It seems to me immaterial whether he is a soldier who has really studied the air or an airman who has really studied land forces. It is the combination of the two . . . that will bring success for a future war. Add to this that the commander . . . must have . . . solid common sense, and a knowledge of humanity, on whose peculiarities, and not those of machines, the. . . practice of warfare is ultimately based.[10]

The General, the Staff, and the Troops

I now want you to consider the general in relation to his troops. [Regarding the staff:] I will give you two simple rules which every general should observe: . . . never to try to do his own staff work; and . . . never to let his staff get between him and his troops. What a staff appreciates is [to get] clear and definite instructions, and then be left to work out the details without interference. What troops and subordinate commanders [want] is that a general . . . be constantly in personal contact with them, and . . . not see everything . . . through the eyes of his staff. The less time a general spends in his office and the more with his troops the better.[11]

Relations with Subordinate Commanders

As to a general's relations with his subordinate commanders, it is important to him to know their characteristics: which must be held back and which urged on, which can be trusted with an independent mission, and which must be kept under his own eye. Some want very detailed and precise orders, others merely a general indication. There are many generals who are excellent executive commanders as long as they are controlled by a higher commander, but who get out of their depth . . . and sometimes lose their nerve, if given an independent command. Others are difficult subordinates, but may be trusted on their own. It is important not to get the two sorts mixed: . . . a higher commander must be a good judge of character. It is interesting to observe the practice of Napoleon and of Wellington in this respect. There were few of his marshals whom Napoleon trusted away from his immediate command—Davout, Masséna, and Marmont were the principal exceptions. Wellington was perfectly happy to give Graham an independent mission, but did not let Craufurd, Beresford, or Picton have much latitude.

The Troops

Now to come to the general's relations with the troops themselves. . . . The outlook of the . . . regimental officer . . . differs naturally from that of the men. And different nationalities demand different treatment. "Mes enfants"—My children"—says the Frenchman, and may speak of glory and the Fatherland; "Men," says the Englishman on the rare occasions when he . . . [addresses] his troops . . .; "Comrades," says the Soviet Russian. . . . But whatever the nationality, whatever the conditions, there remains the basic problem: *What induces the man to risk his life bravely, and what is the general's part in fostering his endurance?* . . . what causes him to face death? Maybe hope of loot or glory, discipline and tradition, devotion to a cause or country, devotion to a man. Glory or loot appeals to few these days; nor, indeed, is much . . . to be had. Decorations and promotion count for something, but may cause much heart-burning unless carefully distributed. *Belief in a cause may count for much, especially if fostered by mass propaganda*; yet there is truth in the following from a book on the late War: A man does not flee because he is fighting in an unrighteous cause, he does not attack because his cause is just; he flees because he is the weaker, he conquers because he is the stronger, or because his leader has made him feel the stronger. . . . *But tradition and discipline, anyway so far as the British are concerned, are the real root of the matter.* I have not the time here to enter into any discussion on the subject of discipline; I will only remark that with national armies—as all armies, even the British, will be in a future war—and general education, discipline should be a different matter from . . . traditional military discipline. . . . But, whatever the system, it is the general's business to see justice done. The soldier does not mind a severe code provided it is administered fairly and reasonably. As an instance [to quote] private soldier on Craufurd in the retreat to Corunna: "If he flogged two, he saved hundreds from death." *Discipline apart, the soldier's chief cares are:—First, his personal comfort*—i.e., regular rations, proper clothing, good billets, and proper hospital arrangements . . . and *secondly, his personal safety*—i.e., that he shall be put into a fight with [the best] chance . . . possible of victory and survival. Guns and butter, in other words. . . . Russian [morale] in the late War broke through lack of guns, Germans largely through lack of butter.

The general who sees that the soldier is well fed and looked after, and who . . . wins battles, will naturally have his confidence. Whether he will also have his affection is another story. Wellington was most meticulous about his administrative arrangements, and was a most successful general. . . . But he was certainly not popular, though on one occasion some of his troops, put into a tight place by . . . one of his subordinates, gave a spontaneous cheer at his arrival. . . . Kitchener, who . . . never courted popularity, received the same tribute . . . of a spontaneous cheer on the field of battle, at the Atbara. Marlborough . . . careful of administration . . . and also successful, was . . . popular, and affectionately [called] Corporal John by his men.[12]

Respect and Confidence Better Than Affection

But does it matter to a general whether he has his men's affection so long as he has their confidence?. . . If he has their appreciation and respect it is sufficient. Efficiency in a general his soldiers have a right to expect; geniality they are usually right to suspect. Marlborough was perhaps the only great general to whom geniality was always natural.[13]

————

The following extract from the Australian Official History shows the impression made by Allenby:—

> There was nothing familiar about Allenby's touch with his regiments and battalions. He went through the hot dusty camps of his army like a strong fresh reviving wind. He would dash up in his car to a Light Horse regiment, shake hands with a few officers, inspect hurriedly, but with a sure eye to good and bad points, the horses of perhaps a single squadron, and be gone in a few minutes, leaving a great trail of dust behind him. His tall and massive, but restlessly active, figure, his keen eyes and prominent hooked nose, his terse and forcible speech, and his imperious bearing radiated an impression of tremendous resolution, quick decision, and steely discipline. Within a week of his arrival Allenby had stamped his personality on the mind of every [cavalry] trooper . . . and every infantryman of the line [in the Middle East Command].

Addressing the Troops

Should a general address his troops . . .? Only, I think, if he has a gift that way, a gift not of eloquence necessarily but of saying the right thing. He must be very sure of himself. He risks more loss of reputation than he is likely to gain. An unfortunate remark or tone, or even appearance, may . . . do more harm than good.[14]

"Privileged Irascibility"

Explosions of temper do not necessarily ruin a general's reputation or influence with his troops; it is almost expected of them ("the privileged irascibility of senior officers," someone has written), and it is not always resented, sometimes even admired. . . . But sarcasm is always resented and seldom forgiven. In the Peninsula the bitter sarcastic tongue of Craufurd, the brilliant but erratic leader of the Light Division, was much more wounding and feared than the more violent outbursts of Picton, a rough, hot-tempered man.[15]

Sense of Humor

Should the high commander have a sense of humour? Certainly [that] is good for anyone; but he must not display it too much or too often. I cannot find . . . that a sense of humour is a very frequent quality in great generals. Allenby certainly had one, though it was not safe to jest with him. But he kept it for his unofficial moments. So did Wellington. . . . I find [none] attributed to Napoleon. The only great commander I can find who was consistently a humorist was that eccentric genius Suvorov, the Russian. . . . Yet the British soldier himself is one of the world's greatest humorists.[16]

Study the Soldier . . .

The man is the first weapon of battle: let us then study the soldier in battle, for it is he who brings reality to it. Only study of the past can . . . show us how the soldier will fight in the future.

When you study military history don't read outlines on strategy or the principles of war. Read biographies, memoirs, historical novels, such as "The Road to Glory" or "Schönbrunn." Get at the flesh and blood of it, not the skeleton. To learn that Napoleon won the campaign of 1796 by manoeuvre on interior lines . . . is of little value. If you can discover how a young unknown man inspired a ragged, mutinous, half-starved army and made it fight, how he gave it the energy and momentum . . . how he dominated and controlled generals older and more experienced than himself, then you will have learnt something.

Napoleon did not gain [high] position . . . so much by a study of rules and strategy as by a profound knowledge of human nature in war. A story of him in his early days shows his knowledge of psychology. [As] an artillery officer at the siege of Toulon he [put] a battery in such an exposed position that he was told he would never find men to hold it. He put up a placard, "The battery of men without fear," and it was always manned.

Discipline, Encouragement, and Care for Troops

Here are a few principles that seem to me to embody the practice of successful commanders in their relations with their troops. A general must keep strict . . . discipline. He should give praise where praise is due, ungrudgingly, by word of mouth or written order. He should show himself as frequently as possible to his troops, and as impressively as possible. . . . He should never indulge in sarcasm, which is being clever at someone else's expense, and always offends. He should tell his soldiers the truth, save when absolutely necessary to conceal plans, &c. Few things annoyed the soldier more in the late War than [publications] by . . . Intelligence to make out that the German soldiers were fighting badly . . . when the soldier knew [better]. To sum up, the relationship between a general and his troops is very much like that between the rider and his horse. The horse must be controlled and disciplined, and yet encouraged . . . according to an old hunting maxim, "be cared for in the stable as if he was worth £500 and ridden in the field as if he were not worth half-a-crown." And the horse knows . . . if his rider is bold or frightened, determined or hesitating. A general must drive his men at times. Some of the best and most successful riders . . . are not those who are fondest of horses. A general may succeed . . . in persuading his superiors that he is a good commander: he will never persuade his army that he is a good commander unless he has the real qualities of one.[17]

War Requires Improvision and Fighting Spirit

My . . . lectures are done. All I have hoped to do in them is to persuade you to a flesh-and-blood study . . . of military history, and that *war is not a matter of diagrams, principles, or rules.* The higher commander who goes to Field Service Regulations for tactical guidance inspires about as much confidence as the doctor who turns to a medical dictionary for his diagnosis. And no method of education, no system of promotion, no amount of commonsense ability is of value unless the leader has in him . . . the fighting Spirit. Whatever mistakes they committed, however they differed from each other, the great leaders of . . . War, civil or military . . . had this in common, an unconquerable spirit. As one of them has said: *"No battle was ever lost until the leader thought it so": and this is the first and true function of the leader.* . . . The ancient Romans put up a statue to the general who saved them in one of Rome's darkest hours, with this inscription: "Because he did not despair of the Republic."

One word more. The pious Greek, when he had set up altars to all the . . . gods by name, added one more . . . "To the Unknown God." So whenever we speak . . . of the great captains and set up . . . altars to Hannibal and Napoleon and Marlborough . . . let us add one more altar, "To the Unknown Leader," . . . to the good company, platoon, or section leader who carries forward his men or holds his post, and often falls unknown. It is these who in the end do most to win wars.[18]

Personal Command

I believe firmly in a "personal" command, i.e. that a commander should never attempt to control an operation or a battle by remaining at his H.Q. or be content to keep touch with his subordinates by cable, [radio,] or other means of communication. He must as far as possible see the ground for himself to confirm or correct his impressions of the map; his subordinate commanders to discuss their plans and ideas with them; and the troops to judge of their needs and their morale. All these as often as possible. The same of course applies to periods of preparation and periods between operations. In fact, generally, the less time a commander spends in his office and the more he is with his troops the better.

There are certain rules a commander must observe when he goes forward to his subordinate commanders. [The first of these is]: . . . He must leave at his H.Q. someone who can deal with changes in the situation and developments during his absence. This will nearly always be the senior General Staff officer. It is not enough that he should be at the H.Q. when the commander is away, he must be thoroughly in the mind of the commander, who should therefore discuss with him possible developments and leave him in no doubt of his intentions.[19]

Orders Must Be Followed Up

However much personal visits and liaison officers are used, command has very largely to be exercised, especially in higher commands, by means of written messages sent by Signals. The error most frequently committed by commanders and staff is to assume that their responsibility ceases when the message is handed to Ciphers or Signals, and to take no action to trace the progress of a message. It should be a matter of drill that all important orders or messages are traced.[20]

Intelligence and Propaganda

There are certain principles in the use of Intelligence staff that are sometimes neglected. Intelligence must have as good accommodation as possible and peace and quiet. Too often Intelligence officers are given inadequate facilities and everyone on or off the staff crowds in to "see the latest news." Intelligence staff cannot function properly in such conditions. They must be able to sift information, refer it to previous reports, spread their maps, etc., in peace. As Divisional

Commander I made it an absolute rule that no one except the G.S.O.I. or myself was allowed to enter the Intelligence office.

The above give some of the most important factors in the proper working of the machinery of command. As to the moral factors in command, it is always worth while to bear in mind the following:

>   (a) Two-thirds of the reports which are received in war are inaccurate; never accept a single report of success or disaster as necessarily true without confirmation.

>   (b) Always . . . devise means to deceive and outwit the enemy and throw him off . . . balance; the British in war are . . . lacking in . . . cunning.

>   (c) Attack is not only the most effective but the easiest form of warfare and the moral difference between advance and retreat is incalculable. Even when inferior in numbers, it pays to be as aggressive as possible.

>   (d) Finally, when things look bad and one's difficulties appear great, the best tonic is to consider those of the enemy.[21]

"Ruses and Stratagems" of War

Always mystify and mislead the enemy.—Stonewall Jackson

———————

Practically all ruses and stratagems in war are variations or developments of a few simple tricks that have been practised . . . since man has hunted man, i.e. since the existence of the human race. They can be roughly divided under the following heads . . .: False information or disguise . . . Feigned retreat . . . Encouragement of treachery . . . [and] Weakening of morale.[22]

Conclusions

In the post–Great War era, Wavell was something of a radical in the British armed services. He did not attribute god-like qualities to the British Imperial or any other General Staff—or respect lower staffs. He thought that the best military leaders were "naturals,"—men who loved to fight, loved their profession and—most importantly—their men. He believed in "leading from the front," and that good generals were calculating gamblers—and should on occasion ignore regulations.

He predicted that developing technology would produce wars of ever greater speed and scope—the *blitzkrieg*. He wanted generals familiar with the army, navy, and air force—so that joint operations could be effective. He envisioned the day when generals might command from the air (as Americans later did in Vietnam). In North Africa, in 1941–42, *Rommel* continually scouted in aircraft, and often came close to commanding from the air. He was Wavell's true disciple.

VII

Erwin Johannes Eugen Rommel

(1891–1945)

NO BETTER EXEMPLAR of military leadership can be found than Erwin Rommel. As a lieutenant and captain in World War I, he led infantry on the Western and Italian fronts, in the latter often penetrating enemy lines and in the final days capturing thousands of prisoners. As a general and field marshal in World War II, Rommel made legend as the "Desert Fox" in North Africa at the head of his Afrika Korps. He was a "natural." Major General von Mellenthin, a lieutenant colonel in Africa, wrote: "Between Rommel and his troops was that mutual understanding which cannot be explained and analyzed, but which is the gift of the gods. The Afrika Korps followed Rommel wherever he led, however hard he drove them . . . the men knew that Rommel was the last man to spare Rommel."[1]

The son of a Württemberg mathematics teacher, Rommel decided he wanted to be a soldier as a boy, although his family had no military tradition. At 18 he volunteered into the Imperial German Army as an officer-cadet, and was made a lieutenant in 1912. In World War I, he became one of Germany's most highly decorated officers, winning the Iron Cross (2nd and 1st Class) on the Western front, and *Pour le Mérite* in 1917 on the Italian front.[2] By that time, he had been wounded three times, and was relegated to staff duty for the rest of the war. Between campaigns he married Lucie-Maria Mollin, his "Dearest Lu," to whom he wrote almost daily during both world wars.[3]

Rommel was physically ordinary—about 5′8″ tall, slender, well muscled, with brown hair and eyes—but was a born leader, fearless and imaginative, with *coup d'oeil* or *Fingerspitzengefühl*—the ability to size up a battlefield instantly and capitalize on it. In 1917 in Italy, "Detachment Rommel" repeatedly penetrated enemy lines, destroying positions and taking prisoners. At war's end he was a captain, and served for nine years more without promotion.

After 1933, and in the early years of World War II, Hitler, who admired Rommel, promoted him rapidly.[4] When the United States entered the war (December 1941), Rommel, at age 50, was already famous. He had commanded a panzer division in the *blitzkrieg* against France in 1940, bested British armies in North Africa in 1941–42, briefly invaded Egypt, and had risen to field marshal.[5]

Rommel was sent to "the desert" in February 1941 to help Germany's Italian ally. Field Marshal Rodolfo Graziani had invaded Egypt; General A. P. Wavell, British Middle East commander, loosed Sir Richard O'Connor, with the Western Desert Force (soon renamed Eighth Army), which drove the Italians far into Libya, capturing 130,000 men. Rommel, with the Afrika Korps—initially fewer than 20,000 men—landed in Tripoli in February 1941.[6] Despite his small force, Rommel went on the attack on 24 March.[7] By 15 June he had driven the British 500 miles east—to the border of Egypt—but had bypassed Tobruk. In July, General Claude Auchinleck replaced Wavell in the Middle East;[8] Eighth Army was under Sir Alan Cunningham (later N. M. Ritchie). Cunningham was reinforced to about 750 tanks (vs. Rommel's 400, half Italian) and in November relieved the Tobruk garrison and forced Rommel to retreat into western Libya.

Rommel's Afrika Korps had become Panzer Gruppe Afrika and then Panzer Armee Afrika, with three German divisions (2 tank, 1 infantry), and two Italian Infantry corps. His tank strength was half that of the enemy, but he supplemented tanks with 88mm guns.[9] In early 1942, Rommel advanced again, and in May, at Gazala, scored a spectacular victory. Leaving a holding force on the coast, he attacked from the south through the British rear, was trapped, but broke out and drove north to the sea. On 21 June, he took Tobruk, and was promoted to field marshal (*General Feldmarschall*).

Auchinleck took personal command of Eighth Army and on 28 June made a stand at Mersa Matruh—100 miles into Egypt—but again retreated. Rommel pressed forward to within 60 miles of Alexandria, but he was short of everything; half his troops rode in captured vehicles. Meanwhile Field Marshal Harold Alexander took command in the Middle East; General Bernard Montgomery took over Eighth Army. "Monty" had been monumentally reinforced with men and American tanks. During 31 August–7 September 1942, in a vicious battle at Alam Halfa, Montgomery stopped Rommel, who retreated to El Alamein and dug in. Hitler promised rockets and Tiger tanks (88mm guns), but none came.

Montgomery won the Battle of El Alamein (23 October–4 November 1942); he had 195,000 troops and 1,000 tanks against Rommel's 50,000 Germans, 54,000 Italians, and 510 tanks (300 Italian). Moreover, the RAF controlled the air. After nine days of pounding, Rommel retreated—eventually into Tunisia. Monty was on his heels and Americans and more British had landed in Morocco and Algeria—threatening from the west. Rommel could only delay the Allies; he was replaced before the Germans surrendered in May 1943.

Rommel had routine assignments until 1944, when an allied invasion of Europe loomed. He was then sent to shore up Hitler's "Atlantic Wall," then given command of one of two army groups under Field Marshal Gerd von Rundstedt, charged with defeating the Allied invasion force. Rundstedt wanted to keep the panzers back from the coast, ready to strike wherever the Allies landed. Rommel insisted they should be concentrated near the coast, since Allied airpower would prevent their moving in daylight. Privately, he felt that if the Allies got ashore, the war was lost. Hitler, who had taken over command of German forces, ordered a compromise, dooming his own defense.

After the D-Day landings (6 June 1944), Rommel fought hard, despite premonitions of defeat. En route home for his wife's birthday on 17 July 1944, his staff car was strafed by a British fighter and he was severely wounded. Before he recovered, he was arrested for implication in the bomb plot of 20 July that almost killed Hitler. (Apparently he knew of it, but was not involved.) Offered the choice of suicide or public disgrace and destitution, he took the poison offered—for the sake of his family.

Rommel reached his greatest fame in 1942, in North Africa. Yet he commanded only a few divisions. Other field marshals, such as Erich von Manstein in Russia, had army groups of up to 130 divisions. Rommel's notoriety was based primarily on his mastery of desert war and his victories against great odds. However, it was also a product of German propaganda (though he was never a Nazi) and partly of the publicity of his enemies, who lauded his humanity and chivalry.[10]

Rommel is the best remembered of the German generals, and deservedly so. He was a man of character, a general both feared and respected by his enemies, and revered by his troops.

———

Rommel's *Infantrie greift an* (my translation) will get short shrift below. Based on his experiences in the Great War, it is largely a "how to" book for small-unit infantry. Most of the material quoted is from B. H. Liddell Hart's *Rommel Papers*, with clarifications from his major source, Rommel's *Krieg ohne Hass* (1950), edited by his wife, Lucie, and General Fritz Bayerlein, his chief of staff in North Africa. The British translation of the *Rommel Papers* has *not* been "Americanized," by changing petrol to gasoline, and the like.

———

Retrospective Views and Observations on Actions

[*From* Infantrie greift an (*Infantry Attacks*).]

Digging In

[*France, Doulcon Woods, September 1914.*]

In view of the power of today's weapons, troops must be dispersed and each man must dig himself in. Dig in before the first enemy shells fall! Better too much spadework than too little. Such work saves blood. [*Diese Arbeit spart Blut.*] . . . In the attack, there should be as many machine guns up front as possible. [Men should be ready] to fire MG while in motion if there are collisions with the enemy and in the final assault [*beim Zusammenschloss und Sturm am Platz*].

[*France, Defuy Woods, September 1914.*]

Stone-hard ground in [our] battalion area made digging in very difficult. The officers and NCOs of all grades—by command, harassment, and personal example—had to make tired and hungry men dig [until our position was secure].

Duties of Officers and NCOs

[*France, Defuy Woods, September 1914.*]

Believing the enemy was beaten, we brought up the reserves and machine guns [from lines behind the front]. . . . They were very quickly hit by devastating "revenge" fire from the enemy. In such situations men often lose their nerve and run for cover. Leaders of all grades (officers and NCOs) must confront them with stubborn force, and use weapons if necessary [to make them fight]. . . .

Personal Leadership

[*Romania, Kurpenul village, 1917. The enemy, superior in numbers and well equipped with machine guns and mountain artillery, resisted to the maximum.*]

The battle was won by committing every man at the enemy's most vulnerable point. In such cases the leader must be very active. [*Rommel knew where to commit his men, and led in person.*]

[*Romania near Ungureana Peak, 9 August 1917.*]

By using the smallest irregularities in the terrain for cover [Rommel's detachment] was able to get 1 Km. behind the enemy front, dig in on a ridge and fight off attacks. During the night the Romanians had to withdraw from their front opposite R.J.R. 18 [18th Reserve Infantry] and W.G.B. [Württemberg Mountain Battalion].

Personal Reconnaissance

[*Preparations for assault on Mt. Cosna, 11 August 1917.*]

The attack plan [*Angriffsplan*] for 11 August was made on the basis of personal reconnaissance during the night [before] and the earliest morning hours. [*Although Rommel was wounded, he followed the scouting party, led by a senior sergeant, which found positions for outflanking the enemy line. As a result, Mount Cosna was taken on 12 August.*]

Care of Troops: Rommel Prepares While Men Rest

[*Italy: Preparations for assault on Mt. Cragonza, 25–26 October 1917.*]

While the exhausted troops rested, the officers worked ceaselessly to find out about the enemy and the terrain. At midnight they sent scouts toward Jevscek.

In that way they laid the basis for a breakthrough in northwestern Jevscek and for storming Mount Cragonza.

[*This was standard procedure in Rommel's detachment (three companies—battalion size) and why Detachment Rommel led the way through the Alps into Italy. Once Germans entered the northern valleys, Italian troops, never enthusiastic over the war, surrendered in droves.*][12]

From the *Rommel Papers* and *Krieg ohne Hass*

Leadership "From the Front"

The duties of a commander are not limited to his work with his staff. He must also concern himself with details of command and should pay frequent visits to the fighting line, for the following reasons:

(a) Accurate execution of the plans of the commander and his staff is of the highest importance. It is a mistake to assume that every unit officer will make [the most] of his situation; most of them soon succumb to . . . inertia. Then it is simply reported that for some reason or another this or that cannot be done—reasons are always easy enough to think up. People of this kind must be made to feel the authority of the commander and be shaken out of their apathy. The commander must be the prime mover of the battle [*Der Befehlshaber muß der Motor des Kampfes sein*] and the troops must always have to reckon with his appearance in personal control.

(b) The commander must [constantly] keep his troops abreast of all the latest tactical experience and developments, and must insist on their practical application. He must see . . . that his subordinates are trained in accordance with the latest requirements. The best form of taking care of troops [*truppenfürsorge*] is first-class training, for this saves unnecessary casualties.

(c) It is also greatly in the commander's own interest to have a personal picture of the front and a clear idea of the problems his subordinates are having to face. It is the only way in which he can keep his ideas permanently up to date and adapted to changing conditions. . . . Success comes most readily to the commander whose ideas have not been canalised into any one fixed channel, but can develop freely from the conditions around him.

(d) The commander must have contact with his men. He must be capable of feeling and thinking with them. The soldier must have confidence in him. There is one cardinal principle which must always be remembered: one must never make a show of false emotions to one's men. The . . . soldier has a surprisingly good nose for what is true and what false.

Troop Morale

There are always moments when the commander's place is not back with his staff but up with the troops. It is sheer nonsense to say that maintenance of the men's morale is the job of the battalion commander alone. The higher the rank, the greater the effect of the example. The men tend to feel no kind of contact with a commander who, they know, is sitting somewhere in headquarters. What they want is what might be termed a physical contact with him. In moments of panic, fatigue or disorganisation, or when something out of the ordinary has to be demanded from them, the personal example of the commander works wonders, especially if he has had the wit to create some sort of legend round himself.

The physical demands on the troops [in Egypt, 1942] approached the limits of endurance. This placed a particular duty on the officers to provide a continual example and model for their men.[13]

Tactical Boldness and Military Gambles

It is my experience that bold decisions give the best promise of success. But one must differentiate between strategical or tactical boldness and a military gamble. A bold operation is one in which success is not a certainty but which in case of failure leaves one with sufficient forces in hand to cope with whatever situation may arise. A gamble, on the other hand, is an operation which can lead either to victory or to the complete destruction of one's force. Situations can arise where even a gamble may be justified—as, for instance, when in the normal course of events defeat is merely a matter of time, when the gaining of time is therefore pointless and the only chance lies in an operation of great risk.

Improvision

The only occasion when a commander can calculate the course of a battle in advance is when his forces are so superior that victory is a foregone conclusion; then the problem is no longer one of [with what, *womit*] but only of [how, *wie*]. But even in this situation, I still think it is better to [strike a killing blow] rather than to creep about the battlefield anxiously taking . . . security measures against every conceivable enemy move.

Normally, there is no ideal solution to military problems; every course has its advantages and disadvantages. One must select [what] seems best . . . pursue it resolutely and accept the consequences.[14]

Take Military Doctrine "with a Grain of Salt"

Prejudice against innovation is a typical characteristic of an Officer Corps which has grown up in a well-tried and proven system. Thus it was that the Prussian

Army was defeated by Napoleon [*Die preußische Armee unterlag aus diesem Grunde Napoleon*]. This attitude was also evident during this war, in German as well as British officer circles, where, with their minds . . . on complicated theories, people [could not] come to terms with reality.[15] A military doctrine had been worked out [in] detail and it was now regarded as the summit of all military wisdom. The only military thinking which was acceptable was that which followed their . . . rules. Everything outside the rules was regarded as a gamble; if it succeeded . . . it was the result of luck and accident. This [cast] of mind creates fixed preconceived ideas, the consequences of which are incalculable.

Take Advantage of Technical Advances

For even military rules are subject to technical progress. What was good for 1914 is only good to-day where the majority of the formations engaged on both sides, or at least on the side which is attacked, are made up of non-motorised infantry units. Where this is the case the armour still acts as the cavalry . . . outrunning and cutting off the infantry. But in a battle . . . between two fully-motorised [armies], quite different rules apply. I have dealt with this already.

However praiseworthy it may be to uphold tradition in . . . soldierly ethics, it is to be resisted in . . . military command. For to-day it is not only the business of commanders to think up new techniques which will destroy the value of the old: the potentialities of warfare are themselves being continually changed by technical advance. Thus the modern army commander must free himself from routine methods and show a comprehensive grasp of technical matters, for he must be in a position continually to adapt his ideas of warfare to the facts and possibilities of the moment. If [necessary], he must be able to turn the whole structure of his thinking inside out.[16]

Importance of Air Power

[*Reference to the growing presence of the RAF before El Alamein.*]

From the command point of view [the British] would gain the following advantages:

(a) Through total command of the air, he alone would have access to complete and unbroken reconnaissance reports.

(b) He would be able to operate more freely and boldly, since, if an emergency arose, he [could], by use of . . . air-power . . . break up the approach march and assembly and . . . every operation of his opponent, or . . . delay them until he had [taken] effective counter measures.

(c) . . . [A]ny slowing down of one's own operations tends to increase the speed of the enemy's. Since speed is . . . important . . . in motorised warfare, it is easy to see what effect this would have.[17]

Air Superiority before Ground Action

The first essential condition for an army to be able to stand [in] battle is an adequate stock of weapons, petrol and ammunition. . . . A second essential condition . . . is parity or . . . something approaching parity in the air. If the enemy has air supremacy and makes full use of it, then one's own command [must] suffer the following limitations and disadvantages:

> By using his strategic air force, the enemy can [drastically reduce] one's supplies. . . .
> The enemy can wage the battle of attrition from the air.
> Intensive exploitation . . . of his air superiority [makes for] far-reaching tactical limitations (already described) for one's . . . command.

In future the battle on the ground will be preceded by the battle in the air. This will determine which of the contestants has to suffer the operational and tactical disadvantages detailed above, and thus be forced, throughout the battle, into adopting compromise solutions.

Principles of Tank Warfare in the Desert (1941)

[From experience in motorized/ armored warfare in North Africa],

. . . principles were established [which are] fundamentally different from those applying [elsewhere]. These principles will become the standard [in] future, [when] fully-motorised [units] will be dominant.

Encirclement of the Enemy

The envelopment of a fully-motorised enemy in the flat and [easy-driving] terrain of the desert has the following results:

> (a) For a fully-motorised formation, encirclement is the worst tactical situation imaginable, since hostile fire can be brought to bear on it from all sides; even envelopment on only three sides is a tactically untenable situation.
> (b) The enemy [is] forced, because of the bad tactical situation [encirclement], to evacuate the area [he holds].

The encirclement of the enemy and his subsequent destruction in the pocket can seldom be the direct aim of an operation; more often it is only indirect, for any fully-motorised force [which remains organized] will normally and in suitable country be able to break out . . . through an improvised . . . ring. Thanks to his motorisation, the commander of the encircled force [can] concentrate his weight unexpectedly against any likely point in the ring and burst through it. This fact was repeatedly demonstrated in the desert.

It follows therefore that an encircled enemy force can only be destroyed

(a) when it is non-motorised or has been rendered immobile by lack of petrol, or when it includes non-mobile elements . . . ;

(b) when it is badly led or its command has decided to sacrifice one formation in order to save another;

(c) when its fighting strength has already been broken. . . .

Except for cases (a) and (b), which occurred . . . frequently in other theatres of war, encirclement of the enemy and his . . . destruction . . . can only be attempted if he has first been so heavily battered in open battle that the . . . cohesion of his force has been destroyed.

Divide and Destroy

I shall term all actions which have as their aim the wearing down of the enemy's power of resistance "battles of attrition." In motorised warfare, material attrition and the destruction of the . . . cohesion of the opposing army must be the . . . aim of all planning.

Tactically, the battle of attrition is fought with the highest possible degree of mobility. The following points [demand] attention:

(a) The main endeavour should be to concentrate one's own forces . . . while . . . seeking to split the enemy forces . . . and destroy them.

(b) Supply lines are particularly sensitive, since all petrol and ammunition . . . must pass along them. Hence, everything possible must be done to protect one's own supply lines and to upset [or] cut the enemy's. [Hitting] the enemy's supply area will lead . . . to his breaking off the battle elsewhere, since . . . supplies are [essential to] battle and must be given priority of protection.

(c) Armour is the core of the motorised army. . . . [O]ther [arms] are . . . auxiliaries. The war of attrition against the enemy [tanks] must . . . be waged [if] possible by the tank destruction units. One's . . . armour should . . . be used [for] the final blow.

(d) Reconnaissance reports must reach the commander in the shortest possible time; he must [make] decisions . . . and put them into effect as fast as he can. Speed of reaction decides the battle! Commanders of motorised forces must . . . operate as near as possible to their troops, and . . . have the [best] possible signal communication with them.

(e) Speed of movement and the organisational cohesion of one's own forces are decisive. . . . Any [hitch] must be dealt with . . . quickly. . . .

(f) Concealment of intentions is of the utmost importance . . . to [achieve] surprise . . . and thus make it possible to exploit the time taken by the enemy command to react. Deception measures of all kinds should be encouraged, if only to make the enemy commander uncertain and . . . hesitate and hold back.

(g) Once the enemy has been [altogether beaten], success can be exploited by attempting to overrun and destroy major parts of his disorganised formations. Here again, speed is everything! The enemy must never be allowed time to reorganise. Lightning regrouping for the pursuit and [supplying of] the pursuing forces [is] essential.

Tanks, Artillery, and Infantry in Desert Warfare

Concerning the technical and organisational aspect of desert warfare, particular regard must be paid to the following points:

(a) The prime requirements in the tank are *maneuverability, speed and a long-range gun* . . . the side with the more powerful gun has the longer arm and can [hit first at] the enemy. Weight of armour cannot make up for lack of gun-power, as it can only be provided at the expense of maneuverability and speed. . . .

(b) The artillery must have great range and must, above all, [have] great mobility and [carry] ammunition in large quantities.

(c) The infantry serves only to occupy and hold positions designed either to prevent the enemy from particular operations, or to force him into other ones. [That] achieved, the infantry must be able to get away quickly for employment elsewhere. It must . . . be mobile and be equipped . . . rapidly to take up defence positions in the open at tactically important points on the battlefield.[18]

Rommel's Use of Weapons

[*The Afrika Korps, reinforced with their Italian allies, penetrated into Egypt (the Halfaya Pass) in early 1941, by dint of bypassing Tobruk. Leaving a holding force on the Egyptian border, Rommel concentrated on Tobruk, which he needed for proper supply by sea. Meanwhile the British built up to seven divisions, 700 tanks, and 1,000 aircraft. Rommel had three German and six Italian divisions; 414 tanks (157 Italian "self-propelled coffins") and 320 aircraft (200 Italian). In late 1941 he was forced to retreat across Libya to Agedabia—but there he stopped a massive but uncoordinated British offensive. Faced with greater numbers of tanks and superior artillery, Rommel resorted to decoying enemy tanks into the field of fire of his 88mm antitank guns (actually anti-aircraft guns firing flat). He then withdrew to El Agheila to refit, and in January 1942 began a new offensive that netted him Tobruk and took him to within 60 miles of Alexandria.*]

Against [British tanks and long range artillery] the Germans had in hand the 88mm Pak-Flak, a weapon of unmatched versatility and the envy [of the enemy].[19]

The three-day tank battle at Agedabia at year's end 1941 was a model of mobile battle leadership and the mutual support of tanks and the [88mm] anti-aircraft gun [as a tank killer]. . . . The winter battle in Marmarica is of particular importance, because there the tactical plan of the desert war was born, consolidated, and proved. All [my] successes of the next battles were based on these experiences and finally led to the highlight in the summer offensive, where, in terms of tactics and troop leadership, [we] celebrated improbable triumphs.[20]

[*The improbable triumphs turned into inevitable defeat, however, since the German High Command left him without sufficient armor or supplies. "In the summer of 1942, given six German mechanized divisions, we could have smashed the British so thoroughly that the threat from the south would have been eliminated for a long time to come," Rommel wrote.[21]*

The Russian front was eating up weapons and supplies, and the Royal British Navy and RAF blocked much of what was sent to Rommel. On the Allied side Montgomery took over Eighth Army, and for the climactic Battle of El Alamein he had 195,000 troops and 1,000 tanks—two-thirds American Shermans with 75mm guns. Rommel had 50,000 German and 54,000 Italian troops. Of his 510 tanks, about 300 were Italian, and the German tanks were mostly older models with 37mm, 50mm, and low-velocity 75mm guns. Rommel fought hard all the same, but was forced into retreat, which led to German surrender (after Rommel had been relieved) in May 1943.]

Conclusions

Rommel was a thorough professional, but not one to speak of the "art of war" or the like. His emphasis, both in *Infanterie greift an* and *Krieg ohne Hass*, was on execution, not theory. In both—at the platoon and company or army level—he emphasized centralized command, massing forces, up-front *personal leadership*, speed, surprise, daring, and the calculated military "gamble." Rommel knew his weapons as well, and compensated for his shortage of tanks by heavy use of the 88mm anti-aircraft gun as an anti-tank weapon—using his tanks to draw the British into the field of fire of the 88's. He recognized that airpower was vitally important, and believed the commander must continually adjust his thinking to the realities of his situation and new technology. He felt that both officers and soldiers should know how to improvise in unexpected situations.[22]

In his Storch light aircraft, Rommel continually observed the British positions and movements until the summer of 1942, when the RAF took control of the air, and then occasionally. He came closer than any commander in World War II to commanding from the air.

VIII

George S. Patton, Jr.

(1885–1945)

IN WORLD WAR II, George Patton was the general deemed most dangerous by the German High Command. During the planning for the Allied invasion of Normandy (D-Day, 6 June 1944), the Allies created a bogus Army Group with an active radio network opposite the *Pas de Calais*, and let slip that Patton would command it. As a result, a large part of the German Army on the Atlantic Wall was held in that area.[1] Rommel believed the invasion would come in Normandy, but could not persuade Field Marshal Gerd von Rundstedt or Hitler to let him concentrate the panzers there.[2] After the D-Day invasion Rommel praised the *blitzkrieg* tactics of the *Patton-Armee*.[3]

Called "Old Blood and Guts" by his men, Patton was hated by many for his obdurate discipline, but he won their respect—even devotion—by *winning battles*. He was known by his towering presence, ivory-handled revolvers, cavalry boots and spurs, and his profanity, raised to a "high art," that bonded him with the roughest soldiers. Some newsmen considered him a brute; most enjoyed his cruel wit, such as his mimicking (at news conferences) of General Bernard Montgomery, replete with mannerisms and an overdone British accent.[4]

The same George Patton was an urbane "aristocrat"—*rich*, French-speaking, and well-read.[5] He remained in the Army in the lean years of the 1920s and 1930s because he preferred being an "officer and a gentleman" over anything else—and because he loved combat. Asked by actress Lynn Lunt what he was fighting for, Patton replied, "I, dear Lady, have been fighting all my life . . . for the simple reason that I love fighting."[6] "Compared to war, all other forms of human endeavor shrink to insignificance," he shouted to Colonel Charles Codman over the din of artillery fire (in Europe, 1944), "God, how I love it!"[7]

Patton was a Californian, but venerated his grandfather, the first George Patton, Colonel, 22nd Virginia Infantry, CSA, mortally wounded at Winchester in 1864. "Georgie" inherited Grandpa's saddle, and began riding and shooting at age five. In the Episcopal Church, he developed a strong faith in God and was drenched in the magnificent English of the King James version of the Bible. He would later astonish World War II comrades by quoting at length from the Bible, Homer's *Iliad*, Kipling's *Barrack-Room Ballads*, and other classics.[8]

Patton went to Virginia Military Institute, then West Point, graduating in 1909, and was assigned to the cavalry. In 1910 he married pretty Beatrice Ayer, who shared his love of riding and sailing. Schooled in France and Switzerland, she was a model of social grace. She never complained during their postings out west, but found her element in Washington (1911–13), where she and *Lieutenant* Georgie entertained, among others, Army Chief-of-Staff General Leonard Wood and Secretary of War Henry L. Stimson.

In 1912, Patton competed in the pentathlon for the U.S. Olympic Team and came in a respectable fifth. In 1913 he studied swordsmanship at the French Cavalry School at Saumur. However, his passion was polo; it was like "a good war," he said.

When the Great War began in 1914, Patton was dissuaded from going to fight with the British, and served as an aide to General John J. Pershing in the U.S. "punitive action" against Pancho Villa on the Mexican border. He managed to see action, however, and even had a shoot-out with a guerrilla chieftain.

In 1917, Pershing commanded of the American Expeditionary Force (AEF) dispatched to France. Patton went with him, was trained in tanks by the Allies, and headed the AEF Tank School. In September 1918 he saw action at St. Mihiel, leading the 1st Tank Brigade of the U.S. First Army. He often went forward to coordinate attacks with the infantry. Patton wrote of one action: "Five tanks of my right battalion . . . came up so I told them to go through Essey. Some damed [sic] Frenchman at the bridge told them to go back as there were too many shells [falling] in the town. The Lt in command obeyed. This made me mad so I led them through on foot."[9]

On 26 September 1918, in the Meuse-Argonne offensive, Patton was severely wounded; the war ended before he recovered. He went home a colonel with a Distinguished Service Cross (DSC) for valor and a Distinguished Service Medal (DSM) for his work at the Tank School. He reverted to captain, however, and in 1921 left the Tank Corps (which was rotting for lack of support) for the Cavalry.

Between world wars, Patton was seldom happy. His division commander in Hawaii wrote on his efficiency report: "This officer would be invaluable in time of war but is a disturbing element in time of peace."[10] He threw himself into work, polo, sailing—and had the one extramarital affair of his life. When World War II loomed, he was too old to command tanks (53; the limit was 50), but friends got him assigned to train the first troops for the new tank arm (Armor).

In November 1942, Patton commanded the American landings in Morocco, where the Vichy French resisted, if briefly. It took him three days, to take Casablanca, because the landings were chaotic. Patton was on the beach and in the water, pushing and shoving at landing craft and kicking soldiers who lingered.[11] When all was quiet, Georgie entertained Churchill and Roosevelt during their conference at Casablanca, and shot boar with the sultan of Morocco.

Meanwhile, the U.S. II Corps was put to flight by Rommel at Kasserine Pass (14–22 February 1943). General Dwight "Ike" Eisenhower, Allied commander, called Patton to take over the corps. He arrived with flags flying and sirens screaming (which became standard with him) and could not resist a bit of stage play: "Let me meet Rommel in a tank and I'll shoot it out with the son-of-a-bitch."[12] But the "Desert Fox" had been replaced. Patton, by harassing his officers day and night and by personal example, turned disheartened troops into fighting men. His corps did well, and he was made commander of Seventh Army for the invasion of Sicily alongside the British Eighth Army under General (later Field Marshal) Bernard Montgomery. Patton "invented" a race for Messina, took risks, and won.

A hero one day; a villain the next. Visiting the wounded, Patton, in two hospitals, found tearful soldiers who had been admitted for "exhaustion." He called them cowards, cursed them, and slapped them with his gloves. Doctors sent reports to Eisenhower, who decided to privately discipline Patton. "[If I can't], they'll be howling for Patton's scalp, and that will be the end of Georgie's service in this war. I simply cannot let that happen. Patton is indispensable to the war effort—one of the guarantors of our victory."[13]

The press got the story, however, and the "howling" began. Eisenhower got permission to dismiss Patton from the Army chief of staff, George Marshall, in Washington, but did not. Instead, Ike ordered Patton to England, and in January 1945, gave him command of Third Army (part of 12th Army Group, under colorless Omar Bradley, earlier Patton's chief of staff.) The press still pursued Patton, but he escaped any serious trouble.

Third Army arrived in Normandy on 8 July 1944 and fell in on the right flank of Allied forces. "All of a sudden," says Alistaire Horne, "the mighty German army in France seemed to have disappeared into *Nacht und Nebel*. With extraordinary speed, Patton's Third Army was sweeping south and east of Paris, heading for the grim First World War battlefields of Verdun and the . . . Rhine."[14] By September, most Allied commanders thought the Germans were beaten. Patton was eager to cross the Rhine; Ike could hold him back only by cutting his gas supply. Even then, Patton moved forward on captured German gas.

At Christmastime, the German Army suddenly launched a drive through the Ardennes. U.S. Airborne divisions reinforced the sector. The Germans bypassed Bastogne, but kept driving for the Meuse. Patton, on 22 December, turned three divisions of his army northward—drove 40 miles through snow, mud, and ice—and broke into Bastogne on 26 December.[15] Hitler's final gamble had been lost.

Returning to his push for the Rhine, Patton crossed on 23 March 1945; Montgomery the next day. Both wanted to drive on Berlin, but Eisenhower ordered them to leave it to the Russians. They protested, but Ike stood firm— on orders from Washington. Patton drove across Germany to Czechoslovakia, but it too had been allotted to the USSR, and he was ordered back into Austria.

Patton's undisguised contempt for the Russian generals, his merry neglect of anti-fraternization orders (which banned U.S. soldiers from dating German girls), and more serious opposition to denazification policies lost him command of Third Army, then the governorship of Bavaria. (Certain that war between the

United States and the USSR was inevitable, he wanted the German Army on his side.) Patton spoke to friends of the "horrors of peace," and schemed to go to the Far East to fight the Japanese,[16] but was given command of the "paper" Fifteenth Army. Near Mannheim, on 9 December 1945, going for a day of hunting, he was mortally injured in an automobile accident, and died twelve days later with his wife by his bedside.

Patton would surely have preferred death in combat.

The material quoted below is from the *Patton Papers*, edited by Martin Blumenson.[17] Clarifications are mostly Blumenson's, but I have occasionally modified them to provide information that was unnecessary in the original. The punctuation is General Patton's and Blumenson's; misspellings are Patton's. Putting [*sic*] after the latter seemed heretical; thus all "[sic]'s" are Blumenson's, most of which mark the unusual use of words or expressions.

No Formulae for Warmaking

[*Schofield Barracks, Hawaii, 26 March 1926:* lecture, "The Secret of Victory."]

Despite the years of thought and oceans of ink which have been devoted to the elucidation of war its secrets still remain shrouded in mystery.

Indeed it is due largely to the very volume of available information that the veil is so thick.

War is an art and as such is not susceptible of explanation by fixed formulae. Yet from the earliest time there has been an unending effort to subject its complex and emotional structure to dissection, to enunciate rules for its waging, to make tangible its intangibility.

The Importance of Great Captains

To understand [that impalpable something that can produce victory] we . . . shall perchance find it in the reflexes [sic] produced by the acts of the Great Captains. . . .

Not in the musty tomes of voluminous reports or . . . recollections wherein they strove to immortalize and conceal their achievements. Nor yet in the countless histories where lesser wormish men have sought to snare their parted ghosts.

The great warriors were too busy and often too inept to write contemporaneously of their exploits save in the form of propaganda reports . . . biographies were retrospects colored by their vain striving for enhanced fame, or by political conditions then confronting them. War [is] . . . violent simplicity in execution [and] . . . pale and uninspired on paper. . . .

Disregarding wholly the personality of Frederick [the Great] we attribute his victories to a tactical expedient, the oblique order of battle . . . [A]ccounts of valor mellow with age.

Yet . . . the history of war is the history of warriors; few in number, mighty in influence. Alexander, not Macedonia conquered the world. Scipio, not Rome destroyed Carthage. Marlborough not the allies defeated France. Cromwell, not the roundheads dethroned Charles.

Lessons of the Last War

The tendency . . . [is] to consider the most recent past war as the last word, the sealed pattern of all future contests to insure peace . . . all unconscious of personal bias we of necessity base our conceptions of the future on our experience of the past. . . . personal knowledge is a fine thing but unfortunately it is too intimate. . . . So with war experiences . . . [we forget that] it was the roads and consequent abundant mechanical transportation PECULIAR to western Europe which permitted the accumulation of enough gas shells to do the strangling. . . .

Due either to superabundant egotism and uncontrolled enthusiasm or else to limited powers of observation . . . [the specialists] advocate in the most fluent [manner] . . . the vast FUTURE potentialities of their own weapon. In the next war, so they say, all the enemy will be crushed, gassed, bombed or otherwise speedily exterminated, depending for the method of his death upon whether the person declaiming belongs to the tank, gas, air or other special service.

. . . [M]any [specialists] possess considerable histrionic ability and much verbosity [and] they attract public attention. The appeal of their statements is further strengthened because . . . they deal invariably in mechanical devices which intrigue the simple imagination . . . [and their schemes have] a strong news interest which insures their notice by the press. . . .

[Newspapers have a] tendency to exploit the bizarre. . . .

To . . . [pacifists] the history of the race from the fierce struggles in primordial slime to the present day is a blank . . . the lion loses his appetite and the lamb his fear, avarice and ambition, honor and patriotism are no more, all merge in a supine state of impossible toleration. The millions who have nobly perished for an ideal are fools, and a sexless creature too debased to care and too indolent to strive is held up for emulation.

Unchanging Means of Winning

There is an incessant change of means [in warfare] . . . [but] the unchanging ends have been, are and probably ever shall he, the securing of predominating force, of the right sort, at the right place, at the right time.

German Dependence on Staff in World War I

[N]o soldiers ever sought more diligently [than the Germans] for prewar perfection. They builded and tested and adjusted their mighty machine and became so engrossed in its visible perfection, in the accuracy of its bearing and the compression of its cylinders that they neglected the battery till when the moment came their masterpiece proved inefficient through lack of the divine afflatus, the soul of a leader.

Leadership and Knowledge

We require and must demand all possible thoughtful preparation and studious effort possible. . . . Our purpose is not to discourage such preparation but simply to call attention to certain defects in its pursuit. . . .

All down the immortal line of mighty warriors . . . [they] were deeply imbued with the whole knowledge of war as practised at their several epochs. But also, and mark this, so were many of their defeated opponents, for . . . the secret of victory lies not wholly in knowledge. It lurks invisible in that vitalising spark, intangible, yet as evident as the lightning—the warrior soul. . . .

Dry knowledge like dry rot destroys the soundest fiber. A constant search for soulless fundamentals, the effort to regularise the irregular, to make complex the simple, to assume perfect men, perfect material and perfect terrain as the prerequisites to war has the same effect on the soldier student.

Plans and Execution

War is conflict, fighting an elemental exposition of the age old effort to survive. It is the cold glitter of the attacker's eye not the point of the questing bayonet that breaks the line. It is the fierce determination of the driver to close with the enemy, not the mechanical perfection of a Mark VIII tank that conquers the trench. It is the cataclysmic ecstasy of conflict in the flier not the perfection of his machine gun which drops the enemy in flaming ruin. . . .

Hooker's plan at Chancellorsville was masterly, its execution cost him the battle. The converse was true [for Napoleon] at Marengo.

Command and Staff

Staff systems and mechanical communications are valuable but above and beyond them must be the commander; not as a disembodied brain linked to his men by lines of wire and waves of ether; but as a living presence, an all pervading visible personality. . . .

Napoleon Bonaparte and Stonewall Jackson stand preeminent in their use of
. . . time. . . .

In war tomorrow we shall be dealing with men subject to the same emotions
as were the soldiers of Alexander; with men but little changed . . . from the
starving shoeless Frenchmen of 1796. With men similar save in their arms to
those who the inspiring powers of a Greek or a Corsican changed at a breath to
bands of heroes. . . .

There are certainly born leaders but the soldier may also overcome his natal
defects by unremitting effort and practice.

Taking Care of the Troops

Loyalty is frequently only considered as faithfulness from the bottom up. It has
another and equally important application that is from the top down. One of
the most frequently noted characteristics of the great who remained great is . . .
loyalty to their subordinates. It is this characteristic which binds with hoops of
iron their juniors to them. A man who is truly and unselfishly loyal to his
superiors is of necessity so to his juniors and they to him.

The Commander as Actor

A man of diffident manner will never inspire confidence. A cold reserve cannot
beget enthusiasm . . . there must be an outward and visible sign of the inward
and spiritual grace.

It then appears that the leader must be an actor and he certainly must
be. . . .

The fixed determination to acquire the warrior soul and . . . to conquer or
perish with honor is the secret of victory.[18]

"School Solutions," Unity of Command, and Leadership

[Letter to Dwight D. Eisenhower, 9 July 1926.]

Dear Ike: Your letter [following Eisenhower's graduation from the Command
and General Staff College] delighted me more that [than] I can say. As soon as
[I] saw the list I wrote you congratulating you on being honor[ed] but I had no
idea that . . . you were no [number] ONE.

I am convinced that as good as leavenworth [C&GSC at Leavenworth, KS] is it
is still only a means not an end and that we must keep on. I have worked all
the problems of the two years since I graduated and shall continue to do so.
However I dont try for approved solutions any more but rather to do what I
will do in war. This applies both to formations and to verbage of the order.

Orders in battle must be written wholly by the general him self not by a committee of his staff. Hence they must be short. Further in battle par 3 [operations] not par 2 [intelligence] is the important point.

As for par 4 [supply] let them live off the country and in par 5 state that the CP is the head of the maine blow. [He was speaking of the paragraphs of the standard field order.]

You know that we talk a hell of a lot about tactics and such and we never get to brass tacks. Namely what it is that makes the Poor S.O.B. who constitutes the casualtie lists fight and in what formation is he going to fight. The answer to the first is Leadership that to the second—I don't know. But this I do know that the present Infantry T.R. [Training Regulations] based on super trained heroes is bull. The solitary son of a bitch alone with God is going to skulk as he always has and our advancing waves will not advance unless we have such superior artillery that all they have to do is to walk. . . .

First Read Battle Studies by Du Pique (you can get it at Leavenworth) then put your mind to a solution. The victor in the next war will depend on EXECUTION not PLANS and the execution will depend on some means of making the infantry move under fire. I have a solution for the Artillery and cavalry but only a tentative one for the infantry. After you tell me what you can make of it I will send you mine.

You did not say in your letter where you were going? I think probably an instructor ship is the best. The G.S. [General Staff] is punk. You and I will never have a G.S. [assignment] . . . as now invisioned.

With renewed congratulations and best wishes, I am

Most Sincerely, G S Patton Jr.

P.S. I gave you the last copy of my notes. Since they have been so useful I should like to get hold of a copy. Do you think you can locate one for me. If so I would like it. GSP[19]

Psychology of Attack

[Letter to Major Jack W. Heard (Cavalry Board, Fort Riley), 12 August 1926.]

[. . . I have however decided that it is the enemies soul rather than his body which is defeated. For the same reason the formation which a charge is executed is immaterial; determination and speed are the only requisite. *The leader must be in front.* It is interesting to remember that the mounted bowmen never closed nor did the pistol fighters of Maurice of Nassau—Reason—the weapons they used could be discharged at a distance. In both cases they were put out of business by the charge with the steel NOT because the steel was more *deadly* but because the determination to use it, being of a higher order, broke the spirit of the enemy. Pistol fire, if effective, would kill more enemy than the saber. Rifle fire from the hip would kill more enemy than the bayonet but man, being what he is, will never close to effective range unless he knows that his weapon is useless at any other. It is the apparent menace of death rather than actual death which wins battles. The vicious saber charge wins long before the lines touch; and having won, anything is sufficient to stick the enemy in the back. Sincerely yours,[20]

Realistic Training

[Report of Major Patton—as division G-3 (Operations) on a Brigade maneuver in Hawaii which offended the brigadier general in command and other senior officers as well.]

The normal purpose of an attack is the infliction of death wounds and destruction on the enemy troops with a view to establish both physical and moral ascendency over them. The gaining of ground in such a combat is simply an incident; not an object.

The following remarks are not confined to advance guards nor are they wholly orthodox. They are submitted for what they may be worth . . . [The attempt by soldiers to use cover was not warranted in most cases, for the] primary efforts are directed to fancied self preservation rather than towards killing his enemy . . . In battle a man going forward enters a lottery, with death the stake, and the odds the laws of probability. The only saving clause in his venture are the time and the effect on the enemy's nerves of his rapid approach; why waste these benefits in futile sacrifices to lost Gods of Indian wars.

In battle the dead do not run but the living do and for them to so perform it is necessary that they be scared. These considerations seem to indicate that the present method of using machine guns is not . . . the best arrangement. Serious thought should be given to supplying each platoon with . . . man transported machine guns.

[Howitzer platoons] seem to absorb more men from our depleted regiments than their killing value justifies.

There is much talk to the effect that the fire of guns, machine guns, stokes mortars, etc make certain places impassable. History proves that fighting men can go anywhere. The technique of deploying, fire, cover, etc [in our training exercises] seems to overshadow the paramount idea of KILLING. Advances are too unenthusiastic. This . . . is enhanced by the fact that most exercises stop at the deployment. Actually it is . . . [after] deployment where the fighting . . . starts. It is thought that all exercises should be conducted with this idea in view.[21]

Evils of Large Staffs

[Letter to Brig. Gen. Harold B. Fiske, 30 September 1927.]

My dear general Fiske: While I fully realise that generals do not require the approval of majors I am presuming on the fact of my acquaintance with you in

France to tell you how very timely your article in the last issue of the Infantry Journal appears. Both my experience in the World War as a training officer and my present occupation as a General Staff Officer . . . have forcibly impressed me with the slowing and emasculating effect on operations and personal leadership [of] large staffs. As you point out, one of the chief defects in staff work arises from the fact most recent graduates from the different schools seem over impressed with formularism. Their chief concern is to write an order in the nature of an approved solution without regard to the men who must execute it and without considering that successful combat depends on energetic and timely execution rather than on wordy paragraphs.[22]

Why Men Fight

[*Lecture, "Why Men Fight," 27 October 1927.*]

BLUMENSON:

[*Patton believed that*] Superiority in all endeavors, particularly in war, was hereditary. A man's class would show in gentlemanly behavior and sacrifice and leadership. The lower classes had to be schooled to instant and unquestioning obedience to authority. Men fought for food and sex, out of patriotism, habit, or simply obedience, and decorations for valor were important.

PATTON:

[A] coward dressed as a brave man will change from his cowardice and, in nine cases out of ten, will on the next occasion demonstrate the qualities fortuitously emblazoned on his chest . . . We must have more decorations and we must give them, [generously]. . . . War may be hell; but for John Doughboy there is a heaven . . . in anticipating what Annie Rooney will say when she sees him in his pink feather and his new medal.

[The truly great military men] were biological incidents whose existence is due to the fortuitous blending of complementary blood lines at epochs where chance or destiny intervenes to give scope to their peculiar abilities.

It may well be that the greatest soldiers have possessed superior intellects, may have been thinkers; but this was not their dominant characteristic . . . [they] owed their success to indomitable wills and tremendous energy in execution and achieved their initial hold upon the hearts of their troops by acts of demonstrated valor . . . the great leaders are not our responsibility, but God's.[23]

Eagerness to Fight

[*Diary, 28 October 1942, aboard ship for Morocco.*]

I have been giving everyone a simplified directive of war. Use steamroller strategy, that is make up your mind on a course and direction of action and stick to it. But in tactics do not steamroller. Attack weakness. Hold them by the nose and kick them in the arse.

[*Diary, 30 October 1942.*]

I finished the Koran—a good book and interesting.
    It begins to look like we will get ashore without a fight. I am sorry. The troops need blooding; also, it would be better for [my] future prospects.

[*Diary, 3 November 1942.*]

Perhaps when Napoleon said, *Je m'engage et puis je vois* [I start the fight and then I see], he was right. It is the only thing I can do in this case as I see it. I have no personal fear of death or failure.

[*Diary, 6 November 1942.*]

Things are looking up. It is calmer and the wind has fallen to about 20 miles and is northeast, which is O.K. The forecast is for a possible landing condition. The intercepts [of enemy messages] indicate that the French will fight.[24]

[*The landings began on 8 November 1942—Patton's in Morocco and two others in Algeria. The French resisted strongly in Morocco, but surrendered on 11 November (and changed sides) as a result of military force and high-level negotiations.*]

Pride and Discipline

[*Letter to all subordinate commanders, 15 November 1942.*]

The following memorandum will be read to all troops:
    I fully appreciate the danger and hardships you have been through and the lack of conveniences and clothing which you face. On the other hand, you, each one of you, is a representative of a great and victorious army. To be respected, you must inspire respect. Stand up, keep your clothes buttoned, and your chin straps fastened. Salute your officers and the French officers, now our allies. Keep your weapons clean and with you. Your deeds have proven that you are fine soldiers. Look the part.

Religious Faith

[*Letter to all commanding officers, 15 November 1942.*]

It is my firm conviction that the great success attending the hazardous operations carried out on sea and on land by the Western Task Force could only have been possible through the intervention of Divine Providence manifested in many ways. Therefore, I should be pleased if, in so far as circumstances and conditions permit, our grateful thanks be expressed today in appropriate religious services.[25]

Again, Pride and Discipline

[*Letter to Gen. Thomas T. Handy (Office of the Army Chief-of-Staff, Gen. George C. Marshall), 31 January 1943.*]

I am firmly of the opinion that the discipline, military bearing, and neatness of the troops trained in America is not up to the standard necessary. . . . The soldiers are sloppily dressed, they do not salute, they do not take care of themselves, and their officers do not insist that they correct these defects. It takes us about a month . . . to get them up to anywhere the standard of the 2d Armored Division. . . . In the training of the troops to make a landing, viciousness and speed must be stressed. They must hit the beach running and continue to run . . . Languorously meandering over the sand hills will not get anyone anything but a grave.[26]

Discipline and Command Deficiencies

[*Patton (as noted above) was called from Morocco (5 March 1943) to take over II Corps after Rommel scattered it at Kasserine Pass.*]

[*Diary, 8 March 1943.*]

The discipline, dress, and condition of weapons at 34th [Division] very bad— terrible. On the other hand, elements of the division have fought well. Inspected their positions and found it weak, particularly in the emplacement of the 37[mm] anti-tank guns, which are on the crest instead of on the reverse slope where they belong. . . . All division commanders, field artillery brigade commanders, and heads of corps staff sections came to supper. . . . After dinner [II Corps] G3 and G2 gave plan and enemy situation. [Terry] Allen and [Orlando] Ward [division commanders] gave their tentative plans. I finally approved plans, as altered, and fixed H hour.

My concern is for fear that the enemy will attack us first. This command post was situated . . . too far in the rear. I will change it as soon as the. . . operations start.[27]

BLUMENSON:

Patton was to be ready by March 15, to reoccupy and reopen the Thelepte airfields, then move through Fériana and capture Gafsa. Once Gafsa was secure, he was to send other troops to Maknassy and seize a pass through the Eastern Dorsale. Meanwhile, because everyone was wary of what Rommel might do, Patton had to hold two divisions in the rear. . . . Actually, the II Corps attack was distinctly subsidiary and minor in purpose and scope. Patton was merely to mount a threat against the Axis in order to help Montgomery [*who had beat*

Rommel at El Alamein (in Egypt) and pursued him to Mareth, in south Tunisia. The British Allied Field Commander, Gen. Harold] Alexander had been so disappointed by the performance of the American troops during the Kasserine battle that he had little confidence in their ability to fight. Patton preferred not to notice.

Dying for One's Country vs. Killing the Enemy

Soldiers: All of us have been in battle. But due to circumstances beyond the control of anyone, we have heretofore fought separately. In our next battle we shall . . . have many thousands of Americans united in one command. . . . In union there is strength!

Our duty . . . is plain. We must utterly defeat the enemy. Fortunately for our fame as soldiers, our enemy is worthy of us. The German is a war-trained veteran—confident, brave, and ruthless. We are brave. We are better-equipped, better fed, and . . . we have with us the God of Our Fathers known of Old. The justice of our cause . . . makes us confident. But we are not ruthless, not vicious, not aggressive, therein lies our weakness.

Children of a free and sheltered people who have lived a generous life, we have not the pugnacious disposition of those oppressed beasts our enemies who must fight or starve. Our bravery is too negative. We talk too much of sacrifice, of the glory of dying that freedom may live. Of course we are willing to die but that is not enough. We must be eager to kill, to inflict on the enemy—the hated enemy—wounds, death, and destruction. If we die killing, well and good, but if we fight hard enough, viciously enough, we will kill and live. Live to return to our family and our girl as conquering heroes—men of Mars.

The reputation of our army, the future of our race, your own glory rests in your hands. I know you will be worthy.[28]

Discipline, Pride, and Leadership

BLUMENSON:

On June 5 [1943], Patton issued a letter of instructions to his subordinate commanders. In it he set forth the principles he wished them to follow in the approaching Sicilian campaign.

PATTON:

In view of your long experience and demonstrated ability, I have certain diffidence in writing this letter; nonetheless . . . I would be remiss in my duty if I failed to express my views and outline as briefly as may be, certain points in the conduct of operations which I expect you to observe.

There is only one sort of discipline—perfect discipline. . . .

Discipline is based on pride in the profession of arms, on meticulous attention to details, and on mutual respect and confidence. Discipline must be a habit so ingrained that it is stronger than the excitement of battle or the fear of death.

Discipline can only be obtained when all officers are so imbued with the sense of their lawful obligation to their men and to their country that they cannot tolerate negligence. Officers who fail to correct errors or to praise excellence are valueless in peace and dangerous misfits in war.

Officers must assert themselves by example and by voice.

The history of our invariably victorious armies demonstrates that we are the best soldiers in the world. Currently, many of you defeated and destroyed the finest troops Germany possesses. This should make your men proud. This should make you proud. This should imbue your units with unconquerable self-confidence and pride in demonstrated ability.

Tactics and Improvision

There is no approved solution to any tactical situation.

There is only one tactical principle which is not subject to change. It is: "To so use the means at hand to inflict the maximum amount of wounds, death, and destruction on the enemy in the minimum of time."

Never attack [enemy] strength [but rather his weakness].

You can never be too strong. Get every man and gun you can secure provided it does not delay your attack. . . .

Casualties vary directly with the time you are exposed to effective fire. . . . Rapidity of attack shortens the time of exposure. . . .

If you cannot see the enemy, and you seldom can, shoot at the place he is most likely to be. . . .

Our mortars and our artillery are superb weapons when they are firing. When silent, they are junk—see that they fire!

Battles are won by frightening the enemy. Fear is induced by inflicting death and wounds on him. Death and wounds are produced by fire. Fire from the rear is more deadly and three times more effective than fire from the front.

Few men are killed by bayonets, but many are scared by them. Having the bayonet fixed makes our men want to close. Only the threat to close will defeat a determined enemy.

In mountain warfare, capture the heights and work downhill. Never permit a unit to dig in until the final objective is reached, then dig, wire, and mine. . . .

Never take counsel of your fears. The enemy is more worried than you are. Numerical superiority, while useful, is not vital to successful offensive action. The fact that you are attacking induces the enemy to believe that you are stronger than he is.

A good solution applied with vigor *now* is better than a perfect solution ten minutes later. . . .

Mine fields, while dangerous, are not impassable. They are far less of hazard than artillery concentrations. . . .

Speed and ruthless violence on the beaches is vital. There must be no hesitation in debarking. To linger on the beach is fatal.

In landing operations, retreat is impossible.

Weapons will be kept in perfect working order at all times.

Vehicles will be properly maintained in combat as elsewhere.

We can conquer only by attacking. . . .

Continued ruthless pressure by day and by night is vital.

We must be . . . emphatic in the ruthless destruction of the enemy.[29]

Battle as Sport

[*Talk to 45th Division, 27 June 1943 (before the Allied invasion of Sicily).*]

Clearly all of you must know that combat is imminent. . . . You are competing with veterans, but don't let that worry you. All of them, too, fought their first battle, and all of them won their first battle just as you will win yours. Battle is far less frightening than those who have never been in it are apt to think. . . .

Battle is the most magnificent competition in which a human being can indulge. It brings out all that is best; it removes all that is base.

All men are afraid in battle. The coward is the one who lets his fear overcome his sense of duty. . . .

Remember that the enemy is just as frightened as you are, probably more so. . . . The attacker wins. You cannot win by parrying. Yet the enemy, being uncertain of our intentions, must parry. . . .

Booby traps are what the name implies—boobies get trapped

You have a sacred trust in your men and to your country, and you are lower than the lowest thing that lives if you are false to this trust. An officer . . . must always be willing and anxious to take the chances his men must take. He must lead . . . and he must assert himself. . . .

Pride is the greatest thing a man can have. . . .

We Americans are a competitive race. . . . We love to win. In this next fight, you are entering the greatest sporting competition of all times . . . for the greatest prize of all—victory.[30]

Patton's "Fighting Principles," Part I

[*As edited by Blumenson. Patton's words are in quotation marks. In "Letters of Instruction" issued in England in March and April 1944, prior to D-Day.*]

BLUMENSON:

His first letter of instruction, dated March 6, had the purpose of orienting the "officers of the higher echelons in the principles of command, combat procedure, and administration which obtain in [Third Army] and which were to "guide you in the conduct of your several commands." Among them were:

> Everyone was to "lead in person." A commander who failed to obtain his objectives and who was "not dead or severely wounded has not done his full duty."

> Commanders and staff members were to "visit the front daily . . . to observe, not to meddle. . . . Praise is more valuable than blame . . . your primary mission as a leader is to see with your own eyes and be seen by your troops while engaged in personal reconnaissance."

> Issuing an order was worth only about 10 percent. "The remaining 90 percent consists in assuring . . . proper and vigorous execution" of the order.

> Persons who did not rest did not last. When the need arose, "everyone must work all the time, but these emergencies are not frequent."

> The farther forward the command posts were located, the less time was wasted in driving to and from the front.

> Everyone was "too prone to believe that we acquire merit solely through the study of maps in the safe seclusion of a command post. This is an error."

> Maps were necessary "in order to see the whole panorama of battle and: to permit intelligent planning. . . . A study of the map will indicate where critical situations exist or are apt to develop, and so indicate where the commander should be."

> Plans had to be "simple and flexible. . . . They should be made by the people who are going to execute them."

> There could never be too much reconnaissance.

> Information was "like eggs: the fresher the better."

> Orders were to be short to tell "what to do not how." An order was "really a memorandum and an assumption of responsibility by the issuing commander."

> "In battle it was always easier for the senior to go up [to the front than for the junior to come back."

> Warning orders were vital and had to be issued in time, "not only to combat units but also to the Surgeon, the Signal Officer, the Quartermaster, the Ordnance Officer, and the Engineer Officer who . . . too have plans to make and units to move. If they do not function, you do not fight."

> Every means had to be used "before and after combats to tell the troops what they were going to do and what they have done."

> The responsibility for supply rested equally "on the giver and the taker."

> *Commanders were to "visit the wounded personally" and frequently.* Decorations were to be awarded promptly.

> *"If you do not enforce and maintain discipline, you are potential murderers."*

Walking wounded and stragglers sought "to justify themselves by painting alarming pictures."

Fatigue made "cowards of us all. Men in condition do not tire."

And finally, "Courage. DO NOT TAKE COUNSEL OF YOUR FEARS."[31]

Make the Enemy Die for *His* Country

[*Letter to Beatrice, 24 March 1944.*]

I have just finished "inspiring" them. . . . Things are shaping up pretty well now but I wish we had more . . . killer instinct in our men. They are too damned complacent— willing to die but not anxious to kill.

I tell them that it is fine to be willing to die for their country but a damned sight better to make the German die for his. No one has ever told them that.[32]

Patton's "Fighting Principles," Part II

BLUMENSON:

[Patton's] second letter of instructions appeared on April 3. Addressed to corps, division, and separate unit commanders, it stressed [*among other things*]:

> "Those tactical and administrative usages which combat experience has taught myself . . . to consider vital. You will not simply mimeograph this and call it a day. You are responsible that these usages become habitual in your command."

Among the items were the following:

> *Formal guard mounts and retreat formations*, as well as regular and supervised reveille formations, were "a great help and, in some cases, essential to prepare men and officers for battle, to give them that perfect discipline, that smartness of appearance, that alertness without which battles cannot be won."
>
> *Officers were always on duty*, and their duty extended to every individual, junior to themselves, in the U.S. Army—"not only to members of their own organization."

> "*Never yield ground*. It is cheaper to hold what you have than to retake what you have lost.
>
> . . . There was "no such thing as 'Tank country' in a restrictive sense. Some types of country are better than others, but tanks have and can operate anywhere."[33]

The successful soldier won his battles cheaply so far as his own casualties were concerned, "but he must remember that violent attacks, although costly at the time, save lives in the end."

Improvision

BLUMENSON:

On April 15 [1944] Patton issued his third letter of instruction, this one pertaining to the separate tank battalion attached to each infantry division. Once again he enumerated the thoughts that governed his ideas of tactics. Some of them were:

> Because of "a slavish adherence to the precept that 'Tanks should be used in mass,' we are not gaining the full advantage from the separate tank battalions."
>
> "Any weapon which is not actively engaged in killing Germans is not doing its duty."
>
> "Battles . . . practically never develop according to pre-conceived notions. Therefore our killing weapons must be as close as possible to the fighting zone."
>
> Whether tanks or infantry should lead an attack was always a problem. In general, the infantry went first "against emplaced and known antitank guns, large antitank minefields, and terrestrial obstacles such as bridges and defiles."
>
> Tanks usually preceded infantry "against scattered minefields or minefields of the new, so-called Boot type mines, against normal artillery and infantry positions, and . . . any type of counter-attack."
>
> Tanks were to "keep out of villages, where they are at a tremendous disadvantage and cannot utilize their power. Block houses and strong points without anti-tank guns are duck soup for tanks."
>
> Finally, the skillful commander used "the means at hand, all weapons, for the accomplishment of the end sought, the destruction of [the enemy]."[34]

Use of Weapons and Cooperation of Arms

BLUMENSON:

Patton issued his fourth letter of instructions on April 17, this on the employment of tank-destroyer units. Some of his strictures were:

> The main purpose of tank destroyers was "to knock out tanks. Secondary usages include direct or indirect fire to reinforce artillery fires; destruction of anti-tank weapons, pill boxes, permanent defensive works; and the support of infantry. . . ."
>
> Tank-destroyer units were "not self-supporting, consequently they will

be employed in close cooperation with other arms"—infantry, armor, and artillery.

The use of tank destroyers in defense "must not be stereotyped."[35]

Definition of Leadership

[Letter to son George at West Point, 16 January 1945.]

Leadership . . . is the thing that wins battles. I have it—but I'll be damned if I can define it. Probably it consists in knowing what you want to do and then doing it and getting mad if any one steps in the way. Self confidence and leadership are twin brothers. . . .

One of these damned jet planes that goes 470 miles an hour just dropped a bomb. It shook this house . . . and scared Willie. They also shoot rockets at us, but one gets used to such things. It is like a thunder storm. You are not apt to be in the way. And if you are, what the Hell, no more buttoning and unbuttoning.[36]

Fighting: Who Will Write Instructions?

[Diary, 8 August 1945.]

At the close of the Sicilian Campaign I talked to a group of officers from each division . . . to obtain from the men who did it, the means they used to fight, because having studied war since I was about sixteen years old, I have only come across some twelve books which deal with fighting, although there are many hundreds which deal with war.

This is because the people who fight either are killed or are inarticulate.

With this end in view, I talked to a selected group . . . and intend to repeat it. . . .

Of course, the horrid thought obtrudes itself that, in spite of my efforts—which will probably be filed and forgotten—the tactics of the next war will be written by someone who never fought and who acquired his knowledge by a meticulous study of the regulations of this and the last World War, none of which were ever put into practice in battle. However, I console myself with the thought that I have, in so far as the ability within me lay, done my damndest.[37]

Farewell Speeches to Divisions Going Home from Germany, 1945

BLUMENSON:

It often appeared to be an empty exercise, for even here the old magic was gone. According to [Col.] George Fisher, who accompanied Patton on one of these trips, the division was lined up and waiting at the airfield when Patton's plane landed.

With the precision of a familiar maneuver the General hit the ground, strode a few paces, and mounted a platform that had been set up. . . . Patton, resplendent as always, proceeded to give the troops the works.

He never talked very long and he certainly followed no conventions of finished oratory. He would start off rather slowly, and his squeaky, high-pitched voice did not carry very well. . . .

I had the personal feeling that the General regularly got himself punch-drunk with profanity. His sulphurous son-of-a-bitching, I thought, was a habit he had permitted himself to form in days when there might have been some reason for him to strike a pose.

The reaction of the troops was somewhat mixed. There were many, of course, to whom roughness of [language] was normal and habitual, and it was Patton's habit to act as if this were true of every man in uniform.

Stripped of bitching and damning, Patton's farewell to the troops came down to something like this: You have served with the greatest group of soldiers ever assembled anywhere at any time. . . . Never forget that you are heroes. And if any civilian—here one must fall back into Pattonese—and if any goddamned civilian ever tries to make fun of your uniform, you are to knock the son of a bitch down. . . .

Patton was eternally ready to fight; and if there was no enemy in front of him, there were still some lily-livered civilians back home to be attended to. But . . . these men who were on their way back home had their own notions about how the civilian situation in the States should be handled. They were willing enough to have their Army commander remind them of the glories of their service under him, but as for the future—well, they had come to a parting of the ways with Patton and all that he stood for. . . .

Patton was forever preaching a gospel of warfare that was somehow alien and antipathetic to young Americans who had reluctantly and only temporarily suffered themselves to become soldiers. If in North Africa and Sicily they had listened gravely to his words, it was because they had to. . . . [Later] they began to see that *Patton was a consistent winner.* That was the true basis of Patton's esteem among the rank and file of Third Army. As the war progressed, he was . . . an eagerly followed commander—not because of his theatrics but simply because he had demonstrated beyond question that he knew how to lick Germans better than anybody else.[38]

Patton's Last "Notes on Combat"

[*Five days before his fatal accident.*]

BLUMENSON:

On November 4 [1945], Patton issued what would be his final "Notes on Combat," ten single-spaced typed pages devoted to divisions and their organizations, formations, and tactics. Among his comments:

Violent and rapid attack with the marching fire is the surest means of success in the use of armor.

[One should not think] that there is practically no difference between an infantry division and an armored division. The difference is very real and two fold. First, the purpose of the tanks in an infantry division is to get the infantry forward, while the purpose of the infantry in an armored division is to break the tanks loose.

Second, the mental characteristics of the commander of an infantry division who has to conduct the slow bitter slugging tactics essential to that arm may not, and probably will not, have the attributes essential to the commander of an armored division where rapidity of movement and reckless operation are the criteria of success.

The primary function of war has not within historic time been materially changed by the advent of new weapons. The unchanging principle of combat is to inflict on the enemy the maximum amount of wounds and death in a minimum of time and as cheaply as possible. If future leaders will remember that nothing is impossible, that casualties received from enemy action in battle are a function of time and effective enemy fire, and that any type of troops can fight any place, they will not go wrong.[39]

Conclusions

Patton was a man of execution, not planning. He believed that the secret of victory was the "vitalizing spark" of the "soul of a leader." He pronounced that great leaders won wars. ("Alexander, not Macedonia conquered the world," etc.) Yet, he conceded that a staff could be useful. Patton preached that great commanders were loyal to their troops. His diary shows that despite his emphasis on minute points of discipline he was aware of the trials and discomforts of his men, and saw to their needs. Much of his bombast was purposeful—to show confidence in himself and his troops.

Codman wrote that Patton excelled in making men do what they "would not do" unless he was there.[40] Gerald Astor, describing his role in the Battle of the Bulge, said: "His true genius lay in his ability to put the show on the road, to move men and machines."[41] Men who at first hated him came to respect, if not to love him. Everyone likes to be on a winning team, and Patton was a *winner*. Whatever his faults, Patton's talents as a combat leader rate among the finest in history.

IX

Charles de Gaulle

(1890–1970)

CHARLES ANDRÉ-MORIE-JOSEPH DE GAULLE[1] is best know as the leader of the Free French in World War II and as a politician afterward. However, he was a combat officer in World War I, was wounded and captured, and was in the first fruitless battles against the Germans in World War II. Moreover, the professional army he favored in the 1930s in many ways resembles the special operations forces that in major nations stand ready today (2002) to fight small wars and conduct antiterrorist operations.

DeGaulle was born in Lille, in the Département du Nord, which the French historian Michelet called the "land of battles." His family was of minor nobility, and boasted many intellectuals. His grandmother had been a famous novelist. His father, Henri de Gaulle, was a graduate of the prestigious Ecole Polytechnique, and taught at various *collèges*. DeGaulle attended the Collège Stanislas and St. Cyr (at the time the "French West Point").

A junior officer in World War I, he was wounded and taken prisoner at Verdun (1916), and was released only at war's end in 1918. Between the world wars, DeGaulle graduated from L'Ecole Supérieure de Guerre (Staff College), and served on the staff of Marshal Henri Pétain, in the occupied Rhineland, and in Lebanon.

Influenced by his experience in the Great War, DeGaulle bitingly criticized the defensive attitude of the High Command, which eventually produced the Maginot Line.[2] He summed up his ideas in *Vers l'armée de métier* (1934), which called for a small, highly trained army of armored units and motorized infantry with covering airpower. He expected it to fight the first battles, while, if necessary, conscripts and reserves were mobilized. His scheme was rejected despite the support of politicians such as Paul Reynaud, later premier.

When the Second World War began in 1939, DeGaulle was in command of a tank brigade of the 5th Army in Alsace. In 1940 he was given a division, and during the German *blitzkrieg* fought well, but was called to Paris and appointed Under Secretary for National Defense by Premier Reynaud. DeGaulle was in London when France was defeated and Reynaud resigned to allow Marshal Pétain to form a new government, make peace with Germany, and establish a puppet French state with the capital at Vichy.

DeGaulle stayed in London. Though initially almost ignored by the British government, he managed to organize exiled Frenchmen, and tried—at first with little effect—to encourage the French at home to resist German rule. His arrogance and abrasive personality did not help him with the Allies, but by 1942 he was recognized by Britain and the United States as leader of the "Free French." Though the French in North Africa initially opposed the Allies (notably in Syria and Morocco), they were persuaded by diplomacy and force to change sides, and fielded troops for the Allies in North Africa and in Europe.

However, the Allies initially appointed General Henri Giraud commander of French forces in North Africa (1942); DeGaulle took command in April 1944, only weeks before the Allied invasion of Normandy (6 June 1944). Meanwhile DeGaulle had concentrated on building up a non-Communist French resistance movement in France, which got British and American support because so much of the resistance was French Communist, backed by Moscow.

In 1944, after the Normandy invasion, DeGaulle's stock was given a boost by U.S. forces. Patton, whose Third Army was nearest Paris, got orders from Eisenhower to let the Free French Forces enter the capital first. Before war's end, with the support of the Allies, DeGaulle was able to form a French government, which excluded most Communists, and was recognized by the Allies. In the face of grave economic problems, however, combined with the French Assembly's refusal to consider a constitution with a stronger executive, DeGaulle resigned in 1946.

In 1947 he was back in politics, leading a conservative party, *Rassemblement du Peuple*. In 1958, as premier of France, he was able to set Algeria free in the face of violent opposition led by some of the more popular generals in the French Army—something perhaps only he could have done. Then, in 1959, in Napoleonic fashion, he installed a new constitution by vote of the people—ignoring the legislative chambers—which gave the executive (DeGaulle) greater power. He then "reigned" as president from 1959 to 1969. As early as 1940, he had proclaimed "*Je suis La France*" (I am France). A "bigger than life" figure, he was mourned by friend and foe when he died in 1970.

This chapter differs from the others in that General de Gaulle is not quoted *in extenso*. It consists of a summary of the central ideas in his *Vers l'armée de métier* (1934) with key quotations (in my translation) from that book.[3] It is not a period piece, but has insights applicable to war today.

DeGaulle's Professional Army

In *Vers l'armée de métier* [Toward a Professional Army] DeGaulle argued for a small, elite army. He recognized that he was flying in the face of the army establishment, whose ideas were based on experience in World War I. That war, he wrote, made "numbers the basis of tactics." France needed, he said, an army geared to "autonomous enterprise, surprise, exploitation"—a new well-drilled, professional army [*l'instrument nouveau*].

Such an army would be "sharp and mobile, [using] motorized and tracked vehicles . . . able to appear and disappear very quickly . . . capable of changing . . . its emplacement, direction, disposition." It could attack while the enemy was mobilizing and deploying his forces, and give France an initial advantage. He conceded, in effect, that the next war would require masses of troops, but held that his new army would give France time to muster her troops efficiently.[4]

He expected his army to be ready to strike first at any enemy, cooperating with air forces, and if needed, naval forces. It would take key points and wrack disorder in the enemy ranks.

Leadership Benefits

His fondest hope was that his new army would give commanders true control in the field, first off "to restore the 'moment' [*evénément*] which could be sensed by great captains [as the time for action] and which, during [World War I], was lost due to excess preparation."[5]

"Surprise, the old queen of the [military] art" and speed would be the earmarks of the new army [*instrument*].[6] Instead of centralized command fighting by the map, there would be "direct observation" together with "mobility . . . [and] initiative."[7] Air power would extend the effect of the "shock troops" in "combined operations."[8]

Command

"Changes in the employment of a force modifies the exercise of command," De Gaulle wrote—not in its principles, but in techniques. In olden times, he said, a commander could see the whole battlefield. "The tactic was [based on] the *coup d'oeil* . . . Hannibal won his battles by a glance [at the field] and personal example." Later, when the field and armies were larger, commanders such as Condé, Hoche, and Napoléon inspired troops by appearing at the front at critical times. World War I strategy and tactics were geared to masses of men and "material elements"—heavy artillery, machine guns, tanks, and aircraft. Planning was done by huge staffs.

"During battles, the commander's eye saw nothing but a map. . . . In short, everything conspired to give to command a remote character . . . [and] anonymity, which allowed no place for genius and sentiment." This, he lamented, resulted in the loss of "that imponderable coefficient, the devotion that soldiers gave to their captains."

However, DeGaulle reasoned, if the "perfection of machines" since World War

I had accentuated the "technical character of war," it had also restored "to the exercise of command . . . haste and audacity, which should bring back the factor of personality in war." This was because with swift movement and sudden changes in the situation, commanders at the front would have to make judgments quickly, without councils of war and the resulting delays. He continued:

> Now [we must have] perpetual improvision, rapid orientation of very mobile units, commanders eager to see what is going on, who move about the field and survey their zone. In short [there must be] personal and instantaneous action . . . at all levels of command.
>
> A parallel transformation in the methods of troop leadership will evolve. . . . In an army where autonomous action is the rule, the commander will make [most] decisions. . . . There will be more means . . . to consult before action with superior officers, and to coordinate his ideas with those of his neighbors. Initiative . . . will become sovereign—but not in defiance of orders. Character . . . will resume its place on the shield of battles in all its glory.
>
> In addition, there [will be] a rebirth in the *armée élite* of the reciprocal understanding between the troops and the commanders which was ruined by [mass warfare]. . . .
>
> The reciprocal and equally profound influence of [the new form of] combat will bring generals and soldiers closer together. . . . Personal command [*l'action de présence*], which in the [last war] was not practiced by even the most ardent of our commanders, will be restored. . . . In place of depending on staff guidance . . . [commanders] would be at the head of troops, literally, not figuratively. . . . The risks run would increase, but so would the honor of setting the example. The effects produced on the combatants in times past by appearance in [the fight] of the sash of Condé, of the golden costume of Murat . . . would be replaced by the sight of the command car or airplane of the commander. And if, in future lists of those lost in action feature . . . a long list of generals, perhaps that would be better for that *camaraderie des armes*, . . . the most noble gem of the military crown.[9]

Conclusions

DeGaulle's ideas on command, if in part based on tradition, seem particularly applicable to war in the twenty-first century. It seems likely that most wars will be small and fought by close-knit units, where the officers and men work together as proud professionals. Some of his ideas have been put into practice. As noted in chapter 4, the United States and most major countries have special forces, which are professional first-strike units. However, the days of extended mobilization are not over, as the preparations for the Gulf War of 1991 demonstrated, and as have those for "America's New War" of 2001.

X

Erich von Manstein

(1887–1973)

FIELD MARSHAL Erich von Manstein is included here because he has been rated as the greatest German commander of World War II by his fellow German generals, his opponents, and military historians.[1] He planned the *blitzkrieg* against France in 1940. Then he fought in Russia for most of the war, under conditions more terrible than in any other theater. Manstein did not have the magnetism of Rommel, but he led from the front, never spared himself, and took care of his men, who respected his judgment. Throughout, whatever Hitler ordered, he refused to allow his troops to execute civilians. In 1943 and 1944, he saved the lives of uncounted German troops by blatant disobedience to Hitler's orders to "stand or die" in the face of superior forces. He commanded many more troops than Rommel: in turn a corps, an army, and army groups of as many as 130 divisions.

Manstein was born Erich Lewinski in Berlin (1887), son of General Eduard Lewinski. His father soon died, and his mother, left with *ten* children, allowed Erich to be adopted by their childless friends, General George von Manstein and his wife. Erich assumed his adopted father's name. In 1907 he was commissioned in the 3rd Foot Guards, the old regiment of his uncle, Field Marshal Paul von Hindenburg. In due course, he attended the *Kriegsakademie* and did staff duty during World War I.

Manstein moved up rapidly between the wars. In 1933 he was a major general; in 1935 operations chief of the Great General Staff (*Grosse Generalstab*), and in 1936 deputy chief. In 1939 he was chief of staff to General (soon Field Marshal) Gerd von Rundstedt in the invasion of Poland. In 1940, Manstein planned the *blitzkrieg* through the Ardennes that defeated the French army in three weeks—but he commanded infantry in it because of envy in the OKH (*Oberkommando des Herres*, Army High Command).[2]

For the rest of his career, he commanded on the Russian front—in 1941 a panzer corps, then 11th Army, with which he took Kerch (May 1942)[3] and Sevastopol (July 1942), the major Soviet naval base on the Black Sea. Hitler made him a field marshal, and gave him (November 1942) Army Group Don

(South). He tried to rescue General Friedrich Paulus's army, trapped in Stalingrad—and might have but for Hitler's orders that Paulus was to "stand or
die" rather than break out to meet Manstein's panzers.[4] (In January 1943, his
army bled white, Paulus surrendered to the Soviets.) In early 1943, Manstein
launched a successful counteroffensive at Kharkov, but German impetus was
lost in the largest tank battle of the war at Kursk (5–23 July 1943).

From mid-1943 onward, German forces conducted a fighting retreat from the
USSR. Manstein argued to Hitler that they should give ground in some sectors
in order to concentrate forces and overpower the Soviets in others. But Der
Führer ordered his armies to hold every inch of ground they had taken. Nevertheless, German forces had to withdraw steadily. Hitler blamed Manstein's
"fluid defense," and in March 1944, relieved him of command, but sent him
into retirement wearing Swords to his Knight's Cross.

Four years after the war ended (1949), Manstein was put on trial for war
crimes at the demand of the Soviets. In Britain, a fund was raised for his defense, but he was convicted of minor offenses and imprisoned. After his release
(1953), he advised the new West German government on military matters until
his death in 1973.

―――――――

Most of the text below is from Erich von Manstein's *Lost Victories*, edited and
translated by Anthony G. Powell (1958) from *Verlorene Siege* (1955). (There are
later editions in German and English and even Chinese.) I have not changed
Powell's British spelling and punctuation. Manstein's keen sense of humor will
be evident in the passages below. Not so well demonstrated is his acute appreciation of history,[5] but his views on leadership are of primary interest here.

―――――――

A Point of Law and Ethics

[*June 1941: Manstein heads 56 Panzer Corps, leading the army of Colonel-General
Busch from East Prussia toward Leningrad (St. Petersburg).*]

A few days before the offensive started we received an order from the Supreme
Command of the Armed Forces (O.K.W.) which has since become known as the
'Commissar Order'. The gist of it was that all political commissars of the Red
Army whom we captured were to be shot out of hand as exponents of Bolshevik
ideology.

Now I agree that from the point of view of international law the status of
these political commissars was extremely equivocal. They were certainly not
soldiers, any more than I would have considered a *Gauleiter* [NAZI civilian
official] attached to me as a political overseer to be a soldier. Neither could they
be granted the same non-combatant status as chaplains, medical personnel or

war correspondents. On the contrary, they were—without being soldiers—fanatical fighters, but fighters whose activities could only be regarded as illegal according to the traditional meaning of warfare. Their task was not only the political supervision of Soviet military leaders but, even more, to instil the greatest possible degree of cruelty into the fighting and to give it a character completely at variance with the traditional conceptions of soldierly behaviour. These same commissars were the men primarily responsible for the fighting methods and treatment of prisoners which clashed so blatantly with provisions of the Hague Convention. . . .

Whatever one might feel about the status of commissars under international law, however, it inevitably went against the grain of any soldier to shoot them down when they had been captured in battle. An order like the *Kommissarbefehl* was utterly unsoldierly. To have carried it out would have threatened not only the honour of our fighting troops but also their morale. Consequently I had no [choice] but to inform my superiors that the Commissar Order would not be implemented by anyone under my command. My subordinate commanders were entirely at one with me in this, and everyone in the corps, and acted accordingly. . . . [M]y military superiors endorsed my attitude.[6]

Up-front Leadership

World War II . . . called for [new] methods of command, especially in the case of highly mobile formations. In [mobile warfare], situations changed so rapidly, and favourable opportunities came and went so fast, that no tank-force commander could afford to bind himself to a command post any great distance to the rear. If he waited too far back for reports from his forward units, decisions would be taken much too late and all kinds of chances would be missed. Often, too, [after] a successful action . . . it was necessary to counteract the only too natural phenomenon of battle fatigue and instil new life into the men.

It was even more vital, in view of the unprecedented demands which the new war of movement made on the energies of officers and men, that higher commanders should show themselves as often as possible to the front-line troops. The ordinary soldier must never have the feeling that the 'top brass' are busy concocting orders somewhere to the rear without knowing what it looks like out in front. It gives him a certain satisfaction to see the Commanding General in the thick of it once in a while or watching a successful attack go in. Only by being up with the fighting troops day in and day out can one get to know their needs, listen to their worries, and be of assistance to them.[7]

Troop Morale

A senior commander must not only be the man who perpetually has demands to make in the accomplishment of his mission; he must be an ally and a comrade as well. . . . Apart from anything else, he himself derives fresh energy from . . . visits to the fighting troops. Many's the time, when visiting a divisional headquarters, that I have heard anxieties voiced about the diminishing battle morale of the fighting troops, the excessive strain to which they were often . . . subjected.

Such worries inevitably preoccupied commanders more and more as time went on, for it was they who ultimately bore the responsibility for the regiments and battalions. Yet once I had gone forward [to the] troops in the line, I was often overjoyed to find them more confident and optimistic than I had been led to expect—not infrequently because they had fought a successful action in the meantime. And then, I smoked a cigarette with a tank crew or chatted with a rifle company. . . . I never failed to encounter that irresistible urge to press onward, that readiness to put forth the very last ounce of energy, which are the hallmarks of the German soldier.

Experiences like this are among the finest things a senior commander can ask for. The higher one rises, unfortunately, the rarer the [opportunities to visit troops at the front]. An army or army group commander is quite unable to mix in with the fighting troops to the same extent as the general commanding a corps.[8]

Commander and Staff

Even the corps commander, of course, cannot be permanently on the road. A man who is constantly rushing around his forward area, and can never be found when required, virtually hands over his command to his staff. This may be . . . a good thing in [some] cases, but it is still not the role for which he was intended.

Everything ultimately hinges—particularly with highly mobile formations—on a rational organization of command duties, the continuity of which must be maintained at all costs. It was indispensable that the Corps Q [quartermaster/supply] branch should usually remain stationary for several days at a time in order to keep the flow of supplies moving.

The Commanding General and his operations branch, on the other hand, had to move their tactical headquarters forward once or even twice a day if they were to keep in touch with the mechanized divisions. This called for a high degree of mobility on the part of Headquarters. The only way to achieve it was to cut the [HQ equipment and supplies] to a minimum—always a salutary measure where command is concerned, and to do without any of the usual comforts. Needless to say, the Patron saint of Red Tape, who, [among] her other activities, I fear, likes to tag along behind armies in the field [was ignored] when we were operating under conditions of this kind.[9]

"Roughing It" with the Troops

We did not waste time looking for accommodation [in Russia]. . . . The small wooden huts of the east held little appeal, particularly in view of the ubiquity of . . . 'domestic pets' [rats, lice, etc.]. Consequently our tactical headquarters lived almost the whole time in tents and the two command wagons which, together with a few wartime Volkswagen and the vehicles of the [radio] section and telephone exchange, carried our other ranks when we changed location. I myself slept in a sleeping-bag in the small tent I shared with my [aide-de-camp], and do not remember having used a proper bed more than three times throughout this panzer drive. The one man with any objection to living under canvas was our senior military assistant, who preferred to sleep in his car. Unfortunately he had to [sleep with] his long legs sticking out through the door, [and] could never get his wet boots off after a rainy night.

We always used to pitch our little camp in a wood or a copse near the main axis of advance—if possible by a lake or stream so that we could take a quick plunge before breakfast or whenever we came back covered with dust and grime from a trip to the front.[10]

Staff and Commander: Activities

While the Chief-of-Staff naturally had to stay behind the command post to deal with the work and telephone calls, I spent the days, and often part of the nights, out on the road. I usually left early in the morning, after receiving the dawn situation reports and issuing any orders that were necessary, to visit divisions and forward troops. At eleven, I would return to the command post for a while and then go out to visit another division, for as often as not it is just around eventide that success beckons or a fresh impetus is needed. By the time we returned to our tented camp, which would meanwhile have been shifted to a new location, we were dead tired and as black as sweeps. On such occasions it was a special treat to find that, thanks to the forethought of Major Niemann, my second assistant, we were to have a roast chicken or even a bottle of wine from his own small stock instead of the usual evening fare of rye bread, smoked sausage and margarine. I am afraid that however far forward we were, chickens and geese were very hard come by, having as a rule been snapped up by other fanciers before we appeared on the scene. When, with the onset of the early autumn snows, it became rather too chilly to sit in the tents, we found it both pleasant and refreshing to use the sauna baths which, however primitive in form, were to be found on almost every farmstead.[11]

Communication with Staff and Lower Units

Such flexible leadership on my part was, of course, possible only because I was able to take a [radio] vehicle along with me on trips [courtesy of] our excellent signals officer Kohler, who later became a Staff major. Thanks to the admirable speed with which he could get our tactical staff or any divisional headquarters on the air, I was continuously informed of the situation throughout the corps and decisions taken by me on the spot could be passed back with a minimum of delay. I might add that during my imprisonment after the war Kohler proved a most unselfish friend and helper to my [family].[12]

The Perfect Aide, Pepo

Apart from my faithful drivers Nagel and Schumann and the outriders, my constant companion on these trips was my A.D.C., Lieutenant Specht. We called him 'Pepo' because of his short, wiry figure and his youthful freshness and happy-go-lucky nature. He was a young cavalry officer of the best type. Brisk, vigorous, somewhat irresponsible where danger was concerned, shrewd and quick on the uptake, he was always cheerful and slightly saucy. All these qualities had endeared him to me. He rode brilliantly (his father was a keen horse-breeder, his mother a first-class horsewoman) and had won several big events as a newly commissioned officer just before the war. He was game for anything, and would have liked nothing better than to take his Commanding General out on skirmishing patrols. As long as we belonged to 56 Panzer Corps and could be daily at the scene of action, Pepo was content with me and his lot, but when I became an army commander and could no longer be up at the front so often, he began to champ at the bit. [Later] I again sent him to a division, but this time he crashed on his way there in a Fieseler Storch [light aircraft]. The loss was a heavy blow to me.[13]

[On 30 September 1941, General Hans Guderian, whose leading unit was 40 miles from Moscow, was ordered to stop and hold. Hitler had given priority to taking Leningrad and Stalingrad; tanks and air cover were allocated accordingly.[14] This was probably the turning point of the Russian campaign.[15] OKH (Army HQ) changed Hitler's mind, but by that time, winter was setting in. In November, the army foundered; tanks were frozen in mud and snow; the men were hungry and freezing. Hitler blamed Field Marshal Walther von Brauchitsch, Army CIC, dismissed him (and the Army chief of staff, General Franz Halder), and took command himself. Thus from January 1942 until his suicide in 1945, Hitler was CIC of both the Wehrmacht and the Army, and (if from afar) personally commanded the army in Russia. Field Marshal Wilhelm Keitel remained nominal chief of the Wehrmacht, and proposed that Manstein be made chief of staff to Hitler and the Wehrmacht (OKW). Hitler declined. "Mit Manstein, das geht nicht gut aus."[16] Nevertheless, as noted in the biographical sketch above, Manstein was soon advanced to Army Group commander and promoted to field marshal].

On Hitler as Supreme Commander

Hitler's strategic aims [in Russia] were based primarily on political and economic considerations. These were: (a) the capture of Leningrad, which he regarded as the cradle of Bolshevism, by which he proposed to join with the Finns and dominate the Baltic, and (b) possession of the raw material regions of the Ukraine, the armaments centres of the Donetz Basin, and later the Caucasus oilfields. By seizing these territories he hoped to cripple the Soviet war economy. . . .

The O.K.H. [Army HQ], on the other hand, rightly contended that the conquest and retention of these undoubtedly important strategic areas depended on first defeating the Red Army. The main body of the latter . . . would be . . . [on] the road to *Moscow* . . . [which was the] focal point of Soviet power . . . whose loss the regime dare not risk. There were three reasons for this. In contrast to 1812—Moscow [was] the political centre of Russia. Loss of armaments [factories] around and east of Moscow would . . . inflict extensive damage on the Soviet war economy. Moscow was the nodal point of European Russia's traffic network. Its loss would split the Russian defences in two and prevent the Soviet command from ever mounting a single, co-ordinated operation.

Viewed strategically, the divergence of views between Hitler and O.K.H. amounted to this: Hitler wanted to seek the issue on both wings (a solution for which, in view of the relative strengths involved and the vastness of the theatre of operations, Germany did not possess adequate forces), whereas O.K.H. sought it in the centre of the front.

It was on this divergence of basic strategy that the German conduct of operations ultimately foundered. Although Hitler agreed to the disposition of forces proposed by O.K.H., according to which the bulk of the Army was to be committed in two army groups in the north and one in the area south of the Pripet Marshes, the tug-of-war over strategic objectives continued throughout this campaign. The inevitable consequence was that Hitler not only failed to attain his aims . . . but also confused the issue for O.K.H.

The 'General Intention' laid down by Hitler in his 'Barbarossa' Directive ('destruction of the bulk of the Russian Army located in western Russia by bold operations involving deep penetration by spearheads; prevention of the withdrawal of battleworthy elements into the Russian interior') was in the last analysis nothing more than a strategic or even tactical formula.[17]

Personal Failure

The absence of a "war plan" permitting the timely preparation of an invasion [of the USSR revealed] a failure of Wehrmacht leadership—in other words, on the part of Hitler himself.

"Give the Devil His Due"

In considering Hitler in the role of a military leader, one should certainly not dismiss him with such cliches as "the lance-corporal of World War I." He undoubtedly had a certain eye for operational openings.

There can be no question that his insight and unusual energy were responsible for many achievements in the sphere of armaments. Yet his belief in his own superiority . . . ultimately had disastrous consequences.[18]

However . . .

His interference prevented the smooth and timely development of the Luftwaffe, and it was undoubtedly he who hampered the development of rocket propulsion and atomic weapons.

What he lacked . . . was simply military experience—something for which his 'intuition' was no substitute.

And so this active mind seized on almost any aim that caught his fancy, causing him to fritter away Germany's strength by taking on several objectives simultaneously, often in the most dispersed theatres of war.[19]

The rule that *one can never be too strong at the crucial spot*, that one may even have to dispense with less vital fronts or . . . radically weaken them in order to achieve a decisive aim, was something he never . . . grasped. As a result, in the offensives of 1942 and 1943 [in Russia] he could not bring himself to stake *everything* on success [in one area].

Hitler [also] overlooked . . . that . . . [holding a] territorial objective presupposes the defeat of the enemy's armed forces. [In] the Soviet Union [the capture] of economically valuable areas [was] problematical and their long-term retention [an] impossibility.[20]

Overestimation of Power of the Will

[Hitler's failure as a commander may be attributed to his] . . . over-estimation of *the power of the will*. . . . Hitler had little inclination to relate his own operations to the probable intentions of the enemy, since . . . his will would always triumph in the end. He [also refused] to accept any reports . . . of enemy superiority. . . . Hitler either rejected them or minimized them with assertions about the enemy's deficiencies and took refuge in endless recitations of German production figures.

In the face of his will, the essential elements of the 'appreciation' of a situation on which every military commander's decision must be based were virtually eliminated. And with that Hitler turned his back on reality.[21]

Hitler's Fear of Risk

During the Russian campaign Hitler's fear of risk manifested itself in two ways. One . . . was his refusal to accept that elasticity of operations which, in the conditions obtaining from 1943 onwards, could be achieved only by a voluntary, if temporary, surrender of conquered territory. The second was his fear to denude the secondary fronts or subsidiary theatres in favour of the spot where the main decision had to fall, even when a failure to do so was palpably dangerous.

Whenever he was confronted with a decision which he did not like taking but could not ultimately evade, Hitler would procrastinate as long as he possibly could.

Obstinate defence of every foot of ground gradually became the be all and end all of [his] leadership.

Yet because the Soviet counter-offensive in that winter of 1941 had been frustrated by the resistance of our troops, Hitler was convinced that his ban on any voluntary withdrawal had saved the Germans from the fate of Napoleon's Grand Army in 1812.

His way of thinking conformed more to a mental picture of masses of the enemy bleeding to death before our lines than to the conception of a subtle fencer who knows how to make an occasional step backwards in order to lunge for the decisive thrust. For the art of war he substituted a brute force which, as he saw it, was guaranteed maximum effectiveness by the will-power behind it.[22]

Self-Deception by Numbers

He was possessed of 'la rage du nombre.' He would intoxicate himself with the production figures of the German armaments industry . . . [overlooking] . . . that the enemy's . . . figures were higher still.

In just the same way Hitler was constantly ordering new divisions to be set up. Though an increase in the number of our formations was most desirable, they had to be filled at the cost of replacements for the divisions already in existence, which in course of time were drained of their last drop of blood. At the same time the newly established formations initially had to pay an excessively high toll of killed because of their lack of battle experience. The Luftwaffe Field Divisions, the unending series of SS divisions and finally the so-called People's Grenadier Divisions were the most blatant examples.[23]

Hitler, Front-Line Soldier

A final point worth mentioning is that although Hitler was always harping on his 'soldierly' outlook and loved to recall that he acquired his military experience as a front-line soldier, his character had as little in common with [that of] soldiers as had his party with the Prussian virtues which it was so fond of invoking.

It was hard enough to persuade him to visit our Army Group headquarters; the idea of going any farther forward never occurred to him. It may be that he feared such trips would destroy those golden dreams about his invincible will.

Despite the pains Hitler took to stress his own former status as a front-line soldier, I still never had the feeling that his heart belonged to the fighting troops. Losses, as far as he was concerned, were merely figures which reduced fighting power. They are unlikely to have seriously disturbed him as a human being.[24]

Central Command by Hitler

All . . . theatres were gradually turned over to O.K.W. [Armed Forces HQ under Hitler]. Only the Eastern one remained as an O.K.H. [Army HQ] . . . and . . . it had Hitler at its head. Hence the Chief-of-Staff of the Army was left with just as little influence on the other theatres of war as were Commanders-in-chief of the two other services.

Misunderstanding of German Leadership

[Hitler] attempted more and more . . . in separate orders of his own [to run] subordinate formations. It has always been the special forte of German military leadership that it relies on commanders at all levels to show initiative and willingness to accept responsibility and does everything in its power to promote such qualities. That is why, as a matter of principle, the directives of higher commands and the orders of medium and lower commands always contained . . . 'assignments' for subordinate formations. The detailed execution of these assignments was the [task of] the subordinate commanders.

Ability to Mesmerize

His faculty for inspiring others with his own confidence—whether feigned or genuine—was quite remarkable. This particularly applied when officers who did not know him well came to see him from the front. In such cases a man who had set out to "tell Hitler the truth about things out there" came back converted and bursting with confidence. In . . . disputes I had with Hitler on operational matters in my capacity as an army group commander, what impressed me was the incredible tenacity with which he would defend his point of view.

I was fully alive to the fact that Hitler would never be prepared to relinquish the supreme command officially. . . . [It would have been an] intolerable loss of prestige.[25]

[Manstein decided that the next best thing would be to persuade Hitler nominally to remain Supreme Commander, but to leave operations in each military theater to one responsible chief of staff, and to name a single commander-in-chief for Russia (the

Eastern theater). Hitler declined, surely fearing the Army would favor Manstein for CIC East. Though Manstein thought that under Der Führer's command the German Army in Russia was doomed to defeat, he fought on until dismissed.]

Conclusions

It is easy to see why German generals rated Manstein their top commander. He was both an outstanding General Staff man and a field commander of talent and decision. He was as successful as anyone could have been on the Russian front, where the Germans were overcommitted, surely considering Hitler's decisions in 1941–42 to open fronts in Yugoslavia, Greece, and North Africa as well. Matters were made worse when Hitler assumed control as commander of the *Wehrmacht* and the Army, as Manstein makes plain in the work quoted above.

Manstein valued his troops, provided for them as best he could, and kept in personal contact with them at corps level, and as much as possible when he moved to command an army, then army groups. His defiance of Hitler's orders to violate the Geneva Convention mark him as an officer and gentleman of the "old army," who somehow survived in Hitler's Wehrmacht. During his last years in Russia, he regularly violated Der Führer's orders to stand at all costs, and organized orderly withdrawals to save the lives of German troops.

Perhaps he was a patriot for too long, but he was not a Nazi. He was a professional soldier and a superb leader of men. Brett-Smith wrote: "Manstein was that *rara avis* . . . who combined the genuine intellectual equipment and precision of the good staff officer with the authority, decisiveness and imaginative flair of the good field commander."[26] He was an officer and gentleman in the old Prussian tradition, admired as a man and commander by friend and foe. Field Marshal Gerd von Rundstedt has been called the "last of the Teutonic Knights";[27] perhaps Manstein deserves the title more.

We shall reserve for the general conclusions any comparing of his techniques and his attachment to his men to those of our other commanders.

XI

Bernard Law Montgomery

(1887–1976)

FIELD MARSHAL Viscount Montgomery of Alamein ("Monty") was one of the more famous—some would say successful—army and army group commanders of World War II, and a favorite of British troops. His campaign against Rommel in North Africa was a sensation in its time, even to those aware of his advantages in men, tanks, airpower, supplies, and intelligence (details below). His performance in Italy cannot be faulted. In Europe, he was considered too cautious by many American generals,[1] and his record was sullied by his "Bridge Too Far" maneuver (September 1944), which ended with eighty percent of the British airborne force killed or captured. He outraged Americans by seeming to take untoward credit for the victory in the Battle of the Bulge (December 1944), in which the British role was minimal. But at his fighting best, Monty's attitude resembled Patton's. His ideas on leadership are worth considering.

Montgomery was of an Ulster Irish family with distant Norman-French connections. When he was two, his father, Henry Montgomery, was made Anglican bishop of Tasmania. Monty spent his early years there, under the stern domination of his mother, née Maud Farrar, also of a clerical family.

When Monty was ten, his father was recalled to London, and he was sent to St. Paul's School, where he was called "Monkey," but with respect; he was a savage fighter.[2] He went on to Sandhurst, where he had a mediocre record and again a reputation for violence. Yet he did not drink or smoke, and was a regular church-goer. Later, as a commander, he tried to keep his already strictly disciplined men from the fleshpots of cities (notably Cairo). Lewin says: "Churchill called Montgomery a 'Cromwellian figure'. . . . He was indeed one of Cromwell's plain russet-coated captains, 'such men as had the fear of God before them, and as made some conscience of what they did'."[3]

In World War I, Montgomery, as an infantry lieutenant, bested a German in hand-to-hand combat and took him prisoner; won the DSO; was wounded and sent to hospital in England. He later wrote: "I had time for reflection . . . and came to the conclusion that the old adage was probably correct: the pen was mightier than the sword. I joined the staff."[4] At war's end, he was a Lieutenant

Colonel. Between the wars, he attended and instructed at the Staff College, served in posts around the world, and married a widow with two small sons who gave him a third before dying prematurely—a tragedy that made him totally work-centered.

In 1940, heading a division in France, he survived the British Expeditionary Force's Dunkirk evacuation. In August 1942, he was given command of the British Eighth Army, which had been driven into Egypt by Field Marshal Erwin Rommel's Afrika Korps (so called; it had grown into a German-Italian army). Monty stopped Rommel at Alam Halfa—thanks to superior numbers, new American tanks, RAF air superiority, and ULTRA intelligence.[5] Rommel retreated to El Alamein (7 September 1942) and dug in.

Monty had 195,000 troops and 1,000 tanks (two-thirds American with 75mm guns) against Rommel's 104,000 troops and 510 tanks (half of both Italian). Yet he spent over six weeks preparing to attack, which gave Rommel time to build bunkers and trenches and lay thousands of mines. When Monty finally advanced on 23 October, he had to fight the Battle of El Alamein in World War I style; it lasted thirteen days and took 13,000 casualties. On 4 November Rommel began retreating westward; Monty pursued cautiously, and most of Rommel's army escaped.[6]

Rommel's withdrew, fighting doggedly, over 1,200 miles into Tunisia, where at Mareth, in early February 1943, he ordered a defense line prepared. Meanwhile, Anglo-American troops landed in Morocco and Algeria in November 1942, and drove east toward Tunis. United States forces got a taste of Rommel's fury at Kasserine Pass (19–20 February 1943), but he was recalled (9 March 1943).[7] Montgomery began his attacks on the Mareth line on 20 March 1943. From the west, the U.S. II Corps, under George Patton (part of British First Army), played a part in forcing Rommel's successor, Colonel-General Jürgen von Arnim, to retreat northward to consolidate his lines. Arnim surrendered to the Allies on 13 May 1943.

The Allies next invaded Sicily with two armies—Monty's and an American, under that "flamboyant Californian millionaire, that pistol-packing, cavalry-man-turned-tankman . . . General George S. Patton. . . . The Supreme Allied Commander . . . was to be the nicotine-addicted General Eisenhower." These are a biographer's words, but could have been Monty's,[8] although he respected Patton as a general, and vice versa. They drove the Germans from Sicily. Monty took Eighth Army to Italy, then was ordered to England. Patton followed from Sicily after enduring the furor over the "slapping incidents" (see "Patton" above). Monty was given command of Allied ground forces in the invasion of Europe (6 June 1944). General Dwight "Ike" Eisenhower was Supreme Commander (American troops outnumbered all others), and after the landings was to command the two army groups: Montgomery's 21st, and U.S. General Omar Bradley's 12th. In Europe, however, Monty pressed for field command over both army groups, and wanted a "narrow front," with both army groups driving for the Rhine north of the Ardennes. Eisenhower planned a "broad front," with Monty north and Bradley south of the Ardennes.

While Monty argued for a narrow front, his army made very slow progress.[9] His pace was bitterly resented, especially by Patton, commanding Third Army (in Bradley's Army Group).

Hurt by American attitudes, Monty kept pressing Ike for a single thrust at the Ruhr. Meanwhile V-1 rockets, launched from Belgium, were devastating London. On condition that Monty knock out the V-1 sites and take Antwerp en route, Eisenhower (23 August 1944) gave him orders to strike for the Ruhr, much of Patton's(!) supplies, and the entire Allied Airborne Army (US 82nd and 101st Divisions and British 1st and Polish Brigade). In September Montgomery took Antwerp, the V-1 launch sites, and Brussels, but by then better V-2 rockets were striking London from Holland and Denmark.

He then proposed a daring plan, called MARKET GARDEN, to use the Airborne Army to seize bridges at Eindhoven and Nijmwegen in Holland, and at Arnhem, across the lower Rhine in Germany. Horrock's British XXX Corps would link up with the airborne—and the way would be open to Berlin.[10] Ike allowed Monty to begin the operation on 17 September 1944. Meanwhile, the Germans had moved the 15th Army (which Monty was accused of letting escape from Calais), General Kurt Student's Parachute Division, and II S.S. Panzer Corps into positions beyond the lower Rhine.[11]

The 101st Airborne took the bridge at Eindhoven on 17 September; the 82nd, with the aid of the British Armoured Guards Division, captured the bridge at Nijmwegen on the 20th. At Arnhem, Major General Robert Urquhart's 1st British Airborne was dropped seven miles northwest of the bridge.[12] Then the weather turned ugly, Allied air support failed, and the fury of the German forces fell on Urquhart's men. The British-trained Polish Airborne Brigade (General Sosabowski) went to their aid, but was cut to pieces. The British lost 8,300, killed or captured, of 10,500 men in their airborne units.[13]

Despite the valor of the airborne troopers, the Allies had not crossed the Rhine. Monty's stock fell. It dropped further during the German Ardennes offensive (December 1944). The panzers split Bradley's Army Group, and Ike put the northern U.S. armies under Monty. U.S. airborne forces and Patton's Third Army broke the enemy's back, but Monty, in statements to the press, seemed to claim he had saved the Allies. He vowed to the contrary, but many Americans, including General Bradley, never forgave him.[14]

Monty and Patton, once across the Rhine (March 1944), were suddenly in agreement. Both wanted to march on Berlin. Eisenhower ordered them to leave it to the Soviets. They protested, but to no avail; the decision had been made in Washington and London—and was political. The war ended with the Soviets in possession of Eastern Europe, including eastern Germany.

After the war Monty was chief of the Imperial General Staff and NATO deputy commander. He died at his home in England in 1976.

―――――――

The material below is from *The Memoirs of Field-Marshal the Viscount Montgomery of Alamein* (1958).

Doctrine of Command

My own definition of leadership is this: "The capacity and the will to rally men and women to a common purpose and the character which inspires confidence."

A leader must speak the truth to those under him; if he does not they will soon find it out and then their confidence in him will decline.

The good military leader will dominate the events which surround him; once he lets events get the better of him he will lose the confidence of his men.

The degree [of a leader's "influence"] . . . will depend on [his] personality . . . —the "incandescence" of which he is capable . . . the magnetism which will draw the hearts of men towards him.

What I personally would want to know about a leader is: Where is he going? Will he go all out? Has he the talents and equipment . . . ? Will he take decisions, and take risks where necessary? Will he then delegate [authority after designating] . . . points of decision so that the master plan can be implemented smoothly and quickly? The matter of "decision" is vital.

The leader must know what he himself wants. He must see his objective clearly . . . he must let everyone else know what he wants and . . . the basic fundamentals of his policy. He must . . . give firm guidance and a clear lead.

To succeed, a C.-in-C. must ensure from the beginning a very firm grip on his military machine; only in this way will his force maintain balance and cohesion and thus develop its full fighting potential. This firm grip does not mean . . . cramping the initiative of subordinates; . . . it is by the initiative of subordinates that the battle is . . . won.

The master plan must never be so rigid that the C.-in-C. cannot vary it to suit the changing . . . situation; but nobody else may be allowed to change it at will . . . especially, not the enemy.

[The commander] should never bring [his subordinates] back to him for . . . a conference; he must go forward to them. Then nobody looks over his shoulder. A conference of subordinates to collect ideas is the resort of a weak commander.

It is a mistake to think that once an order is given there is nothing more to be done; you have got to see that it is carried out in the spirit which you intended. . . . The commander should himself draft the initial operational order . . . and not allow his staff to do so.

No leader, however great, can long continue unless he wins victories. The battle decides all.

In Sir Winston Churchill's study of Marlborough we note that: "The success of a commander does not arise from following rules or models. It consists in an absolutely new comprehension of the . . . facts of the situation . . . and all the forces at work. Every great operation of war is unique. . . . There is no surer road to disaster than to imitate the plans of bygone heroes and fit them to novel situations."

The real strength of an army is, and must be, far greater than the sum total of its parts; that extra strength is provided by morale, fighting spirit, mutual confidence between the leaders and the led and especially with the high command, the quality of comradeship, and many other intangible spiritual qualities.

If the approach to the human factor is cold and impersonal, then you achieve nothing.

The morale of the soldier is the greatest single factor in war and the best way to achieve a high morale in war-time is by success in battle. The good general . . . wins his battles with the fewest possible casualties; but morale will remain high even after considerable casualties, provided the battle has been won and the men know . . . that every care has been taken of the wounded, and the killed have been . . . reverently buried.

Some think that morale is best . . . when the British soldier is surrounded by . . . clubs, canteens, and so on. I disagree. . . . Men dumped in some out-of-the-way spot in the desert will complain less of boredom, because they have to shift for themselves.

[The British soldier] will do anything you ask of him so long as you arrange he gets his mail from home, the newspapers, and, curiously enough, plenty of tea. . . . He likes to see the C.-in-C. regularly in the forward area, and be spoken to and noticed. He must know that you really care for him and will look after his interests.

The miners from Durham and Newcastle, the men from the Midlands, the Cockneys, the farmers from the West Country, the Scot, the Welshman all are different. Some men are good at night; others . . . in daylight. Some are best at the . . . mobile battle; others are more temperamentally adapted to the solid killing match in close country. Therefore all decisions are different.

A division develops an individuality of its own . . . the higher commander must . . . learn the type of battle each is best at.

It is exactly the same with generals. . . . Generals must also be matched to the job. In fact, I spent a great deal of time in [considering] this . . . problem. . . . I always used . . . the general and the troops best fitted [for a] particular task. As a result each battle was already half-won before it ever began.

I kept command appointments in my own hand, right down to . . . battalion or regimental level. Merit, leadership, and ability to do the job, were the sole criteria.

Commanders once chosen must be trusted and "backed" to the limit. . . . If, having received the help he might normally expect, a man fails—then he must go.

My whole working creed was based on the fact that in war it is "the man" that matters. Commanders in all grades must have qualities of leadership.

Probably one of the greatest assets a commander can have is the ability to radiate confidence in the plan . . . (perhaps especially) when inwardly he is not too sure about the outcome.

A battle is, in effect, a contest between two wills—your own and that of the enemy general.[15]

It is absolutely vital that a senior commander should keep himself from becoming immersed in details. . . . No commander who has not time for quiet thought and reflection, can make a sound plan of battle . . . or conduct large-scale operations efficiently. . . .

He has got to strive to read the mind of his opponent, to anticipate enemy reactions to his own moves, and to take quick steps to prevent enemy interference with his own plans. . . .

He has got to be . . . able to sort out the essentials from the mass of factors which bear on every problem. If he is to do these things he must . . . not be a heavy smoker, or drink much, or sit up late at night. He must have an ice-clear brain at all times.

The plan of operations must always be made by the commander and must not be forced on him by his staff, or by circumstances, or by the enemy.

The first piece of advice I would give any senior commander is to have a good Chief of Staff.

[The commander] must make the enemy dance to his tune from the beginning, and never vice versa. . . . His own dispositions must be so balanced that he can utilise but need not react to the enemy's move but can continue relentlessly with his own plan.

[Also vital] was "grouping," i.e. seeing that each corps, which has to fight the tactical battle, is suitably composed for its task. Skill in grouping before the battle begins, and in re-grouping to meet the changing tactical situation, is one of the hall-marks of generalship.

A commander must be very thorough in making his tactical plan; once made, he must be utterly ruthless in carrying it out and forcing it through to success.

Before the battle begins an Army Commander should assemble all commanders down to the lieutenant-colonel level and explain to them the problem, his intention, his plan, and generally how he is going to fight the battle and make it go the way he wants. . . .

And when the troops see that the battle has gone exactly as they were told it would go, the increase in morale and the confidence in the higher command is immense—and this is a most important factor for the battles still to come.

The troops must be brought to a state of wild enthusiasm before the operation begins. . . . They must enter the fight with the light of battle in their eyes and definitely wanting to kill the enemy. In achieving this end, it is the spoken word which counts, from the commander to his troops; plain speech is far more effective than any written word.

Operational command . . . must be direct and personal, by means of visits to subordinate H.Q. where orders are given verbally.

A commander must train his subordinate commanders, and his own staff to work and act on verbal orders. Those . . . who want everything in writing, are useless. . . . There is far too much paper in circulation in the Army, and no one can read even half of it intelligently.

Finally, I do not believe that today a commander can inspire . . . armies . . . or even individual men, and lead them to victories, unless he has a . . . sense of religious truth; he must . . . acknowledge it, and . . . lead his troops in the light of that truth.[16]

Changes in Warfare and the Commander

It has been my unique privilege to have commanded during my career every echelon from a platoon up to and including a Group of Armies. I say "unique" because I doubt if there is any other [active] soldier . . . in the free world who has had the same experience.

Times have changed since the campaigns of Marlborough and Wellington; it could almost be said that they won their campaigns single-handed. Certainly they were not bothered with the enormous amount of detailed staff work involved in modern armies. Today a C.-in-C. in the field is the captain of a team, and a large team at that. In the summer of 1945 the question arose whether the nation should make grants of money to the principal commanders in the field in recognition of their services, following the precedent of previous wars. But in modern war, once you start picking out individuals who have really made a first class contribution to the war effort, great problems arise. What about those responsible for radar, anti-submarine devices, intelligence, medical work, and the many whose devoted work in lower grades made possible the winning of the contest?

Leadership Unlike That of World War I

High Command today is more complicated than formerly and a C.-in-C. has got to have a good staff, and a superb Chief of Staff to co-ordinate its activities. He must also pick his subordinate commanders with the greatest care, matching the generals to the jobs. He must know his soldiers, and be recognised by them. I do not believe the leadership displayed on the Western Front in World War I would have succeeded in World War II. I would remind the reader that in World War I although I served in France, I never once saw French or Haig [*the British high commanders*].

Medical Services

An army today is a self-contained community; it contains everything its members need for war, from bullets to blood banks. I will always remember Churchill's anger when he heard of several dentist's chairs being landed over the beaches in Normandy! But we have learnt since the 1914–18 war that by caring for a man's teeth, we keep him in the battle. The good general must not only win his battles; he must win them with a minimum of casualties and loss of life. I learnt during the 1939–45 war that four things contributed to the saving of life:

1. Blood transfusion.
2. Surgical teams operating well forward in the battle area, so that a badly wounded man could be dealt with at once without having to be moved by road to a hospital.
3. Air evacuation direct to a Base hospital many hundreds of miles in rear, thus saving bumpy journeys by road or rail.
4. Nursing sisters working well forward in the battle area. When I joined the Eighth Army in 1942, nursing sisters were not allowed in the forward battle area. I cancelled the order. Their presence comforted and calmed the nerves of many seriously wounded men, who . . . knew they would be properly nursed.

Administration

All these things, and many others like them, have to be in the mind of the modern general. On the administrative side there must be a clear-cut, long-term relationship established between operational intentions and administrative resources. Successful administrative planning is dependent on anticipation of requirements. A C.-in-C. in the field must, therefore, always keep his staff fully in his mind as regards forward intentions, so that the essential administrative preparations can be completed in time. Many generals have failed in war because they neglected to ensure that what they wanted to achieve operationally was commensurate with their administrative resources; and some have failed because they over-insured in this respect. The lesson is, there must always be a nice balance between the two requirements.

Decision and Drive

The acid test of an officer who aspires to high command is his ability to be able
to grasp quickly the essentials of a military problem, to decide rapidly what he
will do, to make it quite clear to all concerned what he intends to achieve and
how he will do it, and then to see that his subordinate commanders get on with
the job. Above all, he has got to rid himself of all irrelevant detail; he must
concentrate on the essentials, and on those details and only those details which
are necessary to the proper carrying out of his plan—trusting his staff to effect
all the necessary co-ordination.

When all is said and done the greatest quality required in a commander is
"decision"; he must then be able to issue clear orders and have the "drive" to get
things done. Indecision and hesitation are fatal in any officer; in a C.-in-C. they
are criminal.

Rapport with Troops

No modern C.-in-C. can have any success if he fails to understand the human
approach to war. Battles are won . . . in the hearts of men; if he loses the battle
for [mens'] hearts . . . he will achieve little.

Unity of Command

[*Monty here is still making his case against Eisenhower, noted in the Introduction.*]

Throughout any force the organisation for command and control must be simple and clear cut. In the desert campaign, in Sicily and in Italy it was so. In the
campaign in North-West Europe the organisation worked well at the start [*when
Monty was in command*], and with it we won one of the greatest battles of
modern times—in Normandy. Then it was changed, and smooth and efficient
command and control disappeared.[17]

Conclusions

Most commanders of World War II were religious, but Montgomery had no peer
as a moralist. He not only lived free of vices, even petty ones like an occasional
drink, but tried to induce his men to do the same. He is quoted above to the
effect that overt religious faith is necessary to leadership in battle.

Montgomery believed with Napoleon that it was "the man," not men, who
mattered in battle. That was one reason he begged Eisenhower to put him
in command of all ground troops in Europe—or Bradley, under whom he volunteered to serve.[18] (Patton would have agreed that a single commander

was needed, and with Monty's assessment that Eisenhower "commanded by committee.")

At the same time, Monty thought subordinates should be able to use initiative, and agreed with Patton (et al.) that the commander should go forward and not ask his subordinates to come to the rear for conferences. He believed in taking care of the troops (but thought that American soldiers had too many creature comforts). He deemed in-person speeches to the troops a necessity, as well as visits.

He valued a good chief of staff; he believed in plans, and in carrying them out "ruthlessly," but averred that plans often had to be changed—that is, a commander had to know how to *improvise*. Our introduction says that, at his best, he was like Patton. Monty once wrote Patton: "George, let me give you some advice. If you get an order from Army Group that you don't like, why, ignore it. That's what I do."[19] Like Patton, he loved War. Horne wrote: "His 'enjoyment' of battle was always something that was confounding, if not . . . shocking, to his critics."[20] Carlo d'Este compared Patton and Montgomery:

> Both played to win; both were equally contemptuous of convention; both had highly developed histrionic tendencies. Both were ardent Episcopalians; both were communicants; both avidly read the Bible including the blood-thirsty chapters of the Old Testament; both believed profoundly in the efficacy of prayer as an aid to victory. Their attitude to women was chivalrous. . . .
>
> Both were masters of manipulation, each influential in convincing their soldiers that what each of them did was important. The notion, perpetuated endlessly . . . by historians on both sides of the Atlantic—that Montgomery and Patton detested one another—is based . . . on a misinterpretation of their private remarks. . . .
>
> Although a feud between the two most controversial Allied generals over the war's most contentious issues makes great copy, it does not always make good history.[21]

Battle, to Monty, was a contest of wills—his and enemy commander's.[22] He saw *winning* as the greatest secret of leadership.

His opinion of himself was high, but perhaps an overblown ego is necessary for command. He once told cadets at Sandhurst (c. 1970) that he would be rated among the Great Captains of all time.[23]

During World War II, with a headquarters full of lackeys and pets, where he repaired to his van at 9:00 PM, no matter what, he seemed, at times, like a relic-general of World War I. But in fact he was a general for his time.

XII

William Joseph Slim

(1891–1970)

LORD LOUIS MOUNTBATTEN pronounced William Slim "the finest general the Second World War produced."[1] His army in Burma comprised British, Gurkha, Burmese, African, and at times American and Chinese troops. He welded this mixture of nationalities into an effective fighting force, and coordinated its operations with British and American air forces. His memoirs (quoted below) contain a wealth of good advice.

The future Field Marshal Viscount Slim saw action as a lieutenant in 1915 in the Gallipoli campaign. He fought at Cape Helles and Sari Bair, attacking up steep hills and surviving in trenches hacked in solid rock in oppressive heat. His battalion had 414 casualties; Slim took a bullet that barely missed his spine. He knew all too well the shortcomings of command in the Great War—generals out of touch with troops, poor planning, inadequate supplies—and their effects on morale.

As an army commander in Burma in World War II, he knew his troops, prepared them for combat, and saw to their needs and *esprit*.[2] He spoke Gurkhali, Urdu, and Pushtu as well as English. In whatever language, wrote General O'Carroll-Scott: "It was always as one man to another—never the great commander to his troops."[3] And Slim did not have the passion for endless preparation that infected so many British generals. He did not delay attacking until he had every possible necessity for victory. Otherwise, says Evans, he would not have given the Japanese in Burma "the greatest land defeat in their history."[4]

Slim was born in Bristol, England, the son of a businessman. He attended King Edward's School, where he joined the Officer Training Corps, and finished training at Birmingham University.

After serving in World War I, he was commissioned in the Indian Army. In the 1920s and 1930s, he commanded Gurkha and Indian troops, with stints at staff college as a student and instructor. When the Second World War began, he commanded of the 10th Indian Brigade, then an Indian division, with which he took Baghdad (June 1941). He was next given the I (First) Burma Corps (Indian and Burmese troops), formed to defend Burma, but was driven into India (April

1942). U.S. Lieutenant General Joseph "Vinegar Joe" Stilwell, nominally commanding the Chinese Army of Chiang Kai-shek, tried to help, but could do little.

Placed in command of 14th Army, Slim prevented the Japanese from invading India (1943–early 1944), then launched an offensive into Burma. By December 1944 he had recaptured northern Burma, following inroads by irregulars—Major General Orde Wingate's "Chindits" (British, Gurkhas, Burmese, and Africans)[5] and "Merrill's Marauders," under Brigadier General Frank Merrill, American volunteers of Stilwell's command who led the advance of his Chinese troops.[6]

Slim managed two of the most difficult commanders in the world—"Vinegar Joe" Stilwell and Orde Wingate. Stilwell was not under Slim's command and averred to hate "limies." Yet Slim got his cooperation:

> My method with Stilwell was based on what I had learnt of him in the Retreat [from Burma in 1942] . . . whenever I wanted anything, to fly over and discuss it with him, alone. Stilwell, talking things over quietly with no one else present, was a much easier and more likeable person than Vinegar Joe with an audience.[7]

Wingate was under Slim's command, but barely. He was in direct touch with British Prime Minister Winston Churchill, who favored eccentrics—if they got things done. Wingate could have been "king of the strange"; slender, of average height, with a tangle of black hair and the beard of a prophet, he snacked on raw chicken and sometimes briefed his officers while stark naked. However, his LRPG (Long Range Penetration Groups) performed prodigies—striking the Japanese behind their lines with small air-supplied detachments. Slim wrote of him:

> Wingate and I agreed better than most people expected, perhaps because we had known one another before, or perhaps because we had each . . . arrived at the same conclusions on certain major issues, the potentialities of air supply, the possibility of taking Burma from the north, and . . . estimates of the strengths and weaknesses of the Japanese.[8]

The Battle for Myitkyina (August 1944), however, badly depleted the Chindits (Wingate was killed in a plane crash during preliminary actions); it virtually wiped out Merrill's Marauders, who were deactivated.[9] Stilwell was promoted to full (four-star) general, a grade long deserved, and ordered home. Only elements of the 14th U.S. Army Air Force, under General Claire Chenault (recently of the freebooting "Flying Tigers," serving Chiang Kai-shek),[10] remained to support Slim.[11]

Slim went forward, nevertheless, to bring the Japanese to a battle of decision at Meiktila and capture Mandalay (March 1945) and Rangoon (May 1945). He was made Chief of Southeast Asian Ground Forces (August 1945). After Japan surrendered, Slim restored order in Malaysia and Indonesia. In 1948 he was made Chief of the Imperial General Staff and shortly promoted field marshal and knighted. He was governor general of Australia (1952–60), then returned to England, where he held ceremonial posts; he retired in 1970 and died the same year.

———————

The following passages are from Field Marshal Slim's memoirs, largely of World War II in Burma, entitled *Defeat into Victory*.[12] The segments quoted deal with his general ideas on leadership.

Personal Command

Our organization at Army Headquarters was basically the same as I had used for 15 Corps. I never adopted the "Chief of Staff System", which, following the German and American lead, had been introduced in some British armies. Under this system the Chief General Staff Officer not only co-ordinates the work of the whole staff, but is the mouthpiece of the commander to the other principal staff officers and heads of Services, interpreting to them his Commander's intentions and wishes. I preferred to stick to the old British method of the Commander dealing directly himself with his principal staff officers. Command is the projection of the commander's personality and, as such, is an extremely [individual matter].

The Staff

In Fourteenth Army . . . my senior staff officer was actually my major-general in charge of administration. For an army engaged in a campaign in Burma this was logical . . . administrative possibilities and impossibilities would loom as large, [or] larger than strategical and tactical alternatives. In any case the immense supply, transport, medical, and reinforcement organizations that we were beginning to build up more than justified a major-general's rank.

Planning

The principles on which I planned all operations were:

> (i) The ultimate intention must be an offensive one.
> (ii) The main idea on which the plan was based must be simple.
> (iii) That idea must be held in view throughout and everything else must give way to it.
> (iv) The plan must have in it an element of surprise.

Refining the Plan

My method of working out such a plan was first to study the possibilities myself, and then informally to discuss them with my Brigadier General Staff, Major-General Administration, and my opposite number in the Air Force. At these discussions we would arrive at the broadest outline of possible alternative courses of action, at least two, more often three or four. These alternatives the B.G.S. would give to our team of planners, specially selected but comparatively junior officers, representing not only the general and administrative staffs, but the air staff as well. They would make a preliminary study, giving the practicability or otherwise of each course and its advantages and disadvantages. They were quite at liberty to make new suggestions of their own, or to devise permutations and combinations of the originals. The results of the planners' examination of the proposals were put up to me as a short paper, largely in tabular form, and from it I decided on the main features of the plan to be followed.

Studying the Enemy

At this stage I usually discussed with the intelligence officer whom I had selected to represent the Japanese command . . . what the enemy's reactions to this plan were likely to be. I was, of course, kept daily in the picture of the Japanese actions, intentions, and dispositions, as far as we knew or could surmise them, but I intentionally waited until I had selected my plan before considering the enemy response to it, as I intended him to conform to me, not me to him. A consideration of these possible Japanese counter-moves never, I think, caused a major alteration in a plan, but they did affect such things as the location and expected tasks of reserves.

Air Support and Transport

As few of our plans were not dependent on air support and air transportation, this was the stage at which general agreement between us [Slim's headquarters and Air Operations Command] had to be reached.

This done—and thanks to the generosity and unselfishness of the air commanders, British and American, with whom I was lucky enough to work, it always was done—the next step was a meeting of my principal staff officers.

Briefing the Staff

At this, besides the Major-General Administration and the B.G.S., would be present my chief gunner, engineer, signaller, doctor, ordnance and R.E.M.E. officers. To them I would put over my plan, meet or override any special difficulties they might have, and send them off to their own staffs to hold their own conferences and to get the thousand and one things required moving. Meanwhile the B.G.S. and the Senior Air Staff Officer got down to the dovetailing of the land and air aspects on which so much would depend. There was still more for the B.G.S. to do. He had to produce the operation order or directive for the corps and other commanders who were to carry out the operations. This he prepared in conjunction with the administrative staff and the Services.

The Operations Order

I suppose dozens of operation orders have gone out in my name, but I never, throughout the war, actually wrote one myself. I always had someone who could do that better than I could. One part of the order I did, however, draft myself—the intention. It is usually the shortest of all paragraphs, but it is always the most important, because it states—or it should—just what the commander intends to achieve. It is the one overriding expression of will by which everything in the order and every action by every commander and soldier in the army must be dominated. It should, therefore, be worded by the commander himself.

Up Front: Briefing the Commanders

The next step was to take the operation order myself to the subordinate commanders who were to act on it. On principle . . . it is better to go forward to them, than to call them back; to give them their orders at their headquarters rather than at your own. That applies whether you command a platoon or an army group.[13]

Personal: Saving Strength

I must have ample leisure in which to think, and unbroken sleep. Generals would do well to remember that, even in war, 'the wisdom of a learned man cometh by opportunity of leisure.' Generals who are terribly busy all day and half the night, who fuss round . . . wear out . . . their subordinates [and] themselves. Nor have they, when the real emergency comes, the reserve of vigour that will then enable them, for days if necessary, to do with little rest or sleep.[14]

Morale

Morale is a state of mind. It is that intangible force which will move a whole group of men to give their last ounce to achieve something, without counting the cost to themselves; that makes them feel they are part of something greater than themselves. If they are to feel that, their morale . . . must . . . have . . . foundations. These foundations are spiritual, intellectual, and material . . . [in]

order of their importance. Spiritual first, because only spiritual foundations can stand real strain. Next intellectual, because men are swayed by reason as well as feeling. Material last—important, but last—because the very highest kinds of morale are often met when material conditions are lowest.

1. *Spiritual*

> (a) There must be a great and noble object.
> (b) Its achievement must be vital.
> (c) The method of achievement must be active, aggressive.
> (d) The man must feel that what he is and what he does matters directly towards the attainment of the object.

2. *Intellectual*

> (a) [The soldier] must be convinced that the object can be attained; that it is not out of reach.
> (b) He must see, too, that the organization to which he belongs and which is striving to attain the object is an efficient one.
> (c) He must have confidence in his leaders and know that whatever dangers and hardships he is called upon to suffer, his life will not be lightly flung away.

3. *Material*

> (a) The man must feel that he will get a fair deal from his commanders and from the army generally.
> (b) He must, as far as humanly possible, be given the best weapons and equipment for his task.
> (c) His living and working conditions must be made as good as they can be.

Religion and Belief in a Cause

[It was easy] thus neatly to marshal my principles but quite another to develop them . . . and get them recognized by the whole army.

At any rate our spiritual foundation was a firm one. I use the word spiritual [to mean] belief in a cause. Religion has always been and still is one of the greatest foundations of morale, especially of military morale. Saints and soldiers have much in common. The religion of the Mohammedan, of the Sikh, of the Gurkha, and of the fighting Hindu—and we had them all in the Fourteenth Army—can rouse in men a blaze of contempt for death. The Christian religion is above all others a source of that enduring courage which is the most valuable of all the components of morale. Yet religion . . . is not essential to high morale. Anyone who has fought with or against Nazi paratroops, Japanese suicide squads, or Russian Commissars, will [know] this; but a spiritual foundation, belief in a cause, there must be. . . .

Nor [is] it enough to have a worthy cause. It must be positive, aggressive, not a mere passive, defensive, anti-something feeling. So our object became not to defend India, to stop the Japanese advance, or even to occupy Burma, but to destroy the Japanese Army, to smash it as an evil thing.[15]

Motivating both Fighting and Support Soldiers

The fighting soldier facing the enemy can see that what he does, whether he is brave or craven, matters to his comrades and directly influences the result of the battle. It is harder for the man working on the road far behind, the clerk checking stores in a dump, the headquarter's telephone operator monotonously plugging through his calls, the sweeper carrying out his menial tasks, the quartermaster's orderly issuing bootlaces in a reinforcement camp—it is hard for these and a thousand others to see that they too matter. Yet every one of the half-million in the army—and it was many more later—had to be made to see where his task fitted into the whole, to realize what depended on it, and to feel pride and satisfaction in doing it well.

Now these things, while the very basis of morale,because they were purely matters of feeling and emotion, were the most difficult to put over, especially to the British portion of the army.

Personal Contact with the Troops

The problem was how to instil or revive their beliefs in the men of many races who made up the Fourteenth Army. I felt there was only one way to do it, by a direct approach to the individual men themselves. Not by written exhortations, by wireless speeches, but by informal talks and contacts between troops and commanders. There was nothing new in this; my corps and divisional commanders and others right down the scale were already doing it. It was the way we had held the troops together in the worst days of the 1942 retreat; we remained an army then only because the men saw and knew their commanders.

Efficacy of Appeal to "Higher Things"

One of the most successful of British commanders once told me that you could make an appeal to these higher things successfully to officers, but not . . . the rank and file. He underestimated his countrymen, and he had forgotten history. His dictum was not true of the England of the Crusades, of Cromwell, of Pitt, nor of Churchill. It was not true of my army, of either the British, Indian, Gurkha, or African soldier.

Up-front Appearances

I made a point of speaking myself to every combatant unit or at least to its officers and N.C.O.s. My platform was usually the bonnet of my jeep with the men collected anyhow round it. I often did three or four of these stump speeches in a day. I learnt, or perhaps I had already learnt in 15 Corps, the various responses one got from the different nationalities. Even the British differed. A cockney battalion saw the point of a joke almost before it came, a north country unit did not laugh so easily but when it did the roar was good to hear. All responded at once to some reference to their pride in the part of Britain they came from or in their regiment. A lot more could be made of this local pride; it is a fine thing. All the British were shy of talk of the spiritual things. This was most marked in the English; the Welsh and Irish had fewer inhibitions on these subjects, and the Scots, who are reared more on the romance of their history, least of any. While Indian races differed in almost everything, they all were more ready than the British to respond openly to direct appeals on . . . abstract grounds. They had not only a greater feeling for personal leadership, but their military traditions, their local patriotisms, and their religions were much more part of the everyday fabric of their lives than such things are with us. Their reaction was immediate and often intense. The Gurkha, bless him, made the most stolid of all audiences. He had a tendency to stand or sit to attention and his poker face never changed its expression until it broke into the most attractive grin in Asia at a rather broad jest. . . . The African . . . responded much as an Indian. Language was a difficulty [but was overcome].

Food and Minor Luxuries before "Higher Things"

I found that if one kept the bulk of one's talk to the material things the men were interested in, food, pay, leave, beer, mails, and the progress of operations, it was safe to end on a higher note—the spiritual foundations—and I always did.

Every Man Important

We played on this very human desire of every man to feel . . . himself and his work important, until . . . the administrative, labour, and non-combatant units acquired a morale which rivalled that of the fighting formations.[16]

Building Morale after Retreat [*From Burma, 1942*]

A victory in a large-scale battle was . . . not to be attempted. We had first to get the feel through the army that it was we who were hunting the Jap, not he us.

All commanders therefore directed their attention to patrolling. In jungle warfare this is the basis of success. It not only gives eyes to the side that excels at it, and blinds its opponent, but through it the soldier learns to move confidently in the element in which he works. Every forward unit, not only infantry, chose its best men, formed patrols, trained and practiced them, and . . . sent them out.

Sometimes they brought back even more convincing exhibits, as did the Gurkhas who presented themselves before their general, proudly opened a large basket, lifted from it three gory Japanese heads, and laid them on his table.

The Value of Easy Victories

[To instill confidence] [w]e attacked Japanese company positions with brigades fully supported by artillery and aircraft, platoon posts by battalions.

We had laid the first of our intellectual foundations of morale; everyone knew we could defeat the Japanese, our object was attainable. The next foundation, that the men should feel that they belonged to an efficient organization, that Fourteenth Army was well run and would get somewhere, followed partly from these minor successes.[17]

Conclusions

Slim finished World War I with a disdain for staffs, and scars of wounds attesting to poor high-level decisions. Nevertheless, he saw the necessity for minimal staffs, so long as they did not separate the commander from his men. He depended heavily on personal contact to build morale among the troops, and to control his subordinates. His operations were planned for offensive action, with an element of surprise; to achieve the latter he studied the dispositions and habits of the enemy (the Japanese). No operation was begun without adequate supply and air support, but he did not carry preparations to extremes.

Slim understood well that *winning* was important, and arranged easy victories for his troops when they embarked on the recapture of Burma from the Japanese. His men were untried and/or demoralized by seemingly unbroken Japanese victories. He believed that men were motivated by religion—of their choice or into which they were born—but that religion, per se, was not essential to morale and therefore victory. He thought that it could be replaced by belief in a cause, which could unite men of different religions, such as he commanded, and evidently he was right.

However, in speaking to the troops, he emphasized—along with the mutual goal of beating the Japanese—"food, pay, leave, beer, mails, and the progress of operations." And he worked steadily at making every man feel he was important to victory, whether fighting in the front lines or providing support in the rear.

He took care of his men, and stayed in contact with them, never hesitating to risk his own life for the mission or to motivate the troops (although he does not say so in his memoirs). His sympathy for the eccentric but effective Wingate, who was always courting death, well illustrates his general attitude. His position against excessive preparation, which made for victory in the field, had gotten him into trouble at the staff college—along with his lack of interest in gentlemanly sports, notably riding and hunting. But: "In the end, the Commandant decided that on sheer merit alone Slim deserved the highest grading and this he was given."[18]

That was the story of Slim's life. From humble beginnings, he had to convince his superiors at all stages of his worth, and despite his outstanding record in Asia, was not made a field marshal and knighted until three years after the war.

XIII

Joseph Warren Stilwell

(1883–1946)

"VINEGAR JOE"

GENERAL JOSEPH W. STILWELL was hated by many—both those above and below him in the command chain, and casual acquaintances. Irascible, acerbic, he was not a man to "suffer fools lightly," even if one of his "fools" was the president of China, Chiang Kai-shek, whom he called "Peanut." He was one of the great characters of World War II, who earned the nickname "Vinegar Joe" a hundred times over. He was tough, blunt, hard, and yet a man of unchallenged integrity—and a fighter who marched with his men and allowed himself nothing they did not have. Those who really knew him loved him; his staff knew that his leathery face and sharp tongue protected a man who worried about his troops and felt a responsibility to their parents. The few words he wrote on leadership are worth considering.

Stilwell was born in Florida but reared in Yonkers, New York. He graduated from West Point in 1904, and was posted to the Philippines, where he made a reputation for testiness. He also showed an uncanny talent for languages. As a result, although he served as liaison officer with a French corps in Europe in World War I, most of his service was in the Far East. When World War II arrived, he was the best available "China Hand." He was sent in 1942, as a lieutenant general, to be chief of staff to General Chiang Kai-shek, president of China, then allied with the United States. Stilwell was also Supremo of the [American] China-Burma-India theater (CBI), and Deputy Supreme Allied Commander, South East Asia to Admiral Lord Louis Mountbatten.

The war in the China-Burma-India theater was complicated by the fact that Britain was fighting to recover Burma, a commonwealth of her Empire, from the Japanese. Americans wanted Burma for roads to China, to facilitate helping Chiang to beat the Japanese by sending weapons and supplies (flown over the Himalayas, "the Hump"), to train his troops, and later to prepare them for a postwar battle against Mao Tse-tung's (Mao Zedong's) Chinese Communists.[1]

"Vinegar Joe" Stilwell had many eighteenth-century American attitudes. He believed generals should wear the same uniforms as men, live under the same conditions, and eat the same food. He was often found standing with his men in "chow lines," and declined most privileges of rank. He seldom wore the three stars of his grade or decorations. He vocally disliked "limies" (the British), especially aristocrats, except, curiously, Lord Mountbatten, 20 years his junior, whom he decided was "a good egg."[2] He despised Chiang Kai-shek because he was devious. The Chinese Generalissimo repeatedly undercut Stilwell's authority by giving orders directly to his generals.[3]

Despite his eccentricities, Stilwell was a leader of men. He went out of his way to walk every step with the infantry—Chinese or American—and saw to his men's needs. He shunned even the simplest comforts for himself; General Slim (who liked the cynical old man) thought he carried austerity to extremes.

Slim and Stilwell collaborated in a drive that ended with the capture of Myitkyina in August 1944—the only Burma campaign that included American ground troops. There, Stilwell proved that to win, he could be as cruel as necessary. He utterly destroyed "Merrill's Marauders" (under Brigadier General Frank Merrill) by withdrawing them, then sending them—many staggering with dysentery or malaria or wounded—back into battle to clinch the victory; Merrill suffered two heart attacks.[4] Orde Wingate's Chindits (British, Gurkha, Burmese, and African) fared better, but Wingate was killed in a plane crash, after which they were never the same.

Nevertheless Myitkyina was a significant victory. Stilwell was promoted to general, but in November 1944, was recalled by President Roosevelt (at the request of Chiang Kai-shek).[5]

In 1945, Stilwell was commander of U.S. Ground Forces, but in June, General Simon Buckner was mortally wounded on Okinawa, and Stilwell took over his Tenth Army. He completed the victory, and prepared to lead the army in the invasion of Japan, which never occurred. Stilwell died in 1946, trying to walk off an incurable cancer.

"Vinegar Joe" was a man of few words. What follows is essentially all he had to say of leadership in the letters, diaries, and other items that make up *The Stilwell Papers* (1948).[6]

Attributes of the Good Commander

[*Diary—May 1944.*] A good commander is a man of high character (this is the most important attribute), with power of decision next most important attribute. He must have moral backbone, and this stems from high character; and he must be physically courageous, or successfully conceal the fact that he is not.

He must know tools of his trade, tactics and logistics. He must be impartial. He must be *calm under stress*. He must reward promptly and punish justly.

He must be accessible, human, humble, patient, forbearing. He should listen to advice, make his own decision, and carry it out with energy.

Unless a commander is human, he cannot understand the reactions of his men. If he is human, the pressure on him intensifies tremendously. The callous man has no mental struggle over jeopardizing the lives of 10,000 men; the human commander cannot avoid this struggle. It is constant and wearing, and yet necessary, for the men can sense the commander's difficulty. There are many ways in which he can show his interest in them and they respond, once they believe it is real. Then you get mutual confidence, the basis of real discipline.

Generals get sharply criticized. They are [said to be] birds who shelter themselves in dugouts and send the soldiers out to get killed. They cover themselves with medals, won at the expense of the lives of their men, who are thrown in regardless, to compensate for faulty or poorly thought-out plans.

There are really not many [generals] like that. The average general envies the buck private; when things go wrong, the private can blame the general, but the general can blame only himself. The private carries the woes of one man; the general carries the woes of all. He is conscious always of the responsibility on his shoulders, of the relatives of the men entrusted to him, and of their feelings. He must act so that he can face those fathers and mothers without shame or remorse. How can he do this? By constant care, by meticulous thought and preparation, by worry, by insistence on high standards in everything, by reward and punishment, by impartiality, by an example of calm and confidence. It all adds up to character.

Q: If a man has enough character to be a good commander, does he ever doubt himself? He should not. In my case, I doubt myself. Therefore, I am in all probability not a good commander.[7]

Problems of Generalship

[*Diary, August 1944.*] Principal load is standing disappointment and upsetting of plans. Everything conspires against him—dumb execution, weather, breakdowns, understandings, deliberate obstruction, jealousies, etc. Must be prepared to accept fifty per cent results in twice the calculated. One small block delays the entire move—not just the unit affected. Tendency of Chinese commanders to change the plan if easier for them. Constant check. Constant prodding. Constant smoothing. As Foch said, "To accomplish even a little on the battlefield, much effort is needed." All he can hope is to keep going.

Success and Accident

A brilliant success is an accident, because accidents are certain to occur; it is only a happy one, that fits into a mistake, in time or place or disposition by the enemy, that brings a result quickly. A dumb mistake by the enemy may put a unit in an unexpected place and wreck a perfect plan. War is a gamble. All we can do is try and keep a small percentage on our side.[8]

Conclusion

"Vinegar Joe" Stilwell could be called the last of the American pioneer-generals. Although he was a well-travelled, educated, professional soldier, his attitudes were more like those of Andrew Jackson and Davy Crockett than of his contemporaries. Not only was he "not afraid to get his hands dirty"; he went out of his way to do so. He was a true democrat, as well as a leader of men, and deserves to be better remembered than he is.

XIV

Matthew Bunker Ridgway

(1895–1993)

GENERAL MATTHEW RIDGWAY's writings deserve to be quoted here, although for most of his military career, he showed little sign of originality or greatness. He was a solid regular officer—seldom if ever questioning his orders, taking on any assignment, maintaining a positive attitude, and avoiding politics. He did not volunteer for, but was *assigned* to the airborne. Nevertheless, he made history at the head of the 82nd Airborne Division in World War II, and later the XVIII Airborne Corps. In Korea, he took over Eighth Army at a time when General Douglas MacArthur gave it little chance of success, and led it to victory—insofar as his political superiors would allow. He knew something of leadership.

Ridgway was born at Fort Monroe, Virginia, in 1895, the son of a West Point–educated, regular artillery colonel. His early life was spent on army posts in the United States and abroad. In due course, Matt went to the United States Military Academy (West Point), graduating in 1917. He spent World War I on the Mexican border, but was a captain in 1918, all the same, although he was not promoted to major until 1932.

When the U.S. Army began preparing for World War II, he was assigned (1939–42) to the War Plans division of the War Department, and rose to colonel. In 1942 he was made assistant commander, under Major General Omar Bradley, of the 82nd "All American" division of World War I. It had become a "paper" division, but they resurrected it, and for its first review, brought in its greatest hero, Sergeant Alvin York, "who, single-handedly, had destroyed a German battalion."[1]

In June 1942, Ridgway was given command of the 82nd, then ordered to convert it into an airborne division. He made his first parachute jump at Fort Benning, Georgia, with more than usual apprehension; he had a spinal injury from a fall during horsemanship classes at West Point, which he had kept secret. Ridgway came down hard and got some bruises, but was exultant that it was nothing worse.[2]

Nevertheless, he trained the 82nd, jumped with it into Sicily in 1943, and led elements of the division at Salerno. He was then called to England, and jumped with the 82nd in the dark early hours before the D-Day landings (6 June 1944).

Ridgway was made commander of the XVIII Airborne Corps—the 82nd and the 101st divisions.[3] In General Montgomery's attempt to skip over the Rhine (September 1944), the 82nd and 101st had 3,542 casualties, but accomplished their missions; the equally elite British airborne, landed seven miles from the Arnhem "bridge too far," was destroyed.[4]

When the Germans launched their offensive through the Ardennes at Christmas, 1944, Ridgway was in England, but flew back. Meanwhile James Gavin, commanding the 82nd, had rushed it and the 101st "Screaming Eagles" to the front. They were key to blocking the Germans until George Patton's armor swept into Bastogne from the south. After the war, Ridgway rose to be deputy chief of staff of the U.S. Army.

In 1950 the Korean War broke out, and on the death of General Walton Walker in December, Ridgway was called to take over the U.S. Eighth Army in Korea (EUSAK), comprising all U.S. and Allied troops.[5] General Douglas MacArthur, Far East commander, had told the Joint Chiefs of Staff that he would lose Korea if not heavily reinforced. They had denied him more troops and authorized him to withdraw if necessary. When Ridgway reported in, MacArthur told him dolefully, "The Eighth Army is yours, Matt. Do what you think best."[6]

In the first days of Ridgway's command Chinese and North Korean troops recaptured Seoul (4 January 1951). But Ridgway was soon making plans for an offensive. In a light plane flown by the 5th Air Force commander, General Earle "Pat" Partridge, he spent days viewing the lines from above. Intelligence (G-2) in Tokyo told Ridgway that his Eighth Army was opposed by 174,000 Chinese troops and as many North Koreans. (The actual number of Chinese exceeded 300,000; the NKPA 130,000). *At any rate, he could not find them.* "Hardly a moving creature did we spot, not a campfire smoke, no wheel tracks, not even trampled snow to indicate the presence of a large number of troops."[7] He had 130,000 U.S. and 100,000 (unpredictable) South Korean troops, about 10,000 from other UN nations—and the advantage of complete control of the air.[8]

Between flights Ridgway visited his troops, telling them they could win, and *must* or shame their fathers. His reputation as an airborne commander preceded him; he appeared wearing live grenades taped to his pack harness and looked tough enough to survive if they went off. They were not for show; he meant to use them if ambushed.[9] Ridgway had presence. General Walter F. Winton, his senior aide, said later: "The force that emanated from him was awesome. . . . You had the impression he could knock over a building with a single blow, or stare a hole through a wall, if he wanted to."[10] He fired up the troops.

On 24 January 1951, Ridgway began a series of offensives, and the Eighth Army steadily advanced. However, what began like a "stroll in the park" met a full-scale Chinese counteroffensive in February. But at Chipyong-ni (13–15 February) three Chinese divisions were stopped by the 23rd Regimental Combat Team (2nd Division), reinforced by the French Volunteer Battalion, and the 1st

Ranger Company (Airborne).[11] Ridgway had "turned EUSAK around."[12] Afterward, the Chinese were able to mount only limited offensives, and soon proved amenable to peace talks, if with intermittent resumption of hostilities.

In April 1951, MacArthur was dismissed by President Truman for acts "close to insubordination."[13] (His sin was determination to win total victory—as in World War II—expressed in letters he knew would be published—in defiance of the orders of his Constitutional commander-in-chief.) Ridgway was named Far East commander. He began peace negotiations with the Chinese in June 1951, but extended talks yielded only an armistice (1953).[14]

Ridgway, meanwhile, had moved to Europe as NATO commander (1952) and then to Washington as Army chief of staff (1953). In 1955, he retired over differences with the secretary of defense, Charles Wilson, who was reducing ground forces and planned to depend on a "Massive Retaliation Policy." Ridgway did very well in business, and lived quietly until his death in 1993 (at 98!).

————————

The short passage below is from *Soldier*, his memoirs.[15]

————————

On Leading Men in Battle

To my mind, the highest service a man can perform is to lead other men in battle. It requires of him courage and competence of the very highest order, and it develops in him a deep and abiding love for the men whose lives are entrusted to his hands—a love that creates in him a complete willingness to sacrifice his own life for them, if need be. To my way of thinking no great battle commander in all history ever reached the heights he might have reached, if he did not feel this love for his men, and a profound respect for them, and for the jobs they had to do.

Regard for Troops above Ambition

In my opinion the commander who in the confusion and the excitement of battle forgets that he is dealing with men's lives, and who through callousness or stupidity sacrifices them needlessly, is more butcher than battle leader. I remember a bitter joke that went the rounds of the Army soon after World War I. . . . At a staff meeting before a big attack some fireeating division commander tapped at a little dot on the map with his riding crop and said: "I'd give ten thousand men to take that hill." There was a moment of silence, and then from the back of the room, where stood the battalion commanders whose men would have to go against the hill, there came an ironic voice: "Generous son-of-a-bitch, isn't he?" I've never admired such generosity, and I shall go to my grave humbly proud of the fact that on at least four occasions I have stood up at the risk of my career and denounced what I considered to be ill-considered tactical schemes which I was convinced would result in useless slaughter. The airborne divisions were particularly vulnerable to . . . noble experiments, for once the airborne had been seen in action in Sicily, every higher commander figured that here was the key to success in combat. They sought to prove to the world, I suppose, that they were bold thinkers, quick to seize upon and utilize a new and dramatic weapon, and some of the plans they dreamed up were fantastic. I knew the airborne's limitations. . . . I saved the 82nd, or large elements of it, from being dropped into situations where it would have been destroyed.

Boldness

I do not wish to convey the impression that I am an advocate of timidity on the battlefield, and I do not feel that I have that reputation among my brother officers. The timid commander, by prolonging combat . . . causes the death of as many men as does the reckless . . . commander. Neither is a true combat leader . . . the finest battle commander . . . can accomplish his mission the quickest, with the least cost in blood.[16]

Building Morale in the Reborn 82nd Division

I am convinced that Sergeant York's visit had a great deal to do with the early inculcation of that supreme confidence, that magnificent esprit, which later was to be the hallmark of the airborne. He created in the minds of farm boys and clerks, youngsters of every station and class, the conviction that an aggressive soldier, well trained and well armed, can fight his way out of any situation. The airborne trooper not only believed in himself, he believed in his comrades. And he was determined that, come what may, he was not going to show up as a man less bold and valiant than they.

Tough Training: For Generals, Too

The rigorous program of physical conditioning we put the men through also had a great deal to do with the development of their fighting spirit. . . . Though neither General Bradley nor myself had ever been in battle, we both knew that to survive the weariness, the long marches, the loss of sleep, the tremendous exertion that men in combat must undergo, each of them had to be as finely trained as a champion boxer. Many a battle has been lost merely because the fighting men have burned themselves out physically, have come up to the last attack too tired to fight. The early days of the Korean War, in which garrison troops, half comatose from sheer physical weariness, were slaughtered in their foxholes, provided many examples of that tragic exhaustion.

An extremely difficult obstacle course, made up of deep ditches, log barriers, high walls, and culverts, was one excellent device we used for hardening the men physically. It was . . . mine and General Bradley's idea that every officer in the division, no matter whether he had a staff job or a field command, should be required to go through the same toughening process as the men. That applied to us as well as to the others. I will never forget the great roar of laughter that went up when Brad and I demonstrated our own skill at traversing the course. The last obstacle was a fairly wide creek, which . . . served as the drainage ditch from the reservation's sewage plant. This was traversed by running full tilt to the bank, grabbing a knotted rope, and swinging across [like] Tarzan of the apes. General Bradley and I ran the course together, with me, as the younger man and his junior in rank, keeping about a half stride behind him. . . . We reached the last obstacle still going strong, but in mid-air General Bradley's hands slipped off the rope and he fell with a tremendous splash into that malodorous stream.

The sight of a two-star general in such a predicament seemed to be a source of vast delight to all ranks, and the incident became one of the memorable highlights of the training period.[17]

The Urge to Jump into the Fight

[*Korea, March 1951.*] Our plan was to drop [the 187th Airborne Regimental Combat Team] in about twenty miles, then to slam an armored column to them over the roads, hoping to catch a large number of Chinese in the jaws of this nutcracker. As an old paratrooper, I had a tremendous desire to jump in with that airborne unit. As an army commander I knew it would be a damn fool thing to do. I was fifty-six years old. My bones had grown more brittle and my joints had stiffened since I had jumped in Normandy. I could easily crack an ankle or a knee on landing, and I'd have to turn over command of Eighth Army. As much as the idea appealed to me, I could find no justification for it.

I was, however, resolved to be there at the moment of the jump, in a light plane that could land among them, so I could get a close-up look at the fight. [*He was there, and his pilot found a place to land.*]

Up-front Leadership

There was a great deal of sporadic shooting going on, here and there, as the assembling troops hunted the [North Koreans and Chinese] down. . . . And I remember feeling that lifting of the spirits, that quickening of the breath and the sudden sharpening of all the senses that comes to a man in the midst of battle.

It was good to be in action again, good to be down on the ground with a parachute assault element in a fight.[18]

Washington's Limited War Policy

The American flag never flew over a prouder, tougher, more spirited and more competent fighting force than was Eighth Army as it drove north beyond the Parallel.[19] It was a magnificent fighting [machine] supremely confident that it could take any objective assigned to it.

Military men, and statesmen, too, will long debate the wisdom of stopping that proud Army in its tracks at the first whisper that the Reds might be ready to sue for peace. To my mind it is fruitless to speculate on what might have been. If we had been ordered to fight our way to the Yalu, we could have done it—if our government had been willing to pay the price in dead and wounded that action would have cost. . . . [T]he effort, to my mind, would have not been worth the cost.[20]

Restoring the Morale of Eighth Army

[January 1951.] General MacArthur had given me full tactical control, which he never abridged, and all the authority a military commander could ask for. It was the sort of challenge—and opportunity—that I suppose every dedicated military man dreams may some day be his. Conscious as I was of the honor such an assignment carried with it, I could not allow my pride to blind me to the full weight of the responsibility.

The very first task I set myself was restoring the fighting spirit of the forces under my command. This meant, in addition to developing confidence in the commander's concern for the safety of every individual soldier, the recruitment of confidence in the soundness of the top commander's decisions.[21]

Responsibilities of Commanders

In combat, every unit commander is absorbed in the accomplishment of his own mission. Be he in command of a squad, a platoon, a company, or any unit all the way up to Corps, his assigned task requires all the professional competence, all the physical energy, and as much strength of spirit as he possesses. He has no time to concern himself with how the higher-ups are carrying out their assignments. And it is often natural that the commanders of the smaller units—from squad up through battalion—should feel that the higher commanders have a relatively simple task—that they just draw lines on a map with a broad black crayon, to mark out objectives, zones of action, boundaries, and phase lines; and that they issue their orders with no understanding of the difficulties provided by weather, terrain, problems of supply and communication, or strength of the opposing forces. The higher-ups, they may sometimes suspect, just press the buttons and leave the commanders of the smaller units to figure out how the impossible may be accomplished.

Planning

But in truth, the larger the command, the more time must go into planning; the longer it will take to move troops into position, to reconnoiter, to accumulate ammunition and other supplies, and to coordinate other participating elements on the ground and in the air. To a conscientious commander, time is the most vital factor in his planning. By proper foresight and correct preliminary action, he knows he can conserve the most precious element he controls, the lives of his men. So he thinks ahead as far as he can.

He keeps his tactical plan simple. He tries to eliminate as many variable factors as he is able. He has a firsthand look at as much of the ground as circumstances render accessible to him. He checks each task in the plan with the man to whom he intends to assign it. Then—having secured . . . his subordinate's wholehearted acceptance of the contemplated mission and agreement on its feasibility—only then does he issue an order.

The Necessity for Improvision

The flow of battle may sometimes change conditions or create new tasks no amount of advance planning could have allowed for. Then the success or failure . . . may well depend on the resourcefulness, the training, the alertness, the decisiveness of the leaders of even the smallest units. The ability to make prompt decisions and to execute them vigorously is best bred in men who, through confidence in their troops and in their superiors, have persuaded themselves that they are unbeatable. Unrelenting attention to detail, concern for the well-being of every member of every unit, painstaking checking out of each assignment with the men charged with performing it—all these help instill that self-confidence, that sense of belonging to a tightly organized and well-led organization, the feeling that can give momentum to a whole force and make it truly unconquerable.[22]

Conclusions

Ridgway was a man of action, not words—although he tried hard to be both. He was a superior field commander, but his writings do not convey the full force of his leadership, which was *personal and up-front*. It is best reflected in the enthusiasm he expressed after joining the paratroopers of the 187th Regimental Combat Team in battle.

All the same, the basics of good leadership are in the short passages given above. He uses his staff, but *he* is in *sole command*, and takes responsibility for success or failure. He believes in *discipline*, tough *training*, and instilling a sense of *camaraderie* and *pride* in his men for their unit and what they are doing. He *takes care of his men*, tries to spare lives, and is attentive to what affects their *morale*. He prefers the *offensive* to the defensive. Launching the Eighth Army on a march northward, despite reports of greater enemy numbers, demonstrates a belief that a smaller force, well led, can triumph over a larger one. (Although in all things, Ridgway is *bold* but judicious). He does his own *reconnaissance*, favors *simple* plans, yet is cognizant that *improvision* still will be necessary at all levels, because plans never work out perfectly. Thus he picks his *commanders at all levels* for ability, stamina, toughness, and the ability to think under pressure. He shows himself *at the front frequently*, partly to raise morale, partly to *follow up* on his orders. His whole demeanor marks him as a fighter leading fighters.

Ridgway undoubtedly would have preferred to *win* in Korea—and thought the Eighth Army could—as did most of his men—but like a good soldier, he bowed to the logic of his Commander in Chief.

XV

Moshe Dayan

(1915–1981)

"MOSHE DAYAN was born to the battlefield," says his biographer, Robert Slater; "He found war exciting, he could not get enough of it."[1] This rings true. After "starring" in the Israeli war of independence (1948–49) and presiding over two more Arab-Israeli wars in 1956 and 1967, he went to see the war in Vietnam as a newspaper correspondent, and slogged into the battle areas with American GIs. As defense minister in 1973, he was surprised by the Yom Kippur War, but the army he had built won it handily.[2] Not only was he a fine soldier, he was remarkably literate, and thus his autobiography is full of lessons (*by example*) in the art of leadership.

Dayan was born in 1915 of Russian-Jewish settlers at Deganiah, on the first kibbutz (collective farm) in Palestine. While Britain ruled Palestine (1919–48), he joined the Haganah (covert Jewish army), formed for *defense* against Arab attacks. During the Arab revolt of 1936, Orde Wingate trained Haganah in *offense*—guerrilla warfare.[3] This Scots-Presbyterian British officer believed that Zionism was a fulfillment of biblical prophecies; he is considered one of the founders of the Israeli Army. Dayan said Wingate taught him both tactics and a "code of life."[4]

When the Second World War began (1939), the Haganah was outlawed, and Dayan was imprisoned at Acre (Akko), but then released to serve in the British Army. Fighting against the Vichy French in Syria, he lost his left eye (and it was a miracle he was not killed) when a sniper scored a direct hit on his binoculars. He left hospital wearing the eye-patch that became his trademark.

In 1948, Britain ended her rule over Palestine and the UN proved unable to partition Palestine between Jews and Arabs. The Jews founded the state of Israel, setting its borders by war; the Haganah was the core of the new Israeli army. In 1948 Dayan formed the 89th Commando Battalion, which won battles and made him famous. In 1949 he was military governor of Jerusalem, of which he took as much as his forces allowed, but participated in negotiations to divide the city, which brought peace with Jordan.

In 1953 he attended the British staff college at Camberly. On his return, he was appointed chief of staff of the Israeli army. Bucking military tradition, he was perpetually with the troops; he made reprisal for Arab terrorist attacks a policy; and he procured new French tanks to augment the British and American World War II models in service. He constantly repeated his major rule to the troops: *"Break through and move, fire and move."*[5]

Meanwhile Egypt, under Abdul Gamal Nasser, had become Israel's most aggressive enemy. It was supplied by the USSR with its latest tanks, the heavy ones with 100mm guns (the Israelis had '75's), and other weapons. In 1956, Nasser nationalized the Suez Canal (owned by an international corporation, dominated by the British and French). He forbade Israeli commerce through the canal, and blockaded the Gulf of Aqaba, Israel's opening to the Red Sea. The UN proved unable to settle the matter. The French and British, who were preparing to invade the canal zone, agreed to a preemptive strike by the Israelis on Egypt.

Beginning on 29 October 1956, Dayan launched blitzkriegs through Gaza, the Sinai, and toward Aqaba. Moving and firing, the Israelis soon had the half-trained Egyptians abandoning their massive tanks and running off across the desert. The passes of the Sinai were taken with paratroops followed by tanks and infantry; finally Sharm el-Sheikh, overlooking Aqaba Bay, was taken on 5 November. Meanwhile the French and British took the Suez Canal Zone with paratroops and amphibious landings of armor and infantry, supported by the RAF. Under pressure (mainly from the United States), the British and French soon withdrew, and the Israelis relinquished their conquests, but retained access to Aqaba. Dayan resigned from the army and went into politics, while Egypt got stronger (courtesy of the USSR).

In 1967 Dayan was made defense minister, and in response to attacks from Egypt, Syria, and Jordan, launched the Six-Day War. This time the Israelis took the entire Sinai peninsula to the Suez Canal, the Golan Heights overlooking Syria, and—most prized by the Jews—all of Jerusalem.

Unfortunately for his military reputation, Dayan was still defense minister when Egypt, then under Anwar Sadat, launched the "Yom Kippur War" in October 1973. The attack came as a total surprise, and the Israelis, in the first days, sustained heavy casualties—for which Dayan was blamed. His intelligence service had failed him (but the American CIA knew no better).[6] Dayan nonetheless came alive and actively "advised" his troops on the fronts, taking risks unusual for a minister. The war had begun on 6 October; by 18 October the Syrians had been driven back and had all their forces guarding Damascus, the Jordanian air force was crippled, and Jerusalem was safe. And in Egypt, Sadat had not only lost, but a massive Israeli armored force was on *his* side of the canal, threatening Cairo.

Dayan resigned as defense minister in 1974, but was soon back in politics. As foreign minister during 1977–79, he helped push through the Camp David agreements, sponsored by President Jimmy Carter, which brought peace between Egypt and Israel. Unable to agree with his prime minister over how to deal with the Palestinians, he then left the government. He died in 1981.

————————

Moshe Dayan was not one to spout theory. What appears below are notes from his *Story of My Life* (1976) on what he *did* as a commander (battalion to army) and chief of staff of the Israeli army. They speak louder than any enumeration of principles of leadership.

————————

1948: Forming the 89th Commando Battalion

When I got back from the Jordan Valley [*where he had defeated a Syrian force*], I set about raising the "mechanized assault battalion," . . . which Yitzhak Sadeh asked me to form before I had left for Deganiah. It was given the number 89 and was to be a unit of Sadeh's armored brigade. This brigade, however . . . never fought as a single formation, and the 89th Battalion, when I was its commander, always operated independently.

Daring and Unorthodoxy

I was happy with this appointment. It was exactly what I wanted. Yitzhak explained that the battalion was to serve as a special commando unit, rather like such British assault units as the Long Range Desert Patrols . . . in World War Two. Ours, of course, would be smaller in scale, without either their resources or the distances they had to cover, but with the same spirit of daring and unorthodoxy. At first I was told that the battalion would be mounted entirely on jeeps and would be lightly equipped, without support weapons and without armor. Its function would be to penetrate deep into enemy territory and operate behind the lines. Later it was decided to include a support company and give the battalion half-tracks as its principal vehicle.

Men Make the Unit

I confess that though table of organization and weaponry were important and would determine the unit's fighting capacity, I concerned myself little with these matters. I left them to my deputy, Yohanan Peitz, an experienced combat officer who had served in the Jewish Brigade of the British army in the world war and who was more of an "organization man". . . . I concentrated on the selection and recruitment of the men.

Morale and Fighting Spirit

Vehicles, weapons, and men reached the base in dribs and drabs. But the most important element was present in full measure—confidence and fighting spirit, the will to get into action and strike at the enemy. This was the very quality I was looking for, and I did everything to encourage it. I truly believed that we could emerge victorious from every battle. There was always some fold in the ground along which we could advance, some rock which afforded cover, and a surprise and judicious military tactic which could give us the advantage over the enemy.[7]

An American Veteran's Advice: Speed and Mobility

[*Dayan talked in New York with Abraham Baum, who had fought in Europe in World War II in the U.S. 4th Armored Division under Colonel (later General) Creighton Abrams (in Patton's Third Army) and led small task forces behind enemy lines.*]

As the legal army of the . . . State of Israel, we had to wield larger formations. I was glad to hear from Baum's combat experience as part of a large army that there was still room for, and indeed great value in, a commando unit like the one I had just organized.

Baum's words well fitted my own ideas. . . . He preached the supreme importance of speed and mobility in battle. According to him, it was best not to undertake preliminary reconnaissance patrols to the projected target of attack, for the information thus received was usually meager, and by tipping off the enemy, the element of surprise was lost. It was best to go straight to the assault positions, with the reconnaissance unit moving ahead, observing, sensing, feeling out the situation, reporting back, and guiding the main force. Baum's experience was born of a different kind of war, but several of his points seemed to me to be applicable to us, too. One was the need to maintain continuous movement. Another was to have the commander direct the action from the front line so that he could see what was happening with his own eyes, rather than rely on second-hand reports.[8]

Personal Reconnaissance, Daring, and Improvision

[*Dayan takes his 89th into battle (He had just returned from New York).*] At Deir Tarif I found Akiva Sa'ar with his half-track company. He had arrived the previous evening to give support to Uri, and now his men were dug in and holding the western and northern slopes of the hill, while the Arab Legion dominated the eastern slope. Akiva tried to dissuade me from going to the top of the hill to survey the situation, since it was under continuous artillery fire and Jordanian snipers were fast on the trigger when they glimpsed a raised head. I ordered my driver to race to the hilltop and park his jeep behind a pile of boulders which I had spotted. The jeep made a wild zigzag dash up the slope, and between the twists and turns I noticed that Akiva was right behind me, as I had expected.

I looked down and saw several of our disabled vehicles stuck on the side of the hill. But I also saw an abandoned Jordanian armored car lying on its side, with its nearside wheels in a ditch. I could hardly believe so beautiful a sight—a real armored car, with thick plating, apparently serviceable, and equipped with a 2-pounder gun! All we had to do was pull it out, get it over to our lines, and use it. True, the Jordanians were shelling and sniping at anyone attempting to get near the armored car, but with ingenuity, a bit of luck, and a tow cable, it could be done.

In the meantime the rest of the battalion had arrived, refueled, and restocked with ammunition. I began to feel slightly uneasy. What were we waiting for? Why weren't we in action? And what was the next target?[9]

Improvision: Acquiring an Armored Car

I jumped onto a half-track and called out to one of the mechanics, asking whether be was prepared to risk it and join me in salvaging the car. "Sure," he said, "with you there's no risk." I had long had my eye on this boy. He was a lean, courteous, baby-faced youth from a farm settlement of the Sharon Plain. For wild driving there was no one like him, and in no time we reached the armored car, hitched it to our vehicle, jerked it out of the ditch and onto its wheels, and towed it back to the bottom of the hill.

The signalmen set to work repairing its radio and the mechanics its engine and, with special reverence, its gun. But we needed training to operate it, so [we sent] to a nearby artillery unit for an instructor. He promptly put some of our men through the fastest gunnery course ever, and within an hour I was informed that the armored car was ready for action. We selected a crew and they dubbed their vehicle "The Terrible Tiger," just the sort of name a Galilean farmer from Yavniel would choose. Dein Tarif grew less noisy. Enemy fire abated. The battalion seemed suddenly less fatigued. All thoughts were on the next move—to Lod.

The Terrible Tiger

I went to inspect the "Tiger." The radio set had been replaced, and the engine was in order. One of the wheels was a bit flat, but there was no spare wheel, and it could not be changed. In the turret stood the new gunner, a private from the jeep company. I told him to . . . fire at a tree 500 yards away. He did so—and whipped off its main branch.

Blond Dov Granek and his company were left behind as a holding and harassing unit, while the rest of the battalion got ready for the Lod action. We set off at 2 P.M. The vehicles were not in ideal shape, but the men were. Heading the column was the armored car. Someone had chalked an arrow on its gun barrel and the words "Straight to the point." Just looking at it gladdened everyone's heart. Following the "Tiger" was a reconnaissance detachment of jeeps, and after them came the half-tracks. Another jeep detachment brought up the rear.[10]

Boldness on Offense

[*Attack on Lod.*] I assembled the unit commanders and issued my orders: The "Tiger" would lead, followed by the first half-track company, then the second half-track company, and finally the unprotected jeeps. I would be with the first half-tracks. If the "Tiger" or any of the half-tracks were hit, or stopped *en route* for any other reason, the rest of the force was to break column, spread, find some way of getting round the halted vehicles, and continue to advance. Once we got past the enemy outposts and entered the city, the battalion was to split up, keep firing left and right, sow panic, and thereby perhaps bring about the enemy's surrender.

Violence, Speed, and Maximum Firepower

I told the officers that I attached the highest importance to the method of attack. If the battalion in column formation was stopped head-on, in effect, the only active elements coming up against the enemy were the first vehicles. The rest were not only passive but they also represented a static, compact target to the enemy. Therefore, if that happened, they were to deploy promptly to the flanks and storm the enemy positions from all sides. We would thus be exploiting our fire power to the full. . . . We had to bear down on our adversary, "run him over," crush him in spirit and body. There were no questions.

The battalion moved. The track was not mined. . . . Movement was slow, for the track was narrow, cut by frequent shallow ditches, and strewn with light banners. The jeeps . . . fired [machine guns] almost without a stop, cutting the thick cactus hedges as with a scythe. We soon picked up speed, crossed the line of enemy posts, and entered Lod. From the police station came heavy fire. The "Tiger" responded on the move, and the rest of the battalion followed.[11]
[*Units of the battalion got separated, but cleared the town of Arab defenders.*]

Personal Leadership

The radio network was again in operation, and I was surprised to hear the voice of Dov Granek, whom we had left behind with his unit at Dein Tarif. He said that the Legion troops had attacked and recaptured the salient. . . . I told him that if he could not hold his position, he should fall back on Tira, and we would deal with Dein Tarif the next day. . . . With a certain hesitancy, he asked: "Perhaps I could organize the rest of my men and try and retake it myself now?" And then I understood that he was not asking for an order but for encouragement. I shouted into the microphone, "Commandos or not commandos?" He did not get it at first. "What? What?" he asked. I repeated: "Are we a commando battalion or not?" This time he caught on, and shouted back: "Commandos. Commandos. We attack." "Take the salient from the east," I told him. "Right," he said.

Care of the Troops

While we had been moving, an undamaged half-track had driven up to mine, and the platoon commander, Charlie, asked permission to return and check whether one of his wounded men had not been left behind near the police station after all. I was inclined to refuse, but the eyes of the other men . . . were fixed on mine. It was as though each imagined himself lying wounded in a ditch and abandoned by his comrades. "Very well," I told him, "but don't get into any trouble." The detachment did not waste a moment. The vehicle screeched a U-turn and raced back into Lod.[12]

Ben-Gurion's Opinion of Dayan and Vice Versa

[*The defense minister called in Dayan and asked if he could break into the Negev, i.e., take on the Egyptians. Dayan said yes, but asked for and was given more vehicles, guns, and ammunition. Before he left, David Ben-Gurion, the Israeli prime minister, asked to see him.*] He [also] . . . asked me about the Lod operation, but [during] my account I noticed that he did not share my enthusiasm. To his mind, this was not "war" but a "prank." He did not agree with my implied thesis that the way to get past the first line of enemy positions was through the fast and daring dash. To him, an attack should be planned and carried out methodically and steadily, like the movement of a steamroller. We ended our brief exchange with his regarding me as a bold enough commander but somewhat of a partisan, and my regarding him as a wise and inspiring political leader who had learned . . . much of the Arabs and of war, but who had no close, personal, first-hand knowledge of either. He knew *about* them, but he did not know them.

More Daring and Improvision

[*The 89th, re-equipped with half tracks, scout cars, and jeeps, and with captured ammunition for the "Tiger," broke through into the Negev, where it fought the Egyptians.*]

H-hour was 10 P.M. In the afternoon I assembled the battalion for a briefing. It turned out, in fact, to be a lesson-learning post-mortem of our Lod action, for we had had no time to hold this discussion earlier. The general lines of our operational plans were to break into the Faluja airstrip, held by Egyptian forces, by driving through and firing on the move; to cross the main Majdal-Faluja road and go on until we reached a Wadi south of the Karatiya mound; to cross the wadi and capture the mound on our vehicles. A road in the top of the mound was marked on the map as negotiable by vehicles. I gave orders that if it were to prove impassable, we were to capture the mound on foot. I emphasized that the most dangerous stretch would be crossing the Egyptiam lines, namely, the airstrip and the road. This stretch had to be traversed at maximum possible speed, with constant fire at the flanks, and, for the men in the armored cars, with heads down.

[*They swept through the airfield, but got stuck in the wadi. The situation was dangerous; they were before their objective, Karatiya.*]

Calmness under Stress

I felt drained. In my briefing I had categorically insisted that "no man is to stop for anyone—except by order—and no time is to be spent tending the wounded until we reach the wadi. If a vehicle cannot move it is to be abandoned. Until we get to the wadi there is only one rule: break through and move, fire and move." Well, here we were in the wadi, and, of course, stuck.

I ordered the men to start digging into the bank of the wadi so as to hack out a path of shallower gradient which would offer the vehicles an exit. It seemed a herculean task—and it had to be done under mortar and machine gun harassment. There was no alternative.

Near the digging site stood a platoon commander, Amos Abramson from Yavniel in Galilee, who had come on the Operation straight from an Officers' Training Course. He was fresher, more sprightly than the others, and he showed no sign of anxiety or dejection. His whiskers curled at just the right angle. He was the man for me. I told him to take matters in hand— to see to it that the diggers dug, the guards guarded, and the rest of the men kept quiet. I then took myself back to the opposite side of the wadi, lay down, wrapped my head in my Arab *kefieh,* and went to sleep.

[*Dayan had picked the right man. When he awoke, after an hour, the path out was ready.*]

Organized Speed and Violence

The battalion came to life when I notified the commanders: "At 04:00 we advance on Karatiya with whichever vehicles manage to get out by then."

The reconnaissance unit led off, followed by the "Tiger," the jeeps, and five half-tracks. In addition to their normal complements, they now carried the men, weapons, and ammunition of the vehicles left behind. Following the column was the Givati infantry company, which . . . had caught up with us in the wadi, as previously arranged.

The "Tiger" advanced toward the mound and shelled the summit. The jeeps moved off to the flanks, and the half-tracks entered the village, taking it without casualty.

The Givati infantrymen now followed. They were to hold this village and enemy base, and they began clearing Egyptian emplacements, neutralizing possible points of opposition, and securing their own defenses.

It was 6 A.M. on July 18 when we left Karatiya and returned to base via Hatta without further incident. I did not know it then, but this was to be my last day with the 89th Commando Battalion.

Building Morale

A few hours later I drove to the hospital to visit the men who had been wounded in the action. Among them were Arik Nehemkin and Micha Ben-Barak, who had suffered eye wounds. I found the two of them in the same ward, lying in adjoining beds, eyes bandaged, pain and misery in their faces. I recalled my own feelings when I had lost an eye. . . . "Boys," I said to them, "for all that's worth seeing in this wretched world, one eye is enough."[13]

Jerusalem: Benefits of Personal Leadership

Five days after the breakthrough in the Negev, on July 23, 1948, I was appointed commander of Jerusalem. A delegation from the 89th, headed by Dov Granek of the Stern Group or Lehi, tried in prevent my posting from the battalion, but without success. The delegation met with Prime Minister Ben-Gurion, explained to him the importance of my remaining with the commando unit, and even threatened to follow me to Jerusalem with the entire battalion. Ben-Gurion heard them out and then asked them how it was that I had gained the trust of dissidents like the men of the Stern Group [earlier anti-British terrorists] Dov said it was because I had always personally led the battalion in battle and had been absolutely straight with the men. At the end of the meeting, Ben-Gurion told them that Jerusalem needed a good fighting commander, and Jerusalem took priority over every other place.[14]

[*However, it was agreed between the Israelis and Jordanians to divide the city and establish a demilitarized zone between their forces. Until the war ended on 7 January 1949, Dayan saw little action.*]

Readiness

[*On 7 December 1952, Dayan was named head of the operations branch of the General Staff. His first job was to prepare the army to deal with terrorist groups striking from Arab villages just across the borders.*]

It was the fighting man I was concerned with, for he was the cutting edge of the army's tool, and a soldier in the army of Israel, under constant threat from its neighbors, had always to be ready for battle.

If we failed in minor border actions, as we had in the previous year, how would we stand up to the Arab armies on the battlefield? No amount of reorganization would alter the basic function of the Israel Defense Forces—to be fit for battle at all times.

It seemed to me that the recent failures were due to altered attitudes since the War of Independence in three spheres: the degree of the soldier's readiness to risk his life in fulfillment of his mission; the place and duties of the officer in battle; and the basic approach of the General Staff to casualty rates in a period of restricted hostilities.

"No Excuses"

It was not difficult to change the approach of the General Staff and I accordingly met with the Operations officers of all the commands. I told them that in the future, if any unit commander reported that he failed to carry out his mission because he could not overcome the enemy force, his explanation would not be accepted unless he had suffered 50 percent casualties. . . . As long as the unit had not lost its combat power, it had to go on attacking. What I left unsaid when I spoke to the officers was transmitted by the expression on my face. They were left in no doubt that if they failed to carry out their assignment, they would have to face a detailed debriefing; and if their explanations did not satisfy me, there would be little future for them in the army.

Special Operations Force 101

The factors that helped to bring about a practical change in combat standards during the year when Makleff was chief of staff and I was head of Operations were the channelling of the better-educated national service recruits to the fighting units and, above all, the establishment of a special unit known as Force 101. This was a volunteer unit which undertook special operations across the border. The commander was the daring and combatwise Maj. Ariel Sharon, whom I had admired and known well since he had been my Intelligence officer at Northern Command.

Again Building Morale

In January 1954 . . . Force 101 was merged with the paratroops, and Arik [Ariel Sharon] became commander of the Paratroop Battalion. For some time thereafter, this unit alone undertook all the reprisal actions against Arab terrorists and raids across the border. Later, there was a growing recognition that such assignments should also be given to other units. The paratroops ceased to be solely an army formation and became a concept and a symbol—the symbol of courageous combat—that other formations in the army tried to live up to. Through the paratroops, the army recovered its [self-] confidence, and it was now rare indeed that a unit commander returned from action having to explain the failure of his mission.[15]
[In December 1953, Dayan was made chief of staff.]

A Better Image for the Chief of Staff

Ben-Gurion pinned on my badges of rank and I received the standard of the chief of staff. . . .

At the end of the ceremony, the secretary of the Cabinet came over to me and casually observed that I would now have to change my partisan character. . . . I would have to "fashion a new Moshe Dayan," he said. I told him he was wide of the mark. It was not I who would change; the image of the chief of staff would change.

Austerity at the Top

I started the change of style in my own office. I abolished the post of aide-de-camp to the chief of staff and I took over his room as my office. I brought in the field table covered by a khaki blanket and a glass top which I had used when I was head of Operations. I turned the large, well-furnished room which had been the office of the chief of staff, with its massive table and upholstered chairs, into a conference room. I wanted the field commanders who came to see me to feel that they had come to the headquarters of a higher command which was not very different and not cut off from their own. When I inspected units in the field, I wore fatigues, sat on the ground with the troops, got dirty and dusty together with them.

Out with the Troops—Surprise and Results

I paid a lot of surprise visits at night, mostly driving alone. I wanted to check whether units were in a constant state of readiness; ensure that there was always a responsible senior officer in every command headquarters; and talk to the soldiers returning from a night exercise or from guard duty at an outpost. Whenever there was an operational problem, I would see the head of the Operations Branch, the unit commander, and his junior platoon commanders. I wanted to hear what had happened, if it was after an action, or what special problems were envisaged, if it was before an operation. I wanted to hear things from them at first hand, without intermediaries, and I wanted the young officers to hear what I had to say directly from me, in my own words and in my own style.

My immediate office staff, my secretary and the head of my bureau, thought I showed too little respect for the chain-of-command principle by my direct contact with lower-echelon units through unexpected visits without prior notification to the intervening commands. They were probably right, but I was unable and unwilling to behave differently. I understood, demanded, appreciated, and approved of ordered and systematic staff work—on condition that it did not erect a barrier between me and the troops.[16]

Teaching Personal Leadership

Since it was through the young officers that we could shape the kind of army we wanted, I would use the occasion of a graduation parade at an Officers'

Course whenever I had something special to say. I remember one such occasion at the end of May 1955. . . . A few days earlier, I had had the unpleasant duty of terminating the service of a young career officer who had ordered a soldier to proceed on a dangerous action while he himself sat in safety. A vehicle of ours was stuck close to the border of the Gaza Strip and was under heavy fire from the Egyptians. The officer . . . sent a driver to retrieve it, while he himself lay behind cover and issued directions from there. I told the cadets: "I would not have dismissed this officer if he bad decided that the danger was too great and it was better to abandon the vehicle rather than endanger lives. But if he decided to take daring action and save the vehicle, he should have advanced with his troops and laid his own life on the line together with theirs. Officers of the Israeli army do not send their men into battle. They lead them into battle."

Liberal Arts or Technical Training

Forging an army, however, requires more than talk, and officers require more than courage and moral leadership. They should also be well educated and of rounded intellect. Most of our officers at that time had fought in the War of Independence and stayed on, having had no opportunity before that war or since of attending the university. I thought that should be corrected, and we accordingly introduced a system of sending officers to the university at the army's expense. They could take a degree in any subject that interested them. . . . One officer who later became commander of the Armored Corps studied philosophy. . . . We also started sending officers in the technical services, such as ordnance and engineering, to the Haifa Technion (Institut of Technology) to study subjects related to their work.[17]

[*Israelis tended to relax, all the same, assuming peace would prevail now that independence was won. Dayan did not believe it. As noted above, he initiated a policy of retaliation against Israel's enemies, particularly Egypt, and strengthened the army. His efforts paid off in the victorious blitzkriegs of 1956, 1967, and the victory of 1973. Finishing his memoirs after the 1973 war, however, he made the rare gesture— for a senior commander—of conceding that the tactics he had pioneered earlier, and used so successfully, had now become obsolete.*]

Honesty, Open-mindedness, and Willingness to Change

When the war started, weak points were revealed in our armored strategy. . . . In several battles, our tanks used tactics based on the experience of the past. These tactics, which worked well in previous wars, favored the rapid dash of our armored forces, unaccompanied by the infantry and without artillery support, right into the heart of the enemy's positions, on the assumption that this would bring about his collapse. This time the assault units found themselves surrounded by enemy infantry equipped with large quantities of . . . anti-tank weapons . . . which were capable of . . . stopping and inflicting heavy casualties on our tank forces.

The fact was that the entire face of war had dramatically changed. Even those who had carefully followed the technical advances that had been made in weaponry in the last few years could not conceive the rate of destruction they commanded. The efficiency of the tanks of both sides in the Yom Kippur War was ten times greater than that of the armor in World War Two.[18]

Conclusions

Dayan had a commando's attitude toward war: "break through and move, fire and move." That tactic worked in the war of 1948–49. Before the 1956 war, he had learned more about logistics, and reequipped the Israeli Army as best he could. That and his old strategy and tactics of rapid movement—blitzkrieg—won the wars of 1956 and 1967.

As chief of staff, his performance was admirable. His headquarters was austere and thinly manned. He spent much time with the troops. His night visits to units, without prior notice, undoubtedly improved alertness of commanders at all levels, and their units' state of preparedness. As Minister of Defense, however, Dayan lost touch with the fighting machine he had created, and left command to his generals. Typically, he took responsibility for the early losses in the 1973 war all the same. But in concluding that his "strategy" of earlier wars was obsolete he went too far. "Fire and move" is still valid, even if armor needs infantry, artillery, and air support.

The Israeli Army still has the smallest ratio of staff men to combat troops of any in the world. Dayan set that laudable pattern.

XVI

Vo Nguyen Giap

(1911–   )

IT SEEMS OBLIGATORY to include something from the writings of Vo Nguyen Giap in this book. General Giap (with Ho Chi Minh, d. 1969) is credited with North Vietnam's victory over the French (1945–54), the founding of the Communist Peoples' Republic of Vietnam (PRVN), and the unification of Vietnam by conquering the Republic of (South) Viet Nam (RVN) (1954–75), supported by the United States. America's goal was to create a democratic RVN, but in the 1960s she had to send ever-greater numbers of U.S. troops to reinforce the Army of South Vietnam (ARVN). Between 1969 and 1973, however, the United States withdrew its troops (details below). Despite U.S. aid, the ARVN could not defend its country, and fell before the PRVN forces in 1975. Giap surely directed the war(s), although his writings make him seem more a Communist politician than a commander; however, he depended on the Party for recruitment, discipline, and insuring a supportive public.

Giap was born in An Xa village in Quangbinh Province, then in French Indochina, in 1911.[1] He attended French high school in Hué, but was jailed as a Communist revolutionary (1928–31). On release, he attended the University of Hanoi, and began teaching. In 1939, he fled into China, where he found senior countryman and revolutionary Ho Chi Minh; "Uncle Ho" sent him to Communist Party School at Yenan for political training, with the advice to learn about the military also.[2] He got informal military training from Mao Zedong's Communist soldiers, and perhaps interviewed Mao himself.

Giap never attended a military academy or staff college, but schooled himself in the "art of war." He revered Mao, but knew that many of his ideas came from Sun-tzu; he also considered Napoleon and Lawrence of Arabia his "tutors."[3] Ho Chi-Minh, Giap's idol, returned from China to Vietnam and organized the *Vietminh* guerrillas to fight the Japanese (who ousted the French, 1940–45); Giap joined him. In 1945, Ho and Giap organized a "national army" that attacked the returning French, but it was driven into the mountains.

However, with help from the USSR and China, the Peoples' Army of Vietnam (PAVN) became a formidable guerrilla force, and then an army, with artillery and armor. Under Giap's command, it ultimately defeated the French at Dien Bien Phu (1954). The People's Republic of Vietnam was founded, with Ho Chi-Minh as president, and Giap prepared to conquer South Vietnam. In the South, the Republic of Vietnam was established by men who professed devotion to western-style democracy, and got aid from the United States for their army (ARVN) and economy.

Despite Giap's aid the guerrillas in the south (the Vietcong) were driven underground. Regular PRVN troops entered the war in 1965; the United States sent American forces, and got deeply involved in the war by 1968, committing 500,000 troops and massive airpower. The PAVN took enormous casualties, to which they seemed indifferent.[4] (In the first battle, against 1st Battalion, 7th Cavalry, in the Ia Drang Valley, 1,800 to 2,000 PAVN were killed; 79 U.S. soldiers.)[5]

In truth, the morale of PAVN troops sagged, but Giap countered with "Marxist-Leninist" indoctrination, while publicizing (questionable) improvements at home, and constantly claiming victories.[6] Giap's "Tet Offensive" of 1968 (combining PRVN and Vietcong forces) *failed miserably*. But its size and intensity, together with the American media's reaction, persuaded the United States to withdraw, while preparing the ARVN to defend its own country. All American troops except Marine guards at the Saigon embassy were sent home by December 1973. In 1975, Giap's forces took Hanoi and unified Vietnam. Giap was moved into government, and held various ministerial posts. Now long retired, he is still influential.

———————

Most of the passages below are from Giap's *Military Art of People's War*, written before the war in South Vietnam was over.[7] Giap refers to the guerrillas in North and South Vietnam as the "National Liberation Force" (*Vietminh*), but in the South they were called Vietnamese Communists (*Vietcong*). A master propagandist, he virtually never admits defeat of any of his forces. At the end are a few quotations from interviews included in the biographies of Giap by Currey and MacDonald.[8]

———————

The Role of the Communist Party

The success of our Party's military line is *typical of the creative application, in our concrete conditions, of the universal principles of Marxism-Leninism on revolutionary war, on the building up of revolutionary armed forces, and of revolutionary bases, and so forth.* Its content reflects the character and the universal laws of revolutionary war in general and the character and the particular laws of revolutionary war in our country. Its content is particularly rich and creative in the combination of political struggle with military struggle, the combination of the entire people's political struggle with the entire people's uprising, with the people's war, in order to win the greatest victories for the revolutionary cause.

This military line *regards the leading role of our Party as most important*, as a sure guarantee of final victory. The reason is that our Party is the vanguard Party of the working class, the most intransigent representative of the interests of the class, the people, and the nation. Our Party is not only determined to carry out a most thorough revolutionary struggle, it is also imbued with the principles of Marxism-Leninism which is the most progressive science. Thus, it is capable of determining the most correct strategy and tactics to ensure victory.

On the one hand, our people's revolutionary struggle in the present period applies the precious experience of fraternal countries in revolutionary struggle; on the other hand, it continues and develops to a high degree our people's *traditions of indomitable struggle against foreign aggression* and the spirit of resolute and heroic struggle of our peasants' uprisings in the past. Marxism-Leninism never disowns the history and the great constituent virtues of a nation; on the contrary, it raises these virtues to new heights in the new historical conditions. During the many thousand years of their history, our people repeatedly rose up to struggle heroically against foreign aggression and reconquer national independence.[9]

The Nature of Revolutionary War

Our nationwide resistance war, which was a people's war, was a new development; it was a *true revolutionary war, a war by the entire people, a total war*. A revolutionary war, because it was carried out [by the] mobilization and organization of the masses, with the aim of achieving a national democratic revolution. A war by the entire people, because it was a war in which a whole nation struggled in unity, each citizen becoming a combatant, a war in which our Party's correct revolutionary line succeeded in grouping all patriotic strata of the population in a broad front based on a strong worker-peasant alliance, and mobilizing together for the struggle. A total war, because armed struggle was . . . combined with political struggle, because at the same time as we engaged in a military struggle, we carried out reduction of land rent, land reform, political struggle in urban centers and enemy-occupied areas, and struggle in the economic and cultural fields.

It should be stressed that during the resistance, we used *armed struggle as an essential form of struggle*, with the countryside as a base. The enemy we faced was the expeditionary corps of French colonialism. . . . It was only through armed struggle that it was possible . . . to decimate and annihilate the enemy, and win victory for the resistance.

Against the United States

In the South of our country, in the conditions of struggle against neocolonialism and the "special war" of United States imperialism, historical conditions present some aspects which are similar to those of the resistance against French colonialism, but others which are peculiar to the liberation war in South Vietnam.

Our people in the South enjoy a clear political superiority over the enemy; they also have traditions of and experience in political struggle and armed struggle and are animated with ardent patriotism and high revolutionary spirit; the enemy are strong materially and technically, but the social bases of the reactionary forces in the service of the United States imperialists being extremely weak, they are in a state of complete political isolation, and their political weakness is irremediable.

Because of our country's temporary partition, a phase has appeared of acute political struggle against the war unilaterally started by the enemy, developing afterward into political struggle combined with armed struggle. The war of liberation now being waged by our countrymen in the South is *a revolutionary war, a war by the entire people, a total war* using simultaneously the two forms of struggle, regarding *both as fundamental and decisive*. Armed struggle has developed on the basis of political struggle brought to a higher level; these two forms of struggle develop simultaneously in a vigorous manner and stimulate each other. Armed struggle which becomes more and more vigorous does not make political struggle decrease in intensity but, on the contrary, gives it a stronger impulse; together they pursue the aim of annihilating and dislocating enemy armed forces, striking vigorously where the enemy is basically weak, on the political ground. The people's war in the South applies at the same time the laws governing revolutionary armed struggle during our nationwide resistance and the laws governing this struggle during the August 1945 general uprising, which makes its content infinitely rich and creative.

The practice of revolutionary struggle in our country in new historical conditions has made an original contribution to Marxist-Leninist theory on revolutionary armed struggle, according to which revolutionary struggle is a dialectic combination of political struggle and armed struggle, sometimes taking the form of political struggle, sometimes the form of a long revolutionary war, sometimes the form of an entire people's uprising, and sometimes combining all the above forms. This is what we mean when we say that the people's uprising and the people's war in our country are new developments in the conception of revolutionary violence.

Marxist-Leninist Doctrine and War

The Marxist-Leninist doctrine holds that revolutionary struggle in general and armed struggle in particular must be the work of the masses who, once they are conscious of the political aims of the revolution, are ready to be organized and resolute in rising up to fight, so that they become capable of defeating the most wicked enemy. As Lenin said, "The masses who shed their blood on the battle-field are the factor which brings victory in a war."

In order to carry out a people's war, the entire people must be mobilized and armed. Our Party's fundamental concept in this matter is that of the *people's armed forces*. This concept is indicative of the revolutionary character, the popular and class character of the armed forces; it is indicative of the Party's absolute leadership of the armed forces.

Political before Military Organization

Because armed struggle is the continuation of political struggle, no powerful armed forces could be built without the people's mighty political strength. Looking back at our people's long and arduous revolutionary struggle, we can clearly see that the years of bitter political struggle after our Party was founded, to enlighten and organize the masses, to build the worker-peasant alliance, to create a People's United Front, to affirm the leading role of the Party, were the years of preparation of forces for the subsequent armed struggle. After our Party had decided to prepare for an armed uprising and later, to wage a long resis-tance war, it continued to attach much importance to propaganda, to mobiliza-tion work among the masses, to stimulating the patriotism of various strata of the people and their hatred of the enemy, organizing the people . . . the workers and peasants, into a strong basis for the great union of the entire people for the resistance. The political force of the masses, of the people, is the strongest possi-ble base on which to develop the armed forces. Furthermore, even in the cir-cumstances of revolutionary war, this political force continues its direct support for the front and participates in the struggle against the enemy, assuming a most important role in the war.

In the first days, when our Party decided to make preparations for an armed uprising, it relied only on the force of the politically conscious masses, having then not even the smallest armed force. In the first days, when our Party called on the entire people to rise up and take part in the resistance war for national salvation, the principal force opposing the aggressors was the united force of the entire people, while the people's armed forces were still weak in numbers, equipment, and experience. In recent years, our countrymen in the South at first also relied basically on their political force when they heroically rose up to fight against a wicked enemy. Their innumerable heroic deeds are further proof that the source of strength of the armed forces in a revolutionary war is the strength of the united struggle of the entire people; that once patriotism and revolutionary ideas have penetrated deep into the people, they become an in-vincible force.

Stages of Military Organization

The People's armed forces are born of the revolutionary people. The worker-peasant self-defense units in the days of the Vietminh [National Liberation Army] soviets, the small semiarmed and armed forces in the period preceding the general uprising, the National Salvation units, the Propaganda Groups for the Liberation of Vietnam, the Ba To guerrillas, the thousands of self-defense and self-defense fighting groups [sic] throughout the country, were built up on the basis of consolidating and developing the political organizations of the masses. During the resistance, the recruiting of cadres and combatants for main-force units and local units, militia and guerrilla groups relied chiefly on that inexhaustible source of supply: the revolutionary people, the best elements in the mass organizations led and educated by the Party. Today, when in the completely liberated North, we have powerful armed forces, we still keep very close relations with the organizations of the masses led by the Party. Born of the people, the people's armed forces can grow in strength only thanks to their unreserved support and by continuously learning from their revolutionary spirit and rich experience in revolutionary struggle. To consolidate and continuously develop blood relations with the people, our armed forces have not only to fight, but also to work and produce, remaining always close to the political movement of the masses.

The people's armed forces are the revolutionary armed forces of the laboring people, of the workers and peasants; they fight to defend the interests of the people, the class, and the nation. These armed forces must be placed under the leadership of the vanguard party if they are to have a revolutionary character and an increasingly high combative spirit. That the armed forces should have a revolutionary character, a class character, is the essential point in our Party's theory on the building of the armed forces. That is the reason why our Party attaches great importance to the role of political work, regarding it as vital to the armed forces. To make unceasing efforts to enhance the class consciousness and patriotism of cadres and combatants, to ensure the absolute loyalty of cadres and combatants to the Party, the people, the fatherland, and their readiness to sacrifice everything for the revolutionary cause—these tasks must be fulfilled to make the armed forces a reliable instrument of the Party and the people in the national democratic revolution and in the socialist revolution. Our People's Army is a heroic army, firstly because it is an army born of the people, fighting to defend the people's interests; because it is determined to carry out a thorough revolution, determined to fight and to win, and has a tradition of heroic fighting, hard work, endurance, determination to overcome difficulties, to fulfill all duties. To firmly maintain and consolidate the absolute leadership of the Party in the armed forces, to intensify the education of cadres and combatants in proletarian ideology and in the Party's line and revolutionary tasks, to realize unity within the army, unity between the army and the people, international unity, to provoke the disintegration of enemy forces, to realize broad inner democracy and at the same time strict self-imposed discipline—these are *the fundamental principles to follow in the building of the people's armed forces in the political aspect*, and the factors which will preserve their class character and ensure their constant growth and victory.

Levels of Forces in a People's War

In order to carry out a people's war, the armed forces must have adequate forms of organization comprising *main-force troops, regional troops, militia, and self-defense units*. The main-force troops are mobile units which may be used in fighting in any part of the country. Regional troops are the mainstay of armed struggle in a region. Militia and self-defense groups are extensive semiarmed forces of the laboring people who, while continuing their production work, are the main instrument of the people's power at the base.

The practice of revolutionary armed struggle by our people has proved that the three above-mentioned forms of organization of the armed forces are wholly adequate for the tasks of promoting a people's war, for mobilizing and arming the entire people for the war. We have to look back at our people's struggle through successive periods to grasp fully the importance and strategic role of those three categories of armed forces. If we had not organized secret self-defense units during the preinsurrection period, the powerful armed forces such as we had later on would never have come into being; if during the resistance we had not organized an extensive network of self-defense groups and strong regional units, guerrilla warfare could not have developed to a high degree, and still less could we have built a powerful main force. On the other hand, if we had not had a large mobile main force when the armed struggle was at a victorious stage, there would have been no great battles to annihilate enemy forces, no victorious campaigns, and the glorious [victory in the] Dien Bien Phu battle would not have taken place.

Forces Developing in the South (c. 1969)

[*At this date, the Vietcong had been driven underground, and was barely active. Giap had been forced to commit PRVN regulars.*]

Today in the South of our country, in the main the armed forces are developing according to the same laws as those discussed above. The extensive semiarmed organizations efficaciously supported the movement of the masses in the countryside, when the people were rising up to free themselves from the enemy's grip, undertake partial uprisings at the base, and promote guerrilla warfare. It was while these political and armed struggles were raging that the three categories of armed forces were formed and developed. The South Vietnam Liberation Army [*Vietminh, called Vietcong—Vietnamese Communists—in the south*] has been growing rapidly and unceasingly. We can say that the above three forms of organization have extremely close, organic relations, which ensure an inexhaustible source of strength from the masses of the people for the people's armed forces, and make it possible for them not only to carry out their task of annihilating enemy forces but also to protect our political and economic bases and preserve the potential of the liberation war.

Victory with Smaller Forces

Our country has no vast territory, no large population; numerically, our armed forces cannot compare with those of large countries. For this very reason, to defend our country efficaciously, to defeat an enemy who is stronger than we materially and technically, we have to apply those three forms of armed forces strictly. Extensively and strongly organized militia and self-defense groups, strong regional troops, powerful and highly mobile main-force troops: that is a *sine qua non* condition for developing our fighting power.[10]

From Guerrilla War to Regular War

According to our military theory, in order to ensure victory for the people's war when we are stronger than the enemy politically and the enemy is stronger than we materially, it is necessary to promote an extensive *guerrilla war* which will develop gradually into a *regular war* combined with a guerrilla war. Regular war and guerrilla war are closely combined, stimulate each other, deplete and annihilate enemy forces, and bring final victory.

Today on the South Vietnam battlefields, guerrilla war in the form of partial uprisings in the countryside has attained an extremely important strategic role and is developing to an increasingly high degree.

Offense Preferable to Defense

In all wars, the activities of the armed forces are either offensive or defensive. A revolutionary war . . . uses both . . . forms but regards offensive activities as the most essential. As a result of concrete practice of revolutionary armed struggle, our military art has created original forms of struggle: *guerrilla warfare, mobile warfare, and positional warfare*. All these forms, in offensive and defensive operations, can raise . . . the determination of the people's armed forces to wipe out the enemy, to defeat what is strong with what is weak . . . to carry out a thorough revolution.

Our military art has also established correct principles of operational direction to guide all war activities by our armed forces. These principles have gradually taken shape in the course of our people's armed struggle. . . . These principles . . . attach the greatest importance to the determination to wipe out enemy manpower and preserve and strengthen our forces; they are, at the same time, penetrated with the thought that everything should be done to gain initiative in offensive operations, achieve great mobility, develop political superiority and heroism in fighting, in order to defeat an enemy stronger than we in equipment and technique. . . .

Our military art must develop continuously if it is to meet the requirements of revolutionary tasks and *the requirements of a people's war in the present conditions*. A war may take place . . . when the enemy has modern equipment and weapons, while our side [does not], as on the South Vietnam battlefield at present. Our countrymen in the South have enhanced their fighting tradition and applied in a creative manner the experience gained during the resistance in order to defeat the enemy. A war may also take place . . . where the enemy has modern equipment and weapons while our equipment and weapons, though still inferior to those of the enemy, are becoming relatively modern. In these circumstances, our military art is still based on the popular character of the war, on politics and heroic fighting spirit, and [thus] the efficaciousness of equipment and weapons will be increased, the organization and direction of operations will be brought to a higher level, and our armed forces will have an increasingly greater fighting power.

Support from the Rear

A strongly organized rear is always a factor of success because it is a source of political and moral stimulation . . . to the front, a source . . . of manpower, materials, and money for the war. As the war grows in scale, the role of the rear becomes increasingly important.

As soon as the question of armed struggle was posed, another question was also posed—that of having places where our people's armed forces could be hidden, trained, supplied, strengthened, and could rest. While revolutionary struggle was developing, we created a rear where there had been none, developed it, beginning with political bases among the masses, and now have a relatively complete system of popular national defense. . . . In the early days when our Party made the decision to prepare for an armed struggle, we did not have a single inch of free territory; at that time, [our] only rear . . . was our secret political bases, and the . . . loyalty of the people who had become conscious of their revolutionary cause. It was from these secret political bases that our Party [organized] our first guerrilla units . . . concentrating on armed propaganda, political activities being regarded as more important than military activities—[built up bases] for the armed struggle, and gradually [waged] partial guerrilla war. . . . Afterward, during the . . . long resistance war, we had vast free zones as . . . [an] organized rear for the armed struggle, besides the guerrilla bases . . . in the enemy's rear. Our rear . . . increasingly strengthened . . . was the starting point from which our concentrated main-force units launched offensive operations on battlegrounds favorable to us; this rear made it possible to prepare and supply . . . the armed forces, in [ever greater] counteroffensive campaigns.

The North is the "Rear" in the Final Struggle

At present, the liberated North . . . is our vast and strong rear; it is the base for the entire Vietnamese people's struggle for their revolutionary cause. In order *to consolidate national defense in every aspect* [and] greatly increase the defense capabilities of the country, we have . . . to build up powerful people's armed forces [and] to consolidate our rear. . . . The most fundamental question is to enhance the people's patriotism, socialist consciousness, awareness of being masters of their own country, and revolutionary vigilance, and . . . to mobilize the entire people for *increasing production and building socialism*, while being always ready to *fight for the defense of the North*. It is necessary . . . to consolidate the . . . dictatorship of the Proletariat, broaden democracy for the laboring people, resolutely repress the counterrevolutionaries. When internal order and security are ensured, no foreign aggressors are to be feared. A powerful people's national defense must have its material and technical bases; therefore, building . . . socialist industry and agriculture . . . means of communication and transportation . . . have a great importance for the consolidation of national defense in the North. While building up the economy, it is necessary *to coordinate better the economic construction with national defense, Peacetime needs with Wartime needs*. Only in this way can we fulfill our revolutionary tasks . . . increase the national defense potential . . . ensure [victory] by our armed forces, [and] foil all enemy maneuvers of provocation and aggression.[11]

The Party, the Army, and Industrialization

In this new phase of the revolution, the people's armed forces, [once] the instrument of the . . . worker-peasant dictatorship, have become the instrument of the . . . dictatorship of the proletariat; [this] requires a deeper ideological transformation, as the socialist revolution is the deepest and most thorough revolution in history. Consequently, the task of heightening the cadres' and combatants' class consciousness, educating them in Marxist-Leninist ideology, becomes all the more urgent. At present . . . the economy in the North is developing gradually and surely [and] we have new capabilities to improve our military equipment and strengthen the . . . bases of the armed forces. And thus . . . studies to grasp modern military technique and science [and] raising the level of organization and command, are becoming an important political task; but the Party . . . must continue to give [priority] to the . . . strengthening of the revolutionary character, the class character, of the people's armed forces.

In order to grasp fully the military line of our Party, we should also be imbued with our viewpoint on practice, because this military line results from an ingenious application of the universal principles of Marxism-Leninism on war and the armed forces to the concrete conditions of our country. . . . The revolutionary war in Vietnam is subject to the general laws of revolutionary war, but, at the same time, it has its specific laws. Our Party has successfully led the war because it has grasped the above general and specific laws and has based itself on the concrete conditions of our country in order to solve all the fundamental military questions.

The Military Line of the Party

[*Here we read Communist propaganda at its most blatant. However, if Giap did not convince the South Vietnamese, his lies must have been effective in the PRVN army and "back home" in the north.*]

To grasp fully the military line of the Party, we should also clearly *see the role of the fighting tradition and experience* of the people and the people's armed forces. Through the practice of an extremely heroic, rich, and creative revolutionary struggle, our people and our people's armed forces have built up a glorious fighting tradition and gained most precious and rich experience.[12]

The South Vietnam people and Liberation Army [*Vietcong*], with their ardent patriotism and deep hatred of the enemy, have gained extremely rich fighting experience, defeated all modern tactics and weapons of the United States imperialists and their agents, and driven them to severe, humiliating defeats in their "special war."

Magnificent heroism, military struggle combined with political struggle, annihilation of enemy troops by hundreds of thousands . . . defeats inflicted on the "heliborne" and "armor-borne" tactics . . . destruction of the system of "strategic hamlets" set up by the enemy and the building of thousands of our own fighting villages and hamlets [with] over a hundred million individuals participating in direct political struggle against the enemy, liberation of three-fourths of the territory with over eight million inhabitants—all these glorious deeds make up the experience that our countrymen in the "Bronze Citadel of the Fatherland" [*South Vietnam; so called by Ho Chi Minh*] and the heroic Liberation Army [Vietcong] have gained at the price of great sacrifices. . . .

We must also carefully study *the advanced experience of the armies of fraternal countries* [*the USSR and China*] which has made a great contribution to our people's armed struggle. But in this study . . . we should be careful to . . . keep in mind the realities of our country and our army, our tradition of armed struggle and our fighting experience . . . guarding ourselves from mechanical imitation and dogmatism.

Developments in the South

[*Here is more blatant propaganda—the deliberate, convincing lie—that kept the Communist movement alive in the South—at a time when the Vietcong had almost ceased to exist as an organized fighting force.*]

At present, our countrymen in South Vietnam are winning increasingly important victories in their liberation war, the United States imperialists and their lackeys are in an extremely severe political and military crisis. In an attempt to save the situation, they are now endeavoring to intensify their "special war" in the South, at the same time increasing their activities of sabotage and provocation against the North, and seeking to expand the war to the North. Now more than ever, our entire people in the North, while exerting the greatest efforts to construct a socialist economy, must endeavor to consolidate national defense, build up powerful people's armed forces, stand ready to take part in the struggle to safeguard peace, defend the socialist North, and actively support the heroic struggle of our countrymen in the South.[13]

Interviews with French Correspondents

[*The interviews were granted by General Giap to Wilfred Burchett and Roger Pic in 1966 and 1967, and translated from the French by the editors/translators of Giap's War.*]

United States Ground and Air War

Since their defeat in Korea, and after the first failures of the GIs in South Vietnam, the American imperialists foresaw the impossibility of a war waged by the American infantry on the Asian mainland. (They see this, yet they go on; they will pay the price.) Accordingly, a war with their air force against the Democratic Republic of Vietnam seemed to them a fortunate discovery [inspiration] at the beginning. . . . They attacked indiscriminately channels of communication, industrial centers, populous regions in North Vietnam, sparing not even day nurseries, schools, hospitals, pagodas, and churches.

The American imperialists have not, for all that, attained the objectives envisaged.

And in South Vietnam . . . ? Our compatriots in the South have wiped out the best American units in Zone D to the north of Saigon, at Pleime, at Ia Drang, in the plains of Central Vietnam; they have successfully attacked bases which are still solidly defended: Da Nang, Chu Lai, and most recently Tan Son Nhut. The South Vietnamese mercenary army has suffered a series of defeats.[14]

United States Aggression

[T]he war which the United States government now wages in South Vietnam is a war of aggression, a war of neo-colonialist aggression. As for our people in South Vietnam, they pursue a fight of legitimate defense in order to safeguard their national rights and to contribute to the maintenance of peace in Asia and throughout the world. Courageous for good reason, united as a single man, knowing how to wield this invincible weapon which is people's war, supported by the socialist countries and by those throughout the world who cherish peace and justice, they have gone from one success to another. . . .

Whatever the means which the Americans put to work or could put to work, they [cannot] modify this irreversible truth: . . . The epoch in which we live [is] the epoch of the triumph of socialism and of the peoples' liberation movements. Our war . . . is a just war. We shall win.

Vietnam is one; it is indivisible. . . . Our people are resolved to fight in order to defend the North, liberate the South, and accomplish the peaceful reunification of the fatherland.[15]

Excerpts from an Article by Giap

American Aggression

[*An abridged version of a long essay, "Great Victory, Great Task," which was serialized in* Nhan Dan, *14–16 September 1967.*]

Newly arrived American troops suffered heavy blows at An Tan, Nui Thanh, Pleiku, Da Nang, and especially at Van Tuong. Their bases were tightly encircled by guerrilla belts. Neither the United States forces nor the puppet forces could halt the huge, persistent, and victorious attacks made by the southern army and people. The United States imperialists and their lackeys were increasingly confused.[16]

In the course of the war, the socialist regime in the North has grown stronger, the North has fought well and has also produced well. Good communications and transportation have been maintained, and the economy and culture have been developed steadily. Despite many obstacles created by the enemy, the living conditions of the people are stable. The determination to oppose the Americans and to struggle for national salvation has grown in strength.

In the South, in the spirit of "the North calls, the South answers," the southern army and people have continued to attack the United States, puppet, and satellite troops everywhere, and have tried to attack their air bases and logistical depots, to inflict heavy losses and to force the enemy increasingly on the defensive.[17]

The American's Inferiority Complex

Following World War II—and especially after their defeats in China, Korea, Indochina, and Cuba—the United States imperialists have begun to sense their inferiority, and that of the imperialist camp, in the global balance of power.

Failing in "Special War," the United States Moves to Limited War

The United States imperialists attempted the special war strategy [*supporting the ARVN against the Vietcong*] in the south of our country and failed. They had to move quickly, while on the defensive, to a strategy of limited war in order to deal with their dangerous military position. This shift . . . revealed their un-yielding, aggressive, and belligerent nature.

. . . Limited war is one of the three forms of aggressive war. It is war actually fought by Americans, but limited in size and scope. While special war is fought mainly by local lackey troops [ARVN], limited war is waged by United States troops themselves.[18]

United States Is Neocolonialist

In general, the aggressive policies of the United States imperialists seek to achieve neocolonialism. . . . The final goal is the consolidation of the puppet army and government and their transformation into effective tools [of] neo-colonialism. The . . . military aim of the limited-war strategy is to destroy the enemy's military forces . . . to attack quickly . . . to end the war quickly.

Since they must limit the number of their troops, the American imperialists are particularly careful to use the forces of the local lackeys [ARVN] well. They believe that by using a small number of United States troops as a core for local lackey units—equipped with modern weapons—they can repress their oppo-nents in a country where the economy is backward or newly developing. . . . Limiting their strategic goals also means limiting their political goals, and, in the military arena, concentrating on destroying the enemy's military forces, partic-ularly the regulars, quickly.

They have frantically carried on the political games of neocolonialism along with the military games of aggressive war. As a result, the present limited war continues to be an aggressive war aimed at achieving the political objectives of neocolonialism.[19]

Vietnamese Guerrillas and Regulars

The American imperialists have a huge military force to use to carry out their aggression in the South. Our people's military struggle has therefore become increasingly important.

Guerrilla activities and large-scale combat are coordinated, help each other, and encourage each other to grow. They are also coordinated closely with the political struggle in order to win victories in both the military and political fields. . . .

Our people truly appreciate the struggle being carried on by the American people against the Johnson administration's aggressive war in Vietnam, and we consider it a real sign of sympathy and support for our people's just resistance.[20]

Vietcong Actions

The Liberation Armed Forces' [Vietcong's] method of attacking cities is being used on the southern battlefields. Small LAF units, supported by the people's political forces, have won huge victories and have destroyed a substantial portion of the enemy's mobility. . . . [A]ttacks launched by the LAF in the heart of Saigon, Hue, and other cities have aided the struggle of the urban compatriots, frightened the enemy, and filled . . . our compatriots with joy. The attacks on the cities have all shown the tremendous courage, skill, and flexibility of the LAF. [*Such attacks were attempted in the Tet Offensive of January–February 1968 and had short-lived terrorist success, but failed.*]

American Imperialists Are Rich but Weak

Revolutionary people the world over have learned that the United States imperialists are rich but weak and that their economic and military potential, although great, has its limits. The American imperialists are being beaten by a small but heroic people. The longer they continue their aggressive war in Vietnam, the more they are isolated in international politics.

In the United States itself, the Johnson administration is faced with a conflict between the ruling clique and the growing protests of the American people.

What plans do the American imperialists have?

1. They will continue to expand the limited war . . . Johnson [will] send another 50,000 men to South Vietnam, bringing . . . United States forces to over 500,000 by July 1968.

2. The United States imperialists may expand their limited war over all our country. . . . If the American imperialists expand the limited war into the North, it is certain that they will be rapidly and totally defeated. Even with over one million men at their disposal, they have failed in the South. If they send infantry troops into the North, how many more would be needed?[21]

Effort Will Make Vietnam Victorious

We must work to increase the fighting power of our armed forces and the different branches of the people's army and to make our fire nets more effective against U.S. aircraft, warships, and artillery units, to destroy as much American force as possible and to protect the socialist North more effectively.

Now that we are confronted with new plots and acts of sabotage by the American imperialists, it is all the more necessary for us to invent more courageous and resourceful tactics to surprise the enemy constantly and to inflict heavy defeats on him. We must also concentrate on perfecting and inventing fighting methods to use against the U.S. naval forces and artillery units. With stalwart, militant determination, with heroism, courage, and intelligence, we can work to make those weapons we have superior and to invent highly effective tactics in order to punish American naval and artillery units as they deserve.

Under President Ho's banner, which calls for "Determination to defeat the

United States aggressors," let our entire army and people take advantage of victories to move ahead.[22]

Army Day Rally Speech

The Heroism of the Vietminh (Vietcong)

[From Giap's speech at an Army Day Rally in Hanoi on 21 December 1968. Official translation furnished by the London representatives of Cuu Quoc *to the editors/ translators of Giap's* War.]

Directly confronting the United States aggressors on the great front of their country, the heroic South Vietnamese people and armed forces, under the banner of the South Vietnam National Liberation Front [*Vietcong, again underground at this juncture*], have braved all hardships and sacrifices and fought valiantly and persistently against the foreign aggressors. Though the United States imperialists have taken their local war to a high level, raising the strength of the United States puppet and satellite armies to 1,200,000 men, our compatriots and Liberation Armed Forces, maintaining and developing their offensive position, have smashed one after another all the counteroffensives of the enemy. Especially since early spring this year [1968], compatriots and fighters in the South . . . have launched repeated general offensives and widespread uprisings and have recorded unprecedentedly big and all-around victories.

The Reduction of American Forces

After four years of . . . war with more than half a million United States troops as the hard core, the United States imperialists have had to think of "de-Americanizing" the war. Thus, they have admitted the error . . . of their decision to bring [American] troops into South Vietnam to save the puppet army and administration from collapse.

The army and people in North Vietnam have shot down more than thirty-two hundred of the most up-to-date aircraft of the United States, killing or capturing a sizable number of top American pilots, and have sunk or set fire to hundreds of enemy vessels. The so-called air superiority of the United States . . . the chieftain of imperialism which used to boast of its wealth and weapons and which is notorious for its cruelty—has received a staggering blow at the hands of the Vietnamese people. They had to stop unconditionally the bombardment of the Democratic Republic of Vietnam. . . . This constitutes a very big victory on our part and a very bitter defeat for the United States imperialists. . . . Our people and army can be proud of the fact that under the . . . leadership of our Party headed by esteemed President Ho Chi Minh, undaunted socialist North Vietnam has really become a steel rampart and our heroic Vietnamese land, a real fortress.

Vietnam Has Won the War

The reality of our victory and of the United States failure on the Vietnam battle-field proves that . . . a nation which has resolutely stood up in arms . . . for independence and freedom along a correct line . . . can . . . defeat any aggressor, even United States imperialism.[23]

All Glory to the Communist Party

Our Party has organized the heroic armed forces of the Vietnamese people composed of the regular army, the regional armed forces, and the militia and guerrillas. These are a wonderful army of our nation which, within only a score of years, has grown from small guerrilla bands into a mighty army and thus, together with the entire people, defeated Japanese fascism and French imperialism and is today defeating United States imperialism.

Long live the Vietnam Workers Party!
Long live President Ho Chi Minh![24]

Giap Interprets the Results of the Tet Offensive (1968)

[*From an interview granted by General Giap to Madeleine Riffaud in May 1968; published in* L'Humanité *on 4 June 1968. Mme Riffaud authorized its publication in the translation of Giap's* War.]

RIFFAUD:
While visiting Vietnam for more than a month I have often heard quoted, not just on Radio Hanoi, but in my conversations with people in the street, this phrase from President Ho Chi Minh's December 25, 1967, message: "It is now clear that the Americans have lost the war. . . . "

GIAP:
In fact, our president correctly stated in his message to the nation: "It is now clear that the United States has lost the war." These words now take on their full meaning not only for us Vietnamese but also for world opinion. They reflect the great reality of our struggle against American aggression.

The spring 1968 offensive revealed abruptly to the Americans that the Vietnamese people do not give up easily and that their military strength has not been in any way impaired by United States aggression, no matter what its forms and its cruelty. Gone, and gone for good, is the hope of annihilating the Liberation forces. Gone are the "pacification" projects. They would have to start all over again from scratch. The United States troops had to entrench themselves on the defensive, blocked in their positions. The "McNamara line" proved its total ineffectiveness.[25] [*As noted above, the Tet Offensive, militarily, was a failure.*]

The Ia Drang Battles

[*The following is excerpted from Cecil B. Currey's biography of Giap,* Victory at Any Cost. *See the next chapter for the American view of the first of these battles.*]

CURREY:

In the Ia Drang campaign, Giap said, "We had trouble with supplies of water and food. We had no helicopters. Our people had to forage in the jungle for food and drink water from the streams. But our foot soldiers had to be very intelligent, very creative, and make their own way." He explained what he had learned. The Americans had fearsome strength: a highly mobile divisions with much flexibility, capable of launching sudden attacks supported by heavy firepower. "But the Americans didn't understand that we had soldiers almost everywhere; that it was very hard to surprise us."[26]

"You Americans were very strong in modern weapons, but we were strong in something else. Our war was people's war, waged by the entire people. Our battlefield was everywhere, or nowhere, and the choice was ours. . . . Being . . . everywhere was the best mobility of all."[27]

Giap thought about American mobility and concluded, "Even advanced weapons [such as helicopters] have weaknesses." American reliance on aerial bombings proved to be an Achilles' heel. "You staged bombing raids in advance of your [helicopter] landings." Then, when Giap's forces heard incoming helicopters, "we went on alert and prepared for battle wherever you landed." During preparatory bombings "our soldiers were in their tunnels and bunkers and took very few casualties. When your armed helicopters came we were still in our shelters. Only when the helicopters brought your troops did we emerge, and only then did we start shooting." Almost as an aside, he added, "In Viet Nam, your commanders never realized that there are limitations on power, limitations on strength.[28]

Principles for the Vietminh

[*The following is excerpted from Peter MacDonald's* Giap: The Victor in Vietnam. *These principles were promulgated while the guerrilla movement against the French was still underground.*]

- The war of liberation is a protracted war and a hard war in which we must rely mainly on ourselves—for we are strong politically but weak materially, while the enemy is very weak politically but stronger materially.

- Guerrilla warfare is a means of fighting a revolutionary war that relies on the heroic spirit to triumph over Modern Weapons.
- It is the means whereby the people of a weak, badly equipped country can stand up against an aggressive army possessing better equipment and techniques.
- The correct tactics for a protracted revolutionary war are to wage guerilla warfare, to advance from guerilla warfare to regular warfare and then closely combine these two forms of war; to develop from guerilla to mobile and then to siege warfare.
- Accumulate a thousand small victories to turn into one great success.[29]

Mao's Seven Steps

- Arouse and organize the people.
- Achieve internal unification.
- Establish bases.
- Expand the bases.
- Recover national strength.
- Destroy the enemy's national strength.
- Regain lost territories.

Giap's Additions

- If the enemy advances, we retreat.
- If he halts, we harass.
- If he avoids battle, we attack.
- If he retreats, we follow.

Laws for Vietminh Framed by Ho Chi-Minh, Giap, and Pham Van Dong

- Fragment the opposition's (either foreign or anticommunist) leadership, if necessary.
- Use assassination and torture.
- Do not destroy the opposition, take it over.
- Do not smash the existing social system entirely.
- Do not try for too much.
- Appear outwardly reasonable while working secretly against the opposition.
- Use overt and covert groups, with little contact between them.
- Do not antagonize if it can be helped, for doing so creates rival groupings.
- Work from small to large, from the specific to the general.
- Win small gains by communism, large gains by nationalism.[30]

Conclusions

It is obvious that Giap's leadership was rooted in the Communist Party's political discipline (and power to punish), to which were added the motivations of class struggle, racism, and nationalism. All three were in play in the struggle against the "colonialists" and "neocolonialists" (the United States). Racism was a factor in both anti-colonialism and nationalism. He acknowledged the necessity of aid from "fraternal countries"—the USSR and Communist China. By contrast, he considered the United States to be "isolated" in South Vietnam, and that the "social bases" of the United States in South Vietnam were weak—weaker than those of the French had been.

Giap was a master of propaganda, as is evident in his diatribes against the United States, in which he claims "victory" for his forces in the Ia Drang Valley (a battle described from the U.S. side in the next chapter), among other places. He admitted to *no* defeats. His major efforts were directed to making good Communists of the workers and farmers. That accomplished, he believed, "war by the whole people" could be mounted, and they would be unbeatable. In the South, he says, "our military art is still based on the popular character of the war, on politics and heroic fighting spirit."

Giap was more a political than military leader. The war, he said, was being fought according to the "Party's Military Line," modified to suit Vietnamese conditions, but he never gave specifics. Battlefield leadership, to which our other combat leaders have devoted much thought, was not a problem for him. Evidently, he felt his men were motivated by their Communist beliefs or indoctrination, plus hatred of westerners and love of country. Giap always placed above all else the cultivation of loyalty to the Party in the people and the army.

XVII

Harold G. Moore

(1924–   )

No one is better qualified to speak on the Vietnam War than Lieutenant General Harold G. Moore, USA (ret.). He had been in the Korean War, and entered Vietnam as a lieutenant colonel, commanding the 1st Battalion, 7th Cavalry (Airmobile)—the "Garry Owen," once George Armstrong Custer's regiment. In November 1965, his unit was the first to fight North Vietnamese regulars in a bloody battle in the Ia Drang Valley. Before Moore left Vietnam he had been promoted to command the 3rd Brigade, 1st Cavalry Division. He asked for another command assignment in Vietnam, but was told he had "had his turn."

In 1992 "Hal" Moore and Joseph Galloway published *We Were Soldiers Once . . . and Young: Ia Drang: The Battle That Changed the War in Vietnam*, considered by many the best book on the Vietnam War.[1] It was praised by Vietnam veterans with such different views as General Norman Schwarzkopf and Colonel David Hackworth, who called it "the best account of infantry combat I have ever read."[2] Segments of it are quoted below.

Born in Bardstown, Kentucky, Hal Moore graduated from West Point, he says, "by the skin of my teeth," but was the first Army officer of his class (1945) to reach the grade of Lieutenant General. He is a Master Parachutist and sometime parachute tester for the Army. His decorations include the Distinguished Service Cross, the Bronze Star (for valor), the Distinguished Service Medal, and many foreign awards.

After His Vietnam service, he commanded the 7th Infantry Division in Korea, was Commanding General of Fort Ord, California, and then was the Army's deputy Chief of Staff for Personnel. Moore retired in August 1977, with thirty-two years' service. He has since been successful in business, helping to develop Crested Butte Ski Resort in Colorado, then forming a computer software company. He and his wife, Julie, have homes in Auburn, Alabama and Butte, Colorado. They have five grown children: sons Steve, Dave, and Greg, daughters Cecile and Julie. The General gives occasional lectures at military schools, colleges, and universities. In his spare time he prefers outdoor sports.

"Advice for Military Leaders" below was provided to the author by General Moore, and has never before been published. The remaining excerpts are from *We Were Soldiers Once . . . and Young*.

Advice for Military Leaders

Preparations

PREPARATIONS could make a book; [here are] only a few items:

1. Read Military History. Read small unit actions. The personality of a big battle is often formed by small unit actions.
2. Visit historic battlefields with maps and books in hand.
3. Instill the *WILL TO WIN* in your unit. Allow no second place trophies in the trophy cases.
4. Build Unit Discipline, teamwork. A team of fighters.
5. Prepare your unit for your death (or being gravely wounded and evacuated) and for your subordinate leader's loss as well. A Squad leader must be ready to command a platoon or the company.
6. Squad leaders and Fire Team leaders must know how to adjust artillery/mortar fire. Live fire is not always necessary. You can do this with marbles and a sandtable; or golf balls and a small piece of ground.
7. Be ready for wounded men yelling "Medic" or screaming for "Mom." Practice reducing the enemy fire—neutralizing it *BEFORE* going out for the wounded.

Train in all these ways, and you'll be a winner.

Conduct in Battle

Four Principles:

1. "Three strikes and you're *NOT* out!" A Leader can either inspire confidence in his unit—or contaminate the environment and his unit with his attitude and actions.

A Leader must be visible on the battlefield. From battalion commander on down, *he must be IN the battle*; brigade and division commanders on occasion. You must exhibit a self-confident, positive attitude. You must exhibit determination to prevail no matter what the odds or how desperate the situation. You must have and display the *WILL TO WIN* by actions, words, tone of voice on the radio as well as face-to-face, by appearance, by demeanor, by countenance, and the look in your eyes. A Leader must remain calm and cool and *SHOW NO FEAR*. A Leader must ignore the noise, dust, smoke, explosions, screams and yells of the wounded and the dead lying around him. That's all NORMAL.

A Leader must never give any hint or evidence that he is uncertain about a positive outcome, even in the most desperate of situations.

Again the principle which must be driven into your own head and the heads of your men is: "*Three strikes and you're NOT out!*"

2. The corollary principle which interacts with the one above is: "There's always one more thing you can do to influence any situation in your favor—and after that, one more thing—and after that, one more—etc. etc."

In battle I periodically mentally detach myself for a few seconds from the noise, the screams of the wounded, the explosions, the yelling, the smoke and dust, the intensity of it all and ask myself: "What am I doing that *I should NOT* be doing, and what am I not doing that *I SHOULD BE* doing to influence the situation in my favor?"

3. "When there's nothing wrong—there's nothing wrong *except—THERE'S NOTHING WRONG!* That's exactly when a Leader must be most alert.

4. Finally, "*Trust your instincts.*" In a critical, fast-moving battlefield situation, instincts and intuition amount to an instant Estimate of the Situation. Your instincts are the product of your education, training, reading, personality, and experience.

"TRUST YOUR INSTINCTS."

When seconds count, instincts and decisiveness come into play. In quick-developing situations, the Leader must act fast, impart confidence to all around him, and must not second-guess a decision. *MAKE IT HAPPEN!* In the process, a Leader cannot stand around slack-jawed when he is hit with the unexpected. He must face the facts, deal with them, and *MOVE ON*.

Style of Leadership

[*What follows are excerpts from* We Were Soldiers Once . . . and Young *that illustrate General Moore's style of leadership.*]

Thoughts the Night Before the Operation

[Eighty men of Bravo Company] would be the only troops on the ground [at LZ X-Ray, in the Ia Drang Valley] until the helicopters returned to Plei Me, loaded another eighty, and returned. . . .

It was a thirty-minute round trip and at the expected rate it would take more than four hours to get all of my men on the ground. The Hueys would also have to divert to refuel during this process, costing even more time; and if the landing zone was hot and any of the sixteen helicopters were shot up and dropped out, that, too, would immediately impact on the timetable.

I ran an endless string of "what ifs" through my mind. . . . Time so spent is never wasted; if even one "what if" comes to pass a commander will be a few precious seconds ahead of the game. My worst-case scenario was a hot LZ—a fight beginning during or just after our assault landing—and I certainly had to assume the enemy would be able to provide it. In any assault into an enemy-held area—whether it's a beachhead or a paratroop drop zone, and whether you have to cross a major river or, as in our case, land in the base area—the hairiest time is that tenuous period before your troops get firmly established and organized, and move out. This is when you are most vulnerable.

I ran through what I could do to influence the action if the worst came to pass. First, I would personally land on the first helicopter, piloted by [Major] Bruce Crandall. That would permit me a final low-level look at the landing zone and surrounding terrain, and with Crandall in the front seat and me in the back we could work out, on the spot, any last-minute diversion to an alternate landing zone, if necessary, and fix any other problems with the lift.

In Vietnam . . . every battalion commander had his own command-and-control helicopter. Some commanders used their helicopter as their personal mount. I never believed in that. You had to get on the ground with your troops to see and hear what was happening. You have to soak up firsthand information for your instincts to operate accurately. Besides, it's too easy to be crisp, cool, and detached at 1,500 feet; too easy to demand the impossible of your troops; too easy to make mistakes that are fatal only to those souls far below in the mud, the blood, and the confusion.[3]

The Operation Begins

[*Morning, 14 November 1965.*]
Major Bruce Crandall [pilot] recalls: "We went low-level and arrived right on schedule at the release point into the landing zone. The landing zone was not as clear of obstacles as we would have liked but we got our flight in without any real problems. The only movement we spotted in the landing zone was something that looked like a dog scampering into some underbrush on the far side. It was probably an enemy soldier." Now the door gunners on the lift ships were firing into the tree line as we dropped into the clearing. I [*Moore*] unhooked my seat belt, switched the selector switch on my M-16 to full automatic—rock 'n' roll—and fired bursts into the brush to the left, toward the mountain, as Crandall came in hot and flared [hovered to land] over the dry five-foot-tall elephant grass. As the chopper skids touched the ground I yelled, "Let's go!" and jumped out, running for the trees on the western edge of the clearing, firing my rifle.

It was 10:48 A.M. Sergeant Major Plumley, Captain Metsker, Bob Ouellette, and Mr. Nik, the translator, were right behind me. [Capt. John] Herren [CO Bravo Company] and his men came out of their Hueys in like fashion. In less than ten seconds Crandall's first lift of eight ships had roared back into the air, banked north, and hightailed it back east. The second wave of eight helicopters was now touching down to disgorge its troops.

I ran across twenty-five yards of open ground, then across a waist-deep, ten-foot-wide dry creekbed, and continued running some seventy-five yards into the scrub brush, leading the command group. We stopped to slap fresh magazines in our rifles. So far we had been unopposed. We were in a lightly wooded area, with scraggly trees twenty to fifty feet tall and dry, brown elephant grass between. The area was dotted with large mounds of red dirt, most with brush and grass growing out of the tops. The size of these old termite hills ranged from that of a small automobile to that of a large pickup, and they offered excellent cover and concealment. The valley was a desolate place, with no villages and no civilians, ten miles east of where the Ho Chi Minh Trail turned left out of Cambodia into South Vietnam.

The heavily forested eastern slopes of the Chu Pong rose steep and dark more than a thousand feet above the clearing. The massif's lower slopes were covered with thick green foliage, elephant grass, and tangles of brush. . . . The creekbed just inside the western edge of our clearing was an excellent route of approach for enemy troops coming from the direction of the mountain or the valley, and for us going the other way. That creekbed was a critical feature. Heading back toward the clearing, we ran into some of Bravo Company's 1st Platoon troopers, led by Sergeant Larry Gilreath, moving out into the brush. Gilreath yelled: "Moore's fire team has already cleared this area." Plumley grinned. He knew that the troops liked to see the Old Man out with them on the ground, sharing the risks. Gilreath and his men headed deeper into the brush to the west. Plumley and I recrossed the dry creekbed and moved around the clearing, checking on the terrain and on the patrols Herren's troopers were conducting. No enemy contact so far, and I was glad of that. We didn't want a fight before we got the rest of the battalion on the ground.

Now I stopped and looked up at the steep slopes of the mountain. I had a strong sense that we were under direct enemy observation. That, and the fact that everything had gone so well so far, made me nervous. *Nothing was wrong, except that nothing was wrong.* I continued reconnoitering. There were no streambeds on the north, east, or south. The southern edge of the clearing was closest to the mountain and to those draws and fingers reaching out from the high ground. The terrain to the north and east was relatively flat. My attention continued to be drawn back to the south and west. . . . I ordered [Captain John] Herren's 1st Platoon to intensify its march to the west of the creek, and checked to make sure that the rest of Bravo Company was gathered in the clump of trees near the creekbed and ready for action. Herren had most of his troops on the ground; the rest were on the way in the second lift.

This clearing was the only decent helicopter landing zone between the slopes of Chu Pong and the Ia Drang and for two miles east or west. Our assault landing had, so far as we could tell, achieved total surprise.

The People's Army commander on the battlefield, then—Senior Lieutenant Colonel Nguyen Huu An [*told Moore after the war*], "When you dropped troops into X-Ray, I was on Chu Pong mountain. We had a very strong position and a strong, mobile command group. We were ready, had prepared for you and expected you to come. The only question was when."

[*Sergeant Larry Gilreath led 1st Platoon of Bravo Company 150 yards west. Sergeant John W. Mingo, a squad leader who had been a Ranger in Korea, spotted a "boy" in the elephant grass whom he recognized as a Vietnamese soldier. He ran him down, tackled him, and tied him up. Colonel Moore came forward to interrogate him.*]

MOORE:

He wasn't much, but he was this battalion's first prisoner in Vietnam . . . maybe twenty years old, scrawny, wild-eyed and trembling with fear. He was unarmed and barefooted; he wore a dirty khaki shirt, partly pulled out of his khaki trousers. There was a serial number on one of the shirt epaulettes. He carried a canteen but it was empty. He had no papers, no food, and no ammunition.

All I wanted to know was "How many of you are there?" and "Where are they?" A look of apprehension spread over [interpreter] Mr. Nik's face as he shakily translated the prisoner's words: "He says there are three battalions on the mountain who want very much to kill Americans but have not been able to find any." [*Moore now knew what he faced.*]

———

Three battalions of enemy added up to more than 1,600 men against the 160-plus Americans currently on the ground here. I turned to John Herren and ordered him to immediately intensify the patrols in the area where we had found the prisoner. I told Herren that as soon as enough of [Captain Ramon A.] Tony Nadal's Alpha Company troops were on the ground to secure the landing zone, Bravo Company would be cut loose to search the lower slopes of the mountain, with special emphasis on the finger and draw to the northwest. If the enemy were headed for us, it was imperative that we engage them as far off the landing zone as possible. [*General Moore adds: To "stiff arm" them*].

Captain Nadal had been hunting for me while I was in the woods with the prisoner. We caught up with each other after the prisoner was [sent to the rear on a helicopter]. I quickly briefed Nadal on the situation and told him that Alpha Company would take over security in the LZ as soon as the next lift brought in the rest of his men.

The Action Begins in Earnest

I heard [an] uproar explode up on the mountainside. There were the steady, deep-throated bursts of machine-gun fire; rifles crackling on full automatic; grenade, mortar, and rocket explosions. All of it was much louder and much more widespread than anything we had experienced thus far. Now John Herren was up on my radio reporting that his men were under heavy attack by at least two enemy companies and that his 2nd Platoon was in danger of being surrounded and cut off from the rest of the company. [*Actually, he faced a PRVN battalion of 500 +.*] Even as he spoke, mortar and rocket rounds hit in the clearing where I stood. My worst-case scenario had just come to pass: We were in heavy contact before all my battalion was on the ground. And now I had to deal with a cut-off platoon. My response was an angry "Shit!"

[*"Old Snake," Major Bruce Crandall, commanding the battalion's 16 Huey helicopters, radioed that he was bringing in the rest of Nadal's Alpha Company and part of Captain Robert H. "Bob" Edward's Charlie Company.*]

As the first eight choppers dropped into the clearing at 1:32 P.M., I told Captain Nadal to collect his men and move up fast on John Herren's left to tie in with him. Then, I said, I want you to lend Herren a platoon to help him get to his cut-off platoon. I ran out into the clearing to locate Bob Edwards. I had decided to commit Charlie Company toward the mountain as fast as they arrived, and take the risk of leaving my rear unguarded from the north and east. There would be no battalion reserve for a while.

Captain Edwards's men of Charlie Company jumped off their choppers and ran for the wooded edge of the landing zone—the southern edge, thank God. I grabbed Edwards, gave him a quick briefing, and then yelled at him to run his men off the landing zone to the south and southwest and take up a blocking position protecting Alpha Company's left flank. I screamed "*Move!*" and Edwards and his two radio operators shot off at a dead run, yelling and waving to the rest of the men to follow. [*Edwards got his company in position 50 to 100 yards off the LZ.*]

By now, my radio operator, Bob Ouellette, and I had rejoined Sergeant Major Plumley and Captain Tom Metsker near the dry creekbed. The interpreter, Mr. Nik, had gone to ground. Captain Metsker dropped to one knee and began firing his M-l6 at enemy soldiers out in the open just seventy-five yards to the south. Within minutes, Metsker suffered a gunshot wound in his shoulder, was bandaged . . . and was sent back to the copse [*for evacuation*].

MOORE:
I was tempted to join Nadal's or Edwards's men, but resisted the temptation. I had no business getting involved with the actions of only one company; I might get pinned down and become simply another rifleman. My duty was to *lead* riflemen.

I was on the radio, trying to hear a transmission over the noise, when I felt a firm hand on my right shoulder. It was Sergeant Major Plumley's. He shouted over the racket of the firefights: "Sir, if you don't find some cover you're going to go down—and if you go down, we all go down!"

Plumley was right, as always.

The sergeant major pointed to a large termite hill, seven or eight feet high, located in some trees in the waist between the two open areas of the landing zone. It was about thirty yards away; the three of us turned and ran toward it with bullets kicking up the red dirt around our feet and the bees still buzzing around our heads. That termite hill, the size of a large automobile, would become the battalion command post, the aid station, the supply point, the collection area for enemy prisoners, weapons, and equipment, and the place where our dead were brought.

Just now, at 1:38 P.M., the second wave of eight choppers dropped in with more Alpha and Charlie Company troops. They picked up some ground fire this time. Edwards and Nadal [sent] their arriving soldiers [to] their respective companies.

Tagging along with this lift was a medical evacuation helicopter bringing in my battalion aid station group. The big red cross painted on each side only drew more fire. On board were Captain Robert Carrara, the surgeon; Medical Platoon Sergeant Thomas Keeton; and Staff Sergeant Earl Keith. . . . The aid station was authorized thirteen personnel. Keeton and Keith were all we had. Period. Captain Carrara and his two sergeants performed miracles for the next fifty hours.

There were now about 250 men of my battalion on the ground and still functioning. Casualties were beginning to pile up. As we dropped behind that termite hill I fleetingly thought about an illustrious predecessor of mine in the 7th Cavalry, Lieutenant Colonel George Armstrong Custer, and his final stand in the valley of the Little Bighorn . . . eighty-nine years earlier. I was determined that history would not repeat itself in the valley of the Ia Drang. We were a tight, well-trained, and disciplined fighting force, and we had one thing George Custer did not have: fire support.

Now was the time to pull the chain on everything I could lay hands on. I radioed [Captain] Matt Dillon and the fire support coordinators overhead and told them to bring in air strikes, artillery, and aerial rocket artillery on the lower part of the mountain, especially on the approaches to the landing zone from the west and south.

Colonel Tim Brown [brigade commander], overhead in his command chopper, came up on my radio and urged me to pull the fires off the mountain and bring them in as close as possible.

John Herren had the biggest problem: trying to pinpoint the location of his missing 2nd Platoon. [Lieutenant Henry T.] Herrick and his men were not only separated from the rest of Bravo Company, but also engaged in a moving firefight. The fact that this platoon was out in front of Nadal and Herren delayed effective delivery of close-in artillery fire.[5]

Our intention with this bold helicopter assault into the clearing at the base of the Chu Pong massif had been to find the enemy, and we had obviously succeeded beyond our wildest expectations. People's Army Lieutenant Colonel Nguyen Huu An, deep in a command bunker no more than a mile and a half away this Sunday afternoon, November 14, was issuing orders by land-line

telephone . . . as well as by old, unreliable walkie-talkie radios and by foot
messenger. His orders to every battalion in the vicinity were simple: Attack!

The reports of continued heavy fighting in both Herren's and Nadal's sectors to
the west reminded me again that the entire north and east sides of the landing
zone were still wide open. I was praying that the next helicopter lift, [with] the
last of the Charlie Company troops and the lead elements of Delta Company,
would arrive soon.

[*This lift brought in Captain Ray Lefebvre, Delta Company; most of his mortar
platoon, under Lieutenant Raul F. Taboada; plus the machine gun platoon and the rest
of Edwards' Charlie Company. Bruce Crandall found his helicopter fired on by enemy
in plain sight, but he "flared out" and dropped the troops anyway. "Old Snake's"
gunners couldn't fire back for fear of hitting Moore's men. He loaded his chopper with
wounded and made for home base at Plei Me. Several of his Hueys were shot up in
dropping troops, but got out.*]

MOORE:
Captain Ray Lefebvre, commander of Delta Company, was about to earn his
Combat Infantryman's Badge, a Silver Star, and a Purple Heart, all in the next
seven minutes.[6]

[*As Ray Lefebvre left the chopper, a bullet creased his neck and killed his radio
operator. By chance, his men were dropped where they could fill in a gap between
Alpha and Charlie companies. He [Lefebvre] led those he could gather toward the
firing, and called in more as they landed, shoring up the battalion position. He was
shortly wounded again.*][7]

[*Moore pays heartfelt tribute to those who gave him fire support—Air Force fighters
and USAF and Navy fighter bombers, which augmented the fire of the Army's assault
helicopters (ARA—aerial rocket artillery). In addition, there were two batteries of
field artillery—12 guns—under captains Robert L. Barker and Donald Davis, that
fired day and night for three days from LZ-Falcon, five miles away, surrounding
Moore's battalion, as he puts it, "with a wall of steel." On the first day alone they fired
4,000 rounds. Their fire was directed by ARTY forward observers—Lieutenant Bill
Riddle, with Herren's Bravo Company, and Lieutenant Tim Blake with Nadal's Alpha
Company (who was killed in action). They brought the fire in as close to U.S. troops
as possible.*]

MOORE:
A major difference between Lieutenant Colonel Nguyen Huu An of the Peo-
ple's Army of Vietnam and Lieutenant Colonel Hal Moore of the 1st Cavalry
Division was that I had major fire support and he didn't.[8]

No matter how bad things got for the Americans fighting for their lives on the X-Ray perimeter, we could look out into the scrub brush in every direction, into that seething inferno of exploding artillery shells, 2.75-inch rockets, napalm canisters, 250- and 500-pound bombs, and 20mm cannon fire and thank God and our lucky stars that we didn't have to walk through *that* to get to work.[9]

I asked Bruce Crandall's brave aircrews of Alpha Company, the 229th Aviation Battalion, for the last measure of devotion, for service far beyond the limits of duty and mission, and they came through as I knew they would. This was the first, and in the view of many of us, the toughest of many missions we would accomplish together in a long, deadly combat tour. We desperately needed ammunition and water and medical supplies—and Crandall's Hueys brought them to us. Our wounded, screaming in pain or moaning . . . in shock, had to be evacuated, or they would die where they lay, on their ponchos behind the termite hill.

Hauling out the wounded was not the slick crews' job. Crandall's people were assault helicopter crews, trained to carry infantrymen into battle. Hauling the wounded off the battlefield was a medical-evacuation helicopter mission. But this was early in the war, and the medevac commanders had decreed that their birds would not land in hot landing zones. . . . Even before I asked, Bruce Crandall had already decided to begin doing everything that had to be done.

Until the LZ went hot, Matt Dillon and Mickey Parrish had controlled all flights into X-Ray from the command chopper overhead. No more. I [*Colonel Moore*] took control because only I knew where my men were, where the enemy ground fire was coming from, and where the safest spot to land was at any given moment. From this point forward, every helicopter coming into X-Ray would radio me for landing instructions.

CRANDALL:

"Moore's people laid down covering fire for us, and as we broke over the trees into the clearing I could see Hal Moore standing up at the far end of the LZ, exposing himself to enemy fire in order to get us into the safest position possible in the LZ. I landed where he directed and our crews and his people began pitching the ammo boxes off the aircraft as fast as they could. At the same time, the wounded were moved up and loaded aboard."

[*Among those loaded onto the helicopter were Captain Lefebvre. While helping Lefebvre into the chopper Captain Tom Metsker, the battalion intelligence officer, already wounded, received a mortal hit.*][10]

Captain [Myron] Diduryk ran up to me and shouted: "Garry Owen, sir! Captain Diduryk and Bravo Company, 2nd Battalion, 7th Cavalry, a hundred and twenty men strong, reporting for duty!"[11] His eyes sparkled with excitement and the challenge of the situation. I told Diduryk to assemble his men in a clump of trees thirty yards northwest of the command post to act as battalion reserve for the time being.

[*Diduryk's company would later see plenty of action.*]

Up in the scrub brush, in the thick of the fight to reach Herrick's cut-off platoon, the Alpha Company commander, Captain Tony Nadal, had come to a decision. He had one platoon pinned down in a hail of enemy fire and he knew that the longer this went on the harder it would be to get them out. It was 5:10 P.M. Nadal ordered his reserve, the 3rd Platoon, to move up on his left in an attempt to circle the enemy forces. It didn't work. They ran into the same buzz saw that was chewing up all the other platoons.

Over on the right, Sergeant Larry Gilreath of Bravo Company wasn't finding the going any easier. Captain John Herren asked Sergeant Gilreath if he knew of any other way that they had not tried. Says Gilreath, "My answer was 'No sir.' Even without all our dead and wounded that had to be taken care of, the time of day was against us."

Captain Nadal says, "The fight continued for another twenty or thirty minutes with neither side making headway. It was getting dark and as the casualties mounted I decided we were not going to be able to break through. I called Colonel Moore and asked for permission to pull back." John Herren, who was monitoring the battalion net, heard Nadal's request and quickly concurred. It was now 5:40. . . . I ordered both companies to withdraw to the creekbed under cover of heavy supporting artillery fires.

With night approaching there was no real choice. I did not want to go into the hours of darkness with my battalion fragmented, with the companies incapable of mutual support, and subject to defeat in detail. The cut-off platoon would have to hang onto their little knoll tonight. We had to pull back, get our wounded and dead out, and resupply ammo and water. Then we had to get all units on line, tied in tight, with artillery and mortar fires registered for the long night ahead.

Closing Down for the Night

For Nadal and Herren, the hardest part would be breaking contact with the enemy and pulling back. Disengagement is always one of the most difficult military maneuvers to accomplish successfully. Doctrine calls for a deception plan, covering elements, fire support, security, mapped routes, a precise schedule, and the use of smoke. We had fire support and we could call down smoke, but we had neither the troops nor the time to work out a school solution.

Captain Nadal, with his artillery observer and artillery radio operator both dead, was now calling and adjusting fire support over the battalion command net. He recalls: "I told all platoon leaders that no one was pulling back until everyone, dead or alive, came back. In order to cover my withdrawal, I called Colonel Moore and asked him to give me a smoke mission and to drop the range about a hundred meters closer to us than the high-explosive fire missions. This would put the smoke almost directly on top of us."

Nadal's request went to the battalion command post and was relayed to the command helicopter overhead, where Captain Jerry Whiteside called it back to the fire direction center at LZ Falcon. In seconds the reply came back: "No smoke available." Drawing on my Korean War experience, I asked if they had white phosphorus (WP) shells. They said yes. I told them to fire the mission using Willy Peter.

The bursting WP shells release thick clouds of brilliant white smoke and spew out fragments of phosphorus, which ignites on contact with air. I reckoned that if the North Vietnamese had never made the acquaintance of Willy Peter it would be a real eye-opener for them. Within a minute the shells whistled in, low over my head. The explosions were instantly effective in breaking up the NVA and silencing their guns.[12]

While the costly effort to reach the remnants of Lieutenant Herrick's platoon was [being attempted] in the brush a hundred yards away, Sergeant Ernie Savage [commanding for his dead lieutenant] and his surrounded buddies were clinging desperately to their little patch of ground. Savage had walked the artillery in tight around them and each time he heard voices or saw any movement he called in the heavy stuff. "It seemed like they didn't care how many of them were killed."

Captain Herren was on the radio keeping Savage informed of the attempts to break through. Finally Herren told Savage they couldn't make it before dark and were withdrawing. Herren told Savage, "Don't worry. You've won this fight already." Savage and Sergeant McHenry seemed confident they would survive if they could hold out through the night. Specialist Galen Bungum and others had their doubts. . . . "PFC Clark kept asking me: 'Do you think we'll make it?' I didn't know, but I said we have to pray and pray hard."[13]

The Second Day

It was 6:20 A.M., Monday, November 15, and in the half-light before dawn, the battalion operations officer, Captain Matt Dillon, knelt rummaging through his field pack for the makings of C-ration hot chocolate. An uneasy feeling nagged at me as I stood nearby peering into the calm dimness around the clearing. It had nothing to do with Sergeant Savage and the Lost Platoon. They had survived the night without further casualties, and Dillon and I had worked out a new plan for their rescue. No. It was something else that bothered me. It was too quiet. Too still. Turning to Dillon, I told him to order all companies to immediately send out reconnaissance patrols forward of their positions to check for enemy activity. Dillon put out that order while his radioman, Specialist 4 Robert McCollums, fired up a heat tab under a canteen cup of water for their hot chocolate.

While the patrols were preparing to ease out of the perimeter to check for enemy infiltrators, I told Dillon to radio all the company commanders to meet us at Bob Edwards's command post just behind the Charlie Company lines to discuss the best attack route out to Savage.

[*Colonel Moore planned a rescue attack with three companies, but the enemy attacked first, as he had half-expected from the eerie quiet.*]

Captain Bob Edwards remembers: "At first light Colonel Moore was planning to attack to reach the cut-off platoon. The company commanders were to meet at my command post to discuss this. He also directed us to patrol out from our positions for possible snipers or infiltrators that had closed in on the perimeter during the night. I passed this on to my platoon leaders and told them to send a squad from each of the four platoons out about two hundred yards. The patrols from 2nd Platoon, Lieutenant Geoghegan, and 1st Platoon, Lieutenant Kroger, had moved about a hundred and fifty yards in the search when they began receiving heavy small-arms fire. They returned fire and started back."

Geoghegan's platoon sergeant, Robert Jemison, recalls . . . "At first light we sent out a patrol. Staff Sergeant Sidney Cohen, Specialist 4 Arthur L. Bronson, and three other men [were picked]," says Jemison. "They saved us from being surprised. They spotted the enemy on their way in to attack our position. They came running back, with Bronson screaming: 'They're coming, Sarge! A lot of 'em. Get ready!' I told the machine gunners to hold their fire until they were close."

At the battalion command post the attack shattered the early-morning stillness like a huge explosion. The intense heavy firing told us with jolting clarity that the south and southeast sections of the X-Ray perimeter were under extremely heavy attack. I yelled to Dillon to call in all the firepower he could get. Fire swept across the landing zone and into my command post. It was 6:50 A.M.

Then—Lieutenant Colonel Hoang Phuong, who was present in the Ia Drang . . . says, "We had planned to launch our attack at two A.M., but because of air strikes and part of the battalion getting lost, it was delayed until 6:30 A.M. The attack was carried out" [*by a battalion of regulars and one of Vietcong*].

Bob Edwards was on the radio desperately trying to get information from his four platoons. The heaviest firing was in the vicinity of his 1st and 2nd platoons, who were holding down the left side of the lines. . . . Captain Edwards and the five men sharing the command-post foxhole began shooting at the onrushing enemy.

Moments later, there was a desperate radio call from Edwards: "I need help!" I [*Moore*] told him no; he would have to hold with his own resources and firepower for the time being. It would be tactically unsound, even suicidal, to commit my small reserve force so quickly, before we got a feel for what the enemy was doing elsewhere around the perimeter. Charlie Company was obviously in a heavy fight but they had not been penetrated.

Bob Edwards estimated that his men were being attacked by two or three companies and, to make things worse, a large number of the enemy had closed with Geoghegan and Kroger's two platoons before the artillery and air could be brought to bear. The North Vietnamese were now safely inside the ring of steel.

My command post and Alpha and Bravo companies, directly across the flat, open ground behind Edwards's foxholes, were now catching the enemy grazing fire, which passed through and over the Charlie Company lines.

The Bravo Company commander, John Herren, says: "I alerted my men to be ready to swing around and defend in the opposite direction if the enemy broke through into the perimeter behind us." In Alpha Company, Captain Nadal's radio operator, Specialist Tanner, remembers: "When morning broke it all started over again. . . . We would fire at any muzzle blast seen."

Bob Edwards [*Charlie Company*] could not raise Lieutenant Kroger or Lieutenant Geoghegan on his radio because the two platoon leaders and their men were fighting for their lives, blazing away at the onrushing enemy.

PFC Willie F. Godboldt, twenty-four . . . was hit while firing from his position twenty yards to Sergeant Jemison's right. Jemison remembers, "Godboldt was hollering: 'Somebody help me!' I yelled, 'I'll go get him.' Lieutenant Geoghegan yelled back: 'No, I will!' Geoghegan moved out of his position in the foxhole to help Godboldt and was shot."

The enemy now closed to within seventy-five yards of Edwards's line. They were firing furiously, some crouched low and at times crawling on their hands and knees. Others, no taller than the elephant grass they were passing through, came on standing up and shooting. They advanced, screaming at each other and at Edwards's men. Leaders were blowing whistles and using hand and arm signals. A few were even carrying 82mm mortar tubes and base plates. This was clearly no hit-and-run affair. They had come to stay.

Playing a key role in keeping Geoghegan's platoon from being overrun were two M-60 machine guns—one manned by Specialist James C. Comer of Seagrove, North Carolina, and Specialist 4 Clinton S. Poley, and the other operated by Specialist 4 George Foxe of Rocky Mount, North Carolina, and Specialist 4 Nathaniel Byrd of Jacksonville, Florida. Comer and Poley were on the left; Byrd and Foxe were off to the right, next to the 1st Platoon. Comer's gun interlocked its field of fire with that of Delta Company on the left, while Byrd and Foxe interlocked their fire with that of the 1st Platoon. Those two machine guns kept cutting down the enemy.

Now Bob Edwards's 3rd Platoon, led by Lieutenant Franklin, came under attack, but fortunately with nothing like the numbers or ferocity of the assault against Kroger's and Geoghegan's platoons. A heavy firefight developed on Franklin's right, involving Lieutenant Lane's reinforcing platoon from Bravo Company, 2nd Battalion. Sergeant John Setelin was in that scrap: "It seemed like half a battalion hit us all at once. He hit us headlong and he hit us strong. I thought we were going to be overrun. When Charlie hit us, he had this strange grazing fire. He shot right at ground level trying to cut your legs off, or, if you weren't deep enough in your foxhole, he shot your head off. When he started firing at us, it came like torrents of rain. You couldn't get your head up long enough to shoot back. You just stuck your weapon up, pulled the trigger, and emptied the magazine."

MOORE:

Back at the battalion command post, I had my ear glued to the radio handset when Captain Bob Edwards's voice broke in with a quick, curt "I'm hit!" I asked him how bad it was and whether he could still function. He replied that he was down and his left arm was useless, but he would do his best to carry on.[14]

[*Edwards was bleeding badly. He called Colonel Moore and asked that he send his executive officer, Lieutenant John W. Arrington, forward to take command (he was at the ammo dump); Moore sent him at a run to Edward's foxhole, only 50 yards from the battalion CP.*[15] *The enemy was right in front of Edwards, within easy hand grenade range.*]

Edwards's artillery forward observer was pinned down in the command-post foxhole, unable to adjust the fires. The battalion fire support coordinator, Captain Jerry Whiteside, calmly stood up, peered over the termite hill in the face of enemy fire, and adjusted the artillery and aerial rocket gunship fire forward of Charlie Company.

Lieutenant Charlie Hastings, our forward air controller, had already swung into action. Sensing disaster, Hastings made an immediate, instinctive decision: "I used the code-word 'Broken Arrow' . . . " [*American unit in danger of being overrun*] and we received all available aircraft . . . for close air support. We had aircraft stacked at 1,000-foot intervals from 7,000 feet to 35,000 feet, each waiting to receive a target and deliver their ordnance."

Now it was 7:15 A.M., and suddenly fighting broke out in front of the Delta Company machine guns and mortar positions. It was a separate, heavy assault on a section of the perimeter immediately to the left of Edwards's Charlie Company. Initial reports estimated two companies of enemy, many dressed in black uniforms. It was a Viet Cong battalion . . . making its first appearance on the battlefield.

Specialist 4 George McDonald, a Charlie Company mortarman, was beside his mortar near Sergeant Adams's position. "When our perimeter was attacked it was so close that we weren't able to use the mortars. I was told to use my M-79 [*a 'grenade launcher,' which also fired high explosive and buckshot rounds*] . . . and was pleased with the results."[16]

MOORE:

By now I was convinced that the enemy was making a primary effort to overrun us from the south and southeast, and I alerted the reserve platoon for probable commitment into the Charlie or Delta Company sectors. The noise of battle was unbelievable. Never before or since, in two wars, have I heard anything to equal it. I wanted to get help to Bob Edwards, but decided it was still too early in the game to commit the reserve force. Instead, I told Dillon to direct

Captain Tony Nadal of Alpha Company to quickly move a platoon across the clearing to reinforce Charlie Company.

Not wanting to weaken his critical left flank, which was closest to Charlie Company and was holding that sharp left turn in the line just east of the creek-bed, Nadal chose to pull out his right-flank 2nd Platoon—Joe Marm's unit, now led by Platoon Sergeant George McCulley—and send them over to help Edwards.[17] Nadal then ordered his 3rd Platoon leader, Sergeant Lorenzo Nathan, to stretch his men out to fill the gap left by the departure of McCulley's men. McCulley and his sixteen men, all that were left of Lieutenant Marm's platoon, came through the battalion command post. I briefed the sergeant and pointed out where Edwards's command post was located.

McCulley and his men headed out at a low crouch, moving fast in short bounds across the open ground under heavy enemy automatic-weapons fire. They lost two killed and two wounded—including Sergeant McCulley, who was wounded in the neck . . . but finally made it to the right center of the Charlie Company sector, about fifteen yards behind their lines. There, taking up positions that gave them good fields of fire, the remnants of the 2nd Platoon men provided some measure of defense in depth to Charlie Company. But the loss of four men crossing the clearing convinced me that further internal movements were inadvisable until we reduced the enemy grazing fire.

The enemy commander was getting better at this. His attacks on Charlie and Delta companies were well planned and came close to achieving complete surprise. And, unlike the first day when he committed his forces piecemeal, today he threw perhaps as many as a thousand men against us in a twenty-five-minute span. Then, too, I had spent too much time worrying about Herrick's platoon and how to rescue them. I should have paid more attention to the enemy's capabilities. If I had, I would have gotten the H-13 scout helicopters up at first light, sweeping the approaches at low level and looking for the enemy.

Clearly the enemy commander had moved his troops and reinforcements all night to get them in position. His objective was to position his assault force right under our noses, so close that our artillery could not be effectively used, and then smash through Charlie Company's lines and on out into the open clearing. With that, he could then roll right into the battalion command post and attack into the rear of Alpha and Bravo companies. Only the recon patrols at first light averted complete disaster.

The enemy troops had Geoghegan's and Kroger's understrength platoons in a deadly bear hug. Americans and North Vietnamese were dying by the dozens in the storm of fire.

The bloody hole in the ground that was Bob Edwards's command post was crowded with men. Sergeant Hermon Hostuttler lay crumpled in the dirt, now dead. Specialist 4 Ernie Paolone [was] bleeding from a shrapnel wound. . . . Sergeant James P. Castleberry, the artillery forward observer [and his] radio operator, PFC Ervin L. Brown, Jr. [were] the only unwounded men. . . . Bob Edwards, shot through the left shoulder and armpit, slumped, unable to move, in a contorted sitting position with his radio handset held to his right ear.

———————

Lieutenant Neil Kroger's platoon had taken the brunt of the enemy attack. Although artillery and air strikes were taking a toll on the follow-up forces, a large group of North Vietnamese soldiers had reached Kroger's lines and the killing was hand-to-hand.

Specialist Arthur Viera was crouched in a small foxhole firing his M-79. "The gunfire was very loud. We were getting overrun on the right side. The lieutenant [*Kroger*] came up out into the open in all this. I thought that was pretty good. . . . He hollered at me to help cover the left sector. I ran over to him and by the time I got there he was dead. He had lasted a half-hour."

Some thirty-five yards to Jemison's right rear, Lieutenant John Arrington had safely negotiated the open clearing and made it to the Charlie Company foxhole to take over from the badly wounded Captain Edwards. "Arrington made it to my command post and, after a few moments of talking to me while lying down at the edge of the foxhole, was wounded. He was worried that he had been hurt pretty bad and told me to be sure and tell his wife that he loved her.

"I thought: 'Doesn't he know that I am wounded, too?' Arrington was hit in the arm, and the bullet passed into his chest and grazed a lung."

At 7:45 A.M. the enemy struck at the left flank of Tony Nadal's Alpha Company, at that critical elbow where Alpha and Charlie Companies were tied in. We were now under attack from three directions. Grazing fire from rifles and heavy machine guns shredded the elephant grass and swept over the battalion command post and aid station.

At about this time fifteen or more mortar and rocket rounds exploded all around the termite-hill command post. We were locked into a fight to the death, taking heavy casualties in the Charlie Company area, and there was no question that we were going to need help. I radioed Colonel Tim Brown to ask him to prepare another company of reinforcements for movement as soon as it could be accomplished without undue risk. Brown, with typical foresight, had already alerted Alpha Company, 2nd Battalion and had it assembled with the helicopters to fly in on call.

JOE GALLOWAY REMEMBERS:

"The incoming fire was only a couple of feet off the ground and I was down as flat as I could get when I felt the toe of a combat boot in my ribs. I turned my head sideways and looked up. There, standing tall, was Sergeant Major Basil Plumley. Plumley leaned down and shouted over the noise of the guns: 'You can't take no pictures laying down there on the ground, sonny.' He was calm, fearless, and grinning. I thought: 'He's right. We're all going to die anyway, so I might as well take mine standing up.'"

The enemy commander's assault into the Delta Company line was not going well. In fact, he would have done a good deal better attacking any other sector of the perimeter. Delta Company now had its own six M-60 machine guns, plus three more M-60s from the recon platoon, stretched across a seventy-five-yard front. Each gun had a full four-man crew and triple the usual load of boxed ammunition—six thousand rounds of 7.62mm. To the left rear of the machine guns were the battalion's 81mm mortars, whose crews were firing in support of Charlie Company and, meanwhile, fending off the enemy at closer range with their rifles and M-79s.

SPECIALIST WILLARD F. PARISH [24, OKLAHOMA]:
I was in a foxhole with a guy from Chicago, PFC James E. Coleman, and he had an M-16. I had my .45 [pistol] and his .45 and I had an M-60 machine gun. . . .
"I was looking out front and I could see some of the grass going down, like somebody was crawling in it. I hollered: 'Who's out there?' Nobody answered so I hollered again. No answer. I turned to Coleman: 'Burn his ass.' Coleman said: 'My rifle's jammed!' . . . I looked back to the front and [enemy troops] were growing out of the weeds. I just remember getting on that machine gun . . . I really don't remember what . . . I did. I was totally unaware of the time, the conditions."
On that M-60 machine gun, according to extracts from his Silver Star citation, Specialist Parish delivered lethal fire on wave after wave of the enemy until he ran out of ammunition. Then, standing up under fire with a .45 pistol in each hand, Parish fired clip after clip into the enemy, who were twenty yards out; he stopped their attack. Says Parish: "I feel like I didn't do any more than anybody else." . . . More than a hundred dead North Vietnamese were later found where they had fallen in a semicircle around his foxhole.[18]

———

[*The fighting continued, with PAVN breaking through at places and shooting wounded lying on the ground, but the battalion tightened its perimeter and held firm. Help was on the way. Colonel Brown had started 2nd Battalion, 5th Cavalry, under Lieutenant Colonel Bob Tully, overland toward LZ X-Ray. Tully's force arrived just after noon (15 November); it was a well-trained battalion. (The 2nd Battalion, 7th Cavalry followed the next morning, 16 November, arriving about 12:00 noon.) Moore called on Tully's men, who were fresh, in battle formation, and moving west, to rescue the "lost platoon," led by Bravo Company 1st Battalion, whose men knew the location of the platoon and the ground to be covered. Tully pulled off the rescue with fair ease. There was some sniper fire, but PAVN casualties had been heavy; the Vietnamese had pulled out to regroup.*]

Just before four P.M. Matt Dillon got the radio call from Tully's operations officer advising that the relief force was now an estimated fifteen minutes away from

X-Ray. Dillon told Lieutenant [Richard P.] Tifft to start calling in the helicopters. Then Tully's force began closing on the perimeter. It was a bittersweet moment. Happy, relieved, and grateful to get that platoon back, I walked over to Tully and thanked him and his men. I shook hands with Ernie Savage and told him that he and his men had done a great job in the worst sort of situation. Then there was the sobering, grim sight of the dead and wounded of Herrick's platoon. The dead lay on their poncho litters. Two or three of the wounded came in on their own feet, half-walking, half-carried on the shoulders of their friends. Some of those who had survived without a scratch were so drained that they also required help.

As Savage, Bungum, and the others came into the command post, Joe Galloway talked briefly to each of them: "They were like men who had come back from the dead. We were all filthy, but they were beyond filthy. Their fatigue uniforms were ripped and torn; their eyes were bloodshot holes in the red dirt that was ground into their faces. I asked each man his name and hometown and wrote them down in my notebook, along with something of what they had gone through."

Within half an hour after the Tully task force had returned to X-Ray, Brigadier General Richard Knowles [*assistant division commander*] came up on the radio asking permission to land. He says, "We came in fast. I jumped out and my chopper departed. Morale was high and the 1st Battalion, 7th Cav was doing a great job."

Before leaving, General Knowles told us that he would direct Tim Brown to pull my battalion and the attached units out of X-Ray the next day and fly us back to Camp Holloway for two days of rest and rehabilitation. But for now we faced the prospect of another long night [15–16 November 1965] defending this perimeter.[19]

The Last Night and the Morning of 16 November

[*Capt. Myron Diduryk's reinforcement company from 2nd Battalion, 7th Cavalry took the brunt of fighting during the night. Amazingly, no Americans were killed and only six men were slightly wounded. The rest of the perimeter, Moore thought, had been too quiet. At dawn, he ordered a "Mad Minute" of fire, when every man on the perimeter would fire for two minutes at anything that bothered him, or just fire. The Mad Minute provoked some PAVN regulars to rise out of the grass and start an attack, probably prematurely. Artillery fire was brought in on them. It also nailed two snipers—one caught on his rope and hung there, dead, the other fell to the ground; a little later a third was shot when he tried to climb down and get away.*][20]

MOORE:

In our Mad Minute we had swept the area outside our perimeter. Now I ordered a sweep inside our lines. At 7:46 A.M. the reserve elements, the recon platoon, and the survivors of Charlie Company began a cautious and very deliberate patrol of the territory enclosed by our troops. I ordered them to conduct the sweep on hands and knees, searching for friendly casualties and North Vietnamese infiltrators in the tall elephant grass. They also checked the trees inside the line of foxholes closely. By 8:05 A.M. they were reporting negative results.

At 8:10 all units on line were ordered to coordinate with those on their flanks and prepare to move five hundred yards forward on a search-and-clear sweep, policing up any friendly casualties and all enemy weapons. There was a long delay before this dangerous but necessary maneuver could begin. Radio checks, ammo resupply, coordination with flanking units—all these took time for men who were slowing down mentally and physically after forty-eight hours of constant tension and no sleep. My last rest had been those five hours of sleep the night of November 13 [*prior to flying into LZ X-Ray*]. I could still think clearly but I had to tell myself what I intended to say before I opened my mouth. It was like speaking a foreign language before you are completely fluent in it.

I was translating English into English. I had to keep my head, concentrate on the events in progress, and think about what came next. The sweep began at 9:55 A.M., and Myron Diduryk's men had moved out only about seventy-five yards when they met enemy resistance, including hand grenades. Lieutenant James Lane, Diduryk's 2nd Platoon leader, was seriously wounded. I stopped all movement immediately and ordered Diduryk's company to return to their foxholes. Sergeant John Setelin, his burned arm still throbbing, was unhappy. "That morning we were ordered to sweep out in front of our positions. I didn't like that. At night I felt fairly safe because Charlie couldn't see me and I was in that hole and didn't have to get out. But when daylight came I wanted to cuss Colonel Moore for making us go outside our holes. We were told to make one last sweep, a final check around. During that sweep, [James] Lamonthe and I brought in one of the last of our dead.

[*Moore called for massive air support.*]

The aerial attack began [*by A-1E Skyraiders from the 1st Air Commando Squadron, Captain Bruce Wallace, flight leader*]. [*Forward air controller, Lieutenant Charlie*] Hastings had also called in a flight of jet fighter-bombers. Within minutes the brush out beyond Diduryk's lines was heaving and jumping to the explosion of rockets, 250- and 500-pound bombs, napalm, 20mm cannon shells, cluster bombs, and white phosphorus.

After several minutes of this I told Charlie Hastings: "One more five-hundred-pounder very, very close to kill any PAVN left out there, then call them *off*." I told Diduryk to order his men to fix bayonets and move out. Within ten seconds we jumped off into the black smoke of that last five-hundred-pound bomb.

LT. RICK RESCORLA [*of Diduryk's reinforcement company.*]:
"We gathered for the last sweep. Suddenly a fighter-bomber plowed down from above. We buried our noses at the bottom of our holes. An express train screamed down and the explosion shook the earth. The bomb landed thirty yards from our holes. We came up cursing in the dust and debris. The call came to move out. Every available trooper, including Colonel Moore, pushed the perimeter out."

This time it was no contest at all. We killed twenty-seven more enemy and crushed all resistance. I looked over a field littered with enemy dead, sprawled by ones and twos and heaps across a torn and gouged land. . . .

RICK RESCORLA (again):
"Colonel Moore, in our sector, was rushing up to clumps of bodies, pulling them apart. 'What the hell is the colonel doing up here?' Sergeant Thompson asked. I shook my head. Later we saw him coming back at the head of men carrying ponchos. By 10:30 A.M. Colonel Moore had found what he was looking for. Three dead American troops were no longer missing in action; now they were on their way home to their loved ones."[21]

[*Lieutenant Colonel Robert McDade with the rest 2nd Battalion, 7th Cavalry, plus Alpha Company of 1st Battalion, 5th Cavalry marched in at noon on 16 November from LZ Columbus, three miles east. In the column was PFC Jack P. Smith, son of TV anchorman Howard K. Smith. Jack Smith wrote of what he saw in a 1967 article for the* Saturday Evening Post.]

"The 1st Battalion had been fighting continuously for three or four days, and I had never seen such filthy troops. They all had that look of shock. They said little, just looked around with darting, nervous eyes. Whenever I heard a shell coming close, I'd duck but they kept standing. There must have been about 1,000 rotting bodies . . . starting at about 20 feet, surrounding the giant circle of foxholes."[22]

By now, late morning, Tuesday, November 16, the personality of Landing Zone X-Ray had changed. What previously had been a killing field had become something else. We moved about with impunity in places where movement had meant death only hours before. Except for our own air and artillery, there was nothing to be heard. It was just too quiet, too suddenly, and that made me uneasy. That old principle: Nothing was wrong except that nothing was wrong. Where was the enemy? Headed back into Cambodia? Still on the mountain, preparing to attack again? . . . Where were the enemy 12.7mm heavy anti-aircraft machine guns? If the enemy commander brought those weapons to bear on us from the mountain above, LZ X-Ray with three American battalions crowding the clearing would present a beautiful target. I told Dillon to step up the harassing artillery fire and . . . air strikes . . . in on the slopes above us. I told him I wanted a picture-perfect helicopter extraction, covered by all the firepower we could bring to bear.

Then, still worried about whether we had accounted for everyone, I ordered the battalion rear command post to do a new accounting on all our dead and wounded. And I told Myron Diduryk to take his company out on one final lateral sweep across his front 150 yards out.

[*Diduryk found nothing, but men of 1st Battalion, 5th Cavalry, attached to 2nd Bn, 7th Cavalry, found one of Moore's dead, in a foxhole.*]

A sergeant ordered his men: " . . . 'Get him by the harness and drag him to the choppers.' Someone came up behind me and said: 'No, you won't do that, Sergeant. He's one of my troopers and you will show respect. Get two more men and *carry* him to the landing zone.' It was Colonel Moore, making a final check of his positions."[23]

Frank McCulloch, *Time* magazine's Saigon bureau chief at the time, says, "A helicopterload of us reporters flew into LZ X-Ray on the third day. A few rounds came in and we all flopped down on the ground. We looked up and there was [Joe] Galloway standing up, saying: 'Bullshit. That stuff ain't aimed at us.'"

Charlie Black, of the *Columbus* (Georgia) *Ledger-Enquirer,* came up and hugged Galloway. . . . Galloway tried to tell Black something of what had happened in this place . . . for one of the long reports he airmailed home [for] the 1st Cavalry Division's hometown newspaper, read by the wives and children of the soldiers: "Charlie, these are the greatest soldiers that have ever gone into a fight! There hasn't been any outfit like this before. It's something I wish every American could understand, what these kids did. Look over there; doesn't that make you feel good?" [The reporters looked] toward . . . where a GI had planted a small American flag atop the shattered trunk of a tree.[24]

MOORE:

Now came the body count. . . . We did the best we could to keep a realistic count of enemy dead. In the end it added up to 834 dead by body count, with an additional 1,215 estimated killed and wounded by artillery, air attacks, and aerial rocket attacks. On my own I cut the 834 figure back to 634, a personal allowance for the confusion and fog of war, and let the 1,215 estimated stand. . . .

On our side, we had lost 79 Americans killed in action, 121 wounded, and none missing.[25]

Evacuation and Muted Triumph

Dean Brelis, an NBC News correspondent, was in LZ Falcon [*where Moore's troops transferred to larger choppers*] that afternoon. He captured the scene in his 1967 book, *The Face of South Vietnam.*

> Hal Moore was the last man to come out of the battle. It was the biggest battle he had ever fought. He was a lieutenant colonel, and he carried himself like a proud man. His sergeant major was at his side. It would need a Shakespeare to describe what happened then, but it was something that was love and manliness and pride. It was the moment of the brave. Hal Moore turned and went from group to group of his men, and only a few bothered to get up because there was no exclusivity now, no rank, and Hal Moore did not want them to stand and salute. He was saluting them. He talked with them. He thanked them. He was not solemn, and he did not bring to his greetings the salutations of a politician.

There was no poverty of spirit in his handshake, and he shook every man's hand. It was a union of the men who had met and defeated the enemy, not forever, not in a victory that ended the war, but in a victory over their uncertainty. When their hour had come they had done their job, and it was this thought, too, that Hal Moore had in his mind. And he said that if they had won no one else's gratitude, they had his.[26]

After forty minutes or so with Herren's company we walked over to the artillery positions, manned by A and C batteries of the 1st Battalion, 21st Artillery, and commanded, respectively, by Captain Don Davis and Captain Bob Barker.

MOORE:

I asked Barker and Davis to gather their gunners. The artillerymen, who had fired more than eighteen thousand rounds over fifty-three straight hours, were exhausted. Huge mountains of empty brass shell casings had grown beside their guns. The gunners who gathered in front of me were stripped to the waist, their skin dyed red from the dirt and sweat. I thanked them from the bottom of my heart. I told them exactly what their barrages of high-explosive shells had done for us in the heat of battle, and what they had done to the enemy.[27]

Later, as the Chinooks began ferrying the troops to Camp Holloway, Plumley and I stayed behind a while longer, talking with the artillerymen, before boarding the Huey for the ride back. We were not present to see what reporter Dean Brelis witnessed at Holloway and recounted in his book:

> *By late afternoon they were all back at Pleiku.* They walked off the big Chinooks and, without anyone giving a command, they straightened up. They were not dirty, tired infantrymen anymore. *Hal Moore's battalion voluntarily dressed their lines, as if they were coming back to life.* And the GI's who had not been in the Ia Drang glanced at them with something approaching awe because these were the guys who had been in it. No cheers, but they could not conceal their admiration. A few GI's were taking pictures as we went by—there was something dramatic in the scene all right, because Hal Moore's men had not yet thrown off what they had been through.

In the cockpit of the Huey flying Plumley, Ouellette, and myself toward Pleiku was Serpent 6, Old Snake, Major Bruce Crandall. Beside Crandall was his copilot, Captain Jon Mills. Old Snake had taken us into this thing and now he was taking us out. When we landed and shut down at Camp Holloway, the sergeant major and I left to make sure that our troopers were being well taken care of. But before walking off I told Crandall that after all that had happened I sure could use a drink. Old Snake pointed out a small, gaudily painted Quonset-hut Officers Club nearby, and we agreed to meet there later.

Plumley and I found that the troops were doing all right. They had been given hot showers, clean fatigue uniforms, hot chow, cold beer, and some pup tents for shelter.

Assured that my men were being taken care of, I rejoined Bruce Crandall and Jon Mills and we headed off for that drink. I was still wearing my grimy, frayed old World War II—style herringbone twill fatigues that I had lived in for the last five days. In *Pleiku: The Dawn of Helicopter Warfare in Vietnam*, J. D. Coleman tells what happened next:

> When they walked up to the bar the bartender told them he couldn't serve them because Moore was too dirty. . . . Moore patiently explained that they had just come out of the field and would really appreciate a drink. The bartender replied: "You're in the First Cav. This Club doesn't belong to you; you'll have to leave." Mills says that was when Hal started to lose his patience. He said: "Go get your club officer and we'll settle this. But right now, I'm here and I'm going to have a drink. And I would like to have it in the next couple of minutes." The bartender beat a hasty retreat to summon the club officer but still refused the trio service. So Moore unslung his M-16 and laid it on the bar. Mills and Crandall solemnly following suit with their .38's. Moore then said: "You've got exactly thirty seconds to get some drinks on this bar or I'm going to clean house." The bartender got smart and served the drinks. By this time, the club officer had arrived. He had heard all about the fight in the valley and knew who Moore was. And, as it turned out, so did most of the customers in the club. From then on, the trio couldn't buy a drink. That was when they knew that the fight on LZ X-Ray was finally over.[28]

Conclusions

General Moore represents the very finest in American combat leadership. His principles, detailed early in this chapter, were clearly those he followed in the Ia Drang battle and afterward. He fought alongside his men; he put their needs before his own; he demanded honor for his heroes and respect for his dead.

It is tragic that men such as Hal Moore and his troopers were asked to fight a war that the United States should not have entered, and which our armed forces were not allowed to win—a fact that gnawed at the American military's morale for two decades.[29]

XVIII

Nicholas F. "Nick" Vaux

(1936–   )

VAUX AND THE HAPPY WARRIORS OF 42 COMMANDO

NICK VAUX is given a chapter here because of he commanded the 42 Commando, Royal Marines, in the Falklands War. Since World War II, the major powers have depended increasingly on Special Operations Forces (SOF) to handle emergencies—"peace-keeping," assisting a given side in a small war, spearheading a larger conflict, damping a terrorist situation, and the like. The British SOF are of the finest. They include the SAS (Special Air Service) and SBS (Special Boat Service), which recruit men largely for covert operations, and the Royal Marine Commandos, who are the "happy warriors." Vaux and "the 42" in the Falklands provide a good example of elite unit operations.

Nicholas Francis Vaux, now Major-General (ret.), CB, DSO, was born in 1936 in (as he puts it) "a remote part of central Africa." He lived in this place of mystery until he was ten, then went off to school in Great Britain. Commissioned into the Royal Marines in 1954, he took part in the British-French seizure of the Suez Canal Zone in 1956.[1]

Vaux went on to serve in various Marine units in the Mediterranean and Far East, and in the West Indies aboard a frigate, and attended the Army Staff College at Camberley. He was able to "stand still" long enough (1966) to marry Zoya Hellings, daughter of a senior marine, and later to father two daughters and a son. Among subsequent assignments were staff officer in the Ministry of Defence and special adviser to the U.S. Marine Corps. Prior to the Falklands emergency, he spent many winters in Norway with the arctic warfare forces of the Royal Marines.

In 1982, as a lieutenant colonel, he commanded 42 Commando, Royal Marines (RM), during the Falklands War, and won the Distinguished Service Order. He attended the Royal College of Defence Studies, London, in 1985, and the same year was appointed chief of staff, Commando Forces Royal Marines. In 1987 he was given command of the Royal Marine Commandos and promoted to major general. He retired in 1990, and since 1993 has been consultant and managing director of the UK-Russia Security Group.

Nick Vaux was once an inter-Service pentathlete and a steeplechase rider, as well as a skier and mountain climber, and still enjoys hunting, fishing, and training hunting dogs. He lives with his wife at Plymouth and on Dartmoor, England.[2]

The passages below are from Nick Vaux's *Take That Hill: Royal Marines in the Falklands War*.

British Ground Forces in the Falklands War

[*Major General Jeremy Moore, RM, commanded the British ground forces that recovered the British Falkland Islands (seized by Argentina in April 1982). The forces comprised the 3 Commando Brigade, under Brigadier Julian Thompson, RM; 5 Army Brigade; and advance units of the SAS and SBS.[3] The 3 Commando Brigade comprised 40, 42, and 45 Commandos with 2 and 3 Battalions of the Parachute Regiment attached. It landed at San Carlos, on the northwestern corner of the main island. The 5 Brigade, composed of Guards Regiments, arrived later, and was hard-hit by the Argentine Air Force. After 3 Brigade had fought its way across the island, the two forces were joined for the three-day march on the capital, Port Stanley. The campaign lasted only six weeks (1 May–14 June 1982). We pick up the "42" as it is about to leave Ascension Island, the staging area for much of the ground force.*]

Camaraderie at the Start

It was now apparent that international diplomacy could not avert conflict. Before leaving Ascension 6 May [1982] each unit chose to have a 'smoker', as they called it, where officers and NCOs joined their troops in the men's canteen for a last 'get-together'. John Ware and his band were at 'Four-Two's', helping to create the boisterous camaraderie which will always be one of my best memories of this time. We were completely at ease with each other, and full of confidence in ourselves. Every now and again the cheerful chatter would die down for a 'Four-Two Special', which might be a solitary comedian unerringly ridiculing the officer establishment, some sort of song, or a musical group. Marine Maurice Toombs was a particular favourite. He had adapted the old Cliff Richard hit 'Summer Holiday' to altogether more sinister verses, predicting a fate that would shortly overtake 'The Spics' on the Malvinas. The song was in the most appalling taste from an outsider's point of view, and unashamedly vicious, too. But aggression had now to be encouraged, and morale fostered, in every way possible. I asked for an encore. Once again, we all roared out those ghastly threats with gusto.

The evening ended when, quite spontaneously, the band launched into a patriotic theme. Suddenly, unexpectedly, certainly out of character for the predominant generation present, we were all on our feet, singing lustily and emotionally. But the songs were those that, nowadays, only have an annual, implausible airing at the last night of The Proms. We might have been a battalion on a troopship to South Africa, the Dardanelles, or India. As I watched those bronzed young faces, raised in martial chorus, it was clear that each and every one had accepted the coming challenge. They knew that, in success or disaster, they were committed together, and felt that this was how it should be. I knew then that, given the chance to close with the enemy, we could unleash a fearful ferocity.

The Commando Attitude

In an article about 42 Commando, John Shirley had quoted me as saying: "You have to have a violent and uncompromising attitude to this job. It's what you get paid for. War is about generating violence and we have to generate more of it more quickly than the other side . . . " Looking about me at the "smoker", with the whole Commando in full voice, I recognized that this was precisely what we could do.

The time had come to stimulate, rather than suppress, the potential for violence that simmers within elite forces. We were going to war.[4]

Combat HQ and Personnel

Tac HQ was made up of a mixture of signallers, drivers, and the Provost for protection, meticulously directed by the indefatigable RSM [Regimental Sergeant Major]. David Chisnall was one of the youngest ever selected in the Royal Marines, and one of the most wary and accomplished field soldiers I have known. For nearly fifteen years he had alternated between unit Reconnaissance Troops across the world, and the Mountain and Arctic Cadre. He had also completed over ten winters in North Norway, climbed to "severe" standard in the Alps, qualified as a ski teacher in a Norwegian school, and completed a bewildering variety of special operations training. Immensely strong and lithe, he moved like a wild animal through cover or at night, with an instinctive awareness of danger that was to save my life at least once. Despite this primeval nature, however, he was invariably well turned-out; indeed, I once wrote in a report that he could be found "as immaculate and unruffled on top of some mountain in a gale, as he was when directing unit ceremonial on the parade ground". WO1 [Warrant Officer 1] Chisnall was younger than me, and we had not served together before, but we liked each other from the outset, a particular advantage in such a crucial relationship within the unit hierarchy.

The RSM is the senior non-commissioned rank, and it is he who safeguards the men's individual interests, using, if necessary, his exclusive access to the CO. This paternalism must be matched by unremitting enforcement of professional standards, especially amongst the SNCOs [Senior Non-commissioned Officers]. . . . David Chisnall was perhaps less imposing than my first RSM in the 1950s, a fearsome figure who would crash to attention with a daunting salute before declaring in stentorian tones: "Mr Vaux, Sir! It's time you had your hair cut again, and have you written to your mother this week?" But Chisnall was just what was needed for 42 Commando in the 1980s. His only drawback, as far as I was concerned, was that he was teetotal—hangovers were never shared experiences on early morning ski trips or at Orderly Room.[5]

The Company Commanders

Until now, there has been only oblique reference to the two men who would lead "K" and "L" Companies. ["M" *Company was detached to take South Georgia Island, with SAS, SBS, and Royal Navy units*] . . . [T]he relationship between a CO and his rifle company commanders . . . must be adapted to the personality and experience of individuals. A frustrated company commander is of little use in battle, when mutual confidence and freedom of action count for all.

Captain David Wheen, who commanded "L" Company, had been a wild young subaltern and Navy skier in the same unit where I first had to accept the restrictions of desk and telephone. I envied him then, and wondered now how he apparently still managed to seem a military "free spirit". This was largely due to his boundless enthusiasm for doing what he enjoyed, as well as to a lively and friendly personality. All of which made him a popular and relaxed company commander, if not always a conscientious administrator. In adversity he was robust and determined, especially in the Arctic, where he was as much at home on a pair of skis as any local. [*The 42 trained in Norway regularly.*] A typical memory of David is of him outfacing a Norwegian major as they hurtled ever faster down an icy, ever-steepening slope. Eventually the Scandinavian prudently turned up his ski tips to slow down and acknowledge defeat, while Wheen swooped on down the slope with a triumphant whoop. The major bone of contention between David and myself, the subject of some amusement to signallers and officers on the unit command net, was that OC [officer commanding] "L" Company seldom responded on the radio as quickly as the CO thought he should.

OC 'K' Company was a very different personality. Peter Babbington was . . . expert in support weapons, as well as an experienced Arctic operator. His dour, single-minded attitude to the parochial interests of his company could be either reassuring or aggravating, depending upon whether these coincided with the Commando's more general intentions. His charges, of course, reciprocated with a fierce loyalty and keen response to all Peter asked of them; nevertheless, his strong convictions and vigorous personality made him a firm disciplinarian. He was a thoroughly practical soldier—imperturbable, resourceful, absolutely determined once embarked on a course of action. Even though there was some truth in the topical joke that 'Four-Two' did this, while 'K Commando' did that, I knew that Peter and his men could be relied upon when it mattered.[6]

42 Commando, RM, in Action

[*When the Commandos landed (21 May 1982), the 42, amid much grumbling, was put in reserve, while other units secured San Carlos and vicinity. However, after ten days of enduring intense cold, rain, and snow, the troops were elated to be airlifted (31 May) to Mount Kent, on the far side of the island, and become spearheaders. They cleaned up after the SAS, which had preceded them, and Vaux began preparations to take the next mountain, Mount Harriet, a step nearer to Port Stanley. We pick up the "42" on Mount Kent.*]

Initial Contact with the Enemy

It was now that we also began to see increasing numbers of prisoners. They were either captured by our patrols, or sometimes just found wandering, apparently eager to give themselves up. The marines were more intrigued by their enemies than actively hostile to them, but could not resist some gentle mockery: '*Hey, José—who cries for Argentina now, then . . .* ?' Most of the captives seemed very young and bewildered, although some of their so-called Special Forces troops inclined to arrogance, a posture swiftly punctured by the caustic wit of our own hard-bitten NCOS. The prisoners' wonder at the high morale of our troops and the rapport between officers, NCOs and marines was very evident. There was much laughter on one occasion, brought about by the FN automatic rifle with which a marine had presented me on Mount Kent. I had kept the weapon, largely because it was handier to carry than my Sterling submachine-gun. A rather cocky Argentine sergeant asked if this meant that the British rifle was inferior to the FN, to which I replied that there had not been a chance to use it yet. 'But', chipped in [his British guard], 'We have really been waiting for someone like you who could run fast enough for the CO to find out. . . .'[7]

Command and "Staff"

For Guy [Sheridan, major, second in command] and myself, the command BV became our workplace and our shelter. [*The Volvo BV was a heavy-duty tracked vehicle.*] Although it was extremely cramped with two of us in there, we could share the monitoring of the radio, [and] co-ordinate our problems much more easily. During the day we hardly saw each other. Guy concerned himself with logistic and administrative preparations, while I was usually away. Occasionally we had to have 'O' Groups with the company commanders. . . . By squeezing up like sardines, all the officers except Phil Wilson and Mike Norman could just fit inside the BV. Those two were so burly that they had to remain outside, peering cheerfully over the back of the vehicle. Although its canvas screen could be draped over their shoulders, the rain and wind lashed at their buttocks.

Humor and a Canteen of Cheer

In the dim red glow of the battle-lights, I could glance round at the fierce, blackened faces, bristling with stubble, drawn with fatigue, and imagine myself among some desperate band of cornered brigands. Then someone would make a characteristic aside, we'd all laugh, and suddenly they were transformed back into the officers of 'Four-Two' whom I knew so well from Orderly Room, mess parties, parades in ceremonial dress. Beneath those grim faces the humour and mutual trust remained untarnished. It was so very important for us all to be reminded of that. It would have been nice to have had 'a glass of comfort' on these occasions. But such things were wistful memories, until one day we were visited by [Colonel] Tom Seccombe . . . Deputy Brigade Commander, dressed distinctively in his own choice of field gear, which included Wellington boots and a blackthorn stave that would have done credit to Little John in Sherwood Forest. He tramped around the positions dispensing gruff encouragement and hilarious observations in appropriate doses, much to the delight of the marines, who knew him well and appreciated seeing him. After putting to me some shrewd suggestions for improving our lot, he turned to leave, heading for his helicopter. 'Oh, by the way, Nick . . . I think we should exchange water bottles,' he suddenly said. I goggled at him utterly mystified. 'Come on, here's mine,' he went on, slightly impatiently. I handed over my battered, half-empty bottle and received a new and very full one in exchange. Only after I had saluted as the helicopter took off did I realize that this was certainly no ordinary bottle of water. The next 'O' Group gave me the chance to share 'Uncle Tom's' kind consideration with the others.

Command from the Front: Julian Thompson

Brigadier Julian, of course, visited 'Four-Two' as often as he could, and he and I looked at Mount Harriet together from various vantage points. We knew little enough then about the enemy strengths, but the position was obviously being held in order to prevent a British advance along the track [path, actually—there were no roads except on the coast] from Goose Green to Stanley. We also concluded that there must be some form of mine barrier, although only patrolling could determine the answers we sought. The Brigadier, however, was obviously more worried just then about whether 42 Commando could survive in its present positions long enough to accomplish such patrolling. Then, a day or so [later] one of his staff visited us. . . . It was a ghastly day of wind and rain, and Commando HQ looked like a shipwreck with the survivors stumbling miserably about in the murk.

Rest in the Rear?

I was not too surprised to be told that the Brigade Commander was coming up again the next morning. Julian Thompson asked me . . . whether I agreed that the Commando should be withdrawn for a 'drying-out period'. Every effort would be made, he promised, to bring us back into the line for the main attack. He left me with twenty-four hours in which to think it over. . . .

It was clear that how I answered would be one of the critical decisions of 'Four-Two's' war. By now there was evidence of real suffering among the troops in the rifle company positions. I could see that if we endured too long in these mountains, we might not be capable of a major attack at the end of that time. Moreover, our patrols were now going to have to fight for the intelligence we needed to plan the main assault. That would require leadership, initiative, aggression and stamina, from increasingly weary and weakened junior leaders and marines. The self-confidence and determination with which we had landed were now being eroded ominously. Morale and fitness are like bank accounts—incessant withdrawals must be compensated for eventually.

No, Thanks. We Deserve a "Proper Battle"

But withdrawal smelt of failure, and spelt obscurity. Whoever took our place would certainly attack Mount Harriet, since they would have patrolled and planned for it. If we came back at all, it would be as a reserve or flanking unit. This was precisely what I sought to avoid. If we must go to war, then 'Four-Two' surely deserved the chance to fight a proper battle. I believed that this was the collective view. All the same it was only fair [to get the opinions of the officers and men]. . . . To a man they turned the offer down, decisively and with confidence. 'Nobody wants out of this mountain, Colonel,' said David Wheen. 'We just want to hurry up and get onto the next one. . . . ' My other sensor of the Commando pulse, the Regimental Sergeant-Major, was equally positive about the will to remain for a fight. I told Julian Thompson. It was clear that he was as relieved . . . as I had been.[8]

Medical Evacuation

[On a patrol to find a way through minefields, Marine Kevin Patterson had his foot blown off. "Casevac"—casualty evacuation, by helicopter—promised to get him to hospital, despite the foul weather.]

So while the pilot, Captain Nick Pounds RM, thrashed through the gusting rain and stygian gloom towards enemy territory in which exhausted, wary men strained to hear his approach, we relayed their terse queries and directions from . . . [42] Commando HQ. Against all odds, a pick-up was made on the track itself [vulnerable to enemy fire]. Nick Pounds's only comment to me later was about the cheerful courage of Patterson, who had joked over the intercom as they flew straight to Ajax Bay and the surgical expertise that would save him.[9]

Strain on the Kidneys

After the casevac had been completed I spoke with [the patrol leader] Sergeant [M.] Collins on the radio. We had a critical decision to make. Although there was now a very serious risk of his patrol being compromised, we must go on seeking a route through the minefields. Unless one could be found, an attack from the right flank would be impossible. They understood that . . . Collins told me calmly; he and the other three were ready and willing to carry on.

Not long after setting out again, when roughly opposite the enemy positions at the western end of Mount Harriet, Collins and his men . . . suddenly . . . realized that their patrol had been spotted. A large group of the enemy loomed out of the darkness and began to move down towards them from the track. Collins retreated rapidly with his group, until he fell into a water-filled peat cutting. The rest of the patrol threw themselves on top of him. . . . The four of them hastily adopted a somewhat optimistic defensive position. At that point, the Argentines went to ground as well. For the next—excruciatingly cold—hour or so, nobody moved! Then, despite the acute tension, Collins turned to Lance-Corporal Steven Sparkes, who lay beside him, and whispered in the troops vernacular, 'How's your bottle [bladder], then?'

Unhesitatingly, Sparkes replied that it had 'gone pop' a long time ago. This apparently reduced all of them to uncontrollable fits of the giggles. . . . Meanwhile, Sergeant Collins had surmised that the winners of this 'Mexican Stand-Off', as he called it, would be the experienced professionals and he was [right]. [The enemy fell back.][10]

Finding Enemy Positions—The Hard Way

[Lieutenant Mark] Townsend and his lads were to harass the enemy's forward positions, attempting to draw their fire and expose the defences. By now we had pinpointed a series of strong-points and machine-gun nests with this tactic which, although dangerous, invariably spooked the enemy's inexperienced conscripts into firing wildly into the darkness. Already we knew that there were at least two companies holding the area, one at either end of 'Zoya' [the west flank of Harriet]. Now it seemed increasingly likely that there were even more Argentines in the vicinity. After our ventures to the south, I was also keen to keep up activity on both flanks, in order to avoid giving any indication of our intended axis of attack. I Troop had a stimulating night out. They killed six enemy and wounded several more, forcing the Argentines to abandon at least one position. Best of all, they spread panic and confusion throughout the area. Marine Graham Fisk unexpectedly had to demolish one wretched defender with a 66-mm rocket at close quarters: 'There was nothing left of him from his kneecaps upwards . . .'

Each time we terrorized the defenders of Mount Harriet, their confidence would be eroded. At the same time, we must seem increasingly ferocious to them. This patrol also managed to pin-point three more machine-gun positions before returning unscathed, under impressively close cover from a series of thunderous barrages. These, we hoped, had punished the defenders as much as they depleted our reserves of gun ammunition. The next day, 'K' Company's morale was sky-high after such a successful 'blooding'. Confidence in Chris Romberg as their artillery controller was also firmly established. Somewhere in all the excitement, [a 42 reconnaissance] patrol had slipped undetected on to 'Katrina' [a ridge north of Harriet], from where they made invaluable sightings throughout the next day.

While all that was going on, the redoubtable [Sergeant] 'Jumper' Collins and Lieutenant Colin Beadon, the Milan [guided missile] Troop Commander, with three other marines, were painstakingly feeling their way through the maze of obstacles across that naked plain south of Mount Harriet. They were no doubt grateful for the chaos beyond the crestline as a distraction for the enemy above them. After some hours they penetrated to the track junction opposite 'Zoya's' western extremity. At this point, Beadon had seen . . . sites for his Milan firing-posts down the track Stanley, along which the enemy could counter-attack with his armoured cars. Collins, however, had one more task, check on a fence that I had hoped could be used as a start-line for our attack. Alone and unarmed . . . he . . . crawled . . . among enemy positions. Half an hour later he was back. The mission had been accomplished.

The 42 Plan of Attack

On Thursday 10 June, I flew to Brigade 'O' Group below Mount Kent. Already [Brigade Operations officer, Captain] Ian McNeill had passed our outline plan to the staff, who now knew our attack would be 'right flanking'. We had asked [to depart from] the silent-attack policy because harassing gunfire might be necessary to distract enemy lookouts across the plain. It was reassuring to be told that this available 'on call'.[11]

[Vaux was unhappy, however, to learn that the Welsh Guards would fall in south of him after 42 took Mount Harriet. The Guards had lost a number of men when their troop ships had been hit by Argentine aircraft fire, and had just reorganized. Vaux was concerned about their morale—but also, he admits, the 42 preferred to go it alone.]

The Brigadier Ignores the Odds

With simple, but comprehensive orders, the Brigadier [Thompson] inspired us . . . to launch our units against a numerically superior enemy, holding formidable . . . positions. Despite the logistic setbacks, . . . consequences of enemy air attacks, the conflicting interests within the Task Force, and . . . pressures from the home base, we were ready. Many of his problems were those that com-

manders in war have always had to face. But some could also be ascribed to twentieth-century communications and the scope that they provided for armchair campaigning. Regardless of all this, Julian Thompson never lost his aim . . . to attack . . . the following night—Friday 11 June.[12]
[42 Commando attacked Mount Harriet from the south, while 40 and 45 Commandos and the Paras took heights to the north—all closing on Port Stanley.]

Attack on Mount Harriet

'K' were the first Company in and the first to go, but even a cool operator like Babbington was obviously troubled by his thoughts and was putting off that initial step of leaving. I found an apprehensive Peter in deep and dilatory thought. I asked 'Have you got everything?' 'I think so', he replied—together we did a quick finger check off, then just stood very close facing each other. I grabbed his hand, shook it and said 'I'll see you at first light at the top, then.' He said 'I'll be there', and disappeared into the darkness with his company. I knew what he'd been thinking because we'd had a very quick word at the end of the 'O' Group. I'm not a particularly religious man, but I offered a silent prayer for my very good friend, but then cursed him soundly as I realised he'd gone without his Milan Section [missiles] and that I would have to tell the CO we'd screwed it up already![13]
[The Milan Section caught up at the track.]

Timings to move out had already been given, so radio codewords would merely confirm progress at various checkpoints. Colin Beadon and his advance party had already set off down to the track below. Guy and Phil Wilson were ensconced in the Mortar Troop HQ where they would remain, unscathed, we hoped, in case they had to take over command. On the Brigade radio net, a staff officer was plausibly and convincingly explaining, in clear speech, that fuel shortages would delay movement forward for several days.

HQ Troops Volunteer for the Attack

Immediately after the Commando 'O' Group, Matt Sturman had taken me aside to urge that he should be allowed to go with 'Porter Troop'. There were, he argued, enough officers of the required experience in Main HQ and so he could be far more useful forward with this untried organization, which we had created to defend against counter-attacks. It was a characteristic request from a dedicated officer who had volunteered to accompany the Commando in the first place. . . . I said that he could go. Soon he [led] 'Porter Troop' off down 'Tara's' rough slope, a tactical distance behind 'K' Company, who had begun their move as soon as Beadon had reported that he had crossed the track.

Now that the concentration area was clearing, Tac HQ could also move out on to its chosen vantage point high on 'Tara's' southern shoulder. . . . The Argentines had obligingly constructed a spacious peat bunker there around a stone sheep-pen, [which might not] have withstood the impact of a 155-mm shell . . . but it gave a little shelter from the piercing wind. . . . From there we had a panoramic view of the plain below, with ghostly trail around the base of the Challenger features.

The Approach Maneuver Begins

The advance party, consisting of 9 Troop from "J" Company [*another improvised group*], with engineers and anti-tank elements in support, was already behind time: the Milan teams could not sustain the pace as they struggled over the rough going under their crushing burdens. There was nothing to do now but wait . . . monitoring progress, reacting to the unforeseen, praying that our luck would hold. As if to emphasize the last aspect, I found myself whispering quietly with Albert Hempenstall, the chaplain, while we gazed out over the plain on which so many lives were now being hazarded. The 'Padre' was popular within the unit, and always present in adversity. . . . The marines also respected him for his long experience with Green Beret. . . .

About an hour after 'K' Company had crossed the silvery three-quarter moon sailed provocatively out from serried banks of cloud. The effect was most disconcerting. Light and shadow were harshly accentuated everywhere, but at that distance we could detect no movement from the direction we knew our troops to be. However, enemy patrols or listening posts in the area would be a major hazard [*if there were any*]. Shortly afterwards, when the Advance Party had just reached the lake in the centre of the plain, the Argentines suddenly put up several starshells. . . . Our own vengeful salvoes wailed above us, to burst among 'Zoya's' nearest crags. . . . Beadon and Babbington reported themselves on the move again, but we held David Wheen's company on our side of the track for the time being. There was silence everywhere else on the 3 Commando Brigade battlefront [*a deliberate silent attack policy*] although hundreds of commandos and paras were stalking through the darkness towards their objectives. [Our] assault would [be] in the middle of the night, [not] the usual dawn attack.

'L' Company had already had their share of problems. In the blackness of the concentration area, someone had accidentally fired his rifle. Such an accident is always a hazard, although the risk of detection at that distance from the enemy was . . . not a worry. Nor, by a miracle, was anyone hurt. But the company had been unsettled by the incident. . . . Then, the Sergeant-Major had begun to sense that all was not well in one of the leading troops, and had gone forward to check. [*He sent back a disabled trooper, game but slowing the march.*]

On two more occasions . . . starshells cast a baleful glow over this wilderness, on which two rifle company groups and assorted teams of supporters skulked in the shadows. Each time we invoked retribution in the form of artillery and naval gunfire support. The shells burst in vicious conflagrations on the crestline, 105-mm with a lurid, red flash, the 4.5-inch shells with an evil greenish glow that seemed to rise up from the stricken target. It was odd to listen to the calm, almost casual exchanges between [Forward observer] Nigel Bedford and HMS *Yarmouth*, almost ten miles out to sea. Under his direction she could put down a devastatingly accurate . . . fire at minimal notice.[14]

The Attackers Move Up Undetected

Despite this increasing disruption to the night, however, we did not seem to have been detected, and no enemy machine-guns or artillery sought to interfere with our progress. 'L' Company crossed track and set off, an hour or so behind 'K'. Not long afterwards, Colin Beadon reported that he reached the forming-up position. This was important news. It indicated that the original route was still clear, and that 9 Troop had now marked it for the rifle companies following. Beadon would now secure the area and deploy his Milan firing-posts covering the route from Stanley, before moving off in search of the Welsh Guards on the start-line. We had heard nothing from them as yet, nor had our liaison officer managed to get through to us on the radio. The various delays were frustrating both company commanders. They were understandably under pressure, and some crisp dialogue had already taken place about holding up advance and maintaining the separation between sub-units. . . . The 'Four-Two' command net was known for its volatility. . . . There was no point in suddenly becoming tactful and sympathetic now—that might . . . have created alarm and despondency!

The Start-line Secured

[Colin] Beadon reported no sign of the Guards along the fence we selected as a start-line. In the event of failing to communicate, we had agreed a rendezvous time with them, but this had long passed. Soon Peter would be approaching the forming up position [FUP], where I was anxious he should not have to linger. 'Shall we secure it ourselves?' asked Colin. 'Yes!' we told him swiftly.

―――――――

While this was happening Colin had secured the start-line with our own people, and was moving back down towards the FUP. Suddenly he detected movement on his left. Peering through his image intensifier, he observed a small group of men in amongst the rocks several hundred metres away. Their hoods resembled British windproofs, but they were west of the fence line. . . . Bravely stepping forward with his hands raised, he found to his relief they were the Guardsmen. . . . But there was no . . . time to be lost. 'K' Company [was] stalled in the FUP. . . . We told Colin to hold [up], and released 'K' Company. Beadon wrote later: '"K" Company filed past us one by one, led by Sergeant Collins from out of the darkness. It was an awe-inspiring sight! I could not help noticing the amazed expressions of the Welsh Guardsmen.'

"L" Company Strays

Meanwhile, we had . . . [an] even more worrying development. 'L' Company suddenly came up on the air to declare that they had strayed off the route. They were still confident of maintaining direction towards the FUP . . . but crossing this unknown ground would be . . . dangerous. One detonation amongst the tip-toeing troops would signal . . . that one of our companies was trapped in a minefield. The area might then be saturated with artillery or mortar fire. . . . For the moment, 'Lima' Company was casting about to see if it could retrace its steps to the marked track. We waited in numbed tension. . . . Already we were well behind time. Any minute now, 45 Commando and 3 Para should start their attacks. Brigade HQ had accepted that we would be late, but were concerned that our surprise might be lost when the others clashed. The first firing had just begun from the direction of Mount Longdon when David Wheen informed us that he was back on track, and within striking distance of the FUP. There would be just time for 'K' Company to move out to make room for them.

The Enemy Reveals His Positions

This was [the time] to activate our deception because, on the far side of 'Zoya', 45 Commando had closed with the enemy on Two Sisters. 'Three-One, this is Nine. "Vesuvius". I say again, "Vesuvius". Over.' 'Three-One. "Vesuvius". Wilco. Out.' As this exchange crackled across the frozen air waves, a spectacular *son et lumière* was enacted above 'Tara's' eastern crags. Explosions, lights, small-arms fire and blood-curdling yells riveted attention in that direction. Almost immediately, these provoked the gratifying sight of Argentine tracer arching out towards the source of disturbance.

Next moment, night turned into day as our mortars illuminated the western end of 'Zoya'. In synchronized sequence the [flares on] parachutes floated down, their accusing arcs of light lingering over the sources of enemy fire. Agonizing moments later, several Milan missiles 'whooshed' up from below and streaked towards their targets. Milan seems to have an almost leisurely time of flight, the missile twisting disconcertingly as the computer corrects it onto the point of aim. That never seemed more nerve-racking than now. Surely the enemy machine-gun teams would cease firing and take cover? . . . But even if the missiles homed in, we were uncertain that they would prove effective amongst the crags.

Missiles on Target; K Company Moves Up

Our doubts proved unfounded. The magnitude of the explosions was overwhelming. . . . For an instant some tracer cartwheeled across the sky, before fading away. Then the chatter of those weapons was stilled. It was a great moment, and as we passed the news to the mortar line I could hear their shouts of excitement in the distance behind us. Later, I was reminded that each Milan missile cost the same as a Renault 17TL estate car. Cheap at the price—

although most of 'Four-Two' couldn't afford to buy a new car themselves! Now
the tension became almost unbearable. 'K' Company had crossed the start-line
and was ascending the exposed half-mile or so of steep uneven slope. At the
top, long established in their rocky fastness, were numerous enemy soldiers . . .
[the threat of whom] would remain uncertain for only as long as surprise could
be maintained. The earlier 'K' Company was detected, the more costly it would
be for them as they closed with the defenders. We did not believe that this
approach from the rear was mined. . . . But a separate concern was whether
wire obstacles protected the actual position. . . . Yard by yard, like some Nelso-
nian leadsman chanting the depth from the bows of a man-o'-war, Peter Babbington began to murmur their progress into the radio: 'One hundred metres,
nothing to report. Two hundred. . . . ' After 500 I began to wonder if the enemy
might have run away. At 700 metres, the silhouette of Mount Harriet's jumbled
ridge began to loom over 'K' Company.

The Fight Begins

Suddenly adrenalin raced with the words everyone had been waiting for: 'One-
Nine. Contact. Wait. Out.' Peter, retaining the initiative, had decided to engage
some enemy to his front seconds before the Argentines would inevitably open
fire. . . .

At last, the fight was on! In Tac HQ we could only monitor the radio nets and
observe the myriad of explosions and tracer now erupting from that area. During planning, we had discussed how the rifle companies could most effectively
maintain radio control. They had opted for having everyone down to the section commanders on the same net; there were, therefore, far more stations than
usual talking to each other. But on the other hand everyone knew what was
going on, which is vital in these circumstances. . . . 'K' Company's command
net now provided a vivid impression of the vicious, close-quarter fighting in
which they were engaged:

'One-Nine. Three. Go left. Go left. They're bugging out behind you. Use
grenades. Use eighty-fours . . . '

Sharkey. We're pinned down, for Christ's sake get a gun group here. . . . 'I've
lost a section commander! One of my corporals is down. . . . '

On the Gunner net the urgent, precise voice of Chris Romberg could be
heard constantly designating new targets for our guns. Their fire was being
brought down with unerring accuracy almost onto the assaulting groups of
marines. Afterwards, none of us doubted the decisive role our gunners had
played in this battle. Over 1,000 shells or bombs would fall on 'Zoya' alone that
night, all of them instantly, precisely laid to cover movement, suppress defensive fire, break up resistance. They gave us an overwhelming advantage.

The Tide Begins to Turn

Peter Babbington told me what was going on when he could, passing crisp, taut
sitreps [situation reports] that could not disguise his excitement. Later, he told

us how he and an elated Romberg had sat upon a prominent rock directing their battle, with the signallers in cover below them. After a while, Babbington had impatiently demanded more microphone lead. He was told stridently that the signallers [were] under heavy fire and certainly did not feel inclined to expose themselves any further. He commented modestly: 'This is where I think people end up getting awards because they don't actually realize they're doing anything particularly brave—they're just doing their job, and this means they get exposed to fire.'

The marines of 'K' Company were wreaking havoc among the enemy positions. In the darkness they flitted amongst the crags keeping staccato contact by voice and radio, reporting their movements to each other and warning which weapon was being used. The 66-mm and 84-mm anti-tank shells provided the shock action upon which they could close with a dazed enemy. Already Argentines were throwing down their weapons and raising their hands. But some were shot by their own side as they threw down their arms. Where this occurred, 'K' Company meted out swift and ruthless retribution to those Argentine officers or NCOs trying to stiffen resistance. From the beginning, we had said that the enemy must be allowed to surrender, or he would fight more desperately. In these crucial minutes the momentum of the rifle sections never faltered as, urged on by eager troop officers, they began to overrun a confused and faltering enemy.

Casualties and Heroes

Inevitably, 'K' Company's casualties began to mount. Corporal Lawrence Watts, a most professional young NCO, was shot through the heart as he led the rush onto an enemy strong-point. Corporal Steve Newland was hit in both legs as he single-handedly took out a heavy machine-gun position. The Company second-in-command, Lieutenant Chris Whiteley, was scythed down by shrapnel. It was, of course, what we had expected, the junior leaders taking the brunt of the casualties as they led from the front. Quoted in Max Arthur's book *Above All Courage*, Corporal Newland's [action] . . . epitomizes that of them all:

> I thought, 'Shit, I'm on my own!' So I sat and had a quick think. Then having made up my mind I picked up my SLR (rifle), changed the magazine and slipped the safety-catch. I then looped the pin of one grenade onto one finger of my left hand and did the same with another. I was ready. So I thought, 'Well, you've got to do something.' I pulled one grenade, WHACK—straight at the spics. I dodged back round the rock and heard two bangs. As soon as they'd gone off I went in and anything that moved got three rounds . . .

"L" Company Joins the Fight

Peter Babbington now confirmed that his company were sufficiently established for 'L' Company to cross the start-line. This they did with text-book alacrity, hardly pausing to change formation. There would be no silent approach for them, though. The enemy on 'Zoya' were thoroughly alerted, immediately the company moved into a deluge of machine-gun fire. Several casualties went down in those first minutes including the second-in-command Ian Stafford . . . and Julian Pusey, one of the troop commanders. . . .

At Commando HQ we listened anxiously as it became clear that 'Lima's' suppressive fire was threatening 'Kilo's' advance down the ridge, but both company commanders resolved that by decisive co-ordination between them. Then David Wheen began a steady advance towards his objective opposite Tac HQ's position, as Captain Nick D'Apice, his FOO [forward observer], brought down surgically accurate fire missions. Under their cover 'Lima's' advance gathered pace. Casualties lessened, although they were to face through the night a series of close-quarter [fights] against a forewarned and more resolute enemy. In the end I had to reallocate the capture of 'Katrina' to 'K' Company, because at dawn 'L' Company was still fighting for its last objectives.

Tableau of Battle

Visually, this tableau of twentieth-century infantry in battle was electrifying. The moon, appearing behind scudding wisps of cloud, cast a chill pallor upon the black-etched silhouette of the bombarded mountain. Raining intermittently upon its summit were concentrations of red and yellow flashes, afterwards obscured in thick smoke or incandescent clouds of phosphorus. The naval shells seemed virtually to drop in the same hole each time, round after round, with a shower of sparks as though there was an iron foundry on the hillside. Rising above the chaos, Argentine flares burst almost hysterically, as if hoping to dispel the fog of battle and freeze the combatants. Red tracer floated aimlessly across the sky, sometimes bouncing abruptly upwards like sparks from a firework display. In the pool of darkness, in which we had our box at this amphitheatre, muffled, shivering figures peered incredulously out towards the inferno. From there, the disembodied voices in our earphones calmly reported progress.

Moving the HQ Forward

Brigade HQ . . . reminded [us] that time to complete our reorganization on 'Zoya' for the next phase was running out. If each unit had gone firm on its objective by first light, the plan was to continue the attacks onto the next Argentine positions. In our case, the next objective would be Mount William. But I doubted whether we could now be ready, and said so. For the moment, it was imperative to get Tac HQ and 'J' Company moving up to 'Zoya', or we would be overtaken by the dawn before we had got there. David Wheen could at last confirm that the enemy opposite on 'Tara' were too preoccupied to interfere with movement below them. The cumbersome, vulnerable Tac HQ was urgently assembled and we lumbered down the mountainside, with Mike Norman and 10 Troop, 'J' Company, providing protection. The 'Strolling Players' of 11 Troop, who had staged such a successful diversion, would hold on to 'Tara' until we were established on 'Zoya'.

Improvision: Taking the Risky Way

On the way down, I realized that we weren't going to reach the far end of 'Zoya' by daylight if we followed the cleared route across the plain. For a time I kept this to myself while the risky alternative raced through my mind. Eventually I revealed the stark option to Ian McNeill, hoping that he would talk me out of it; 'Yes, Colonel, that's what we'll have to do', was how he replied. He then reminded me that our assault engineers, who could clear mines, were in the FUP with Colin Beadon. Next I tried the RSM. 'Very good, Sir. Presumably 10 Troop will provide protection in front of us?' was all he said. At the track Mike Norman was waiting, so I told him too. Was it my imagination, or did that massive bulk seem to sway momentarily? But he asked only 'Are you sure that's what you want to do?' 'Yes, we must,' I said reluctantly. 'Right!' he replied in ringing tones, 'I'll lead a buggers' rush down the road and we won't stop for anything.' Before anyone could argue, he was off. We all followed in varying degrees of trepidation. Half-way along what seemed to be an illuminated race-track, I realized Marine Green did not appreciate that the road might be mined. It would have been cruel to have spoiled his blissful ignorance; I merely hoped the others were equally unaware. Above us. 'L' Company's battle raged noisily on. It was . . . obvious that 'Zoya' was now being heavily shelled by the enemy as well as ourselves.

In Position—and Engulfed by Prisoners

Breathless but unscathed, we arrived at the original forming up position where confusion seemed to reign. Amidst the lightening gloom, a mass of dishevelled . . . figures meandered listlessly about at the edge of the road. *It took me a moment to realize they were prisoners*, [and] that they outnumbered us! A marine swathed in a poncho and sitting on some rocks, smoking casually, seemed to be in charge. The RSM stalked indignantly over, to find that it was the irrepressible Corporal Newland. He had been carried down by some of the POWs and was now constructively awaiting casevac. . . .

Even as we stood talking to an elated Matt Sturman, sending 'Porter Troop' forward up 'Zoya' and co-ordinating the evacuation of casualties . . . more and more prisoners surged on to the road. But here they could be rounded up by Sergeant Shiel, revelling in his [duties] as Provost Sergeant. Eventually 'Four-Two' [took] nearly 300 POWs. . . . Somewhere among them, although I did not realize it at the time, was my counterpart, Lieutenant-Colonel Diego Alejandro Sona, 4th Infantry Regiment. He was later flown back to Brigade HQ where I eventually read the report of his interrogation.

Care for the Casualties

In chilling contrast to the satisfying spectacle of columns of dejected POWs, the RSM led me to a shallow quarry where several rows of recumbent figures forlornly lay. These were our wounded, already nearly a dozen, eventually to be almost twice that. . . . Now their prospects of recovery depended upon immediate stabilization, followed by timely casevac. Already Ross Adley, the doctor, and his medical team were descending down to the track from 'Tara'. These casualties could be moved back once the Regimental Aid Post had been set up beside the track to give immediate treatment. Afterwards they would be flown out as soon as the helicopters could come forward.

It was a harrowing sight. We stepped carefully among the wounded men, crouching down to talk with those who were conscious. Marine Vincent of 'K' Company was engaged to the previous RSM's daughter. I made some pathetic remark about her wheeling him down the aisle soon. Chris Whiteley, who had shrapnel in both legs, was in considerable discomfort. His morphine had not yet taken effect. But Ian Stafford was as high as a kite on his pain-killer, making jokes and complaining that Highland dancing and skiing wouldn't be so easy from now on. For others . . . merciful oblivion had insulated them from pain and shock.

Pressing On

It seemed so callous to leave them now, but we must press on or Tac HQ would never reach the top by first light. 'J' Company had been sent on already, so that 'K' could fight through on to 'Katrina'. We began our weary ascent.

For the first time in this war I began to worry about my physical endurance. During the night everyone else had seemed to be shivering constantly but, for once, I had felt indifferent to the cold. . . . This must have been because of my total preoccupation with the attack. Now I seemed drained of energy following our gallop along the track, which had proved quite arduous. Perhaps it wasn't too surprising, because the attack had now been going for ten hours and, like most people, I had had several jarring falls in the dark on the way down. As our pace slackened I feared that this time it was not just an overloaded signaller slowing us down. Ian reassured me that everyone was flagging. This encouragement was then compromised by the indefatigable Chisnall, who paced up beside me to offer to carry my equipment as well as his own! He probably could have done, but such selflessness goaded me to press on through what had . . . become a . . . blizzard.

As the slope steepened into the rocky outcrops of 'Zoya's' upper ridge, we seemed like pilgrims wandering in some biblical wilderness. Out of the swirling murk we would suddenly come across small groups assisting disabled figures to stumble down the mountainside. Sometimes they were Argentine, made all the more macabre by their dark, flapping cloaks. All too often it was 'Porter Troop' bringing back our own wounded. Beyond the snow flurries, shells howled and crashed among the crags. Small-arms fire crackled continuously in the background. We began to come upon abandoned weapons and equipment, which meant that we must be entering the defensive positions. Not much further on this was confirmed when we found the first bodies.

"I Reckon We've Done It!"

Unexpectedly the jubilant voice of Peter Babbington came down to us from what seemed to be a fifty-foot cliff. For so long he had been an insubstantial voice from the chaos of battle that it seemed unreal we should meet again now. A last . . . scramble, then there he was, standing jauntily on a humped ridge that ran off on both sides into the darkness. 'Colonel', he said, 'I reckon we've done it. . . . '

I ought to relate that we shook hands, danced a jig, drained Argentine 'dram', or slapped each other on the back. The fact that we didn't shows how jaded I must have been, because Peter and his team positively glowed with energy and aggression. They had 'a real buzz on', as he subsequently described it. This seemed to override completely all the fatigue and strain of their approach and the vicious fighting. 'J' Company was now firm at this end, while 'L' Company had pushed the enemy off the positions facing 'Tara', although there was still some resistance from the depth positions towards Two Sisters [another peak]. I couldn't see any last-minute resistance stopping 'K' Company now. So we released them and they swarmed towards 'Katrina' like hounds from the meet. Mount Harriet ours![15]

Vaux Reflects

[*Mount Harriet fell on the morning of 12 June. The same day, 5 Brigade (Army) joined 3 Commando Brigade in force for the final drive on Port Stanley. On 14 June 1982 the Argentine commander surrendered.*]

The Troops

But why had we prevailed? How had outnumbered, exhausted, British infantry so easily driven the enemy from his mountain strongholds? Where did this apparent invincibility come from?

In 'Four-Two', the average age of marines was less than twenty. They were 'teenagers'. By all modern criteria their youth and inexperience should have been highly susceptible to insecurity or depression. For weeks they had remained afloat, exposed in the glare of uncertain publicity. Finally, they were precariously disembarked under air attack. But amongst today's youth is an awareness of the media. . . . [They] scrutinize politics or strategy. Many of them had realized the risks of this venture long before the air attacks in San Carlos. Afterwards they had never faltered once. At no time was there the slightest indication that resolve was diminishing; indeed, during their ordeal in the mountains they had positively rejected any suggestion of a respite. The only times morale became a worry were when we waited impatiently for the breakout at San Carlos. Or now, here in Stanley, while we anticipated repatriation.

Leadership, Esprit, Tradition, Pride—and Sense of Humor

Leadership, of course, was the key. This began at the level of section commander, and was most prominent within the companies. That was why so many of our casualties had been young officers or NCOs. It was the explanation for the concentration of decorations between captain and corporal. Team spirit came next: the cohesive thread of military history; the *raison d'être* of Special Forces. The section, platoon, or company forms a separate identity, while their parent unit provides security in exchange for commitment, pride as the reward for loyalty. Last, but never least, came the peculiarly British, sardonic humour. An instinctive inheritance from one generation of servicemen to the next, we could not have won without it. Forgiving mistakes, dispelling frustration, mocking at fear, it eased our burden, made light of adversity. In the turn of a phrase, the roll of an eye, disaster could be mocked, misery uplifted.

Public Support

Retrospectively, there was one other important influence. Through radio, newspapers, video and letters, we had always sensed approval and encouragement from home. Naively, almost undeservedly, we took it for granted. Even when the tears were slipping unashamedly on *Canberra*, as she steamed triumphantly up the Solent to a welcome few in history have been privileged to receive. Even then, I don't believe we knew how fortunate we were![16]

Conclusions

Vaux's commandos required a special kind of leadership, not unlike that of the original U.S. Army Rangers—all volunteers and many very recently civilians—trained by British Commandos during World War II. Of them Colonel W. O. "Bill" Darby, who led the first three battalions, said: "Commanding the Rangers was like driving a team of very high spirited horses. No effort was needed to get them to go forward. The problem was to keep them in check."[17] The Royal Marine Commandos had (and have) the same spirit, although they are professionals, and infinitely better disciplined.

XIX

H. Norman Schwarzkopf

(1934–   )

GENERAL "STORMIN' NORMAN" SCHWARZKOPF commanded Allied (mostly U.S.) forces in the Persian Gulf War (1991), America's largest "limited war" since Vietnam, and a successful one. Thus he surely deserves inclusion here

Born in New Jersey and brought up in Lawrenceville, he was the son of Herbert Norman and Ruth Gordon Schwarzkopf—a "West Pointer" and a nurse from West Virginia. His father named him "H. Norman" so that if he went to the U.S. Military Academy (and he did), he would be called Norman.

Schwarzkopf's father served in France during World War I, and was gassed, but recovered. Back home, he left the army and, at the request of the New Jersey governor, founded the N.J. State Police and commanded it during the 1920s and 1930s. In 1940, he was recalled to the Army, and served through World War II and beyond, retiring as a brigadier general in 1957. His father's assignments allowed Norman, as a boy, to live in such places as Iran and occupied Germany. He went to prep school in Switzerland, an American High school in Germany, Valley Forge Military Academy in Pennsylvania, and West Point. At the U.S. Military Academy, he was big enough for football, but slow: "I kept getting in the way of our running backs."[1] He quit, but lettered in wrestling, soccer, and track, graduated in 1956, and chose to "go Infantry."[2]

He shortly won his jump wings, and was assigned to the 101st Airborne Division. His size (6'3", 240 pounds) proved a definite advantage.[3] In 1964–65 he did a tour in Vietnam as adviser to the ARVN[4] Airborne Brigade; he returned with a chest full of medals, and was sent to teach at West Point. As "resident hero" (few officers had been to Vietnam at the time) he got on famously, but let the cadets know that he was not "career faculty": "You'll hear some teachers at West Point call themselves 'academic officers.' I want to make it clear to you I am not an academic officer. . . . I'm a United States Army infantryman and damn proud of it!"[5] In 1968 he married Brenda Holsinger, a TWA stewardess from Virginia; in time, they had children—two girls and a boy—and a model family life.

Schwarzkopf voluntarily left West Point for a second tour in Vietnam (1969–

70) as a battalion commander—and was a good one. At one point he used his strength and 240 pounds to hold a panicky soldier still until a helicopter could lift them from a minefield.[6]

Later, he served in Alaska, Hawaii, West Germany, posts in the continental United States, and the Pentagon. A major general in 1983, he was made deputy commander of the invasion of Grenada—at the last minute—and had little hand in the planning, which was poor. He did well, but "Stormin' Norman" told everybody off afterward. After serving as deputy assistant chief of staff in Washington, he became a lieutenant general and was given a corps, then returned to Washington as Deputy Chief of Staff for Plans and Operations (1987–88). As a four-star general he took over the U.S. Central Command.

When Iraq invaded Kuwait in 1990, he became commander of the Allied forces arrayed against Iraq, which, after months of preparations, demolished Iraq's forces in only four days (24–27 February 1991). He retired in July 1991.

———

The passages below are from General Schwarzkopf's *Autobiography: It Doesn't take a Hero* (1992), written with Peter Petre. Very often, as in the first paragraphs, his actions speak louder than words.

Schwarzkopf Takes Over

[*December 1969, Lieutenant Colonel Norman Schwarzkopf takes over the 1st Battalion, 6th Regiment, 23rd (U.S.) Division in Vietnam.*]

"Interview" with the Outgoing Commander

On the table sat a bottle of Johnnie Walker Black Label scotch. "This is for you," he said. "You're gonna need it." I was expecting a two- or three-hour discussion of the battalion, its officers, its NCOs, its mission—but he only said, "Well, I hope you do better than I did. I tried to lead as best I could, but this is a lousy battalion. It's got lousy morale. It's got a lousy mission. Good luck to you." With that he shook my hand and walked out.[7]

The Helicopter

[*Schwarzkopf sought out the battalion executive officer, who offered to have the staff brief him.*] I said, "I don't want briefings now. I want to visit the companies."

"Sir?"

"I want to visit the companies. Don't we have a command-and-control helicopter?"

"Sir, we do, but Major Lee has it." Major Will Lee was the operations staff officer. "As a matter of fact, sir, he has the helicopter all the time."

"What do you mean? Isn't that a command-and-control helicopter for the battalion commander? Get it back here right now." There was a stunned silence in the operations center. "Sir, may I talk to you for a minute outside?" said the exec. We stepped out and he explained, "I know this is unusual, but the chopper isn't here because your predecessor never went out in the field."

It would require half an hour for the helicopter to return. I went back inside to wait and discovered that there was no place in the operations center for the battalion commander—no desk, no chair, nothing! I went back to my little cabin where I sat desperately trying to figure out what to do next. "How does this outfit function?" I wondered. "Who's in charge?" Finally the helicopter landed. Walking back into the operations center I overheard someone say, "What the hell did you guys call me in for? I've got work to do out there!"

I had visions of this Major Lee as some kind of tin-pot Napoleon who'd taken advantage of his commander's weakness and transformed the battalion into a little empire of his own. I was dead wrong. He was an enthusiastic veteran officer, eager to follow orders, who'd simply been trying to hold the operation together in the absence of any real leadership. When I introduced myself and told him I wanted to go out in the field, he exclaimed: "That's great, sir! Let's go! Which company do you want to see first?"

"Well," I said, "how about A Company?" The battalion had four rifle companies, A through D, and a heavy mortar company, E, and I intended to inspect them all. As we flew out, Lee explained over the intercom that the rifle companies all had the same mission: to intercept the VC rocket teams. They'd set up a camouflaged daytime position, known as a day laager,[8] where the men would eat, rest, clean their weapons, and make plans; then they'd send "ambush patrols" into the countryside at night. Lee said, "Sir, we're about to come up on A Company. As a matter of fact, you can see them."[9]

Shaping Up Company A

And I thought, "You sure as hell can," because A Company's day laager looked like a damn gypsy camp. Nothing was camouflaged: as we circled I saw red cloth and white paper everywhere, and to my further consternation most of the men were up and moving around instead of resting for night operations. The guy who guided us in to land wore a pair of bright red shorts, flip-flops, and a yellow bandanna around his head, and had a three-day growth of beard. I jumped off and walked over to a lieutenant standing nearby—he had no helmet and no weapon, even though this was supposedly enemy territory. He did salute.

"Lieutenant, where the hell's your weapon?"

"Sir, it's over there, near my hammock." "Are you the company commander?"

"No, sir. That's him, in front of the helicopter."

The guy in the red shorts. I motioned him over and ordered him to put on his uniform and get his weapon. That caused a ten-minute delay. Meanwhile the helicopter pilot took off; standard procedure in combat zones was to limit the time helicopters spent on the ground, since they drew fire. With the noise of his turbines gone, I suddenly heard loud rock and roll from transistor radios, echoing out into the hills. The captain came back—still wearing no helmet.

"Sir, I don't have one," he explained.

"What do you mean, you don't have one?"

"Sir, we don't use helmets. You've got to understand that our mission . . . "

"Wait a minute. Don't start telling me how to conduct military operations. The first thing I want to do is check your security. Do you have security posted around your perimeter?"

"Uh . . . yes, sir."

"You've got security out, right? You made an analysis of the enemy avenues of approach, and you've put out security to protect your position. Is that right?"

"Yes, sir."

"Okay, take me to it."

We started walking into the bushes. As we moved further and further out, the captain was calling, "Security? Security?" After a couple of hundred yards I said disgustedly, "We're wasting our time. Let's go back and ask your platoon leaders where security is."

A second lieutenant led us out of the camp in a different direction. No more than ten yards down the trail we almost tripped over a private sitting in the dirt.

"What are you doing here, soldier?" I asked.

"Sir, I'm security." The latrine was probably farther into the bushes than this guy.

"Where's your foxhole?"

"Here, sir." He pointed to a little furrow he'd scraped in the ground, maybe three inches deep. I said, "Okay. Pretend you're under attack. Get in the foxhole." He got down in it—he knew it wasn't big enough for him—and lay there looking up at me sheepishly.

"Let me ask you something, soldier. Does that give you any protection at all? Why even bother digging this much?"

"The lieutenant told me to." So I looked at the lieutenant and said, "Why didn't you make him dig a fighting position?" The bottom line was that they had no security. The enemy could have strolled in, opened fire, and killed dozens of men.

We retraced our steps and I inspected the camp itself. I walked up to a machine gunner whose weapon had no bullets in it and was coated with rust. When I asked why the gun wasn't loaded he hung his head and explained that his ammunition was in his rucksack. I wasn't angry with him—it was his sergeant who was responsible—but I said, "Okay, soldier. Let's do a simulation. You're under attack. Get your ammunition." The guy scrambled over to his rucksack and turned it upside down. Out tumbled a portable radio, cans of food, books, and a hopeless tangle of ammunition belts, all rusty and caked with the crumbs of cookies from home.

I knew I had to put an end to this carelessness before men started dying. I took the company commander, the guy who had been wearing red shorts, aside.

"Things are going to start changing around here, Captain, right now. *Right now.* My inclination is to relieve you of your command, but I can't do that because apparently this is the way you've been allowed to operate. But I'm telling you: you know what to do and it had better happen. First, when you stop some-place, you will put out security, and I mean *good* security. Second, I want every portable radio out of the field. Third, I want every weapon in this outfit cleaned, and I'd better never come in again and find anybody without a weapon. Ever! In his hand! With clean ammunition! Fourth, I want every man, starting with you, shaved, cleaned up, and in proper uniform. With a helmet! And fifth, there is no way these men can go on ambush patrol tonight and stay awake . . . they're all awake now."[10]

On to B Company

Major Lee, who had been glued to my side during the entire inspection, could barely contain himself as we got in the helicopter: "Goddammit, Sir! You're right, sir!"

We next flew to B Company, at the other end of the Rocket Pocket about twenty miles away. With its ragtag uniforms, it looked like Cox's army. They'd arrived at a new position an hour before and immediately lost two men to a booby trap. The entire force was milling around in shock, so we spent an hour talking to the troops and helping the young captain disperse his men, put out security, and make new plans for the night, since the company hadn't reached its . . . position. The captain impressed me as a sincere, caring commander. By this time, it was raining and almost dark, so we flew back to LZ [Landing Zone] Bayonet.[11]

Shaping Up Battalion Headquarters

By the time I got to the mess hall there was a long line—troops standing in the rain. . . . I took my place at the end of the line, which caused a mess sergeant to trot over: "Sir, you don't have to stand in line. We've got a special section for officers."

"Sergeant," I said, "if my troops have to stand in line out here in the rain, I'll stand here, too." He seemed confused by that and went away. Meanwhile the troops were staring at me. They had all sorts of weird crap on their necks—bandannas and beads and gold chains—but they started talking to me and for the first time I felt encouraged.

"You the new battalion commander?" asked one. "You gonna make a lot of changes?" asked another. A third added, "This is the first time we've ever talked to our battalion commander. It's good to talk to you, sir." The line moved along, and once I got inside I discovered that the officers didn't even have the same dinner hour as the men. They waited until the troops were done, then sat down and got served. I sent for the exec and told him that from now on all officers would eat with the troops. Then I had my supper.

That evening I held my first meeting with the twenty-man battalion staff. Their briefings confirmed all my fears: the 1/6 was failing in its mission. The Vietcong were able to wend their way into the Rocket Pocket and launch at will—not surprising, given the way we were advertising our positions. Horribly, we were also losing lives. Two weeks before, a platoon from D Company had wandered casually into a village and been ambushed. Six men had died—without accounting for a single Vietcong. I didn't have to convince the staff that our ways had to change.

I walked out of the operations center and gazed down the hillside. Something had been gnawing at me all day about the operations center and my cabin, and now all of a sudden it hit me. Son of a bitch! The barbed wire and bunkers that made up the LZ Bayonet security perimeter were below where I was standing— the operations center and my cabin were *outside the wire!*

I called the executive officer outside and demanded an explanation. "Sir, the former battalion commander was afraid of rockets. He moved the operations center and his hooch up here because this hill shields us from the launch sites."

I thought, "This layout is absolutely crazy." The odds of a rocket randomly landing on the operations center were minuscule, but if the Vietcong ever attacked the base on foot, which was not so improbable, my staff and I would have no protection whatever.[12]

One Source of the Problem

For a long time afterward I tried to figure out how the situation could have been allowed to deteriorate so far. Perhaps the answer was ticket punching. In those days all a lieutenant colonel needed to get promoted to colonel was to command a battalion in Vietnam "successfully"—that is, to come back alive with a decent efficiency report. Officers were rotated through battalion command every six months, which enabled the maximum number to punch their battalion-command ticket, but also meant that many unqualified officers were put in charge of men's lives. It was common practice to reward a loyal staff officer at higher headquarters by assigning him a battalion (I was an example). Because officers remained in command for such a brief time, they didn't have to suffer the results of their incompetence. These ills were inherited by the next commander, and even *his* successor.[13]

Further Evidence of Vulnerability

The next day I was awakened with the news that a dawn patrol had shot a Vietcong sneaking through the wire along our perimeter. On his body they'd found detailed sketches of LZ Bayonet—the sort of reconnaissance needed for one of the Vietcong's most devastating tactics, called a sapper attack.[14] At night, guerrillas who had memorized the layout of a base would sneak through the wire at one end, sprint across the compound throwing grenades and explosive charges into bunkers and sleeping hooches, and make it out the other end, having inflicted huge casualties. Finding those sketches of our base made everybody's pucker factor increase considerably, mine included—not least because the drawings clearly indicated the locations of the operations center and my hooch.[15]

Two Encounters with the Brigade Commander

[A]s I finished dressing, there was a knock on my cabin door. It was my brigade commander—a legendary combat infantryman named Joe Clemons, who had become a national hero and won the Distinguished Service Cross in the battle of Pork Chop Hill during the Korean War. The battle had been the subject of a best-seller . . . and a Hollywood movie. . . . Colonel Clemons was also new to the brigade, and I was looking forward to working for him, but we hadn't met because he'd been away on leave. He'd heard about the Vietcong in our wire and wanted to make sure I knew how to protect my base.

I saluted, and he asked me to brief him on the dead Vietcong. Then he said, "Let's go inspect your perimeter."

I hadn't seen the LZ Bayonet perimeter the night before, but I had no illusions about what we'd find. Clemons was furious within fifteen minutes. The bunkers had long since caved in. All along the barbed wire were yawning gaps where anyone could enter. The Claymore mines, which had originally been positioned to cut down enemy soldiers charging the wire, had mostly rusted away from their detonating wires, so they'd have been useless during an attack. Worse, some had been turned around so that if we had set them off, their shrapnel would have blown back into the camp. Joe Clemons chewed me out. I was furious, too, but all I could say was, "Sir, I'll take care of it."

"Didn't you inspect the bunker line yesterday?"

"No, sir."

"Why the hell not?"

"There were a lot of other things I was inspecting, sir."

"This is a disgrace! I've never seen anything this bad in all my years in the Army." We walked the whole perimeter, and the colonel berated me the entire way. I knew he was right: if there had been a sapper attack the night before . . . many of my men would have died.

As soon as he left, I rounded up the officers and NCOs and we spent the entire day making sure sandbags got filled, foxholes dug, and Claymores replaced so we could defend the camp. We extended the perimeter to take in the operations center and my cabin, although I had decided that eventually both would be moved down into the base. Clemons's reproaches kept echoing in my mind. I decided I couldn't work with a commander who doubted my competence. I called and asked if we could meet. He received me at his headquarters that evening but did not offer me a seat.

"Sir, you had every reason to be angry at what you found at my unit today," I said. "But I want you to know that I was angry, too. I was as shocked as you at the state of that perimeter. And I recognize I was at fault not to have inspected it as soon as I took command."

Clemons locked eyes with me as I spoke and didn't say a word. I took a breath and continued, "I don't know what you know about my unit. But on the basis of two days' experience, I can tell you I've probably inherited the worst battalion in the United States Army. I know what's wrong and I will fix it, but that can't happen overnight. And it won't do any good for you to chew my ass every time you come around. You'll just slow me down."

He didn't say anything, just kept staring at me with his icy blue eyes. Finally he said, "Colonel Schwarzkopf, I want to tell you that *I've* inherited the worst *brigade* in the United States Army. I'm willing to believe you know what needs to be done. Now let's do it together." There was no smiling or backslapping— we were both under the gun.[16]

Disasters, and Norman Storms

In the weeks that followed, disaster piled on disaster. In D Company in late December, a veteran sergeant who had just joined the battalion after a year of advanced training in the United States, and whom I had personally briefed on what I expected of him, led a dozen GIs into the jungle on night ambush patrol. Completely ignoring all the rules, they moved into their position in broad daylight, blew up their air mattresses . . . and . . . all fell asleep. The Vietcong found them within hours and killed them all, except for one private who ran away and was able to tell us what had happened.

I had to be a complete son of a bitch to get any results, which often entailed losing my temper five or six times in a day. Being calm and reasonable just didn't work. For one thing the antiwar protests were mounting in the United States and a lot of our draftees knew they'd been sent to an unpopular war and didn't want to fight. Then there was the Army's policy of keeping Vietnam tours to one year, which meant a constant stream of raw recruits and a constant exodus of experienced men. When these new kids arrived, they'd immediately be exposed to a bogus combat-veteran culture that was in reality no more than an accumulation of bad habits. Some other troops would tell them: "Forget that crap you learned in basic training. This is how we do it around here. This is the real thing."

Because the war had put such strain on the Army personnel system that experienced junior officers and NCOs were scarce, I didn't have enough leaders to set everybody straight. At the rank of sergeant first class or above, for example, our battalion had slots for thirty-five NCOs, but we had only five. Even our lieutenants were mostly draftees—college kids who'd been offered the chance to go to instant officer school and who'd decided that if they had to go to war, they'd rather do it as lieutenants than privates. But psychologically they were unprepared to take responsibility for men's lives. . . .

We had no choice but to treat troops almost like raw recruits and teach them to wear their helmets and flak jackets and to carry their weapons and keep them clean. After discovering many of the men couldn't shoot straight, I had each company build a little rifle range and required the troops to train there. At the same time we began moving more aggressively in the Rocket Pocket, patrolling areas we'd never entered and pushing the VC farther back into the hills. It was dangerous, uncomfortable work, and to help the troops decompress I set up a rotation system that let units come back . . . and spend a week manning bunkers in the rear. That gave the men a chance to relax, shower, wear clean clothes, and eat three square meals a day.

I was flying out every day to supervise my field forces and holding staff meetings every night, pounding on the officers and NCOs about things we needed to fix—all this while LZ Bayonet was still under threat of attack by the VC organization that had sent the scout who carried the map of our base. After a few weeks, the pressure really started getting to me. One afternoon I confided in First Sergeant Walsh, a highly experienced, competent, crusty old NCO who was a big reason B Company had its act together:

"Jesus, Top, I have to operate on such a short fuse . . . the battalion's in such lousy shape . . . there's a million things that need to get done. I'm not normally like this."

"But you're right, sir. Everybody knows you're right," he said. Then he paused and studied my face. "Sir, I know you're worried about having to be a son of a bitch. But don't worry about that. I've worked for lots bigger sons of bitches than you." And he smiled and saluted and walked away. I didn't know whether to feel relieved or depressed.

The one day I knew I could be a nice guy was Christmas. I ordered the mess hall to prepare a huge meal for the troops and starting late Christmas morning, we loaded food onto helicopters in insulated cans and flew dinner to each company.[17]

Chasing a Phantom Vietcong Battalion

One of our sister battalions, the 5/46, was assigned to the Batangan Peninsula, a rectangle that protruded into the South China Sea between Chu Lai and Quang Ngai. The Batangan was what the troops called a "bad-ass" place—loaded with booby traps and minefields from one end to the other. One of the peninsula's villages was My Lai, where two years before American forces had killed more than three hundred Vietnamese villagers in an incident that was still under investigation. Supposedly the 5/46 had gone to the Batangan to fight a VC battalion known as the "Phantom 48th"—"phantom" because nobody ever actually found it—but the troops had become so demoralized by the mines and booby traps that they'd lost their will to fight. When patrols were sent out at night, they'd go two hundred yards outside their perimeter and stop, and the next morning they'd come in and report that they'd completed their mission and encountered nothing.

Colonel Clemons called me in and said, "The Fifth of the Forty-sixth isn't cutting it down there. They're scared to death. I want you and your unit to trade places with them." As word got around our battalion, a lot of the kids thought I'd volunteered for the mission. I was a gung-ho commander, but not *that* gung-ho. My feelings weren't much different from many of the men's: while it was a compliment for our unit finally to be handed a real assignment, the Batangan was a horrible, malignant place.

We moved in during the last week of March 1970.[18]

Discipline and Personal Leadership

By that time Major Lee had been reassigned to brigade headquarters and I had a new operations officer, a West Pointer named Slade Johnson. He was big (six feet five, 240 pounds), tough, and smart. We dug through the records of the 5/46 and plotted the sites of mine incidents on the map, trying to make sense of the place. It ended up showing lethal little red dots from one end of the peninsula to the other. But we found patterns—for instance, abandoned night defensive positions, where a force had previously camped, were among the most treacherous spots. So from the minute we arrived we gave mine maps to the troops and preached three rules: Avoid known roads and trails. Avoid ready-made openings in hedgerows between rice paddies. Avoid previous night defensive positions.

At the beginning . . . we averaged one mine incident per day. Every time a mine went off, I flew immediately to the site. Mostly I did this to make my helicopter available—it took a medevac half an hour to come down from Chu Lai, and if we could eliminate that delay we could save lives. But I also wanted to talk to the men who'd just lost a buddy. Mines have an insidious effect on morale—the troops are walking along and suddenly somebody is dead or has lost a limb; a helicopter swoops in and takes him away, and there is nothing the men can do to even the score. While I abhorred the massacre at My Lai, I could also imagine how it might have happened. I could read the emotions in the faces of my own men. If I'd said, "The people in that village . . . knew this mine was here; in fact, one of them probably planted it. Go clear the place out," they'd have killed everyone in sight. So I'd move among the troops, asking, "How did it happen?" and saying, "Hey, you know, you can avoid these things if you stay off the roads and trails." I could reduce the tension just by being there, by talking and reassuring and reminding. Our efforts paid off—the men became very good at avoiding mines, and after the first month, if we had one incident in a week that was a lot.[19]

The Softer Side of "Stormin' Norman"

Visiting the wounded was gut wrenching, especially when the casualties came day after day. The hospital at Chu Lai was a cluster of long, low, prefab buildings linked by wooden ramps. I tried to get there while the wounded were still in the recovery room. Unless there was a medevac helicopter on the helipad next to the emergency receiving building, we'd land there and I'd walk in. Both sides of the large room in the receiving building were always lined with wounded soldiers on stretchers set upon what looked like metal sawhorses. Each man had an IV in his arm and medics hovering over him trying to determine how badly he was hurt. The medics welcomed commanders who came to see their troops and would help me find [my] men. . . . If they were in surgery I'd have to wait, but if they were in the emergency room, the recovery room, or the wards I could see them right away.

I'd go up to a kid who'd just lost his leg lying there in shock and in pain, and the first thing he'd do would be *apologize.* "Sir, I'm sorry. I fucked up. I knew better than to do that." Then he'd want to know, "Did anybody die because of me?" I'd tell him how proud I was of him and tell him everything would be okay. If he was in good enough shape, I'd try to arrange for him to talk to his parents on the phone, so they could at least have the reassurance of hearing his voice. I'd usually put my hand on his shoulder and silently pray that somehow my strength would flow into his broken body so that he would live and heal quickly. I'd also know it was probably the last time I'd see him—we moved seriously wounded soldiers to Japan as soon as they were stable. I never broke down in front of a wounded man—it would have embarrassed both him and me—but I frequently found myself outside afterward, on one of those wooden ramps, coughing and choking back tears. Once a doctor came by and asked if I was all right. "Hell, yes, I'm all right," I growled. But I wasn't. These were *my* men, and when they got hurt, I was responsible.

I knew I had to give the men a chance to let off steam. Periodically we'd pull each company from the field and send it back to Chu Lai, where the men could lie around on the beach for three days and drink beer. Before returning them to the Batangan, I'd meet with the whole company. I'd sit . . . on a stage in front of them and talk about whatever they wanted to discuss, whether it was the minefields we were facing or how soon they would be going home. I believed that the better informed a soldier was, the better he'd fight.

Those rap sessions were no fun, however. In a better organization the junior officers would have dealt with a lot of the misinformation and grievances that surfaced. The men would ask, "Why do we have to go out in these minefields? Did you volunteer us for this mission?" And, "Why do I have to wear my helmet and flak jacket all the time? It's hot out there." They hated the mine-fields. They hated the heat. They hated their helmets and flak jackets. Most of the time they hated *me.* But I never made the mistake of confusing their comfort with their welfare. I'd say, "Look, guys, I ain't here to win a popularity contest. My primary concern is keeping you alive. If on the day you leave for the United States your last thought of me is, 'I hate that son of a bitch,' that's fine. Actually, I'll be *happy* if that happens. Because an alternative is for you to go home in a metal casket, and then you won't be thinking anything at all. That's why I make you put on your helmets and flak jackets."[20]

No Breaks for the Battalion Commander

When we moved to the Batangan Peninsula we also moved to a new fire base, called FB Dottie, after the wife of the officer who had commanded the battalion [earlier]. . . . Our tactical operations center at FB Dottie was in a large bunker and next door was another bunker where my staff lived. I slept in a cubicle right in the operations center. I could lie on my cot and hear the radios and know exactly what was going on in the battalion. I'd learned to sleep with one ear cocked during the siege of Duc Co five years before, but now I listened for incoming problems instead of mortar rounds. Working the reins twenty-four hours a day was the only way my staff and I could make sure that the 1/6 kept pulling in the right direction.

Study of the Vietcong

Though we were now a good battalion, we knew we'd never be a great one because we never had enough seasoned junior officers and NCOs.

The enemy dictated my peculiar schedule. During the dry season, which started in April, they moved at night and attacked at night, a tactic that protected them from our helicopter gunships and air strikes. So generally I'd be up until about 4 A.M.—close enough to dawn so that I could hit my cot reasonably confident that there would be no attack that night. Then I'd sleep three or four hours and try to catch a short nap again in the afternoon. I became quite a student of the communist calendar, because the VC had a penchant for striking on holidays or on the anniversaries of past victories. On those dates, we'd string extra barbed wire willy-nilly through the camp and stage "mad minute" barrages: we'd rake our own perimeter with machine-gun and artillery fire to forestall any sapper attacks.

My view of the Vietcong never changed. I saw them as opportunistic brigands who with guns and encouragement from the North Vietnamese oppressed the peasants, stole their money and crops, and bullied them into cooperation. I'd have loved to fight a full-scale battle against the Phantom 48th. We had a competent battalion staff and I was quite confident we could have outmaneuvered and destroyed them. But the war had degenerated by then into piecemeal engagements that played to our weaknesses: our shortage of capable junior officers and NCOs, and our draftees' reluctance to fight.

On a couple of occasions, troops on ambush patrol simply let the Vietcong walk by. The men had figured out that if they didn't shoot at the VC, the VC wouldn't know they were there and so wouldn't shoot either. Good NCOs never would have let them get away with this, but we couldn't count on ours. So we devised a different solution: we beefed up the ambush patrols to fifteen or twenty men instead of the usual six or eight. That gave the men sufficient confidence to attack.[21]

Problems with Higher Command

We had an assistant division commander in charge of operations, a general, who was convinced we should be killing more Vietcong.

One day while Colonel Clemons was visiting my headquarters the general flew in from Chu Lai and announced, "I've figured out why you're not making more enemy contact. The VC have broken up into two- and three-man groups. So I want you to break your battalion into two- and three-man groups as well, and station them all over the area. You'll kill a lot more enemy."

I explained that I'd just found it necessary to *increase* the size of our patrols. "Sir, if you send these men out in two- or three-man groups, they'll be scared to death and won't fight. On top of that, very few know how to read a map. They won't be able to tell us where they are, and we won't be able to fire our artillery without endangering our own men."

This made the general furious: "Well, that just sounds like a leadership problem to me! Obviously you need to exercise firmer control over the men in this battalion."

Stung, I was on the brink of saying, "General, I'm sorry, but I cannot obey your order."

Luckily, Joe Clemons stepped in and said, "Sir, Schwarzkopf's analysis is absolutely correct. What you're suggesting would not be a wise course of action." The general stormed out of the bunker, too angry to speak.

If Clemons hadn't interposed himself, my career might have ended on the spot.[22]

Alaska: General Willard Latham

[Schwarzkopf served as deputy commander to Latham in Alaska, 1974–76.]

In early January 1975, Latham arrived. He was short, tough, and stocky, and there was nothing about him—at least on the surface—for a good old boy to like. He was a nondrinking, nonsmoking moralist who expected to see his commanders in church every Sunday. "I don't care whether you believe in it or not," he told us. "When you're in combat and you're holding a dying soldier in your arms, you owe it to him to know how to pray." Latham was also a fanatic about fitness: he'd fought in Korea when the Chinese came across the Yalu River, and had seen men die or get captured during the retreat because they couldn't keep up. So one of his rules was that everybody in the command had to be able to run five miles in fifty minutes. That shook up headquarters something terrible, because most of those colonels hadn't exercised in years. But within days they were out there, huffing and puffing and getting in shape. There was no way for them to fake it, either: Latham worked out right alongside them.

He was relentless in his demands and stingy with praise, and when he didn't get results, he could be extremely harsh. Yet I sensed this was a man I could learn from.[23]

Division Commander at "Camp Swampy" (Fort Stewart, Georgia)

Schwarzkopf's Big Five List of Goals

Number one was obvious: to make sure my division was combat ready. I knew that the 24th [Mechanized Infantry Div.] was already damned good. . . . My job would be to keep it sharp.

Number two was . . . to take care of the soldiers.

Number three was . . . to take care of the soldiers' families.

Number four was based on what I'd learned in war: that loyalty to one another was what motivated soldiers to fight. Camaraderie and cohesion at every level of the 24th had to be encouraged.

Finally . . . I would have a responsibility to teach my subordinates, just as my mentors had taught me. That gave me my "big five."[24]

Preparations to Attack Iraqi Forces, 1990–91

Once we knew we'd have the units we needed, the plan for the ground war took shape quickly. On November 14, less than a week after the President announced the further buildup of U.S. forces in the gulf, I was able to call my senior commanders to Dhahran to outline how we were going to defeat Iraq. I knew this would be my most important meeting of the war: these were the men who would have to execute the plan. . . . I stood before a fifteen-foot-wide map of Kuwait and Iraq in the "Desert Inn," a run-down building that the Army had converted to a dining hall, and watched as they took their seats. Of the twenty-two generals and admirals present, almost all wore two or three stars.

Briefing the Generals and Admirals

I'd worked myself up into a ferocious state. Only a few of the commanders had any idea of the plan I was about to present or of the tough assignments I was going to mete out. I needed every man in the room to embrace his mission and be breathing fire by the time he went out the door. I began by emphasizing the necessity of maintaining the secrecy of what we were about to discuss. I described how a Washington press leak about an upcoming amphibious exercise in the gulf had prompted Iraq to load a bomber with Silkworm antiship missiles. "You are going to be bombarded with questions by the press. I do not want you to discuss military operations. Period. I do not want you to discuss your capabilities. Period. And you should teach every one of your officers the same thing. . . . I'm telling you I am going to deal absolutely brutally, *brutally*, with anyone I feel compromises classified information." I was harsh, but I was also convinced that our own newspaper and TV reports had become Iraq's best source of military intelligence. We had already cut off all other sources.

I recounted Central Command's long struggle to get Washington to acknowledge that kicking Iraq out of Kuwait was going to require more troops. Now that VII Corps was here, I said, "My written orders from Washington are still to deter Iraq from attacking Saudi Arabia. But there is no doubt about the fact that we are getting ready to go on the offensive. That's what we are here to talk about today. Forget the defensive bullshit, we are now talking offensive. And we're going to talk offense from now until the day we go home."

I walked them through my analysis of Iraq's forces and our own, curtly noting what we were up against: "There are a whole hell of a lot of them—450,000 right now in the Kuwaiti theater, twenty-six divisions' worth, and their divisions are the same size as ours. So they've got mass on their side. Another strength I would say is their chemical capability. They have used it in the past and there is no doubt in my mind they're going to use it on us." I pointed to the weaknesses that would be Iraq's undoing and reminded the commanders of our military strengths. Finally I laid out our battlefield goals. "The first thing that we're going to have to do is, I don't like to use the word 'decapitate,' so I think I'll use the word 'attack,' leadership, and go after his command and control. Number two, we've got to gain and maintain air superiority. Number three, we need to cut totally his supply lines. We also need to destroy his chemical, biological, and nuclear capability. And finally, all you tankers, listen to this. We need to destroy—not attack, not damage, not surround—I want you to *destroy* the Republican Guard. When you're done with them, I don't want them to be an effective fighting force anymore. I don't want them to exist as a military organization." For the benefit of the Vietnam vets—practically the whole room—I emphasized that "we're not going into this with one arm tied behind our backs. We're not gonna say we want to be as nice as we possibly can, and if they draw back across the border that's fine with us. That's bullshit! We are going to destroy the Republican Guard."[25]

———————

[Generals referred to below are: Colin Powell, chairman of the Joint Chiefs of Staff; Charles "Chuck" Horner, USAF Commander; Walter "Walt" Boomer, Commander of U.S. Marines; Gary Luck, commanding the U.S. XVIII Airborne Corps (82nd and 101st Divisions); Binney Peay, 101st Airborne Division; Barry McCaffery, 24th Infantry; Frederick Franks, VII Armored Corps. General John Yeosock had overall command of U.S. Army units.]

"I'm now going to tell you all some stuff that not very many people know about, in Washington particularly," I said, and described the four phases of attack we'd mapped out for Desert Storm: strategic bombing first; then gaining control of the Kuwaiti skies; then bombing Iraqi artillery positions, trench lines, and troops. At last I turned to the plan for the ground offensive—a fully realized version of the envelopment I'd proposed to Powell three weeks before. Using the map, I showed the commanders where I wanted them to maneuver their units. The plan covered a huge area: in order to make sure we fought the campaign on our own terms, we had extended the boundary of the battlefield westward so that it encompassed a rectangle roughly the size of Pennsylvania. Saddam's forces were concentrated at the eastern end, in and around Kuwait. Desert Shield forces would keep them from moving south; to their east was the natural barrier of the gulf, to their north was the Euphrates, which would become a natural barrier once Chuck Horner's air force dropped the bridges that crossed it; and to the west were hundreds of miles of desert that would become our main avenue of attack.

I anticipated, I said, a four-pronged ground assault. Along the Saudi-Kuwaiti border near the gulf, I wanted two divisions of U.S. Marines and a Saudi task force to thrust straight into Kuwait, with the objective of tying up Saddam's forces and eventually encircling Kuwait City. Nodding in Boomer's direction, I said, "I'll leave it to Walt Boomer to figure out how he wants to do that, but it also gives him the capability to come in from the sea with his amphibious forces."

I'd reserved a second corridor, in the western part of Kuwait, for a parallel attack by the pan-Arab forces led by two armored divisions from Egypt and another Saudi task force. Their objective would be the road junction northwest of Kuwait City that controlled Iraqi supply lines. Eventually they would enter Kuwait City and have the dirty job of fighting the Iraqis house to house if necessary.

Meanwhile from the west would come the U.S. Army's power punch. Looking at Gary Luck, I indicated a section of Saudi-Iraqi border more than three hundred and fifty miles inland. "I am probably going to send the XVIII Airborne Corps very deep," I said, showing how I wanted Luck's divisions to race north from that area to the Euphrates, blocking the Republican Guard's last route of retreat. Once that sector was secured, I told him, he would hook his forces east, ready to join the attack on the main body of the Iraqi army. Finally I turned to Fred Franks. "I think it's pretty obvious what your mission is going to be," I said, moving my hand along the desert corridor just to the west of Kuwait, "attack through here and destroy the Republican Guard." I wanted to pin them with their backs against the sea, then go in and wipe them out. I couldn't resist adding, "Once they're gone, be prepared to continue the attack to Baghdad. Because there isn't going to be anything else out there." I allowed that taking Baghdad would probably be unnecessary, because by then the war would have ended.[26]

Reaction and Questions

The effect was electric. When we broke for coffee, the commanders rushed up and were climbing all over the map. Peay and McCaffrey, who had been handed challenging missions far out on the flank, told me: "You know, sir, we thought we were still going to use that ho-hum plan of slogging into Kuwait. This is fantastic!" Walt Boomer, whose Marines were being called upon to do some of that very slogging in order to free up the Army for the flanking attack, accepted the assignment because he knew it had to be done. The only dissonant note was from Freddie Franks: "The plan looks good, but I don't have enough force to accomplish my mission." He argued that I should give him the 1st Cavalry Division [Airmobile] which I was holding in reserve. I said I'd consider it when the time came.

When we reconvened I told them to expect D-day sometime in mid-February. That immediately focused everybody's attention on two huge logistical challenges. The first was that the bulk of our armor was still in Germany and the

United States: we still had to transport more than three divisions to the gulf, give the soldiers time to acclimate, and then move them and their equipment hundreds of miles north to the Saudi border. The second was a decision I'd made to wait on moving into position for the flanking attack until we launched the air campaign. I didn't want the Iraqis to learn of our battle plan and then be able to shift their defenses. I knew that once our Air Force stopped the Iraqis' reconnaissance flights, they would be blind, and even if they did finally figure out our plan, the Air Force would make it impossible for them to shift enough forces to counter it. So I insisted Franks and Luck keep their corps in staging areas near Kuwait. "You'll be allowed to move as soon as we launch the air campaign," I promised. "You have to trust me that I'll give you enough time." That mollified them somewhat. But we all knew that shifting two corps and all their supplies and ammunition two hundred miles or more laterally across the desert would be a mammoth undertaking. I told them, "I'm going to be drilling you guys unmercifully between now and D-day to convince me that you are logistically prepared."

After a question-and-answer session I tried to set a tone for the coming months. "Let me leave you with one thought, guys. In order for this to succeed—because the enemy is still going to outnumber us—it is going to take, for lack of a better word, killer instinct on the part of all of our leaders out there." I pointed again at the map. "What I'm saying is when the Marines hit the wire right here and when the Army forces hit the wire over here, there's going to be none of this bullshit, 'Well, I think we're going to go in and probe a little bit and see if we can get through.' We need commanders in the lead who absolutely, clearly understand that they *will get through*. And that once they're through they're not going to stop and discuss it. They are going to go up there and destroy the Republican Guard. I cannot afford to have commanders who do not understand that it is attack, attack, attack, attack, and destroy every step of the way. If you have somebody who doesn't understand it, I would strongly recommend that you consider removing him from command and putting in somebody that can do the job, because, let's face it, the prestige of the United States military is on our shoulders. But more importantly, the prestige of the entire United States of America rests on our shoulders. There isn't going to be anybody else in this thing except us. There are no more forces coming. What we got is what's going to do the job. And for our country we dare not fail. We cannot fail, and we will not fail. Anybody in here who doesn't understand that, get out of the way. Any questions? Okay, good luck to you. You know what needs to be done."[27]

Conference with the Commander of Moslem Troops

I was still riding high from the commanders' conference when I went to brief [General Prince] Khalid two days later.[28] He was initially shocked by how deeply we intended to invade Iraq, but soon embraced the concept enthusiastically. I hadn't left this to chance: I'd heard him speak often of his wish that

Saudi forces liberate Kuwait, so we'd scripted his troops into both prongs of the attack into the emirate. Two Saudi armored brigades would fight alongside the Egyptians and Syrians on the western thrust and two more would attack in the east, up the coastal highway toward Kuwait City, parallel with Boomer's Marines. Khalid expressed concern about the border barriers Iraq had thrown up—high sand embankments, minefields, razor-wire fences, and other obstacles. I promised advisors who would teach the Saudis the tactics they'd need to breach the enemy lines, as well as armored excavators, mine plows, and other breaching equipment.

Now I faced the ticklish business of enlisting the support of our coalition partners. Even though the United States was supplying two-thirds of Desert Storm's ground force, for the plan to work I needed the combat power of the entire coalition. When Iraq declared on November 19 that it was deploying 250,000 more soldiers "as defensive measures in southern Iraq, the provinces of Kuwait and Basra," I felt even greater urgency to get everyone on board. If Saddam went through with the buildup, his force in the theater would number 680,000. My intelligence staff was skeptical of the announcement, but soon we were picking up a frenzy of military construction along the Kuwaiti border, as the Iraqis added to the defenses they'd already built. More troops flowed in too, though not as many as advertised: the Iraqis ended up with 545,000.[29]

Briefing the British Commander

Just after Thanksgiving I approached the British, presenting our battle plan to Lieutenant General Sir Peter de la Billière, their commander in the gulf. A legendary soldier and adventurer, Sir Peter was former chief of the Special Air Service and the most decorated officer in the British armed services. It was no coincidence that I'd gone to him first: Great Britain had been our closest western ally in the crisis, and he and I had become good friends. I trusted his brains and judgment so much that I asked his advice on even the most sensitive military issues. I wanted de la Billière's newly arrived 1st Armored Division, the Desert Rats, to attack with Walt Boomer into Kuwait. He nodded approvingly as I laid out the details of the offensive plan, but finally remarked bluntly that British voters would object to seeing their boys relegated to a supporting role. Could I reassign his force to the major attack with VII Corps?

[*Schwarzkopf felt he could not refuse. Besides, Billière already had SAS units behind enemy lines. Schwarzkopf added U.S. Special Forces, Rangers, and Navy SEALS to the covert force.*][30]

[*Of course, Schwarzkopf's plan worked perfectly. The war lasted 100 hours—from 4:00 A.M., 24 February 1991 (Gulf time) to roughly 8:00 A.M. on 28 February.*]

Conclusions

General Schwarzkopf's style of personal leadership is best shown by his actions as a battalion commander in Vietnam in 1970. Despite the adverse opinions of troops who were less than eager to fight, he knew that they must—or be killed—and forced them to be ready—flack vests, helmets, clean arms and ammunition at the ready, defenses in order, routine perimeters on patrol—while allowing them time for rest and enjoyment of a few luxuries. His discipline doubtless saved the lives of many potential victims of the Vietcong or PRVN troops.

As commander of Allied forces in the Gulf War, he was the ultimate professional soldier. Some detractors have called his plan "straight out of the book" of the Command and General Staff College. But the enthusiasm of the airborne and other commanders speak to the contrary. It involved a wide-sweeping "left hook"—past Kuwait and into Iraq—with the French armored division and U.S. airborne divisions farthest to the west, then U.S. infantry, armor, and airmobile cavalry divisions and the British "Desert Rats" (1st Armored Division) filling in toward Kuwait City, on which the Saudi Arabian, Egyptian, and Syrian forces, under Prince Khalid, marched directly, supported by the U.S. Marines (1st and 2nd Divisions) and U.S. infantry. USAF fighters and bombers prepared the way and supported the ground troops throughout. The enveloping forces were well into Iraq, having sent thousands of prisoners to the rear, when the "Hundred Hour War" was declared over by President Bush at 9:00 P.M. (Washington time) on 27 February 1991. There was no battleworthy Iraqi force in view. When Schwarzkopf asked that the USAF maintain an "obvious presence" over Baghdad after the cease-fire, General "Chuck" Horner replied: "We have two options, subsonic or supersonic." (There was no effective opposition.)[31]

General Schwarzkopf depended largely on trained regulars from the United States and her allies, reinforced by American Reserve and National Guard units. All were superbly equipped with the best weapons, vehicles, and aircraft that modern technology could produce. (See the Introduction for details.)[32] He struck ruthlessly, and downed an army of superior numbers.

Questions remain, but none that do not have logical answers. For example: Why did the United States require seven months to mobilize an Allied force before attacking Iraq? Diplomacy to secure international support took time, and Allied (including U.S.) forces required time to assemble. The top generals were Vietnam veterans, and wanted to insure that if the United States got into another war, her forces (with her allies') would be allowed to *win*; that required solid support—long-term if necessary—from Washington, and necessary forces, arms, and equipment—and allies. Moreover, Special Operations forces were in action behind enemy lines (British SAS, U.S. Special Forces, Rangers, and Navy SEALS). U.S. forces in the area were never very vulnerable, considering the firepower of the ground troops, the USAF, U.S. Navy aircraft carriers, and Army,

Navy, and Marine air. Why not assemble (taking their weapons into account) overwhelming armed forces?

General Schwarzkopf was surely a dyed-in-the-wool regular; he may have wounded the psyches of some reporters and subordinates, but very few troops, with whom he was popular. His leadership cannot be faulted.

Conclusions ─────────────────────────────

THIS BOOK has attempted to cover the leadership concepts of combat commanders—not their experiences—unless their ideas can best be represented by their actions. It was written in expectation that readers would draw their own conclusions—and it is hoped that they will.

What follows are the author's conclusions, devoted to the practices in war on which most of our commanders agree, citing exceptions. Under these headings are comments on the matter of "presence" and the differences in the exercise of command depending on the era, the type of troops, their backgrounds, morale, and other factors. Special attention will be paid to commanding citizen-soldiers, means of boosting their morale, and factors affecting morale (both derived from opinion at home and in the context of war). The special aspects of leadership will be noted for line troops, special operations forces, and guerrillas, and how command techniques vary depending on the military technology available, and the character of a given war, whether total, limited, guerrilla, antiguerrilla, or police action. All the quotations have appeared in one chapter or another, above; thus most are not footnoted.

─────────

There is general agreement on basic tenets of the art of war. Except perhaps for Giap, the details of whose combat experience are obscure, all our commanders led in person and from the front (as the size of their units allowed), improvised according to the situation, held to unity of command, took care of their troops, took risks, preferred the offensive, and knew the value of *winning*.

On *personal leadership*, Rommel said: "The personal example of the commander works wonders, especially if he has had the wit to create some sort of legend around himself." According to Patton, "The history of war is the history of warriors; few in number, mighty in influence." Manstein left most of his staff in the rear, but moved forward himself with a skimpy operations staff, and even as a corps commander went on "skirmishing patrols." Manstein remarked, as had Sherman before him, that morale at the front was always better than in the rear.[1] Slim wrote, "In the worst days of the 1942 retreat [out of Burma], we remained an army . . . only because the men saw and knew their commanders." Ridgway jumped with his paratroopers in World War II. Dayan was always in the forefront in his younger days; as Israeli chief of staff, he refused a plush office, cut the staff, and continually visited combat units. Moore (planning for Ia Drang): "First, I would personally land on the first helicopter. . . ."

All our commanders had *presence*, normally assumed to facilitate taking over bodies of troops. However, presence can be an asset or a disability. Commanders without a known reputation had to depend on appearance, bearing, demeanor, and poise. If these gave a negative impression, it had to be overcome. Apparently, Rommel had positive presence and *charisma*, an almost magical quality. We quoted General von Mellenthin: "Between Rommel and his troops was that mutual understanding which cannot be explained and analyzed, but which is the gift of the gods." It could be, however, that Rommel was idolized partly because he was a "natural" and partly because he was already something of a legend when he took over the Afrika Korps in 1941—highly decorated in the First World War, and a celebrated panzer leader in the 1940 *blitzkrieg* against France.

Of course, the others had a presence, but most, perhaps all, of them, had to improve it in some way. Even Frederick the Great had to overcome the fact that he had left his first battlefield (Mollwitz, 1741) in the midst of the fight (on advice of his senior general). Angry with himself, he therafter led in person with almost insane bravery. Stonewall Jackson's initial image was of an unkempt "professor" who gave "crazy" orders, but he overcame it by winning. Schwarzkopf's men in Vietnam saw him initially as an overbearing giant, obsessed with improving security. Most, perhaps, came to appreciate that his discipline was saving their lives.

Some of our commanders were physically big, with a potentially intimidating presence; Sherman, Patton, and Schwarzkopf used this asset blatantly. Others were big men who were seldom harsh, but still disciplinarians: Manstein, Slim, and Moore. Still others had an intensity that demanded attention; Stonewall Jackson, Lawrence, Dayan, and to some extent, Giap.

Though few used the term, *camaraderie* was seen as a major asset to personal leadership. Frederick and Napoleon made concerted efforts to gain the affection of their men—and succeeded. DeGaulle wrote that *camaraderie des armes* was the most powerful binding force of armies.[2] Moore was obviously popular with his men, as were Rommel, Manstein, Vaux, and others. Most leaders, however, had to depend on a *reputation for winning* to cultivate camaraderie—Jackson, Patton, and Montgomery, surely. Ironically, Monty was the only one to mention personality and magnetism (charisma) as factors in leadership.

All thought *the ability to improvise* a necessity. According to Napoleon: "[The first quality of a great general] is the courage of the *improviste*. . . ." Jackson, on his maneuver at Chancellorsville, said: "Most men will think that I had planned it all from the first but it was not so. I simply took advantage of circumstances as they were presented to me in the providence of God." Lawrence wrote: "Nine-tenths of tactics were . . . teachable in schools; but the irrational tenth was like the kingfisher flashing across the pool, and in it lay the test of generals." Rommel made similar, if less poetic, statements. DeGaulle wrote that in his new army there would be "perpetual improvision." Patton wrote in his diary

(3 November 1942) as he contemplated the landings in Morocco: "Perhaps when Napoleon said, *Je m'engage et puis je vois* [I start the fight and then I see], he was right." And later, "Battles . . . practically never develop according to pre-conceived notions." Montgomery stated: "The master plan must never be so rigid that the C.-in-C. cannot vary it to suit the changing tactical situation." Generals Moore and Schwarzkopf had to adapt to very different situations in Vietnam. Moore entered the war before it became unpopular in the United States, and showed a remarkable ability to improvise in the Ia Drang battle. Schwarzkopf took over a battalion that reflected the widespread disaffection back home, and emphasized security and survival as much as offense.

With certain qualifications, combat commanders were unanimously for *unity of command*. The exceptions were Vaux and Giap. Vaux, with veteran Marine Commandos, consulted with his officers and NCOs on every problem—although he made the decisions. Giap, who was both general and politician, attributed major decisions to the Communist Party; that might have been true for strategy, but at the operational level, Giap was surely in charge.

Nevertheless, all, including Napoleon, accepted the necessity for *staffs*—for logistics, personnel, march planning, and the like—but gave them little or no say in operations. Jackson called one council of war during his Valley campaign, felt its decisions ruinous, and never called another. Montgomery wrote: "A conference of subordinates to collect ideas is the resort of a weak commander." Patton lectured that historically commanders, not their troops, made conquests—"Alexander, not Macedonia conquered the world"—but used his staff, all the same, in Europe to search for gasoline for his unauthorized advances. Vaux, heading 42 Commando, comprising many combat veterans, responded to opinions from his small battalion staff—officers and NCOs concerned with every patrol or attack—and, of course, recommendations from above.

Commanders of Special Forces always operated differently. *Vaux* was given commandos—men chosen from among volunteers, with built-in aggressiveness and love of the "game" of combat. "You have to have a violent and uncompromising attitude to this job. It's what you get paid for." Dayan, regarding organizing his commando battalion in 1948, said, "I concentrated on the selection and recruitment of the men." Both improvised and led from the front. In both cases, their leadership was of a kind well described by Colonel William O. Darby, speaking of the Rangers of World War II: "Commanding the Rangers was like driving a team of very high spirited horses. No effort was needed to get them to go forward. The problem was to keep them in check."[3]

Taking care of the troops was a top priority for our commanders, though the means differed. Frederick emphasized feeding the men well; Napoleon let them live off the land, but stressed equipping and arming them, and rewarding the valiant—with praise and "trinkets of glory." All believed in sharing the hardships of the men (commensurate with other duties). It was a factor in their *morale*, and none failed to show himself in the front lines whenever possible. Slim philosophized about morale, but on visits to troops spoke first about food, beer, and the progress of the war. "Vinegar Joe" *Stilwell* was obsessive about eating the same food—in line—with his troops, walking every step they did, and keeping (to Field Marshal Slim) a shockingly bare headquarters, all of which was lost on his troops, especially "Merrill's Marauders," whose sick and wounded he sent into battle at Myitkyina.

It was because Patton regularly visited his wounded that he came upon men in hospitals with "battle fatigue," in which he did not believe. He reacted violently and got into trouble with the press and high command. Patton also was acutely aware that his troops were Americans, recently civilians in an affluent society. He quietly saw to it that they got their mail on time, and had beer, soft drinks, and candy bars as well as regular rations. *Manstein*, with troops less accustomed to luxuries, still got cigarettes to them, and shared one with them when he could. In the snows of Russia, not surprisingly, he found battle fatigue was "normal," and dealt with it as best he could in visits to the front.[4] Moore commanded troops most of whom he had trained. He had brave young officers—regular, reserve, and OCS (from the ranks)—and many good regular army NCO's, like his sergeant major, Basil Plumley. The sergeant major looked after his colonel, and kept watch over reporter Joe Galloway: "You can't take no pictures laying down there on the ground, sonny." Moore's troops were mostly draftees, but they were not yet affected by a peace movement in the United States. Moore pressed them hard in battle, but got their rations and ammunition flown in, and maximum supporting firepower. They fought nobly, and after the Ia Drang battle, Moore went to his men and shook every hand, thanking them for the way they had fought. He also thanked the artillerymen who had supported his battalion. Then he visited the wounded before seeing to his own needs.

As to *training and discipline*, our commanders' opinions were close to Napoleon's:

> A good general, good cadres [officers and NCOs], good organization, good instruction, good discipline makes good troops, independent of the cause for which they fight. It is however true that fanaticism, love of country, national glory, can inspire young troops to advantage.[5]

However, their methods of training and command depended on the era and troops. Frederick and Napoleon were demanding and sometimes brutal with their officers, but comrades to their men. Sherman's troops were volunteers and conscripts (with a few old regulars). They felt their cause was noble, but as Americans, they expected rapid promotion, regular pay, good food, and some luxuries. He gave them all of that, while dealing with a ubiquitous press corps, political generals, and the public. He learned quickly to utilize and guard the telegraph and railroads, and how to best employ rifled weapons, and matched enemy fortifications with his own "earth-forts."

Jackson's troops were a few ex–U.S. Army regulars, volunteers, conscripts, and even cadets. Most lacked training, except for a few weeks of drill that Jackson gave them, but they were country boys who could shoot and often could ride. They felt righteous too—believing that they were defending their homeland from invasion—which explains the length and bloodiness of the Civil War. They expected their officers to lead—and "the professor" did; they asked less in the way of food, pay, and luxuries. Jackson satisfied them with victories, and supplied them as best he could, drawing on captured stores and weapons. On a small scale, he used the railroads and telegraph.

In World War I, Patton and Rommel demanded obedience, alertness, initiative, and *action* of their men; Rommel put heavy responsibility on his officers and NCOs.

In World War II, Rommel's charisma made for easy *discipline*. Patton shocked his citizen-soldiers into obedience—beginning by requiring salutes, ties, and shaves when not actually in combat. He set the example; his officers dared not do the same—not under "Old Blood and Guts." Patton loved war, as we have noted. His officers were mostly reserve or temporary; his men mostly conscripts, who called themselves GIs (Government Issues). They more or less cheerfully accepted Patton's manic discipline because they believed they were on the right side of a "Good War," and Patton was a master of armored warfare and a winner; thus he could inspire them with his bombast. GIs trusted him in war; in peace his thinking was alien to them, but most were proud to have served under him.

The persistence of "regular army" drill and discipline are evident in Schwarzkopf's tirades before the Gulf War. His officers saw nothing unusual in his Patton-like speeches.

Guerrilla leaders put more emphasis on nationalism (in Lawrence's case, ethnic solidarity).

Mosby's rangers comprised civilians, Confederate troops, men on leave, absent without leave, and deserters from the U.S. Army (whose fidelity he tested). The "Gray Ghost" led by example; his presence was icy and unfeeling (except to a few intimates), but he regularly embarrassed the enemy, and men competed to serve him. He trained no one, but picked those with the right skills, and summarily dismissed any who failed in combat. He put his raiders on horseback (improving their mounts with captured horses), and taught them to prefer the deadly Colt .44 to the saber. Guerrillas had to learn to take maximum advantage of the "sea" of sympathizers in which they "swam"—to strike and disappear. Mosby's "sea" was ready-made.

Lawrence had to create a "sea" by uniting tribes. He built a loyal following by bribery (though Emir Feisal did the dirtywork), allowing unchecked looting of captured Turkish trains and facilities—and *winning*. His instructors introduced his Bedouins to Enfield rifles, machine guns, and explosives. Lawrence led them on raids, in Arab dress, sharing their hardships, food from a common pot, and the minimal brackish water. The guerrilla leaders were ruthless, used deception and surprise, and, in Mosby's words, didn't "fight fair."

Giap began as a guerrilla leader, and used nationalism, racism, and the promises of Communism (instilled by indoctrination and intimidation) to build first a guerrilla force, then a North Vietnamese army. He acknowledged help from China and the USSR.

All our commanders saw the value of *winning*. Repeated victory could cover a multitude of faults, including eccentricities (Stonewall Jackson) or overemphasis on small points of discipline (Patton). Winning was necessary even for charismatic leaders like Rommel. Montgomery said, "No leader, however great, can long continue unless he wins victories." and "The best way to achieve a high morale in war-time is by success in battle."

All believed that victory depended on the *determination* to win, courage, the ability to make decisions under pressure, improvise, and take calculated risks. Napoleon said determination was the "first requirement of a commander." Rommel wrote, "A commander's drive and energy often count for more than his intellectual powers—a fact that is not generally understood by academic soldiers." Patton made victory a matter of "determination and speed." Moore's "Three strikes and you're NOT out!" expresses determination forcefully. Schwarzkopf told his Gulf officers: "I cannot afford to have commanders who do not understand that it is attack, attack, attack, attack, and destroy every step of the way."

They also preferred offense over defense. Both Frederick and Napoleon said that in defense one should prepare for offense. Jackson's plan for the Southern armies was based on "counter-invasions" from a secure base. Rommel wrote: "The destruction of the . . . cohesion of the opposing army must be the . . . aim of all planning." Patton's dictum was "When in doubt, attack." DeGaulle's *armée de métier* was designed for attack. Montgomery wrote: "[The commander] must make the enemy dance to his tune from the beginning, and never vice versa." Slim wrote: "The ultimate intention must be an offensive one [for all operations]." Ridgway would not be deterred from taking the offensive in Korea, despite the opposition of MacArthur's staff.[6] Dayan's creed was "Break through and move, fire and move." Giap said: "Revolutionary war . . . regards offensive activities as the most essential." Vaux got angry when the Welsh Guards slowed down the 42 Commando's march on Stanley. Schwarzkopf stormed at the Gulf generals: "Forget the defensive bullshit, we are now talking offensive. And we're going to talk offense from now until the day we go home."

The commanders all tried for the *best use of the most modern weapons*. With Frederick and Napoleon it was (among other things) the innovative use of cannon and light cavalry. Both sides in the American Civil War had touted the revolver over the saber for cavalry. Rommel demonstrated the use of tanks in the desert, converted his 88mm anti-aircraft guns into tank-killers, reconnoitered by air, and pled for more air support. In the Falklands, Vaux had fire support from the guns of the Royal Navy and from naval and RAF aircraft, and closer support from artillery and the Milan missile. Moore used new heavy-caliber infantry weapons (such as the M-79 grenade launcher), and called in support from helicopter fireships, artillery, and Air Force and Navy fighters and bombers.

Religious faith was taken to strengthen determination, though only Jackson, Patton, and Montgomery were vocal about it. However, Frederick the Great joined his men in hymns of praise to God after demolishing enemy armies, and

Napoleon ordered the *Te Deum* to celebrate a victory. But as Field Marshal Slim pointed out, faith in a cause can unite men of various religions. And apparently, a political faith can serve; Giap's "religion" was Communism.

And Finally

Despite technological progress in weapons and equipment of war, the basic canons of leadership have not changed. All our commanders took as models the Great Captains of the past. Frederick recommended reading about Eugene, Condé, Turenne, and Caesar; Napoleon added Frederick to the list. Sherman quoted Napoleon; Jackson was compared to him. Mosby cited Frederick on the preference for attack over defense. Lawrence paraphrased Napoleon on the scarcity of generals willing to fight, and had read Xenophon, Saxe, Clausewitz, and Kolmar von der Goltz, among others. Wavell refers to Hannibal, Alexander, Napoleon, Wellington, Wolfe, Caesar, Cromwell, Marlborough, Turenne, Moltke, and others. De Gaulle chose Condé, Turenne, and Frederick, who *"porte à sa perfection l'art guerrier d'Ancien Régime"*; Hoche of the Revolution, and Napoleon. Manstein was versed in Napoleon's campaigns and his impact on Germany.[7] Montgomery wrote: "Moses and Cromwell believed intensely in a divine mission, which never failed them in battle; Napoleon in a human destiny, which in the end did."[8] In 1945, General Patton wrote his son, George, a cadet at West Point:

> It is quite natural that my speeches should sound like Napoleon's because, as you know, I have studied him all my life. You are wrong in saying he fought a different type of war—he and I fought the same way but my means of progress [transportation] were better than his.[9]

Vaux and Moore show a knowledge of history. Giap cited the battle of Valmy (French vs. Prussians during the French Revolution) to his biographer, Colvin, as proof that inspired citizens could defeat regular troops.[10] Schwarzkopf mentions Hannibal, Caesar, Robert E. Lee, and Lawrence in his autobiography.

The basic doctrines of leadership seem to be unchanging. Nonetheless, the words of Marshal T.-R. Bugeaud de Piconnerie still hold true: *"In war, there are principles, but they are few."*[11]

Notes

Introduction

1. Included in a mass of writings edited by his wife, Marie von Clausewitz. Of the many later editions and translations, the latest and perhaps best is *On War*, ed. and trans. by Michael Howard and Peter Paret (1984).

2. And other works: *Traité des grandes operations militaires* (1805); *Histoire critique et militaire des guerres de la révolution* (27 vols., 1820–24). In 1927, he added a life of Napoleon (4 vols.) to the *Histoire critique*, later published separately.

3. An expression used by, e.g., Dennis Showalter; origin uncertain.

4. To paraphrase Gen. George Patton, *The Patton Papers*, ed. by Martin Blumenson (1972–74). II: 733–34 (*Diary* 8 Aug. 1945).

5. Russell F. Weigley, *The American Way of War: A History of United States Military Strategy and Policy* (1977).

6. See *Les Écrits militaires de Charles de Gaulle: Essai d'analyse thématique*, by Pierre Messmer et Alain Larcan (1985), 400, 597, and passim. Discussed by DeGaulle in his *Vers l'armée de métier* (1934), quoted in chapter IX, and in his *Memoirs* I, 8–9. See also *Legitimacy and Commitment in the Military*, ed. by Thomas C. Wyatt and Reúven Gal (1990), 81; Robert A. Doughty (Col. USA), *The Seeds of Disaster: The Development of French Army Doctrine, 1919–1939* (1985); Guy Chapman, *Why France Fell: The Defeat of the French Army in 1940* (1969); Earnest R. May, *Strange Victory: Hitler's Conquest of France* (2000).

7. For example, the French Revolution of 1789. Because of the population explosion of the 18th century, there were too many peasants for available land. They migrated to cities, notably Paris, which had insufficient industry to employ them. Paris directed the revolution. See my *French Revolution and Napoleonic Era* 3rd ed. (1999), 5–8, 43.

8. Modern society also spawned the press (now the *media*). During the French Revolution, J.-P. Marat's newspaper, *L'Ami du peuple*, helped ruin Lafayette's credibility as a general. On later media roles: Jean Tulard, *Napoléon: Ou le mythe du sauveur*, 83–85; William T. Sherman, *Memoirs* (1891), II, 408; Jeremy Wilson, *Lawrence of Arabia* (1990), 466–67, 489–90; Wolf Heckmann, *Rommels Krieg in Afrika* (1976); 40; Dieter Ose, *Entscheidung im Westen, 1944* (1982), 41; David Fraser, *Knight's Cross: A Life of Field Marshal Erwin Rommel* (1993), 308, 550; *Patton Papers*, II: 326–42; Carlo d'Este, *Patton: A Genius for War* (1995), 533–55; David H. Hackworth and Julie Sherman, *About Face: The Odyssey of an American Warrior* (1989), 817; J. F. Dunnigan and R. M. Macedonia, *Getting It Right: American Military Reforms after Vietnam* (1993).

9. Desertion and evasion were rife. See Alan Forrest, *Conscripts and Deserters: The French Army and Society during the Revolution and Empire* (1989).

10. "*La Garde impériale a toujours marché à la Marseillaise.*" *Correspondance de Napoléon Ier* (1870), XXXI: 225.

11. Prussia had a conscription law in 1814, but only volunteers (20,000) in the Waterloo campaign; the Anglo-Dutch only "regulars." The Russian levies and Austrian Landwehr and militia are considered by some the equivalent of conscripts.

12. French muskets, carbines, and pistols were all .69 caliber. The British musket was .75 caliber. Prussian, Austrian, and Russian all about .74. In the French army, only snipers had rifles. The British army had one rifle regiment. Rifles and muskets were muzzle loading.

13. The French field artillery—4-, 6-, 8-, and 12-pounders designed by the Comte de Gribeauval under the *ancien régime*—were the best in Europe. Their opponents' guns were as powerful, but heavier and less maneuverable. Cannon fired solid shot, bombs (hollow, with a fused charge inside), and canister, often called "grape shot."

14. The cavalry had sabers, pistols, and carbines (French, all .69). Heavy cavalry—big men, wearing body armor, on heavy horses—could be used in attacks, supported by infantry; light cavalry attacked other cavalry, scouted, and pursued.

15. The French, beginning in 1793, built a "wig-wag" telegraph system, but not for field use. It consisted of lines of high towers, within sight of each other, on which long blades were mounted for signalling. In time, messages could be sent to neighboring countries.

16. The Civil War was (per capita) America's bloodiest conflict; North and South together had 215,000 killed in action in a population of 32,000,000; there were 283,000 KIA in World War II, out of 132,000,000 (1940).

17. Twelve pounders. The horse artillery preferred the 3-inch (ordnance) rifled piece, but some used the 10-pounder Parrott.

18. Moltke's victories were facilitated by the Prussian "needle gun," a breech-loading single-shot rifle, superior artillery, and the use of the railroad and telegraph. France had a machine gun, the *mitrailleuse*, with 25 barrels, but her generals did not use it. That helped Moltke to fight a short war, which he favored: "Die grösste Wohlthat im Kriege ist die schnelle Beendigung des Krieges und dazu müssen alle, nicht geradzu verwerfliche Mittel frei stehen."

19. The British Imperial General Staff was subordinate to the War Office; the French *État-Major de l'Armée* under the *Conseil Superieur de la Guerre* of generals and ministers. The United States had a General Staff as of 1903, but the AEF staff, formed in France during the war with the advice of the Allies, was the postwar GS model.

20. British Lee-Enfield .303 caliber; U.S. Springfield .30; the French Lebel rifle, tube-fed. The German Maxim machine gun was 7.92mm; the French was similar, as were the British .303 (7.7mm) and American .30 MGs. The U.S. .30 Browning automatic rifle was used in both world wars.

21. British had 18-pound guns and 4.5″ howitzers with a range of six miles. German 8″ (21cm) guns shelled Paris from 76 miles away. The French .75mm was used by all the Allies. The Germans had 77mm guns, 105mm light howitzers, and 150mm heavy howitzers.

22. To name a few: Germany's "Red Baron," Manfred von Richthofen, Britain's Edward C. "Mick" Mannock and William "Billy" Bishop, and America's "Eddie" Rickenbaker. See Lee Kennett, *The First Air War* (1991); John H. Morrow, Jr., *The Great War in the Air* (1993).

23. In 1918, when the First U.S. Army attacked the St. Mihiel salient, it was supported by an Allied air armada of 600 planes, commanded by Colonel William "Billy" Mitchell.

24. The British had 900,000 killed in action; the French 1,400,000; the Russians

1,700,000; the Germans 1,800,000. The United States (in the war only April 1917–November 1918) had 56,000 KIA.

25. The United States had 293,000 KIA; Britain, 398,000; the USSR 1,000,000; Germany, 2,900,000; Japan 1,500,000. Of civilians: Britain had 65,000 killed; Germany 500,000; Japan 300,000; the USSR 10 to 15 million in and around major cities; most were killed by aircraft bombs.

26. See Reina Penington, "Wings, Women and War: A Comparative Study of Women in Military Aviation in World War II" (Ph.D. diss., Univ. South Carolina, 1999). She interviewed many Soviet women pilots.

27. Americans had tanks with 75mm guns (also used by the British) and, late in the war, some with 90mm guns; the USSR had one with an 85mm gun, also late. German tanks had 37mm guns, then 50, and finally 88.

28. US had 155 and 105mm guns; the British 5.5 and 7.2 inch; the Germans 170 and 78mm.

29. 150mm, then 210, 230, and 310mm.

30. See Ronald W. Clark, *The Man Who Broke Purple: The Life of . . . Colonel William F. Friedman* (1977); Bruce Norman, *Secret Warfare: The Battle of Codes and Ciphers* (1973); Jozef Garlinski, *Intercept: The Enigma War* (1979); Peter Calvocoressi, *Top Secret Ultra* (1980); Ronald Lewin, *American Magic: Codes, Ciphers and the Defeat of Japan* (1982); Peter Cremer, *U-Boat Commander* (trans. by Lawrence Wilson, 1984).

31. Of the vast literature, one might begin with *The Manhattan Project: A Documentary Introduction to the Atomic Age* (1991); Peter Goodchild, *J. Robert Oppenheimer: Shatterer of Worlds* (1981); S. S. Schweber, *In The Shadow of the Bomb: Bethe, Oppenheimer, and the Moral Responsibility of the Scientist* (2000).

32. The 2.36″ bazookas could not stop the PRKA's Russian-built T-34 tank, but were replaced with 3.5″ and jeep-mounted 75mm rockets. World War II artillery (105 and 155mm) and tanks (75 and 90mm guns) served well.

33. 47,393 were killed in action in Vietnam, 1964–73. KIA in Korea were 34,000, 95 percent in 1950–52.

34. Gunships had 2.75″ rockets and .50 caliber and 7.62mm (.30 caliber) machine guns. The 1st Cavalry Division (airmoble) moved by helicopter.

35. Semi-automatic or automatic 5.56mm and 7.62mm rifles; 7.62mm machine guns; fragmentation, white phosphorus, and smoke grenades; jeep-borne .50 caliber machine guns and 106mm rockets (if there were roads). USAF planes had 20mm cannon and machine guns, napalm, and 250- or 500-pound bombs.

36. An 84mm recoilless rocket launcher; the shoulder-fired 5.5″ Stinger and 5″ TOW missile with heat-seeking warheads.

37. Both had .50 and .30 caliber machine guns; the IFV a 20mm cannon, and some a TOW guided missle.

38. 155mm guns, 155 and 205mm howitzers.

39. *Weapons of the Gulf War* (ed. by Graham Smith, 1991) gives details, with pictures, of all weapons, tanks, IFVs, APCs, artillery, planes, and helicopters—even naval weapons.

40. Colin Powell, *My American Journey* (1995), 148–49, 487 and passim; H. Norman Schwarzkopf, *Autobiography: It Doesn't Take a Hero* (1992), 299. See also J. F. Dunnigan and R. M. Macedonia, *Getting It Right: American Military Reforms after Vietnam* (1993).

41. He might have had a few more at Leipzig (1813), but many of his German troops were changing sides during the battle.

42. He let commanders in the air control the battle. Telephone conversation (20 October 1992) with the author.

43. Even Vo Nguyen Giap. Peter MacDonald, *Giap: The Victor in Vietnam* (1993), 23.
44. *The Patton Papers*, II, 734.

I. Frederick the Great and Napoleon

1. Edouard Driault, *Pensées pour l'action* (1943), 95–96. He gives Napoleon's order for the books, specifying the number in religion, epics, novels, histories, etc.—all small, with thin covers and no margins.

2. Frederick the Great, *Oeuvres de Frédéric le Grand* (30 vols., ed. by Johann D. E. Preuss et al., 1846–57), XXVIII: 16.

3. Gerhard Ritter, *Frederick the Great* (trans. Peter Paret), 138.

4. Frederick had 3- and 6-pound battalion guns—lighter and smaller than Napoleon's—backed up by batteries of 10- and 12-pounders. Napoleon used 6-, 8-, and 12-pounders and some 4's. Christopher Duffy, *The Army of Frederick the Great* (1974), 111–12.

5. Ritter, *Frederick the Great*, 140. Also see Hans Delbrück, *History of the Art of War* IV: 310–11, 328–29; Arden Bucholz, *Moltke, Schlieffen, and Prussian War Planning* (1991).

6. Fredrick the Great, *Oeuvres* XXVIII: 84.

7. Delbrück, *The Dawn of Modern Warfare*, 376.

8. Tulard, Jean (ed.), *Oeuvres littéraire et écrits militaires de Napoléon* (1969), I: 249.

9. *Correspondance*, 32: 238.

10. "Frédéric a livré, dans la guerre de Sept Ans, dix batailles; il n'a, dans aucune d'elles, fait exécuter les manoeuvres des revues de Potsdam. . . . Le vieux Frédéric riait sous cape, aux parades de Potsdam, de l'engouement des jeunes officiers français, anglais, autrichiens, pour la *manoeuvre de l'ordre oblique*, qui n'était propre qu'à faire la réputation de quelques adjudants-majors." *Correspondance* XXXII: 240, 242.

11. *Oeuvres de Frédéric le Grand*, 30 vols., ed. by Johann D. E. Preuss et al. (1846–1857); *Politische Correspondenz Friedrichs des Grossen*, ed. by Gustav Droysen et al. (1879–1939); *Instruction militaire du roi de Prusse pour ses généraux* (1761; there are earlier and later editions), translated into German as *Geheime Instruction, enthhaltend de geheimen Befehle an die Officiere seiner Armee* (1780); *Gespräche Friedrichs des Grossen* (1919).

12. *Oeuvres de Frédéric le Grand*, vol. XXVII: *Principes généraux de la guerre*; *Correspondance de Napoléon Ier. Volumes 29–32 of Correspondance* record much of what Napoleon dictated on St. Helena, notably to Generals Henry Bertrand, Charles Montholon, Gaspard Gourgaud, and Count Emmanuel de Las Cases.

13. Ernest Picard, *Préceptes et jugements de Napoléon* (1913); André Palluel, *Dictionnaire de l'Empereur* (1969); Adrien Dansette *Napoléon: Pensées politiques at sociales* (1969). Hereinafter cited by authors' names.

14. Frederick II, *Les Principes généraux de la guerre* in *Oeuvres*, XXVIII: 25.

15. Palluel, 550. *Correspondance de Napoléon Ier*, no. 1976.

16. Palluel, 532. To Montholon on St. Helena.

17. *Oeuvres* XXVIII: 40–41.

18. *Observations sur les campagnes de 1796–1797* (Napoleon at St. Helena). Palluel, 556.

19. *Oeuvres* XXVIII: 88.

20. Ibid., XXVIII: 88.

21. Ibid., XXVIII: 40–41.

22. *Correspondance*, no. 15332 (to Clarke, 11 June 1809), Picard, 114.

23. To the Directory, May 1796, when ordered to combine his army with that of Kellermann (Army of the Alps). He offered to resign, but the government relented. He went on to defeat the Austrians in Italy, march on Vienna, and win the war. *Correspondance*, 29: 107.

24. *Correspondance* 31: 418.

25. "C'est une ancienne règle de guerre . . . si vous séparez vos forces, vous serez battu en détail." *Oeuvres* XXVIII: 36.

26. "L'art de la guerre ne consiste pas à diviser ses troupes." To Marshal Berthier, his chief of staff. *Correspondance*, no. 18512 (21 Feb. 1812). Picard, 22.

27. *Correspondance* 32: 210.

28. *Oeuvres* XXVII: 6.

29. Ibid., XXVIII: 39.

30. C.-J.-T. de Montholon, *Récits* de la captivité de l'Empereur Napoléon (2 vols., 1847). II: 240–41; Picard, 120.

31. *Correspondance*, no. 14283. Picard, 114.

32. Picard, 22; *Correspondance* 31: 365.

33. *Correspondance* 31: 413.

34. Emmanuel Las Cases, *Mémorial de Sainte-Hélène*, 5 December 1815. Palluel, 529–30.

35. *Oeuvres*, XXVIII: 14.

36. *Correspondance*, no. 10558 (July 1806). Palluel, 551.

37. *Correspondance*, 31: 347. "Considerations sur l'Art de Guerre," dictated to Gen. Henri Bertrand on St. Helena.

38. *Oeuvres* XXVIII: 43.

39. Ibid., XXVIII: 44.

40. Ibid., XXVIII: 4.

41. Ibid., XXVIII: 12.

42. *Correspondance*, no. 8209 (12 December 1804), in Palluel, 540.

43. *Correspondance*, no. 20090 (to Bertrand, 1813). Palluel, 554.

44. *Correspondance* 31, 263; Picard, 23.

45. Ibid., 31: 417.

46. Ibid., 31: 410.

47. *Correspondance* no. 15933 (to Clarke, 10 Oct. 1809); Palluel, 533.

48. *Correspondance*, no. 14276. Palluel, 551.

49. *Oeuvres* XXVIII: 16.

50. Ibid., XXVIII: 42.

51. *Correspondance* 31: 417.

52. Dansette, 304 (letter to Joseph Bonaparte, 8 September 1806).

53. Las Cases, *Mémorial de Sainte Hélène*, I: 256.

54. *Correspondance* 31: 415.

55. *Oeuvres* XXIX: 42.

56. Ibid., XXVIII: 40–41.

57. *Correspondance* 32: 286 [*Extraits du Mémorial*].

58. To Eugène, 10 May 1809, in Palluel, 533.

59. *Oeuvres*. XXVIII: 15.

60. Ibid., XXIX: 70.

61. Ibid., XXVIII: 20.

62. " . . . en étant toujours attentif à ce que les troupes ne manquent de rien, soit

pain, viande, paille, eau-de-vie, etc.; . . . en examinant les raisons de la désertion, lorsqu'elle se met ou dans un régiment, ou dans une compagnie, pour savoir si le soldat a reçu régulièrement son prêt et toutes les douceurs qui lui sont assignées, ou si son capitaine est coupable de malversation." *Oeuvres* XXVIII: 6.

63. *Correspondance*, no. 9944. Picard, 20.
64. *Oeuvres* XXVIII: 16.
65. Ibid., XXVIII: 9.
66. *Correspondance*, no. 1976. Picard, 20.
67. *Oeuvres* XXVIII: 54.
68. Ibid., XXVIII: 23, 26.
69. Ibid., XXVIII: 26.
70. Ibid., XXVIII: 30.
71. *Correspondance* 31: 415.
72. Ibid., 31: 411.
73. Ibid., 31: 416.
74. *Oeuvres* XXVIII: 50.
75. Picard, 114.
76. *Oeuvres* XXVIII: 45.
77. *Correspondance* 31: 365; Picard, 22.
78. *Correspondance* 31: 347, 353–54.

II. William Tecumseh Sherman

1. Russell F. Weigley, *The American Way of War* (1973, 1977).
2. Perfected in Prussia by General Helmuth von Moltke (the Elder), as noted in the Introduction.
3. James D. Hittle, *The Military Staff, Its History and Development* (1949), 198.
4. Quotations are from William T. Sherman, *Memoirs of General William T. Sherman, by Himself* (2 vols.; 4th ed., 1892), hereinafter cited as *Sherman*. There are later editions. Grant has been republished recently: *Memoirs and Selected Letters: The Personal Memoirs of U.S. Grant: Selected Letters 1839–1865* (1990).
5. *Sherman* II: 386.
6. *Sherman* II: 402–3.
7. Ibid., II: 404–6.
8. Ibid., II: 387.
9. Ibid., II: 389–90.
10. Ibid., II: 390–91.
11. Ibid., II: 392–93.
12. Ibid., II: 401.
13. Ibid., II: 394–97.
14. Ibid., II: 398–99.
15. Ibid., II: 408–9.

III. Stonewall Jackson

1. Henry Kyd Douglas, *I Rode with Stonewall: . . . The War Experiences of the Youngest Member of Jackson's Staff* (reprint 1940), 93. Claude Crozet (1790–1864) was a graduate

of the *Ecole Polytechnique* who was captured during the Russian Campaign. After Napoleon's fall, he came to the United States, taught at West Point (1816–23), then was State Engineer of Virginia and one of the founders of The Virginia Military Institute (1830).

2. In a letter to his sister. James I. Robertson, Jr. *Stonewall Jackson: The Man, The Soldier, The Legend* (1997), 67.

3. Ibid., 247–51.

4. To General Joseph E. Johnston, the Army commander. John Bowers, *Stonewall Jackson* (1989), 125.

5. Burke Davis. *They Called Him Stonewall* (1954), 9–10.

6. See Robert K. Krick, *Conquering the Valley: Stonewall Jackson at Port Republic* (1996); Robert J. Tanner, *Stonewall in the Valley* (1996); James M. McPherson, *Atlas of the Civil War* (1994); and other works cited in the bibliography.

7. Davis, *Stonewall*, 14.

8. *Grant and Lee: A Study in Personality and Generalship* (1957), 127.

9. Mary Anna Jackson, *Life and Letters of General Thomas J. Jackson* (1892); Henry Kyd Douglas, *I Rode with Stonewall* (published by his nephew, 1940).

10. In quotation marks. Quoted in James I. Robertson, Jr., *Stonewall Jackson* (1997), 36, 156; also in biographies by Vandiver, Bowers, Davis, and others. See bibliography.

11. Douglas, *I Rode with Stonewall*, 68.

12. 1862 June (after the Valley Campaign): To Capt. John Imboden. Quoted by Burke Davis. *They Called Him Stonewall* (1954). 194. James M. McPherson. *Atlas of the Civil War* (1994). 68.

13. Mary Anna Jackson, *Life and Letters of General Thomas J. Jackson*, 42–44. This is from the letter of an eyewitness, identified only as "a brother officer."

14. Quoted by J. Bowers, *Stonewall Jackson* (1989). 124; James M. McPherson, *Atlas of the Civil War* (1994), 33; and many others. Douglas, who was there, has a milder version: "Tell the colonels of this brigade that the enemy are advancing; when their heads are seen above the hill, let the whole line rise, move forward with a shout and trust to the bayonet." Douglas, *I Rode with Stonewall*, 10.

15. Mary Anna Jackson, *Letters*, 178.

16. Ibid., 182.

17. Douglas, *I Rode with Stonewall*, 46–47.

18. Ibid., 48–49.

19. Ibid., 49.

20. Most historians say 16,000. See McPherson, *Atlas of the Civil War*, 68.

21. Douglas, *I Rode with Stonewall*, 50–51.

22. Ibid., 50–52.

23. Ibid., 53–54.

24. Ibid., 54–55.

25. Ibid., 56–57.

26. Ibid.

27. Ibid., 57–58.

28. Ibid., 58–60.

29. Ibid., 70–71.

30. Ibid., 71–72.

31. Robert K. Krick, *Conquering the Valley* (1996), 66–68.

32. Douglas, *I Rode with Stonewall*, 88–90.

33. Anna Jackson, *Letters*, 282–83.

34. Ibid., 310–16.

35. Ibid., 318.

36. Ibid., 320–21.

37. Davis, *Stonewall*, 264. J.F.C. Fuller has a slightly different version: "When someone deplored the necessity of destroying so many brave men, he exclaimed: 'No, shoot them all, I do not wish them to be brave.' . . . Jackson was the Old Testament of War, Lee— the New." *Grant and Lee*, 129.

38. *Letters*, 458.

39. Douglas, *I Rode with Stonewall*, 70.

IV. John Singleton Mosby

1. Others are Robert Rogers, of the French and Indian War, and Francis Marion, "The Swamp Fox" of the Revolutionary War.

2. Quoted in Shu Guang Zhang, *Mao's Military Romanticism: China and the Korean War, 1950–1953* (1965), 13.

3. His term. Mosby, *War Reminiscences [and] Stuart's Cavalry Campaigns* (1887), 45.

4. Recent repetition in Gregory J. W. Urwin. *Custer Victorious: The Civil War Battles of General George Armstrong Custer* (1983), 175.

5. Mosby took advantage of Southerners' deeply held belief that the Union troops were invaders.

6. Mosby, *War Reminiscences*, 220–21; John W. Thomason, Jr., *Jeb Stuart* ([1929] 1994), 141; John Scott (late Major CSA), *Partisan Life with Col. John S. Mosby* (1867), reprinted 1990).

7. Jeffry D. Wert, *Mosby's Rangers*, New York, 1990, 47; Mosby, *War Reminiscences*, 85. Quotes General Lee's order.

8. John Singleton Mosby, *War Reminiscences [and] Stuart's Cavalry Campaigns* (1887), hereinafter cited as *War Reminiscences*. *Memoirs of Colonel John S. Mosby* (1917; reprint 1959), cited as *Memoirs*.

9. *War Reminiscences*, 43–44.

10. Ibid., 79–80.

11. Ibid., 80–81.

12. Ibid., 79.

13. Wyndham, a British soldier-of-fortune, commanded the cavalry with the 1st Vermont [Infantry] Brigade in Fairfax.

14. Ibid., *Memoirs*, 170–71.

15. Ibid., 171–74.

16. Ibid., 174–77.

17. He alludes to Napoleon's remark that the "Sun of Austerlitz" hung in the sky until he destroyed the czar's army there (1805).

18. Ibid., *Memoirs*, 177–81.

19. Ibid., 183–84.

20. *War Reminiscences*, 82.

21. Ibid., 83–84.

22. Ibid., 84, 86–88.

23. Ibid., 88–92.

24. Ibid., 89.

25. Ibid., 99–101.

26. Ibid., 102–3.

27. Ibid., 103–4.
28. Ibid., 104–9.
29. Ibid., 109–10.
30. David Miller, *Special Forces* (1999).

V. Thomas Edward Lawrence

1. Peter MacDonald, *Giap: The Victor in Vietnam* (1993), 23. Currey quotes Giap in a 1946 conversation with General Raoul Salan of France: "My fighting gospel is T. E. Lawrence's *Seven Pillars of Wisdom*. I am never without it." Cecil B. Currey, *Victory at Any Cost: The Genius of Viet Nam's Gen. Vo Nguyen Giap* (1996), 154.

2. Four books on Lawrence have appeared since 1989, including an "authorized biography" of 1,200 pages by Jeremy Wilson, *Lawrence of Arabia: The Authorized Biography of T. E. Lawrence* (1990). On Richthofen: P. Kilduff, *Richthofen: Beyond the Legend of the Red Baron* (1994), and the curious British *Under the Guns of the Red Baron* (1997), by Norman Franks et al. (See bibliography.)

3. Though technically illegitimate. His father left his first wife for Lawrence's mother, presented her as his wife, and lived with her until he died. See Wilson, *Lawrence of Arabia*, 29–30.

4. Save for other descendants, such as Ibn Saud, in the south.

5. *Seven Pillars of Wisdom* ([1935] 1966), 286.

6. Malcolm Brown, *A Touch Genius: T.E. Lawrence* (1989), 121.

7. Lawrence's work influenced many writers, including André Malraux in France and Ernest Hemingway in America. Joel C. Hodson, *Lawrence of Arabia and American Culture: The Making of a Transatlantic Legend* (1995), 97.

8. Actually, quotations were taken from U.S. reprints of Lawrence's *Seven Pillars* (1966) and *Revolt in the Desert* (1927).

9. *Revolt*, 23–24.

10. Ibid., 27.

11. T. E. Lawrence, *Seven Pillars of Wisdom* ([1935] 1966), 74. Hereinafter cited as *Pillars*.

12. *Pillars*, 75–77.

13. Ibid., 77–78.

14. Ibid., 146–48.

15. Ibid., 160–67.

16. Colonel Stewart F. Newcombe, head of the British military mission to the Hejaz; Colonel Cyril Wilson, representative at Jidda; and Captain W. A. Davenport, who brought in Egyptian troops.

17. *Pillars*, 194.

18. Shakir was a nephew of Sherif (King) Hussein, Emir of Mecca.

19. Major H. G. Garland, sent to help Feisal.

20. *Pillars*, 170–74.

21. Ibid., 191.

22. *Revolt*, 108–17.

23. *Pillars*, 285–86.

24. The eventual result—after another world war—was evacuation of Palestine by the British and creation of the state of Israel by the Jewish population.

25. Wilson, *Lawrence*. 442–45. Lawrence's views in 1930 are summarized in John E.

Mack's *A Prince of Our Disorder: The Life of T. E. Lawrence* (1974, 1996), 252–53.
    26. Wilson, *Lawrence*, 671–77.

VI. Archibald Percival Wavell

1. H. E. Raugh, Jr., *Wavell in the Middle East, 1939–1941* (1993).
    2. Wrote Rommel: "What distinguished him from other British commanders was his great . . . strategic courage." B. H. Liddell Hart (ed.), *The Rommel Papers*, 146.
    3. This is listed in Kenneth Macksey, *Military Errors of World War II* (1987), 91. But it was not Wavell's decision.
    4. Archibald Percival Wavell, Earl of Wavell, *Generals and Generalship: The Lees Knowles Lectures Delivered at Trinity College, Cambridge in 1939* (1941); hereinafter *Generals*; *Soldiers and Soldiering; or Epithets of War. Essays* (1953), hereafter *Soldiers*.
    5. *Generals*, 1–3.
    6. Ibid., 4.
    7. Ibid., 5–6.
    8. Ibid., 6–7.
    9. Ibid., 8.
    10. Ibid., 8–10.
    11. Ibid., 11.
    12. Ibid., 12–14.
    13. Ibid., 15.
    14. Ibid., 16.
    15. Ibid., 17.
    16. Ibid.
    17. Ibid., 17–19.
    18. Ibid., 26–27.
    19. *Soldiers*, 127–28.
    20. Ibid., 128–29.
    21. Ibid., 130.
    22. Ibid., 131–32.

VII. Erwin Johannes Eugen Rommel

1. Richard Brett-Smith, *Hitler's Generals* (1976), 263.
    2. The latter was Germany's highest medal for bravery, created by Frederick the Great, and awarded to him after he took 9,000 prisoners at Caporetto and 10,000 at Longarone (November 1917).
    3. David Fraser, *Knight's Cross: The Life of Field Marshal Erwin Rommel* (1993), 563ff. See letters in John Pimlott (ed.), *Rommel in His Own Words* (1994); Rommel, *Krieg ohne Hass*, ed. by Lucie-Maria Rommel and Gen. Fritz Bayerlein (1950); and B. H. Liddell Hart, *The Rommel Papers* (1953).
    4. "Rommel war von der Persönlichkeit Hitlers angetan. Hitler andererseits schätzte diesen Offizier, dessen . . . unkonventionelle Führungsmethoden sich mit seinen Führungstechniken, mit denen er die Blitzkriege gewonnen hatte, vergleichen ließen." Dieter Ose, *Entscheidung im Westen, 1944: Der Oberbefehlshaber West und die Abwehr der Alliierten Invasion* (1982), 41.

5. The envious called him Hitler's *Lieblingsgeneral* ("pet general"). Wolf Heckmann, *Rommels Krieg in Afrika* (1976), 40, passim.

6. Operation *Sonnenblume* (Sunflower). The name was more apt than OKW realized— a bloom on a long fragile stem (the supply line). Heckmann, *Rommels Krieg in Afrika*, 41.

7. General Franz Halder, the *Generalstab* chief, called him a "soldier gone stark mad." Brett-Smith, *Hitler's Generals*, 255.

8. On Wavell's victories and defeats, see Harold E. Raugh, Jr. *Wavell in the Middle East, 1939–1941* (1993). The Italians fought best, curiously enough, when placed directly under Rommel.

9. Antiaircraft guns, which he found were superior anti-tank guns. Later mounted on "Tiger" tanks, the best in World War II, but too few.

10. Brett-Smith, *Hitler's Generals*, 263–64.

11. Erwin Rommel, *Infanterie greift an* (1937), trans. Gustave E. Kidde as *Infantry Attacks* (1944, reprint 1979); intro. to new edition by Manfred Rommel (1990). *The Rommel Papers*, ed. by B. H. Liddell Hart, trans. by Paul Findlay (1953). *Krieg ohne Hass*, ed. by Lucie-Maria Rommel and Gen. Fritz Bayerlein (1950).

12. *Infanterie greift an*, 36–37, 51, 58, 151, 190, 215, 328.

13. *Rommel Papers*, 226, 241. *Krieg ohne Hass*, 154–55, 173.

14. *Rommel Papers*, 201. *Krieg ohne Hass*, 120–23.

15. "Eine gleiche Meinung zeigte sich während des Krieges in deutschen sowie britischen Offizierskreisen, die wegen komplizierter Theorien die Fähigkeit verloren, sich der Realität anzupassen." *Krieg ohne Hass*, 127.

16. *Rommel Papers*, 203–4. *Krieg ohne Hass*, 127.

17. *Rommel Papers*, 285. *Krieg ohne Hass*, 222.

18. *Rommel Papers*, 328, 198–201.

19. "Dagegen war den Deutschen in der 8,8 cm-Pak-Flak eine Waffe in die Hand gegeben, die in ihrer vielseitigen Verwendungsmöglichkeit unerreicht und beneidet blieb." *Krieg ohne Hass*, 105.

20. "Die dreitägige Panzerschlacht von Agedabia zur Jahreswende 1941 ist schließlich ein Musterbeispiel beweglicher Kampfführung und der Zusammenarbeit von Panzer und Pak. . . . Die Winterschlacht in der Marmarica ist aber deshalb von ganz besonderer Bedeutung, weil hier die taktischen Grundsätze des Wüstenkrieges geboren, gefestigt und erprobt worden sind. Alle Erfolge der nächsten Kampfhandlungen bauen sich auf diesen Erfahrungen auf und führen schließlich zu dem Höhe-punkt in der Sommeroffensive, wo Rommels Wüstentaktik und Truppen-führung unwahrscheinliche Triumphe feierte." *Krieg ohne Hass*, 106–7. (Not included in full in *The Rommel Papers*.)

21. Richard Brett-Smith, *Hitler's Generals* (1976), 261.

22. *Rommel Papers*, 119, passim.

VIII. George S. Patton, Jr.

1. *The Patton Papers*, ed. Martin Blumenson (1972–74), II: 438. Apparently, Patton asked for a contingency plan to land his actual command, Third Army, at Calais in case Montgomery's army got "boxed up" in Normandy. He was refused. Carlo d'Este, *Patton: A Genius for War* (1995), 599.

2. Contrary to a persistent belief, Rommel was not in command of Atlantic Wall forces on D-Day. David Fraser, *Knight's Cross: The Life of Field Marshal Erwin Rommel* (1993),

467; Dieter Ose; *Entscheidung im Westen, 1944: Der Oberbefehlshaber West und die Abwehr der Alliierten Invasion* (1982), 51–57.

3. "Die amerikanische Generalität hatte taktisch hier bereits sehr modern geführt, obwohl die auffallendsten amerikanischen Leistungen im Bewegungskrieg von der Patton-Armee in Frankreich vollbracht worden sein dürften." *Krieg ohne Hass*, 399. I do not find this in *The Rommel Papers*.

4. On the subject of Monty's proposed "lightning dagger-thrust" to the Ruhr, "[Patton] in a mock English voice . . . aped Monty, saying, the Germans 'will be off their guard, and I shall pop out at them like an angry rabbit.' The reporters howled." d'Este, *Patton*, 657.

5. Ibid., 316, passim; Hubert Essame, *Patton: A Study in Command* (1974), 25–26; Steve E. Dietrich, "Professional Reading of General George S. Patton, Jr.," *Journal of Military History* 53 (Oct. 1989): 387–418.

6. Charles R. Codman, *Drive* (1957), 142. Robert S. Allen, Third Army deputy G-2 (Intelligence), wrote that Patton, in his first speech, told the staff that "They were fighting the war . . . to preserve traditional liberties, to defeat the Nazis . . . and simply to fight—men liked to fight and always would. Only sophists and crackpots denied the latter. They were goddamned fools, cowards, or both. Whoever disliked fighting would do well to ask for a transfer now, for Patton wanted no part of him and would kick him out later." *Patton Papers* II: 429.

7. Codman was Patton's aide. Quoted from a letter to his wife (8 Aug. 1944). Codman, *Drive*, 159.

8. Este, *Patton*, 4, 599, passim; Essame, *Patton*, 137.

9. *Patton Papers*, I: 585. Also see Blumenson, *Patton, The Man behind the Legend* (1985).

10. Essame, *Patton*, 23.

11. Ibid., 54–55; Este, *Patton*, 435–38.

12. Este, *Patton*, 466.

13. Stephen E. Ambrose, *The Supreme Commander: The War Years of General Dwight D. Eisenhower* (1970), 229.

14. Alistaire Horne (with David Montgomery), *Monty: The Lonely Leader, 1944–1945* (1994), 253.

15. Gerard M. Devlin, *Paratrooper* (1979), 527–28. Gerald Astor, *A Blood-Dimmed Tide: The Battle of the Bulge by the Men Who Fought It* (1992), 226–27.

16. *Patton Papers*, II: 694, 699, 701, 707, passim.

17. Martin Blumenson, *The Patton Papers*. Vol. I: *1885–1940* (1972); vol. II: *1940–1945* (1974).

18. Ibid., I: 794–98.

19. Ibid., I: 801–2.

20. Ibid.

21. Ibid., I: 812.

22. Ibid., I: 816–17.

23. Ibid., I: 817–18.

24. Ibid., II: 96–99.

25. Ibid., II: 119.

26. Ibid., II: 166–167.

27. Ibid., II: 185.

28. Ibid., II: 186–87.

29. Ibid., II: 261–62.

30. Ibid., II: 268–69.
31. Ibid., II: 423–24.
32. Ibid., II: 427.
33. Ibid., II: 432–33.
34. Ibid., II: 436.
35. Ibid., II: 437.
36. Ibid., II: 625.
37. Ibid., II: 733–34.
38. Ibid., II: 736–37.
39. Ibid., II: 803–4.
40. Codman, Drive, 159.
41. Astor, A Blood-Dimmed Tide, 226.

IX. Charles de Gaulle

1. General de Gaulle's surname is generally written "de Gaulle" or "DeGaulle"—a style established during World War II. Normally, in noble names, the "de" is dropped, thus the Marquis de Lafayette is called Lafayette. We will call our subject "DeGaulle," since "Gaulle" would be unfamiliar to most readers.

2. "Impenetrable" fortifications on the German border.

3. I have used as a reference Les Écrits militaires de Charles de Gaulle: essai d'analyse thématique by Pierre Messmer and Alain Larcan (1985), a commentary on DeGaulle's writings that includes excerpts from Vers l'armée de métier, La Discorde chez l'ennemi (1924), Le Fil de l'epée (1932). La France et son armée (1938), Mémoires de guerre. 3 vols. (1940–46), and other books, numerous articles, and speeches.

4. Charles DeGaulle, Vers l'armée de métier. 171–75, 179–82.

5. Ibid., 182–85.

6. Ibid., 188, 191–93.

7. Ibid., 198–99.

8. Ibid., 209–10, 213.

9. Ibid., 216–18, 221–30.

X. Erich von Manstein

1. B. H. Liddell Hart, The German Generals Talk (1948), 63 and passim; Richard Brett-Smith, Hitler's Generals (1976), 221; Klaus-Jürgen Müller, The Army, Politics and Society in Germany, 1933–45: Studies in the Army's Relation to Nazism (1987), 114. Defending Manstein against charges of war crimes: Baron Reginald T. Paget, Manstein: His Campaigns and His Trial (1951; trans. into German 1952). Among later historians: R. D. Palsokar, Manstein, the Master General (1970); Dana V. Sadarananda, The Genius of Manstein: Field Marshal Erich von Manstein and the Operations of Army Group Don, November 1942–March 1943 (1987). Among German generals: Franz Halder, Hitler als Feldherr (1949), 46–54; Wilhelm Keitel, Generalfeldmarschall Keitel . . . Erinnerungen, Briefe, Dokumente des Chefs OKW (1961), 227, 289–90.

2. Halder, Hitler als Feldherr, 32. Liddell Hart, German Generals Talk, 63–64.

3. German casualties were 7,500; Russian, 15,000, and 170,000 captured. Brett-Smith, Hitler's Generals, 224.

4. Erich von Manstein, *Lost Victories* (1958), 362; Brett-Smith, *Hitler's Generals*, 226.

5. Manstein, *Aus einem Soldatenleben, 1887–1939* (1958). See esp. 161 on Kolberg, and 333–34 on Liegnitz.

6. Manstein, *Lost Victories*, 179–80. Hereinafter cited as *Lost Victories*.

7. Ibid., 189.

8. Ibid., 189–90.

9. Ibid., 190.

10. Ibid., 190–91.

11. Ibid., 191.

12. Ibid., 191–92.

13. Ibid.

14. Halder, *Hitler als Feldherr*, 38.

15. R.H.S. Stolfi, *Hitler's Panzers East: World War II Reinterpreted* (1991), x, 114–17.

16. Wilhelm Keitel, *Erinnerungen, Briefe, Dokumente des Chefs OKW* (1961), 289–90.

17. *Lost Victories*, 176–77.

18. Ibid., 274–75.

19. Ibid., 275–76.

20. Ibid., 276.

21. Ibid., 276–77.

22. Ibid., 279–80.

23. Ibid., 280.

24. Ibid., 280–81.

25. Ibid., 284–87.

26. Brett-Smith, *Hitler's Generals*, 221.

27. "Personifikation des letzten teutonischen Ritters." Ose, *Entscheidung im Westen, 1944* 40.

XI. Bernard Law Montgomery

1. See *Patton Papers*, 435, 437.

2. Ronald Lewin, *Montgomery as Military Commander* (1971), 6.

3. Ibid., 17. Montgomery himself wrote: "Moses and Cromwell believed intensely in a divine mission, which never failed them in battle; Napoleon in a human destiny, which in the end did. I believe that the one great commander who did not possess this quality of inner conviction was Wellington. One cannot too much admire his foresight, industry, patience and meticulous care. Yet he sometimes lost part of the fruits of victory through an inability to soar from the known to seize the unknown." *The Memoirs of Field-Marshal the Viscount Montgomery of Alamein* (1958), 316–17.

4. Montgomery, *Memoirs*, 33.

5. From decoded German radio messages; the British broke the German codes in 1939. Throughout the war, the Allies knew the enemy's every move. F. W. Winterbotham, *The Ultra Secret* (1975), 111–13.

6. Alistaire Horne (with David Montgomery), *Monty: The Lonely Leader, 1944–1945* (1994), 51; Lewin, *Montgomery*, 85.

7. Montgomery's extended preparations allowed Rommel to strike at the Americans while his troops were preparing positions at Mareth. He had written his wife in January 1943 that he still hoped to stop the British, and wondered why they didn't attack him. *Rommel Papers*, 383.

8. Horne, *Monty*, 50. Ike met Monty in May 1942 and attended a briefing by Monty after a British field exercise. Monty suddenly stopped, sniffed the air, and asked, "Who's smoking?" Ike said, "I am." Said Monty, "I don't permit smoking in my office." Eisenhower put out the cigarette. Stephen E. Ambrose, *The Supreme Commander: The War Years of General Dwight D. Eisenhower* (1970), 44.

9. Monty moved carefully, hoping to save British lives. Manpower was limited, and he feared losses like those of the Great War. Richard Lamb, *Montgomery in Europe 1943–1945* (1983), 407. Just before his death, he talked to Sir Denis Hamilton about "all those soldiers that I killed at Alamein, and in Normandy." Horne, *Monty*, 352.

10. Bradley later wrote: "had the pious, teetotalling Montgomery wobbled into SHAEF with a hangover . . . I could not have been more astonished than I was by the daring adventure he proposed." Omar Bradley, *A Soldier's Story* (1951), 416.

11. Wrote Monty of the latter: "The 2nd S.S. Panzer Corps was refitting in the Arnhem area, having limped up there . . . [from] Normandy. We knew it was there. But we were wrong in supposing that it could not fight effectively." Montgomery, *Memoirs*, 266.

12. Monty manfully took blame for this, but later wrote: "In my—prejudiced—view, if the operation had been properly backed from its inception, and given the aircraft, ground forces, and administrative resources necessary for the job—it would have succeeded in spite of my mistakes, or the adverse weather, or the presence of the 2nd S.S. Panzer Corps in the Arnhem area. I remain MARKET GARDEN's unrepentant advocate." Montgomery, *Memoirs*, 266–67.

13. Lewin, *Montgomery*, 237.

14. Montgomery's explanation is in his *Memoirs*, 278–82.

15. Montgomery, *Memoirs*, 79.

16. Ibid., 74–83.

17. Ibid., 311–13.

18. Richard Lamb, *Montgomery in Europe 1943–1945: Success or Failure?* (1983), 188. Horne, *Monty*, 284.

19. Carlo d'Este, *Patton*, 480.

20. Alistaire Horne, *Monty*, 56–57.

21. Este, *Patton*, 598–99.

22. *Memoirs*, 79.

23. According to my friend Dr. David Chandler, longtime Head of the Department of War Studies at the Royal Military College. In fact, even Gen. George Patton, despite his snide remarks, rated him highly. *Patton Papers*, II, 171; Este, *Patton*, 598.

XII. William Joseph Slim

1. Geoffrey Evans, *Slim as Military Commander* (1969), 215.

2. Evans, *Slim*, 21. More detail in Ronald Lewin, *Slim: The Standardbearer: A Biography of Field-Marshal the Viscount Slim* (1976).

3. Evans, *Slim*, 87. Michael Calvert, *Slim* (1973), 94.

4. Evans, *Slim*, 27.

5. John W. Gordon, "Major-General Orde Wingate," in John Keegan (ed.), *Churchill's Generals* (1991), 287–94. Wingate's force was called, for security reasons, the 3rd Indian Division, but it had no Indians, and consisted of *two* divisions of troops, courtesy of British Prime Minister Winston Churchill. The Chindits were air-lifted to targets in Japanese territory by U.S. Lt. Col. Philip Cochran's "Flying Circus."

6. The most recent biography of Wingate, *Fire in the Night: Wingate of Burma* (1999) by John Bierman and Colin Smith, almost ignores Stilwell and the Marauders. See the next chapter on Stilwell, with references to both Wingate and Merrill.

7. William Slim, *Defeat into Victory* (1956), 207.

8. Ibid., 216. See also John Bierman and Colin Smith. *Fire in the Night: Wingate of Burma, Ethiopia, and Zion* (1999), 246–47, 344–45, 363. After his death Slim called Wingate a genius and one of the handful of "irreplacable" commanders in the war (ibid., 380).

9. See Charleton Ogburn, *The Marauders* (1956 and 1959), 285 (Ogburn was a lieutenant in the Marauders); Alan D. Baker, *Merrill's Marauders* (1972), 29–33, 39, 114ff; Shelford Bidwell, *The Chindit War: The Campaign in Burma, 1944* (1979), 37–38 and 257ff especially.

10. The literature on Chenault and the Flying Tigers was reviewed in Phillip S. Meilinger, "US Air Force Leaders: A Biographical Tour," *Journal of Military History* 52:4 (Oct 1998): 843–45. Hap Arnold, CG of the USAAF, called Chenault a "crackpot," Stilwell preferred "a jackass." Like Wingate, Chenault was a maverick, disliked by regulars—but loved by the American public. He has a dozen biographies; Arnold has one, by Dik Daso, Major, USAF: *Hap Arnold and . . . American Airpower* (2000).

11. Matters in the CBI were complicated because Britain was trying to recover Burma, part of her Empire. Most Americans, surely Stilwell, were hostile or indifferent to restoring the British Empire. They were there to beat the Japanese, and were helping Chiang in order to strengthen him against them. The matter of Mao Zedong's Communist forces, hostile to Chiang but allied with him against the Japanese, was not addressed by the United States until very late in the war.

12. Field Marshal Sir William Slim, *Defeat into Victory* (1956), Hereinafter cited as "Slim."

13. Slim, 208–11.

14. Ibid., 213.

15. Ibid., 182–84.

16. Ibid., 185–87.

17. Ibid., 188–89.

18. Evans, *Slim*, 27.

XIII. Joseph Warren "Vinegar Joe" Stilwell

1. Chiang and Mao were temporarily allied against the Japanese.

2. Barbara W. Tuchman, *Stilwell and the American Experience in China, 1911–45* (1970), 392.

3. Douglas D. Rooney, *Stilwell* (1971), 101.

4. They fought well—"A pitiful but still splendid sight," according to Merrill. Charleton Ogburn, *The Marauders* (1956 and 1959), 248. Ogburn was a lieutenant in the Marauders. Also see Alan D. Baker, *Merrill's Marauders* (1972). Casualties: KIA 93; other deaths, 30; wounded 293; missing 8; hospitalized, 1,970. Charles F. Romanus and Riley Sunderland, *United States Army in World War II: China-Burma-India Theater: Stilwell's Command Problems* (1946), 240. The survivors went to the 475th Infantry, in China. In 1968 the 475th was reactivated as the 75th Infantry Regiment, and was made the parent unit of Long Range Patrol (LRP or LRRP, LR Reconnaissance) units in Vietnam and elsewhere—later redesignated Ranger companies. Today it is the 75th Ranger Regiment,

which also claims descent from the Ranger battalions of World War II and Korean War Ranger Companies. Susan L. Marquis, *Unconventional Warfare: Rebuilding US Special Operations Forces* (1997).

5. He took it stoically. D. Clayton James and Anne Sharp Wells, *A Time for Giants* (1987), 132.

6. Joseph Warren Stilwell, *The Stilwell Papers* (1948).

7. Ibid., 291–93.

8. Ibid., 302–3.

XIV. Matthew Bunker Ridgway

1. "Armed only with a rifle and a pistol, [he] had killed 20 Germans, captured 132, destroyed 35 machine guns and wrecked an enemy battalion." Ridgway, *Soldier: The Memoirs of Matthew B. Ridgway* (1956), 52. The Tennessee farmer won the Congressional Medal of Honor.

2. Ridgway, *Soldier*, 24–26.

3. The U.S. 17th Division was still in training. The 11th went to the South Pacific.

4. First British Airborne Division along with a British trained Polish Brigade suffered 8,300 casualties of 10,500 men committed. Ronald Lewin, *Montgomery As Military Commander* (1971), 237.

5. Walker was killed in a jeep accident. An hour before, he had said it was ironic "that a man who lived as Patton did would die in a traffic accident." Joseph Goulden, *Korea: The Untold Story* (1982), 424.

6. Matthew B. Ridgway, *The Korean War* (1967), 101.

7. Ridgway, *Korean War*, 105.

8. Clay Blair, *The Forgotten War* (1987, 1989), 569–70. Blair says that "on paper" Eighth Army numbered 350,000, almost half ROKA (81 of 163 Battalions).

9. Ridgway, *Soldier*, 219. In the early weeks of fighting, when the only Americans in the war were from the 24th Division, its commander, Major General William F. Dean, had been captured by the North Koreans. See his account: *General Dean's Story* (1954).

10. Blair, *Forgotten War*, 559. Interview of 6 Nov. 1982.

11. The 1st Ranger Company was not the first to fight. That was Eighth Army Ranger Company, under Lt. Ralph Puckett (USMA, 1949). See Robert W. Black, *Rangers in Korea* (1989), 14ff. The French commander was Lt. Col. Ralph Monclar—actually Lt. General Raoul Magrin-Vernery of the Foreign Legion, a legendary fighter who had taken a reduction to lieutenant colonel so he could head the French battalion. Douglas Porch, *The French Foreign Legion* (1991), 466–67, 473–76, 491. James Wellard, *The French Foreign Legion* (1974), 104.

12. Goulden, *Korea*, 449–51; Edwin P. Hoyt, *Bloody Road to Panmunjom* (1985), 171–80; Black, *Rangers in Korea*, 71–79. T. R. Fehrenbach, *This Kind of War* (1963), 391–96.

13. Public disagreement with administration policy, which favored limiting the war. Ridgway, *Korean War*, 142.

14. General Mark Clark, then EUSAK commander, had the duty of signing. Like MacArthur, he had wanted victory in Korea, and was stonefaced and bitter at the ceremony at Panmunjom (27 July 1953). See Martin Blumenson, *Mark Clark* (1984), 269; A. MacDonald, *Korea: The War before Vietnam* (1987), 225. There is still no peace treaty (2002).

15. *Soldier: The Memoirs of Matthew B. Ridgway* (1956).

16. Ibid., 28–29.

17. Ibid., 52–53.
18. Ibid., 217–18.
19. The 38th parallel; roughly the dividing line between South and North Korea.
20. Ridgway, *Soldier*, 219–20.
21. From Ridgway, *The Korean War*, 101.
22. Ibid., 101–3.

XV. Moshe Dayan

1. Robert Slater, *Warrior-Statesman: The Life of Moshe Dayan* (1991), viii.
2. He exposed himself so much that his friends thought he sought death in battle. Slater, *Warrior*, 363.
3. Mentioned above in the chapters on Slim and Stilwell; perhaps the most famous irregular soldier of World War II.
4. Slater, *Warrior*, 45. Moshe Dayan, *Story of My Life* (1976), 28–30.
5. Dayan, *My Life*, 92.
6. Ibid., 506–7.
7. Ibid., 71–72.
8. Ibid., 75.
9. Ibid., 77–78.
10. Ibid., 79–80.
11. Ibid., 81–82.
12. Ibid., 84–86.
13. Ibid., 89–94.
14. Ibid., 95.
15. Ibid., 140–41.
16. Ibid., 142.
17. Ibid., 145–46.
18. Ibid., 509–10.

XVI. Vo Nguyen Giap

1. Cecil B. Currey, *Victory at Any Cost: The Genius of Viet Nam's Gen. Vo Nguyen Giap* (1996), 7. Other sources say 1909 or 1912.
2. Ibid., 51–52.
3. Ibid., 154–55; Peter MacDonald, *Giap: The Victor in Vietnam* (1993), 23.
4. David H. Hackworth, Col. and Julie Sherman, *About Face: The Odyssey of an American Warrior* (1989), 817. Col. Harry Summers, Jr., in his book *On Strategy*, records that he said to NVA Col. Nguyen Don Tu in 1975: "You know you never defeated us on the battlefield." "That may be so," replied Tu, "but it is also irrelevant." Tu later denied his statement, but it has the ring of truth.
5. Harold G. Moore and Joseph L. Galloway, *We Were Soldiers Once . . . and Young: Ia Drang, the Battle That Changed the War in Vietnam* (1992), 199.
6. Vo Nguyen Giap, *The Military Art of People's War*, ed. Russell Stetler (1970), 111, 278. The book uses official North Vietnamese translations; the French interviews are translated by Stetler.
7. Vo Nguyen Giap, *The Military Art of People's War* (1970).

8. Cecil B. Currey, *Victory at Any Cost: The Genius of Viet Nam's Gen. Vo Nguyen Giap* (1997); Peter MacDonald, *Giap: The Victor in Vietnam* (1993).

9. Giap, *War*, 164–66.

10. Ibid., 168–75.

11. Ibid., 177–81.

12. Ibid., 181–83.

13. Ibid., 183–84.

14. Ibid., 277–78.

15. Ibid., 279–81.

16. Ibid., 285.

17. Ibid., 293.

18. Ibid., 293–94.

19. Ibid., 293–96.

20. Ibid., 301–2.

21. Ibid., 303–6.

22. Ibid., 306–7.

23. Ibid., 308–11.

24. Ibid., 315, 318.

25. Ibid., 319.

26. Currey, *Giap*, 257.

27. Ibid., 257–58.

28. Ibid., 258.

29. MacDonald, *Giap*, 80.

30. Ibid., 81–82.

XVII. Harold G. Moore

1. Joseph Galloway witnessed the battle—*and in fact was in it*, since he always carried a M-16 rifle. In a Special Forces camp, much earlier, Major (later Colonel) David Beckwith told him that there was "no such thing" as a noncombattant. A correspondent for United Press International, Galloway flew in to join 1st Battalion, 7th Cavalry after Moore said OK—if he "was that crazy." *We Were Soldiers Once*, 32, 134. General Moore has checked his "biography."

2. Both are quoted on the dust jacket of the book. "Hack" also thinks Moore was an inspired battalion commander with a sixth sense for danger, and a great soldier who should have risen to chief of staff of the Army. David Hackworth (with Julie Sherman), *About Face: The Odyssey of an American Warrior*, 486–87, 634, 811–12.

3. Moore and Galloway, *We Were Soldiers Once*, 40–41. Hereinafter, *Soldiers*.

4. Ibid., 60–63.

5. Ibid., 72–75.

6. Ibid., 92–94.

7. Ibid., 94–97.

8. Ibid., 104–5.

9. Ibid., 105.

10. Ibid., 106–9.

11. The 7th Cavalry is known as the "Garry Owens."

12. *Soldiers*, 126–27.

13. Ibid., 128–29.

14. Ibid., 144–48.

15. Arrington was a NC native, and 1964 graduate of West Point.

16. It was a 40mm "hand cannon," devastating at close range.

17. Lt. Walter Joseph Marm, Jr. (now Col. USA, ret.), evacuated on the 14th with severe wounds, had charged an enemy machine gun and killed a score of PAVN. He was awarded the Medal of Honor in 1966. He was inducted into the Ranger Hall of Fame in October 2000.

18. *Soldiers*, 149–56.

19. Ibid., 178–79.

20. It was the "Mad Minute" of fire that prompted David "Hack" Hackworth to write that Colonel Moore had a combat-hardened infantryman's "sixth sense." Hackworth, *About Face*, 487.

21. *Soldiers*, 194–95.

22. Ibid., 195.

23. Ibid., 197.

24. Ibid.

25. Ibid., 199.

26. Ibid., 202–3.

27. Ibid., 203.

28. Ibid., 204–6.

29. The words "and his troopers," above, were added at the request of General Moore, who read the first draft of this chapter. That is one more indication of the character of the man.

XVIII. Nicholas F. "Nick" Vaux

1. The Egyptian ruler, Gamal Abdel Nasser, had nationalized the canal, an international property operated for decades by the British. The military operation, aided by an Israeli attack on Egypt, was a success, but diplomatic pressures forced return of the canal to Egypt.

2. Vaux, *Take That Hill: Royal Marines in the Falklands War* (1986, 1990), 261.

3. British usage dictates the use of "3," not 3rd, etc.

4. Vaux, *Take That Hill*, 64–65.

5. Ibid., 74–75.

6. Ibid., 75–76.

7. Ibid., 134.

8. Ibid., 137–39.

9. Ibid., 149.

10. Ibid.

11. Ibid., 154–55.

12. Ibid., 155.

13. Ibid., 170. Vaux quotes here from a letter written later by Mike Norman, "J" company captain.

14. Ibid., 170–73.

15. Ibid., 174–84.

16. Ibid., 232–33.

17. William O. Darby and William H. Baumer, *Darby's Rangers: We Led the Way* (1980), 182.

XIX. H. Norman Schwarzkopf

1. H. Norman Schwarzkopf (with Peter Petre), *The Autobiography: It Doesn't Take a Hero* (1992), 67.

2. His record qualified him for other arms, but he wanted to lead men and knew that most high commanders, such as Dwight Eisenhower, Allied Commander in Europe in World War II, came from the Infantry.

3. Schwarzkopf, *Autobiography*, 74.

4. Army of the Republic of Viet Nam (South Vietnam).

5. Schwarzkopf, *Autobiography*, 137.

6. Ibid., 170.

7. Ibid., 152. Hereinafter cited as Schwarzkopf.

8. A corruption of the German word lager, which means camp or supply dump.

9. Schwarzkopf, 152–53.

10. Ibid., 153–55.

11. Ibid., 155–56.

12. Ibid., 156–57.

13. Ibid., 157.

14. A misnomer in traditional terms. A sapper was an engineer who set explosives to undermine fortifications—or disarmed them.

15. Schwarzkopf, 157.

16. Ibid., 157–59.

17. Ibid., 159–60.

18. Ibid., 163.

19. Ibid., 163–64.

20. Ibid., 164–65.

21. Ibid., 166–67.

22. Ibid., 167. The general gave Clemons a bad report; he was passed over for brigadier general and retired.

23. Ibid., 199.

24. Ibid., 237.

25. Ibid., 380–81.

26. Ibid., 381–83.

27. Ibid., 383–84.

28. Khalid Bin Sultan al-Saud, commander of Saudi, Egyptian and Syrian forces. Schwarzkopf: "He was as big as me." Ibid., 329.

29. Ibid., 380–85.

30. Douglas C. Waller, *Commandos: The Inside Story of America's Secret Soldiers* (1994), 34, 233–38, passim.

31. Schwarzkopf, 474.

32. See also *Weapons of the Gulf War*, ed. by Graham Smith, Doug Richardson, consultant (1991).

Conclusions

1. Sherman, *Memoirs of General William T. Sherman, by Himself* (1892), 407. Manstein, *Lost Victories* (1958), 190.

2. "La camaraderie franche et cordiale et la fraternité des combats." *Les Écrits militaires* (1985), 398.

3. William O. Darby and William H. Baumer, *Darby's Rangers: We Led the Way* (1980), 182.

4. Manstein, *Lost Victories*, 189.

5. "Un bon général, de bons cadres, une bonne organisation, une bonne instruction, une bonne discipline, font les bonnes troupes, indépendamment de la cause pour laquelle elles se battent. Il est cependant vrai que le fanatisme, l'amour de la patrie, la gloire nationale, peuvent inspirer les jeunes troupes avec avantage." *Correspondance XXXI:* 417.

6. Ridgway, *Korea*, 104–5.

7. Erich von Manstein, *Aus einem Soldatenleben* (1958), 162; *Lost Victories*, 179, 283, passim.

8. *Memoirs*, 316–17.

9. *Patton Papers*, II: 803. (3 November 1945).

10. John Colvin, *Giap—Volcano under Snow* (1996), 212.

11. "A la guerre, il y a des principes, mais il y en a peu." quoted in DeGaulle, *Écrits militaires*, 498.

Bibliography

THE FIRST section is on war in general, and the last, references. The balance of the bibliography essentially follows the order of the book. For each commander, sources are listed in the order of primary sources by the commander, primary sources by others, and secondary works, including biographies. There are also listings of sources for major wars and other relevant topics, comprising general works, primary sources, and monographs.

General

Allmayer-Beck, Johann Christoph, et al. *Menschenführung im Heer.* Herford, Westfalen, 1982.

American Military Tradition: From Colonial Times to the Present. Ed. by John M. Carroll and Colin F. Baxter. Wilmington, DE, 1993.

Beaumont, Roger A. *War, Chaos, and History.* Westport, CT, 1994.

Bourke, Joanna. *An Intimate History of Killing: Face to Face Killing in the 20th Century.* London, 1999.

Callwell, Charles E. *Small Wars: A Tactical Textbook for Imperial Soldiers.* London, 1990. [Originally published c. 1925.]

Clausewitz, Carl von. *On War.* Trans. by Peter Paret and Michael Howard. Princeton, NJ, 1986.

Corvisier, André. *Les hommes, la guerre et la mort.* Paris, 1985.

Delbrück, Hans. *History of the Art of War.* 4 vols. Lincoln, NE, 1985. Trans. by Walter J. Renfroe, Jr. of 3rd ed., *Geschichte der Kriegskunst.* . . . Berlin, 1962–66.

Donaldson, Gary. *America at War since 1945: Politics and Diplomacy in Korea, Vietnam, and the Gulf War.* Westport, CT, 1996.

Elting, John Robert. *The Superstrategists: Great Captains, Theorists, and Fighting Men Who Have Shaped the History of Warfare.* New York, 1985.

Fuller, J.F.C. *The Foundations of the Science of War.* C&GSC Reprint. Fort Leavenworth, KS, 1993.

Gantzel, Klaus Jürgen, and Torsten Schwinghammer. *Warfare since the Second World War.* New Brunswick, NJ, 2000. Trans. of *Kriege nach dem zweiten Weltkrieg, 1945 bis 1992.* N.p., 1998.

Grossman, Dave. *On Killing: The Psychological Cost of Learning to Kill in War and Society.* New York, 1996.

Hittle, James Donald. *The Military Staff, Its History and Development.* 3rd ed. London, 1961.

Holmes, Richard. *Acts of War: The Behavior of Men in Battle.* New York, 1986.

Howard, Michael. *The Lessons of History*. New Haven, CT, 1991.

Keegan, John. *The Mask of Command*. New York, 1987.

Liddell Hart, B. H. *Great Captains Unveiled*. London, 1927.

Livesey, Anthony. *Battles of the Great Commanders*. London, 1987.

Maihafer, Harry J. *Brave Decisions: Moral Courage from the Revolutionary War to Desert Storm*. Washington, DC, 1995.

Marshall, S.L.A. *Bringing Up the Rear: A Memoir*. San Rafael, CA, 1979.

——. *Men against Fire: The Problem of Battle Command in Future War*. New York, 1947.

Miller, David. *Special Forces: The Men, the Weapons and the Operations*. London, 1999.

Perrett, Bryan. *Canopy of Wars: Jungle Warfare, from the Earliest Days . . . to the Battlefields of Vietnam*. Wellingborough, UK, 1990.

——. *Impossible Victories: Ten Unlikely Battlefield Successes*. London and New York, 1996.

Perrett, Geoffrey. *A Country Made by War: From the Revolution to Vietnam: The Story of America's Rise to Power*. New York, 1990.

Pick, Daniel. *War Machine: The Rationalization of Slaughter in the Modern Age*. New Haven, CT, 1993.

Puryear, Edgar F., Jr. *Nineteen Stars: A Study in Military Character and Leadership*. 2nd ed. Novato, CA, 1981.

Reardon, Carol. *Soldiers and Scholars: The U.S. Army and the Uses of Military History, 1865–1920*. Lawrence, KS, 1990.

Sturgill, Claude C. *Low-Intensity Conflict in American History*. Westport, CT, 1994.

Sun-tsu. *The Art of War*. Trans. with commentary by Ralph D. Sawyer. New York, 1994.

Tao, Han-chang. *Sun Tzu's Art of War . . . Modern Chinese Interpretation*. Trans. by Yuan Shibing. New York, 1987.

Van Creveld, Martin L. *Command in War*. Cambridge, MA, 1985.

——. *The Training of Officers*. New York, 1990.

Weigley, Russell F. *The American Way of War: A History of United States Military Strategy and Policy*. Bloomington, IN, 1977.

Frederick the Great (1713–1786)

Frederick II, King of Prussia. *Gespräche Friedrichs des Grossen*. Berlin, 1919.

——. *Instruction militaire du roi de Prusse pour ses généraux*, Frankfurt and Leipzig, 1761.

——. *Oeuvres de Frédéric le Grand*. 30 vols. Ed. by Johann D. E. Preuss et al. Berlin, 1846–57.

——. *Politische Correspondenz Friedrichs des Grossen*. Ed. by Gustav Droysen et al. Berlin, 1879–1939.

Asprey, Robert. *Frederick the Great: The Magnificent Enigma*. New York, 1986.

Bernhardi, Theodor. *Friedrich der Grosse als Feldherr*. Berlin, 1881. 2 vols. [Seven Years' War, 1756–63.]

Bleibtreu, Karl. *Geschichte und Geist der europäischen Kriege unter Friedrich dem Grossen und Napoleon*. Leipzig, 1893.

Browning, Reed. *The War of the Austrian Succession*. New York, 1993.

Carlyle, Thomas. *History of Friedrich II, called Frederick the Great.* New York, 1859.

Dorn, Gunter and Joachim Engelmann. *Die Schlachten Friedrichs des Grossen: Führung, Verlauf . . . Gliederungen, Karten.* Friedberg, 1986.

Duffy, Christopher. *The Army of Frederick the Great.* New York, 1974.

————. *Military Life of Frederick the Great.* New York, 1986.

Friedrich der Grosse und das Militärwesen seiner Zeit. Contributions by Johann Christoph Allmayer-Beck et al. Herford, 1987.

Horst, Eberhard. *Friedrich II. der Staufer: Kaiser—Feldherr—Dichter.* 2nd ed. Munich, 1978.

Jomini, Baron de. *Traité des grandes operations militaires ou histoire critique des guerres de Frédéric le Grand.* 4th ed. Paris, 1851.

Knopp, Werner. *In Remembrance of a King: Frederick II of Prussia, 1712–1786* [*Erinnerung an einen König*]. Bonn, 1986.

Kugler, Franz. *Life of Frederick the Great: Comprehending a . . . History of the Silesian Campaigns and the Seven Years' War.* London, 1877.

Longman, F. W. *Frederick the Great and the Seven Years' War.* New York, 1893. 9th impression. London, New York, 1908.

Mittenzwei, Ingrid. *Friedrich II. von Preussen: eine Biographie.* 2nd ed. Cologne, 1980.

Ritter, Gerhard. *Frederick the Great: A Historical Profile.* Trans. with intro. by Peter Paret. Berkeley, CA, 1970.

Schieder, Theodor. *Friedrich der Grosse: ein Königtum der Widersprüche.* Frankfurt am Main, 1983.

Showalter, Dennis E. *The Wars of Frederick the Great.* London and New York, 1996.

Treue, Wilhelm (ed.). *Preussens grosser König: Leben und Werk Friedrichs des Grossen.* Freiburg, 1986.

Venohr, Wolfgang. *Fridericus Rex: Friedrich der Grosse, Porträt einer Doppelnatur.* Bergisch Gladbach, 1985. From the 1840–42 edition.

Wars of the French Revolution

Bertaud, Jean-Paul. *La Révolution Armée: Les soldats-citoyens et la Révolution française.* Paris, 1979. Trans. by R. R. Palmer as *The Army of the French Revolution: From Citizen Soldiers to Instrument of Power.* Princeton, NJ, 1988.

Blanning, T.C.W. *Origins of the French Revolutionary Wars.* London, 1996.

Chuquet, Arthur-Maxime. *Les Guerres de la Révolution,* 11 vols. Paris, 1914.

Forrest, Alan I. *The Soldiers of the French Revolution.* New York, 1990.

Lynn, John A. *The Bayonets of the Republic: Motivation and Tactics of the Army of Revolutionary France, 1791–94.* Urbana, IL, 1984.

Quimby, Robert S. *The Background of Napoleonic Warfare.* New York, 1957.

Rodger, A. B. *The War of the Second Coalition, 1798–1801: A Strategic Commentary.* London, 1964.

Ross, Steven T. *From Flintlock to Rifle Infantry: Tactics, 1740–1866.* Rutherford, NJ, 1979.

————. *Quest for Victory: French Military Strategy, 1792–1799.* South Brunswick, NJ, 1973.

Scott, Samuel F. *From Yorktown to Valmy: The Transformation of the French Army in an Age of Revolution.* Niwat, CO, 1998.

————. *Response of the Royal Army to the French Revolution.* Oxford, UK, 1978.

Soboul, Albert. *Les soldats de l'an II.* Paris, 1959.

Woloch, Isser. *The French Veteran from the Revolution to the Restoration.* Chapel Hill, NC, 1979.

Napoleon (1769–1821)

Napoléon I. *Correspondance de Napoléon Ier.* Publiée par ordre de l'Empereur Napoléon III. 32 vols. Paris, 1858–70.

———. *Mémoires pour servir à l'histoire de France sous Napoléon, écrits à Sainte Helène, sous la dictée de l'Empereur, par les généraux qui sont partagé sa captivité. . . .* 9 vols. Paris, 1823–25.

———. *Memoirs.* [Translation.] 7 vols. London, 1923–24.

———. *L'Oeuvre et l'histoire.* 12 vols. Paris, 1969.

———. *Oeuvres littéraires et écrits militaires,* 3 vols. Ed. by Jean Tulard. Paris, 1969.

———

Arnold, Eric A. *A Documentary History of Napoleonic France.* Lanham, MD and London, 1994.

Dansette, Adrien. *Napoléon: Pensées. . . .* Paris, 1969.

Driault, Édouard. *Napoléon: Pensées pour l'action.* Paris, 1943.

Gourgaud, Gaspard, Baron. *Sainte-Hélène: journal inédit.* 2 vols. Ed. by E. H. de Grouchy and A. Guillois. Paris, 1899.

Las Cases, Emmanuel, *Mémorial de Sainte-Hélène.* 8 vols. Paris, 1823–24.

Montholon, C.-J.-T. de. *Récits de la captivité de l'Empereur Napoléon.* 2 vols. Paris, 1847. First pub. in London as *History of the Captivity of Napoleon at Saint Helena.* (1846).

O'Meara, B. E. *Napoleon in Exile.* 2 vols. London, 1822.

Palluel, André. *Dictionnaire de l'Empereur.* Paris, 1969.

Picard, Ernest. *Préceptes et jugements de Napoléon.* Paris, 1913.

———

Camon, Hubert. *La guerre napoléonienne: précis des campagnes.* 2 vols. Paris, 1925.

Chandler, David G. *The Campaigns of Napoleon.* New York, 1966.

Connelly, Owen. *Blundering to Glory: The Military Campaigns of Napoleon.* Wilmington, DE, 1999.

Elting, John R. and Vincent Esposito. *Military History and Atlas of the Napoleonic Wars.* New York, 1964.

Esdaile, Charles J. *The Wars of Napoleon.* Harlow, Essex and New York, 1995.

Forrest, Alan. *Conscripts and Deserters: The Army and Society during the French Revolution and Empire.* London and New York, 1989.

Haythornthwaite, Philip J., et al. *Napoleon: The Final Verdict.* Foreword by David G. Chandler. London and New York, 1996.

American Civil War

Catton, Bruce. *The Centennial History of the Civil War.* Garden City, New York, 1961–65.

Doubleday, Abner. *Chancellorsville and Gettysburg.* New York, 1882.

Doughty, Robert. *American Civil War: The Emergence of Total Warfare*. Boston, 1996.

Foote, Shelby. *The Civil War, A Narrative*. 14 vols. New York, 1958–74.

McPherson, James M. *Battle Cry of Freedom: The Civil War Era*. New York, 1988.

———. *Drawn with the Sword: Reflections on the American Civil War*. New York, 1996.

Parish, Peter J. *The American Civil War*. New York, 1975.

Simpson, Brooks D. *America's Civil War*. Wheeling, IL, 1996.

Stokesbury, James L. *A Short History of the Civil War*. New York, 1995.

Vandiver, Frank E. *Blood Brothers: A Short History of the Civil War*. College Station, TX, 1992.

Blackford, William W. *War Years with Jeb Stuart*. New York, 1945.

Custer, Elizabeth Bacon. *Following the Guidon*. New ed. Intro. by Jane R. Stewart. Norman, OK, 1966.

Garnett, Theodore Stanford. *Riding with Stuart: Reminiscences of an Aide-de-Camp*. Shippensburg, PA, 1994.

Grant, Ulysses S. *Memoirs and Selected Letters: Personal Memoirs of U.S. Grant, Selected Letters 1839–1865*. New ed. New York, 1990.

Henry, Robert Selph (ed.). *As They Saw Forrest: Some Recollections and Comments of Contemporaries*. Jackson, TN, 1956.

Lee, Robert E. *Lee's Dispatches: Unpublished Letters of General Robert E. Lee, C.S.A., to Jefferson Davis and the War Department of Confederate States of America 1862–65*. From the private collection of Wymberley Jones DeRenne. . . . New York and London, 1915. New ed. by Grady McWhiney, with additional dispatches. New York, 1957.

———. *The Wartime Papers of R. E. Lee*. Virginia War Commission. Boston, 1961.

Long, Armistead Lindsay. *Memoirs of Robert E. Lee; his military and personal history, [with documents] hitherto unpublished*. New York and Philadelphia, 1886.

McClellan, Henry Brainerd. *I Rode with Jeb Stuart: The Life and Campaigns of . . . General J.E.B. Stuart*. Bloomington, IN, 1958.

Stuart, Jeb. *Letters of General J. E. B. Stuart to His Wife, 1861*. Atlanta, GA, 1943.

Barnett, Louise K. *Touched by Fire: The Life, Death, and Mythic Afterlife of George Armstrong Custer*. New York, 1996.

Brown, Dee A. *The Bold Cavaliers: Morgan's 2nd Kentucky Cavalry Raiders*. Philadelphia, 1959.

Buell, Thomas B. *The Warrior Generals: Combat Leadership in the Civil War*. New York, 1997.

Davis, Burke. *Jeb Stuart, The Last Cavalier*. New York, 1957.

Fuller, J.F.C. *Grant and Lee: A Study in Personality and Generalship*. New York, 1929.

Hagerman, Edward. *The American Civil War and the Origins of Modern Warfare*. Bloomington, IN, 1988.

Henry, Robert Selph. *"First with the Most" Forrest*. New York and Indianapolis, IN, 1944.

Hurst, Jack. *Nathan Bedford Forrest: A Biography*. New York, 1993.

Luvaas, Jay. *The Military Legacy of the Civil War: The European Inheritance*, 2nd ed. Lawrence, KS, 1993.

McKenzie, J. D. *Uncertain Glory: Lee's Generalship*. . . . New York, 1997.

McPherson, James M. (ed.). *Atlas of the Civil War*. New York, 1994.

———. *For Cause and Comrades: Why Men Fought in the Civil War*. New York, 1997.

Perret, Geoffrey. *Ulysses S. Grant: Soldier and President*. New York, 1997.

Phillips, David. *Maps of the Civil War: The Roads They Took*. New York. 1998.

Riggs, David F. *East of Gettysburg: Custer vs Stuart*. Fort Collins, CO, 1985.

Royster, Charles. *The Destructive War: William Tecumseh Sherman, Stonewall Jackson, and the Americans*. 1st ed. New York, 1991.

Thomas, Emory M. *Bold Dragoon: The Life of J.E.B. Stuart*. New York, 1986.

———. *Robert E. Lee: A Biography*. New York, 1995.

Thomason, John W. *Jeb Stuart*. Ed. Gary W. Gallagher. Lincoln, NE, 1994.

Trout, Robert J. *They Followed the Plume: The Story of J.E.B. Stuart and His Staff*. Mechanicsburg, PA, 1993.

Urwin, Gregory J. W. *Custer Victorious: The Civil War Battles of General George Armstrong Custer*. Rutherford, NJ and London, 1983.

Wills, Brian Steel. *A Battle from the Start: The Life of Nathan Bedford Forrest*. New York, 1992.

Woodworth, Steven E. *Jefferson Davis and His Generals: The Failure of Confederate Command in the West*. Lawrence, KS, 1993.

Wyeth, John A. *That Devil Forrest: Life of General Nathan Bedford Forrest*. New York, 1889.

William Tecumseh Sherman (1820–1891)

Sherman, William T. *Memoirs of General William T. Sherman, by himself*. 2 vols. New York, 1882.

———. *Sherman's Civil War: Selected Correspondence of William T. Sherman, 1860–1865*. Chapel Hill, NC, 1999.

———. *"War Is Hell!" William T. Sherman's Personal Narrative of His March through Georgia*. Savannah, GA, 1974.

———

Bailey, Anne J. *The Chessboard of War: Sherman and Hood in the Autumn Campaigns of 1864*. Lincoln, NE, 2000.

Coburn, Mark. *Terrible Innocence: General Sherman at War*. New York, 1993.

Conyngham, David Power. *Sherman's march through the South. With sketches and incidents of the campaign*. New York, 1865.

Fellman, Michael. *Citizen Sherman: A life of William Tecumseh Sherman*. New York, 1995.

Glatthaar, Joseph T. *The March to the Sea and Beyond: Sherman's Troops in the Savannah and Carolinas Campaigns*. New York, 1985.

Hirshson, Stanley P. *The White Tecumseh: A Biography of General William T. Sherman*. New York, 1997.

Kennett, Lee B. *Marching through Georgia: The Story of Soldiers and Civilians during Sherman's Campaign*. New York, 1995.

Lewis, Lloyd. *Sherman: Fighting Prophet*. Lincoln, NE, 1993.

Marszalek, John F. *Sherman: A Soldier's Passion for Order*. New York, 1993.

———. *Sherman's Other War: The General and the Civil War Press*. Rev. ed. Kent, OH, 1999.

McMurry, Richard M. *Atlanta 1864: Last Chance for the Confederacy*. Lincoln, NE, 2000.

Walters, John B. *Merchant of Terror: General Sherman and Total War*. Indianapolis, 1973.

Thomas Jonathan "Stonewall" Jackson (1824–1863)

Arnold, Thomas Jackson. *Early Life and Letters of General Thomas J. Jackson, "Stonewall" Jackson*. New York, 1915.

Cooke, John Esten. *The Life of Stonewall Jackson. From Official Papers, Contemporary Narratives, and Personal Acquaintance*. New York, 1863.

Douglas, Henry Kyd. *I Rode With Stonewall, being chiefly the war experiences of the youngest member of Jackson's staff. . . .* Chapel Hill, NC, 1940.

Jackson, Mary Anna. *Life and Letters of General Thomas J. Jackson (Stonewall Jackson)*. New York, 1892.

McClellan, Henry Brainerd. *I Rode with Jeb Stuart: The Life and Campaigns of . . . General J.E.B. Stuart*. Bloomington, IN, 1958.

McClendon, William Augustus. *Recollections of War Times, by an old veteran, while under Stonewall Jackson and Lieutenant General James Longstreet; how I got in, and how I got out*. Montgomery, AL, 1909; San Bernardino, CA, 1973.

Poague, William Thomas. *Gunner with Stonewall: Reminiscences of William Thomas Poague, lieutenant [later] Lieutenant Colonel of Artillery, Army of Northern Virginia, CSA, 1861–65: A Memoir Written for his Children in 1903*. Lincoln, NE, 1998.

Stuart, Jeb. *Letters of General J. E. B. Stuart to his wife*. Atlanta, GA, 1943.

———

Alexander, Bevin. *Lost Victories: The Military Genius of Stonewall Jackson*. Edison, NJ, 1996.

Dabney, Robert Lewis. *Life and Campaigns of Lieut.-Gen. Thomas J. Jackson (Stonewall Jackson)*. Philadelphia, New York, Richmond, 1866.

Davis, Burke. *They Called Him Stonewall: A Life of Lt. General T. J. Jackson, C.S.A.* New York, 1954.

Farwell, Byron. *Stonewall: A Biography of General Thomas J. Jackson*. New York, 1992.

Furgurson, Ernest B. *Chancellorsville 1863*. New York, 1992.

Krick, Robert K. *Conquering the Valley: Stonewall Jackson at Port Republic*. New York, 1996.

McCabe, James Dabney. *The life of Thomas J. Jackson*. 2nd ed. Richmond, 1864.

Mills, Bronwyn. *Thomas J. "Stonewall" Jackson*. Stamford, CT, 1993.

Robertson, James I. *The Stonewall Brigade*. Baton Rouge, 1963.

———. *Stonewall Jackson: The Man, The Soldier, The Legend*. New York and London, 1997.

Tanner, Robert G. *Stonewall in the Valley: Thomas J. Jackson's Shenandoah Valley Campaign. . . . 1862*. Mechanicsburg, PA, 1996.

Vandiver, Frank E. *Mighty Stonewall*. Texas A&M, TX, 1988.

John Singleton Mosby (1833–1916)

Mosby, John Singleton. *Memoirs of Colonel John S. Mosby*. Boston, 1917. Bloomington, IN, 1959.

———. *War Reminiscences [and] Stuart's Cavalry Campaigns*. New York, 1887.

———

Alexander, John Henry. *Mosby's Men.* New York, 1904. Gaithersburg MD, 1987.

McKim, Randolph H. *A Soldier's Recollections; Leaves from the Diary of a Young Confederate, with an oration on the motives and aims of the soldiers of the South.* New York, 1910.

Scott, John. *Partisan Life with Col. John S. Mosby.* New York, 1867; Gaithersburg, MD, 1990.

Williamson, James J. *Mosby's Raiders: A Record of the Operations of the Fourty-third Battalion, Virginia Cavalry . . . from the diary of a private . . . with . . . reports of federal officers and also of Mosby.* New York, 1896.

Daniels, Jonathan. *Mosby: Gray Ghost of the Confederacy.* Philadelphia, 1959.

Jones, Virgil Carrington. *Ranger Mosby.* McLean, VA, 1987.

Ramage, James A. *Gray Ghost: The Life of Col. John Singleton Mosby.* Lexington, KY, 1999.

Siepel, Kevin H. *Rebel, the Life and Times of John Singleton Mosby.* New York, 1983.

Wert, Jeffry D. *Mosby's Rangers.* New York, 1990.

World War I

Falls, Cyril Bentham. *The First World War.* London, 1960.

Gilbert, Martin. *The First World War: A Complete History.* 1st American ed. New York, 1994.

Keegan, John. *The First World War.* New York, 1999.

Robbins, Keith. *The First World War.* Oxford and New York, 1984.

Robson, Stuart. *The First World War.* London and New York, 1998.

Strachan, Hew (ed.). *World War I: A History.* Oxford and New York, 1998.

Becker, Jean-Jacques. *1914–1918: l'autre front: études.* Paris, 1977. Trans. as *The Great War and the French People.* New York, 1986.

————. *1914, comment les Français sont entrés dans la guerre: contribution à l'étude de l'opinion publique printemps-été 1914.* Paris, 1977.

Bond, Brian. *War and Society in Europe, 1870–1970.* New York, 1984.

Bourne, Randolph S. *War and the Intellectuals; Essays, 1915–1919.* New York, 1964.

Clark, George B. *Devil Dogs: Fighting Marines of World War I.* Novato, CA, 1999.

Coffman, Edward M. *The Old Army: A Portrait of the American Army in Peacetime, 1784–1898.* New York, 1986.

————. *The War to End All Wars: The American Military Experience in World War I.* New York, 1968.

Cooke, James J. *The Rainbow Division in the Great War, 1917–1919.* Westport, CT, 1994.

Hallas, James H. *Doughboy War: The American Expeditionary Force in World War I.* Boulder, CO, 2000.

————. *Squandered Victory: The American First Army at St. Mihiel.* Westport, CT, 1995.

Joffre, Marshal J. J., et al. *The Two Battles of the Marne: The Stories of Marshal Joffre, General von Ludendorff, Marshal Foch, Crown Prince Wilhelm.* New York, 1927.

Kennett, Lee B. *The First Air War, 1914–1918.* New York, 1991.

Kohut, Thomas A. *Wilhelm II and the Germans: A Study in Leadership*. New York, 1991.

Kriegel, Annie. *1914: la guerre et le mouvement ouvrier français*. Paris, 1964.

Liddell Hart, B. H. *Reputations: Ten Years After*. London, 1928.

May, Ernest R. *Knowing One's Enemies: Intelligence Assessment Before the Two World Wars*. Princeton, NJ, 1984.

Military College of Canada. *General Staffs and Diplomacy before the Second World War*. London and Totowa, NJ, 1978.

Otto, Helmut. *Schlieffen und der Generalstab. Der preussisch-deutsche Generalstab unter der Leitung des Generals von Schlieffen 1891–1905*. Berlin, 1966.

Porch, Douglas. *The March to the Marne: The French Army, 1871–1914*. New York, 1981.

Prior, Robin. *Passchendaele: The Untold Story*. New Haven, CT, 1996.

————, and Trevor Wilson. *Command on the Western Front: The Military Career of Sir Henry Rawlinson, 1914–1918*. London, 1992.

Samuels, Martin. *Doctrine and Dogma: German and British Infantry Tactics in the First World War*. New York, 1992.

Saunders, Anthony. *Weapons of the Trench War, 1914–1918*. Stroud, UK, 1999.

Schellendorff, Bronsart von, General. *The Duties of the General Staff*. Rev. by Major Bronsart von Schellendorff. 4th ed. [Translated for GS: War Office.] London, 1905.

Showalter, Dennis E. *Tannenberg, Clash of Empires*. Hamden, CT, 1991.

Snyder, Jack. *The Ideology of the Offensive: Military Decision Making and the Disasters of 1914*. Ithaca, NY, 1984.

Travers, Tim. *How the War was Won: Command and Technology in the British Army on the Western Front, 1917–1918*. London and New York, 1992.

————. *The Killing Ground: The British Army, The Western Front, and the Emergence of Modern Warfare, 1900–1918*. London and Boston, 1987.

Van Dyke, Carl. *Russian Imperial Military Doctrine and Education, 1832–1914*. Westport, CT, 1990.

Thomas Edward Lawrence (1888–1935), "Lawrence of Arabia"

Lawrence, T. E. *Revolt in the Desert*. Garden City, NY, 1927.

————. *Seven Pillars of Wisdom: A Triumph*. Garden City, NY, 1966. (1st ed. London, 1935).

————. *The Essential T. E. Lawrence*. New York, 1951, 1963.

————. *Strange Man of Letters: The Literary Criticism and Correspondence of T. E. Lawrence*. Ed. Harold Orlans. Rutherford, NJ, 1993.

Brown, Malcolm. *A Touch of Genius: The Life of T.E. Lawrence.*New York, 1989.

Gardner, Brian. *Allenby*. London, 1965.

Hodson, Joel C. *Lawrence of Arabia and American Culture: The Making of a Transatlantic Legend*. Westport, CT, 1995.

James, Lawrence. *The Golden Warrior: The Life and Legend of Lawrence of Arabia*. New York, 1993.

Liddell Hart, B. H. *Colonel Lawrence, The Man behind the Legend.* Rev. ed. London, 1964.

Mack, John E. *A Prince of Our Disorder: The Life of T. E. Lawrence.* London and New York, 1975.

Morsey, Konrad. *T. E. Lawrence und der arabische Aufstand 1916–18.* Osnabrück, 1976.

Savage, Raymond. *Allenby of Armageddon: A Record of the Career and Campaigns of Field-Marshal Viscount Allenby.* Indianapolis, 1926.

Stewart, Desmond. *T. E. Lawrence.* London, 1977.

Thomas, Lowell. *With Lawrence in Arabia.* New York, London, 1924.

Wavell, Archibald Percival Wavell, Earl of. *Allenby, Soldier and Statesman.* London and New York, 1974.

————. *Allenby, a Study in Greatness: The Biography of Field-Marshal Viscount Allenby of Megiddo and Felixstowe, G.C.B., G.C.M.G.* 2 vols. New York, 1940–44.

Wilson, Jeremy. *Lawrence of Arabia: The Authorized Biography of T. E. Lawrence.* New York, 1990.

The Inter-war Period, 1919–1939

Corum, James S. *The Roots of Blitzkrieg: Hans von Seeckt and the German Military Reform.* Lawrence, KS, 1992.

Doughty, Robert A. *The Seeds of Disaster: The Development of French Army Doctrine, 1919–1939.* Hamden, CT, 1985.

Fussell, Paul. *The Great War and Modern Memory.* New York, 2000.

Horne, Alistair. *The French Army and Politics, 1870–1970.* London, 1984.

Müller, Klaus Jürgen. *Das Heer und Hitler. Armee und national-sozialistisches Regime 1933–1940.* Stuttgart, 1969.

Noble, Dennis L. *The Eagle and the Dragon: The United States Military in China, 1901–1937.* New York, 1990.

Winton, Harold. *To Change an Army: General Sir Burnett-Stuart and British Armored Doctrine, 1927–1938.* Lawrence, KS, 1988.

————, and David R. Mets (eds.). *The Challenge of Change: Military Institutions and New Realities, 1918–1941.* Lincoln, NE, 2000.

Archibald Percival Wavell (1883–1950)

Wavell, Archibald Percival Wavell, Earl of. *Generals and Generalship: The Lees Knowles Lectures delivered at Trinity College, Cambridge in 1939.* London, 1941.

————. *Soldiers and Soldiering; or Epithets of war. Essays.* London, 1953.

————. *Wavell: The Viceroy's Journal.* London, 1973.

————

Connell, John. *Wavell, Scholar and Soldier, to 1941.* London, 1964.

————. *Wavell, Supreme Commander, 1941–1943.* Ed. and completed by Michael Roberts. London, 1969.

Fergusson, Bernard, Sir. *Wavell: Portrait of a Soldier.* London, 1961.

Lewin, Ronald. *The Chief: Field Marshall Lord Wavell, Commander-in-Chief and Viceroy, 1939–1947.* New York, 1980.

Pitt, Barrie. *The Crucible of War: Western Desert, 1941*. London, 1980.
Raugh, H. E., Jr. *Wavell in the Middle East, 1939–1941*. McLean, VA, 1993.
Woollcombe, Robert. *The Campaigns of Wavell, 1939–1943*. London, 1959.

World War II: General

Ambrose. Stephen E. *Citizen Soldiers*. New York, 1994.
Double, Michael D. *Closing with the Enemy: How GI's Fought the War in Europe*. Lawrence, KS, 1994.
Doughty, Robert and Ira Gruber. *World War II: Total Warfare Around the Globe*. Boston, 1996.
Fuller, J.F.C. *The Second World War, 1939–1945: A Strategical and Tactical History*. New York, 1949.
Gilbert, Martin. *The Second World War: A Complete History*. Rev. ed. New York, 1991.
Keegan, John. *The Second World War*. London, 1989; New York, 1990.
Liddell Hart, B. H. *History of the Second World War*. London and New York, 1971.
Purdue, A. W. *The Second World War*. New York, 1999.
Weinberg, Gerhard L. *A World at Arms: A Global History of World War II*. Cambridge and New York, 1994.
Wright, Gordon. *The Ordeal of Total War, 1939–1945*. New York, 1968.

———

Bradley, Omar Nelson. *A General's Life: An Autobiography*. New York, 1983.
———. *A Soldier's Story*. New York, 1951.
Eisenhower, Dwight D. *Crusade in Europe*. Garden City, NY, 1948.
———. *Dear General: Eisenhower's Wartime Letters to Marshall*. Baltimore, 1971.
———. *Eisenhower: The Prewar Diaries and Selected Papers, 1905–1941*. Baltimore, 1998.
———. *The Papers of Dwight David Eisenhower*. 13 vols. Baltimore, 1970–89.
Gavin, James M. *Airborne Warfare*. Washington, DC, 1947.
———. *On to Berlin: Battles of an Airborne Commander, 1943–1946*. New York, 1978.
Smith, Walter Bedell. *Eisenhower's Six Great Decisions: Europe, 1944–1945*. New York, 1956.
Zhukov, Georgii Konstantinovich. *Marshal Zhukov's Greatest Battles*. 1st ed. New York, 1969.

———

Ben-Moshe, Tuvia. *Churchill: Strategy and History*. London, 1993.
Charmley, John. *Churchill's Grand Alliance: The Anglo-American Special Relationship, 1940–57*. New York, 1995.
Gilbert, Martin. *Churchill: A Life*. New York, 1991.
Irving, David J. C. *Churchill's War*. Bullsbrook, Australia, 1987. James, D. Clayton, with Anne Sharp Wells. *A Time for Giants: Politics of the American High Command in World War II*. New York, 1987.
Larrabee, Eric. *Commander in Chief: Franklin Delano Roosevelt, His Lieutenants, and Their War*. New York, 1987.
Manchester, William R. *The Last Lion, Winston Spencer Churchill*. Boston, 1983.

Moskin, J. Robert. *Mr. Truman's War: 1945.* New York, 1996.

Westwood, John. *Strategy and Tactics of the Great Commanders of World War II and Their Battles.* New York, 1990.

The U.S. and German Atomic Bomb Projects

Feis, Herbert. *The Atomic Bomb and the End of World War II.* Rev. ed. Princeton, NJ, 1966.

Goodchild, Peter. *J. Robert Oppenheimer: Shatterer of Worlds.* Boston, 1981.

Hales, Peter B. *Atomic Spaces: Living on the Manhattan Project.* Urbana, IL, 1997.

Lanouette, William. *Genius in the Shadows: A Biography of Leo Szilard: The Man Behind the Bomb.* New York and Toronto, 1992.

Powers, Thomas. *Heisenberg's War: The Secret History of the German Bomb.* New York, 1993.

Schweber, S. S. *In The Shadow of the Bomb: Bethe, Oppenheimer, and the Moral Responsibility of the Scientist.* Princeton, NJ, 2000.

Stoff, Michael B., Jonathan F. Fanton, and R. Hal Willliams (eds.). *The Manhattan Project: A Documentary Introduction to the Atomic Age.* Philadelphia, 1991.

Codes And Ciphers: General

Burke, Colin B. *Information and Secrecy: Vannevar Bush, ULTRA, and the Other Memex.* Metuchen, NJ, 1994.

Haldane, Robert A. *The Hidden War.* New York, 1978.

Handel, Michael (ed.). *Strategic and Operational Deception in the Second World War.* London and Totowa, 1987.

Norman, Bruce. *Secret Warfare: The Battle of Codes and Ciphers.* Washington, DC, 1973.

Smith, Bradley F. *The ULTRA-MAGIC Deals and the Most Secret Special Relationship 1940– 1946.* Shrewsbury, 1993.

Codes and Ciphers: Europe and Mediterranean

Beesly, Patrick. *Very Special Intelligence: The Story of the Admiralty's Operational Intelligence Centre, 1939–1945.* London, 1977.

Bennett, Ralph F. *Behind the Battle: Intelligence in the War with Germany, 1939–45.* London, 1994.

———. *ULTRA and Mediterranean Strategy.* New York and London, 1989.

———. *ULTRA in the West: The Normandy Campaign of 1944–45.* London, 1979.

Bertrand, Gustave. *Enigma; ou, la plus grande enigme de la guerre 1939–1945.* Paris, 1973.

Bonatz, Heinz. *Seekrieg im Äther: die Leistungen der Marine-Funkaufklärung, 1939–1945.* Herford, 1981.

Calvocoressi, Peter. *Top Secret ULTRA.* London, 1980.

Cremer, Peter. *U-Boat Commander.* Trans. by Lawrence Wilson. Annapolis, 1984. [Originally pub. in Berlin, 1984. Cremer was the only U-boat commander to survive the fighting 1939–1945.]

Deavours, Cipher A. *Breakthrough '32: The Polish Solution of the Enigma.* Laguna Hills, CA, 1988.

Garlinski, Jozef. *Intercept: the Enigma War.* London, 1979.

Hinsley, F. H., and Alan Stripp (eds.). *Codebreakers: The Inside Story of Bletchley Park.* Oxford and New York, 1993.

Hodges, Andrew. *Alan Turing: The Enigma.* New York, 1983.

Jones, R. V. *The Wizard War: British Scientific Intelligence, 1939–1945.* New York, 1978.

Kahn, David. *Code Breakers.* London and New York, 1966.

————. *Seizing the Enigma: The Race to Break the German U-boat Codes, 1939–1943.* Boston, 1991.

Kozaczuk, Wladyslaw. *Enigma: How the German Machine Cipher Was Broken, and How It Was Read by the Allies in World War Two.* Ed. and trans. by Christopher Kasparek. Frederick, MD and London, 1984.

Lewin, Ronald. *ULTRA Goes to War.* London, 1978.

Montagu, Ewen. *Beyond Top-Secret U.* London, 1977.

Parrish, Thomas D. *The ULTRA Americans: The U.S. Role in Breaking the Nazi Codes.* New York, 1986.

Skillen, Hugh. *The Enigma Symposium 1994.* London, 1994.

West, Nigel. *GCHQ: The Secret Wireless War, 1900–86.* London, 1986.

Whiting, Charles. *Ardennes: The Secret War.* London, 1984.

Winterbotham, F. W. *The ULTRA Secret.* New York, 1975.

Winton, John. *ULTRA at Sea.* London, 1988.

Codes and Ciphers: Pacific Theater

Ballard, Geoffrey St. Vincent. *On ULTRA Active Service: The Story of Australia's Signals Intelligence Operations in World War II.* Richmond, Vic., Australia, 1991.

Bennett, J. W. *Intelligence and Cryptanalytic Activities of the Japanese during World War II.* Laguna Hills, CA, 1986.

Boyd, Carl. *Hitler's Japanese Confidant: General Oshima Hiroshi and MAGIC Intelligence, 1941–1945.* Lawrence, KS, 1993.

Clark, Ronald W. *The Man Who Broke Purple: The Life of Colonel William F. Friedman.* Boston and London, 1977.

Drea, Edward J. *MacArthur's ULTRA: Codebreaking and the War against Japan, 1942–1945.* Lawrence, KS, 1991.

Holmes, W. J. *Double-Edged Secrets.* Annapolis, 1979.

Lewin, Ronald. *The American Magic: Codes, Ciphers, and the Defeat of Japan.* New York, 1982.

————. *The Other ULTRA.* London, 1982.

Prados, John. *Combined Fleet Decoded: American Intelligence and the Japanese Navy in World War II.* New York, 1995.

Van Der Rhoer, Edward. *Deadly Magic.* Alexandria, VA, 1992.

Winton, John. *ULTRA in the Pacific . . . Codes and Cyphers [and] Naval Operations against Japan 1941–45.* Annapolis, MD and London, 1993.

World War II: Mediterranean and Europe

Ambrose, Stephen E. *Band of Brothers: E Company, 506th Regiment, 101st Airborne: From Normandy to Hitler's Eagle's Nest.* New York, 1992.

Ambrose, Stephen E. *Citizen Soldiers.* New York, 1997.
———. *D-Day, June 6, 1944: The Climactic Battle of World War II.* New York, 1994.
———. *The Supreme Commander: The War Years of General Dwight D. Eisenhower.* Garden City, NY, 1970.
Astor, Gerald. *A Blood-Dimmed Tide: The Battle of the Bulge by the Men Who Fought It.* New York, 1992.
Barnett, Correlli (ed.). *Hitler's Generals.* London, 1991.
Belfield, E.M.G. and H. Essame. *The Battle for Normandy.* London, 1983.
Blumenson, Martin. *Kasserine Pass: Rommel's Bloody Climactic Battle for Tunisia.* Reprint. Lanham, MD, 2000.
Brett-Smith, Richard. *Hitler's Generals.* London, 1976.
Daso, Dik Alan. *Hap Arnold and the Evolution of American Airpower.* Washington, DC and London, 2000.
Davis, Brian L. *Waffen-SS.* London and New York, 1985.
Doubler, Michael N. *Closing with the Enemy: How GI's Fought the War in Europe, 1944–1945.* Lawrence, KS, 1994.
Drez, Ronald J. *Voices of D-Day: The Story of the Allied Invasion Told by Those Who Were There.* Baton Rouge and London, 1994.
Duffy, Christopher, *Red Storm on the Reich: the Soviet March on Germany, 1945.* New York, 1991.
Gelb, Norman. *Dunkirk: The Complete Story of the First Step in the Defeat of Hitler.* New York, 1989.
Gray, Ed. *General of the Army: George C. Marshall, Soldier and Statesman.* Reprint. Lanham, MD, 2000.
Hastings, Max. *Das Reich: The March of the 2nd SS Panzer Division through France.* New York, 1982.
Hoyt, Edwin. *The GI's War: American Soldiers in Europe during World War II.* Reprint. Lanham, MD, 2000.
———. *199 Days: The Battle of Stalingrad.* New York, 1993.
Humble, Richard. *Hitler's Generals.* London, 1973.
Keegan, John. *Six Armies in Normandy: From D-Day to the Liberation of Paris, June 6th–August 25th, 1944.* London, 1982.
Keegan, John (ed.). *Churchill's Generals.* New York, 1991.
———. *Waffen SS: The Asphalt Soldiers.* New York, 1970.
Kennett, Lee B. *G.I.: The American Soldier in World War II.* New York, 1989.
Kissin, S. F. *War and the Marxists: Socialist Theory and Practice in Capitalist War.* London, 1988.
Liddell Hart, B. H. *The German Generals Talk.* New York, 1948.
Luther, Craig W. H. *Blood and Honor: The History of the 12th SS Panzer Division "Hitler Youth," 1943–1945.* San Jose, CA, 1987.
Mansoor, Peter R. *The GI Offensive in Europe: The Triumph of American Infantry Divisions, 1941–1945.* Lawrence, KS, 1999.
McFarland, Stephen Lee. *To Command the Sky: The Battle for Air Superiority over Germany, 1942–1944.* Washington, DC, 1991.
Messenger, Charles. *The Last Prussian: A Biography of Field Marshal Gerd von Rundstedt, 1875–1953.* London and Washington, DC, 1991.
Nobecourt, Jacques. *Hitler's Last Gamble: The Battle of the Bulge.* New York, 1967.
Pitt, Barrie. *Churchill and the Generals.* London, 1988.

Theile, Karl H. *Beyond "Monsters" and "Clowns"—The Combat SS: De-mythologizing . . . German Elite Formations.* Lanham, MD, 1997.

Van Creveld, Martin L. *Fighting Power: German and US Army Performance, 1939–1945.* Westport, CT, 1982.

Warlimont, Walter, *Inside Hitler's Headquarters, 1939–1945.* Trans. by R. H. Barry. New York, 1964.

Weidinger, Otto. *Kamaraden bis zum Ende: der Weg des SS-Panzer-grenadier-Regiments 4 "DF" 1939–1945. Die Geschichte einer deutsch-österreichischen Kampfgemeinschaft.* Göttingen, 1962.

Wilt, Alan F. *War from the Top: German and British Military Decision Making during World War II.* Bloomington, IN, 1990.

Ziemke, Earl F. *Stalingrad to Berlin: The German Defeat in the East.* New York, 1986.

Erwin Johannes Eugen Rommel (1891–1945)

Rommel, Erwin. *Aufgaben für Zug und Kompanie.* 4th ed. Berlin, 1940.

———. *Infanterie greift an.* Potsdam, 1937. Trans. by Gustave E. Kidde as *Infantry Attacks.* Washington, DC, 1944.

———. *Krieg ohne Hass.* 3rd ed. Heidenheim, 1950. [Papers edited by his by wife, Lucie-Maria Rommel, and Gen. Fritz Bayerlein.]

———. *Rommel in His Own Words.* Ed. John Pimlott. London and Mechanicsburg, PA, 1994.

———. *The Rommel Papers.* Ed. B. H. Liddel Hart. Trans. by Paul Finlay. London, 1953; New York, 1982.

—————

Carell, Paul. *Die Wüstenfüchse: mit Rommel in Afrika.* Frankfurt/Main; Berlin; Vienna, 1982.

Kühn, Volkmar. *Mit Rommel in der Wüste: Kampf und Untergang des Deutschen Afrika-Korps 1941–1943.* 2nd ed. Stuttgart, 1975.

Liddell Hart, Basil Henry, Sir. *The Other Side of the Hill: Germany's Generals, Their Rise and Fall, with Their Own Account of Military Events, 1939–1945.* London, 1983.

Luck, Hans Von. *Panzer Commander: The Memoirs of Colonel Hans Von Luck.* Intro. by Stephen E. Ambrose. Westport, CT, 1989.

Ruge, Friedrich. *Rommel und die Invasion: Erinnerungen.* Stuttgart, 1959. Trans by Ursula R. Moessner as *Rommel in Normandy: Reminiscences.* London, 1979.

Schmidt, Paul K. *Die Wüstenfüchse: mit Rommel in Afrika.* Frankfurt, 1958. Trans. as *The Foxes of the Desert.* London, 1960.

Schmidt, Heinz Werner. *With Rommel in the Desert.* London, 1951.

Speidel, Hans, *Invasion 1944: Ein Beitrag zu Rommels und des Reiches Schicksal.* Tübingen, 1949. Trans. as *Invasion 1944: Rommel and the Normandy Campaign.* Chicago, 1950.

—————

Behrendt, Hans-Otto. *Rommels Kenntnis vom Feind im Afrikafeldzug.* Freiburg im Breisgau, 1980. Trans. as *Rommel's Intelligence in the Desert Campaign 1941–1943.* London, 1985.

Bergot, Erwan. L'Afrikakorps. Paris, 1972, 1975. Trans. as The Afrika Korps. London, 1976.

Bertoldi, S. Rommel. Novara, 1976.

Buffetaut, Yves. Rommel: France 1940. Bayeux, 1985.

Douglas-Home, Charles. Rommel. London, 1973.

Esebeck, Hanns Gert, Freiherr von. Afrikanische Schicksalsjahre. Geschichte des deutschen Afrika-Korps unter Rommel. Wiesbaden, 1949.

Forty, George. Afrika Korps at War. 2 vols. London, 1978.

Fraser, David. Knight's Cross: The Life of Field Marshal Erwin Rommel. New York, 1993.

Heckmann, Wolf. Rommels Krieg in Afrika: "Wüstenfüchse" gegen "Wüstenratten." Bergisch Gladbach, 1976.

Irving, David. The Trail of the Fox: The Life of Field-Marshal Erwin Rommel. New York and London, 1977.

Kurowski, Franz. Erwin Rommel: Der Mensch, der Soldat, der General-Feldmarschall. Bochum, 1978.

Leuschner, Bernard. Rommel. Paris, 1977.

Lewin, Ronald. The Life and Death of the Afrika Korps. London, 1977.

———. Rommel as Military Commander. London; Princeton, NJ, 1968.

Macksey, Kenneth. Afrika Korps. New York, 1968.

———. Rommel, Battles and Campaigns. London, 1979.

McGuirk, Dal. Rommel's Army in Africa. London, 1987.

Mitcham, Samuel W., Jr. The Desert Fox in Normandy: Rommel's Defense of Fortress Europe. Westport, CT, 1997.

———. Rommel's Desert War: The Life and Death of the Afrika Korps. New York, 1981.

———. Rommel's Last Battle: The Desert Fox and the Normandy Campaign. New York, 1983.

———. Triumphant Fox: Erwin Rommel and the Rise of the Afrika Korps. New York, 1984.

Ose, Dieter. Entscheidung im Westen 1944: Der Oberbefehlshaber West und die Abwehr der alliierten Invasion. Stuttgart, 1982.

Piekalkiewicz, Janusz. Rommel und die Geheimdienste in Nordafrika 1941–1943. Munich, 1984.

Reuth, Ralf Georg, Erwin Rommel, des Führers General. Munich, 1987.

Rutherford, Ward. The Biography of Field Marshal Erwin Rommel. London and New York, 1981.

Theil, Edmund. Rommels verheizte Armee: Kampf und Ende der Heeresgruppe Afrika von El Alamein bis Tunis. Vienna and Munich, 1979.

Westphal, Siegfried. Heer in Fesseln, aus den Papieren des Stabschefs von Rommel, Kesselring und Rundstedt. Bonn, 1950. Trans as The German Army in the West. London, 1951.

Windrow, Martin. Rommel's Desert Army. New York, 1976.

Young, Desmond. Rommel, The Desert Fox. London, 1950.

George S. Patton, Jr. (1885–1945)

Patton, George Smith, Jr. Les Carnets secrets du général Patton: Ed. by Blumenson, Martin [extraits]. Paris, 1975.

———. The Patton Papers. 2 vols. Ed. by Martin Blumenson. Vol. 1: 1885–1940. Vol. 2: 1940–1945. Boston, 1972–74.

———. *War As I Knew It*. Ed. by Beatrice Ayer Patton and Col. Paul D. Harkins. Boston, 1947.

Codman, Charles R., Col. *Drive*. Boston, 1957. [Diary and letters of Patton's senior aide-de-camp.]

Normandy, The invasion of [1944]. Washington, DC, 1994. [Documents.]

Province, C. M. *Patton's Third Army: A Daily Combat Diary*. New York, 1992.

Allen, Robert S. *Lucky Forward: A History of Patton's Third U.S. Army*. New York, 1947.

[Army Times]. *Warrior: The Story of General George S. Patton*. New York, 1967.

Astor, Gerald. *A Blood-Dimmed Tide: The Battle of the Bulge by the Men Who Fought It*. New York, 1992.

Ayer, Frederick. *Before the Colors Fade: Portrait of a Soldier: George S. Patton, Jr*. Boston, 1964.

Birtle, A. J. *Sicily*. Washington, DC, 1993.

Blumenson, Martin. *The Battle of the Generals: The Untold Story of the Falaise Pocket: The Campaign That Should Have Won World War II*. New York, 1993.

———. *Breakout and Pursuit*. Washington, DC, 1984.

———. *Kasserine Pass*. Boston, 1967.

———. *The Many Faces of George S. Patton, Jr*. USAF Academy, 1972. Harmon Memorial Lectures, vol. 14.

———. *Patton, the Man Behind the Legend*. New York, 1985.

———. *Sicily: Whose Victory?* New York, 1969.

Cole, Hugh M. *The Ardennes: Battle of the Bulge*. Washington, DC, 1984.

Essame, Hubert. *Patton: A Study in Command*. New York, 1974.

Este, Carlo d'. *Patton: A Genius for War*. New York, 1995.

Farago, Ladislas. *Patton: Ordeal and Triumph*. New York, 1964.

Forty, George. *Patton's Third Army at War*. London, 1990.

Howe, George Frederick. *Northwest Africa: Seizing the Initiative in the West*. Washington, DC, 1957.

Keegan, John. *Six Armies in Normandy: From D-Day to the Liberation of Paris, June 6th–August 25th, 1944*. New York, 1983.

Marinello, Edward A. *On the Way: General Patton's Eyes and Ears on the Enemy*. Commack, NY, 1998.

Mellor, William Bancroft. *General Patton: The Last Cavalier*. New York, 1971. Pub. as *Patton, Fighting Man*, New York, 1946.

Patton, Robert H. *The Pattons: A Personal History of an American Family*. New York, 1994.

Prefer, Nathan. *Patton's Ghost Corps: Cracking the Siegfried Line*. Novato, CA, 1998.

Semmes, Harry H. *Portrait of Patton*. New York, 1955.

Shapiro, Milton J. *Tank Command: General George S. Patton's 4th Armored Division*. New York, 1979.

Wallace, Brenton G. *Patton and His Third Army*. Washington, DC, 1948.

Wellard, James H. *General George S. Patton, Jr.: Man under Mars*. New York, 1946.

Charles de Gaulle (1890–1970)

Gaulle, Charles de. *La Discorde chez l'ennemi*. Paris, 1924.
———. *Les Écrits militaires de Charles de Gaulle: essai d'analyse thématique*. Ed. by Pierre Messmer and Alain Larcan. Paris, 1985.
———. *Le Fil de l'epée*. Paris, 1932. Trans. as *The Edge of the Sword*. New York, 1960.
———. *La France et son armée*. Parus, 1938.
———. *Mémoires de guerre*. 3 vols. Paris 1940–46. Trans. as *War Memoirs of Charles de Gaulle*. New York and London, 1955.
———. *Vers l'armée de métier*. Paris, 1971. [1st ed. 1934.]

Lattre de Tassigny, Jean de, Marshal. *The History of the French First Army*. London, 1952.
Weygand, Maxime. *En lisant les Memoires de guerre du general de Gaulle*. Paris, 1955.
———. *Histoire de l'Armée française*. Paris, 1961.
———. *Mémoires*. Paris, 1950–57.
———. *The Role of General Weygand: Conversations with His Son, Commandant J. Weygand*. London, 1948.

Chapman, Guy. *Why France Fell: The Defeat of the French Army in 1940*. New York, 1969.
Clayton, Anthony. *Three Marshals of France: Leadership after Trauma*. London, Washington, DC, and New York, 1991. [Alphonse Juin, 1888–1967; Jean de Lattre, 1889–1952; Philippe Leclerc, 1902–47.]
Lacouture, Jean. *De Gaulle*. 2 vols. Vol. I: *The Rebel: 1890–1944*. Trans. by Patrick O'Brian. Vol. II: *The Ruler, 1945–1970*. Trans. by Alan Sheridan. New York, 1991.
Malraux, André. *Felled Oaks: Conversation with De Gaulle*. New York, 1972.

Erich von Manstein (1887–1973)

Manstein, Erich von. *Aus einem Soldatenleben, 1887–1939*. Bonn, 1958.
———. *Die Deutsche Infanterie, 1939–1945: eine Dokumentation in Bildern*. Bad Nauheim, 1967. [Manstein, W. Buxa, H. Hoppe.]
———. *Nie ausser Dienst. Zum 80.Geburtstag von Generalfeldmarschall Erich von Manstein, 24 Nov. 1967*. Cologne, 1967.
———. *Soldat im 20. Jahrhundert: militarisch-politische Nachlese*. Munich, 1981.
———. *Verlorene Siege*. Bonn, 1955. Trans. as *Lost Victories* by Anthony G. Powell. Chicago and London, 1958.

Halder, Franz. *Hitler als Feldherr*. Munich, 1949.
Keitel, Wilhelm. *Generalfeldmarschall Keitel . . . Erinnerungen, Briefe, Dokumente des Chefs OKW*. Göttingen, 1961.

Barnett, Correlli (ed.). *Hitler's Generals*. London, 1991.

Brett-Smith, Richard. *Hitler's Generals*. London, 1976.

Engelmann, Joachim. *Manstein: Stratege und Truppenführer: ein Lebensbericht in Bildern*. Friedberg, 1981.

Liddell Hart, B. H. *The German Generals Talk*. New York, 1948.

Müller, Klaus-Jürgen. *The Army, Politics and Society in Germany, 1933–45: Studies in the Army's Relation to Nazism*. Manchester, UK, 1987.

Paget, Reginald Thomas, Baron Paget. *Manstein: His Campaigns and His Trial*. London, 1951.

Palsokar, R. D. *Manstein, the Master General*. Poona, 1970.

Robertson, Richard Michael. *Erich von Manstein: The Career of a Soldier in the Third Reich*. London, 1967.

Sadarananda, Dana V. *Beyond Stalingrad: Manstein and the Operations of Army Group Don*. New York, 1990.

———. *The Genius of Manstein: Field Marshal Erich von Manstein and the Operations of Army Group Don, November 1942–March 1943*. Philadelphia. 1987.

Bernard Law Montgomery (1887–1976)

Montgomery of Alamein, Bernard Law Montgomery, Viscount. *The Memoirs of Field-Marshal the Viscount Montgomery of Alamein*. London and Cleveland, 1958.

Brett-James, Antony. *Conversation with Montgomery*. London, 1984.

Samwell, H. P. *An Infantry Officer with the Eighth Army: The Personal Experiences of an Infantry Officer during the Eighth Army's Campaign through Africa and Sicily*. Edinburgh and London, 1945.

Barnett, Correlli. *The Desert Generals*. 2nd ed. Bloomington, IN, 1982.

Baynes, John C. Malcom. *Urquhart of Arnhem: The Life of Major General R. E. Urquhart, CB, DSO*. London and New York, 1993.

D'Este, Carlo. *Decision in Normandy: The Unwritten Story of Montgomery and the Allied Campaign*. London, 1983.

Farrar-Hockley, Anthony H. *Airborne Carpet: Operation MARKET GARDEN*. New York, 1969.

Gelb, Norman. *Ike and Monty: Generals at War*. New York, 1994.

Hamilton, Nigel. *Monty: Final Years of the Field-Marshal, 1944–1976*. New York, 1987.

———. *Monty: The Making of a General, 1887–1942*. London, 1981.

———. *Monty: Master of the Battlefield, 1942–1944*. London, 1983.

Hart, Stephen. *Montgomery and "Colossal Cracks": The 21st Army Group in Northwest Europe, 1944–45*. Westport, CT, 2000.

Horne, Alistaire (with David Montgomery). *Monty: The Lonely Leader, 1944–1945*. London and New York, 1994.

Irving, David J. C. *The War Between the Generals*. New York, 1981.

Lamb, Richard. *Montgomery in Europe 1943–1945: Success or Failure?* London, 1983.

Lewin, Ronald. *Montgomery as Military Commander*. New York, 1971.

MacDonald, Charles B. *The Decision to Launch Operation MARKET-GARDEN*. Washington, DC, 1990.

Majdalany, Fred. *The Battle of El Alamein: Fortress in the Sand*. Philadelphia, 1965.

McGill, Michael C. *Montgomery, Field-Marshal: An Ulster Tribute*. Belfast, 1945.

McKee, Alexander. *El Alamein: ULTRA and the Three Battles*. London, 1991.

Moorehead, Alan. *Montgomery: A Biography*. London, 1946.

Murray, G. E. Patrick. *Eisenhower versus Montgomery: The Continuing Debate*. Westport, CT, 1996.

Newell, Clayton R. *Egypt-Libya*. Washington, DC, 1993.

Phillips, C. E. Lucas. *Alamein*. Boston, 1962.

Sweet, John J. T. *Mounting the Threat: The Battle of Bourguebus Ridge, 18–23 July 1944*. San Rafael, CA, 1977.

Thompson, Reginald W. *Churchill and the Montgomery Myth*. New York, 1968.

———. *Montgomery*. New York, 1973.

William Joseph Slim (1891–1970)

Slim, Sir William, 1st Viscount. *Defeat into Victory*. London, 1956. New York, 1961.

———. *Unofficial History*. 4th ed. London, 1960.

———

Abhyankar, M. G. *The War in Burma, 1943–45*. 5th ed. Dehra Dunn [India], 1977.

Calvert, Michael. *Slim*. New York and London, 1973.

Evans, Geoffrey Charles, Sir, *Slim as Military Commander*. Sydney, 1969.

Gibson, Michael R. *Chiang Kai-shek's Central Army, 1924–1938*. N.p., 1985.

Lewin, Ronald. *Slim: The Standardbearer: A Biography of Field-Marshal the Viscount Slim*. London and Hamden, CT, 1976.

———

Ba Maw, U. *Breakthrough in Burma: Memoirs of a Revolution, 1939–1946*. New Haven, 1968.

Bierman, John and Colin Smith. *Fire in the Night: Wingate of Burma, Ethiopia, and Zion*. New York, 1999.

Burchett, Wilfred G. *Wingate's Phantom Army*. Bombay, 1944.

Calvert, Michael. *Chindits—Long Range Penetration*. New York, 1973.

Fergusson, Bernard, Sir. *Beyond the Chindwin, Being an Account of the Adventures of Number Five Column of the Wingate Expedition into Burma, 1943*. London, 1945.

Le Butt, Paul. *We Too Can Die: Tales of the Chindits*. London, 1947.

Mosley, Leonard. *Gideon Goes to War*. New York, 1955.

O'Brien, Terence. *Out of the Blue: A Pilot with the Chindits*. London, 1984.

Rolo, Charles James. *Wingate's Raiders: An Account of the Fabulous Adventure that Raised the Curtain on the Battle for Burma.* London, 1945.

Sykes, Christopher. *Orde Wingate, A Biography.* Cleveland OH, 1959.

Thomas, Lowell. *Back to Mandalay.* New York, 1951.

Tulloch, Derek. *Wingate in Peace and War.* London, 1972.

Joseph Warren "Vinegar Joe" Stilwell (1883–1946)

Stilwell, Joseph Warren. *The Stilwell Papers.* New York, 1948.

———

Belden, Jack. *Retreat with Stilwell.* Garden City, NY, 1944.

Eldridge, Fred. *Wrath in Burma: The . . . Story of General Stilwell and International Maneuvers in the Far East.* Garden City, NY, 1946.

Hedin, Sven Anders. *Chiang Kai-shek, Marshal of China.* New York, 1940.

Lattimore, Owen. *The Making of Modern China.* Washington, 1944.

Liang, Ching-chun. *General Stilwell in China, 1942–1944: The Full Story.* Jamaica, NY, 1972.

Moser, Don. *China, Burma, India.* Alexandria, VA, 1978.

Prefer, Nathan N. *Vinegar Joe's War: Stilwell's Campaigns for Burma.* Novato, CA, 2000.

Romanus, Charles F. *Stilwell's Command Problems.* Washington, DC, 1956.

———. *Stilwell's Mission to China.* Washington, DC, 1953.

———, and Riley Sunderland. *United States Army in World War II: China-Burma-India Theater. . . .* Washington, DC, 1946.

Rooney, Douglas D. *Stilwell.* New York, 1971.

Tuchman, Barbara Wertheim. *Stilwell and the American Experience in China, 1911–45.* New York, 1970.

———

Baker, Alan D. *Merrill's Marauders.* New York, 1972.

Bjorge, Gary J. *Merrill's Marauders: Combined Operations in Northern Burma in 1944.* Fort Leavenworth, KS, 1996.

Hopkins, James E. T. *Spearhead: A Complete History of Merrill's Marauder Rangers.* Baltimore, 1999.

Ogburn, Charlton. *The Marauders.* 1st ed. New York, 1959.

U.S. Army Center for Military History. *Merrill's Marauders, February–May 1944.* Washington, DC, 1990.

Korean War

Collins, J. Lawton. *War in Peacetime: The History and Lessons of Korea.* Boston, 1969.

Dannenmaier, William D. *We were Innocents: An Infantryman in Korea.* Urbana, IL, 1999.

Dean, William Frishe. *General Dean's Story.* New York, 1954.

Hopkins, William B. *One Bugle, No Drums: The Marines at Chosin Reservoir.* Chapel Hill, NC, 1986.

Knox, Donald. *The Korean War: Pusan to Chosin: An Oral History.* San Diego, 1985.

MacArthur, Douglas. *Reminiscences*. New York, 1964.

Maihafer, Harry J. *From the Hudson to the Yalu: West Point '49 in the Korean War*. College Station, TX, 1993.

Whitney, Courtney. *MacArthur: His Rendezvous with History*. New York, 1956.

———

Blair, Clay. *The Forgotten War: America in Korea, 1950–1953*. New York, 1987.

Cumings, Bruce. *Child of Conflict: The Korean-American Relationship, 1943–1953*. Seattle, 1983.

———. *The Origins of the Korean War*. Princeton, NJ, 1990.

Edwards, Paul M. *The Korean War*. Melbourne FL, 1999.

Fehrenbach, T. R. *This Kind of War*. New York, 1963.

Finn, Richard B. *Winners in Peace: MacArthur, Yoshida, and Postwar Japan*. Berkeley, CA, 1992.

Forty, George. *At War in Korea*. London, 1982.

Goulden, Joseph C. *Korea: The Untold Story of the War*. New York, 1982.

Hastings, Max. *The Korean War*. New York, 1987.

Hoyt, Edwin Palmer. *The Bloody Road to Panmunjom*. New York, 1985.

———. *On to the Yalu*. New York, 1984.

———. *The Pusan Perimeter: Korea, 1950*. New York, 1984.

James, D. Clayton. *Refighting the Last War: Command and Crisis in Korea, 1950–1953*. New York, 1992.

Langley, Michael. *Inchon Landing: MacArthur's Last Triumph*. New York, 1979.

MacDonald, C. A. *Korea: The War before Vietnam*. New York, 1987.

Marshall, S.L.A. *Commentary on Infantry Operations and Weapons Usage in Korea: Winter of 1950–51*. Washington, DC, 1989.

———. *Pork Chop Hill: The American Fighting Man in Action, Korea, Spring, 1953*. New York, 1956.

———. *The River and the Gauntlet: Defeat of the Eighth Army by the Chinese Communist Forces, November, 1950, in the Battle of the Chongchon River, Korea*. New York, 1953.

Matray, James I. *The Reluctant Crusade: American Foreign Policy in Korea, 1941–1950*. Honolulu, 1985.

Pemberton, William E. *Harry S. Truman: Fair Dealer and Cold Warrior*. Boston, 1989.

Perret, Geoffrey. *Old Soldiers Never Die: The Life of Douglas MacArthur*. New York, 1996.

Rees, David. *Korea: The Limited War*. New York, 1964.

Rovere, Richard H. and Arthur M. Schlesinger, Jr. *The General and the President, and the Future of American Foreign Policy*. New York, 1951.

Smith, Robert. *MacArthur in Korea: The Naked Emperor*. New York, 1982.

Stanton, Shelby L. *America's Tenth Legion: X Corps in Korea, 1950*. Novato, CA, 1989.

Toland, John, *In Mortal Combat: Korea, 1950–1953*. New York, 1991.

Tomedi, Rudy. *No Bugles, No Drums: An Oral History of the Korean War*. New York, 1993.

Utz, Curtis A. *Assault from the Sea: The Amphibious Landing at Inchon*. Washington, DC, 1994.

Weintraub, Stanley. *MacArthur's War: Korea and the Undoing of an American Hero*. New York, 2000.

Whelan, Richard. *Drawing the Line: The Korean War, 1950–1953*. New York, 1980.

Whiting, Allen Suess. *China Crosses the Yalu: The Decision to Enter the Korean War*. Stanford, CA, 1968.

Wukovits, John F. *Devotion to Duty: A Biography of Admiral Clifton A. F. Sprague*. Annapolis, MD, 1995.

Zhang, Shu Guang. *Mao's Military Romanticism: China and the Korean War, 1950–1953*. Lawrence, KS, 1965.

Matthew Bunker Ridgway (1895–1993)

Ridgway, Matthew B. *Soldier: The Memoirs of Matthew B. Ridgway*, as told to Harold H. Martin. New York, 1956.

—————. *The Korean War: How We Met the Challenge. . . . Why Today's War . . . Must Be Limited*. Garden City, NY, 1967.

———————

Farrar-Hockley, Anthony H. *The Edge of the Sword*. Stroud, UK, 1993.

Higgins, Marguerite. *War in Korea: The Report of a Woman Combat Correspondent*. Garden City, NY, 1951.

History of the Joint Chiefs of Staff. Vol. III, parts I and II: *The Korean War*. Washington, DC, 1979.

———————

Appleman, Roy E. *Ridgway Duels for Korea*. College Station, TX, 1990.

Blair, Clay, *Ridgway's Paratroopers: The American Airborne in World War II*. Garden City, NY, 1985.

Devlin, Gerard M. *Paratrooper! U.S. Army and Marine Parachute and Glider Troops during World War II*. New York, 1979.

Marshall, S.L.A. *Bastogne: The Story of the First Eight Days in Which the 101st Airborne Division Was Closed within the Ring of German Forces*. Washington, DC, 1988.

—————. *Night Drop: The American Airborne Invasion of Normandy*. Boston, 1962.

Mitchell, Ralph M. *The 101st Airborne Division's Defense of Bastogne*. Fort Leavenworth, KS, 1987.

Soffer, Jonathan M. *General Matthew B. Ridgway: From Progressivism to Reaganism, 1895–1993*. Westport, CT, 1998.

Middle East, 1945–1991

Cordesman, Anthony H. and Abraham R. Wagner, *The Lessons of Modern War*. 3 vols. I: *The Arab-Israeli Conflicts*. II: *The Iran-Iraq Conflict*. III: *The Afghan and Falklands Conflicts*. Boulder, CO, 1990.

Hammel, Eric M. *Six Days in June: How Israel Won the 1967 Arab-Israeli War*. New York and Toronto, 1992.

Marshall, S.L.A. *Sinai Victory: Command Decisions . . . in Israel's Hundred-Hour Conquest of Egypt East of Suez, Autumn, 1956*. New York, 1958.

Ovendale, Ritchie. *Origins of the Arab-Israeli Wars*. London and New York, 1984.
Pimlott, John. *The Middle East Conflicts: From 1945 to the Present*. London, 1983.

Moshe Dayan (1915–1981)

Dayan, Moshe. *Breakthrough: A Personal Account of the Egypt-Israel Peace Negotiations*. New York, 1981.
———. *Living with the Bible*. London, 1978.
———. *Story of My Life*. London, 1976.

———

Dayan, Yael. *My Father, His Daughter*. London, 1985.
Eitan, Raphael. *A Soldier's Story: The Life and Times of an Israeli War Hero*. New York, 1991.
Rabin, Yitzhak. *The Rabin Memoirs*. London, 1979.

———

Curtis, David. *Dayan, A Pictorial Biography*. New York, 1967.
Jurman, Pinchas. *Moshe Dayan: A Portrait*. New York, 1969.
Lau-Lavie, Naphtali. *Moshe Dayan: A Biography*. London, 1968.
Schweitzer, Avram. *Israel: The Changing National Agenda*. London and Dover, NH, 1986.
Slater, Robert. *Warrior-Statesman: The Life of Moshe Dayan*. New York, 1991.
Teveth, Shabtai. *Moshe Dayan*. London, 1972.

Vietnam War

De Groot, Gerard J. *A Noble Cause? America and the Vietnam War*. New York, 2000.
Duiker, William J. *The Communist Road to Power in Vietnam*. Boulder, CO, 1996.
———. *Ho Chi Minh*. New York, 2000.
Joes, Anthony J. *The War for South Viet Nam, 1954–1975*. New York, 1989.
Lind, Michael. *Vietnam, the Necessary War: A Reinterpretation of America's Most Disastrous Military Conflict*. New York, 1999.
Morrison, Wilbur H. *The Elephant and the Tiger: The Full Story of the Vietnam War*. New York, 1990.
Tucker, Spencer. *Vietnam*. Lexington, KY, 1999.

———

Broyles, William. *Brothers in Arms: A Journey from War to Peace*. New York, 1986, 1987. Also pub. as *Brothers in Arms: A Veteran Returns to Vietnam in Search of His Enemy and Himself*. New York, 1986.
Hackworth, David H., Col., and Julie Sherman. *About Face: The Odyssey of an American Warrior*. New York, 1989.
Hoang, Ngoc Lung. *General Offensives of 1968–69*. Washington, DC, 1981.

Hosmer, Stephen T. *The Fall of South Vietnam: Statements by Vietnamese Military and Civil-ian Leaders.* Santa Monica, CA, 1978.

Humphries, James F. *Through the Valley: Vietnam, 1967–1968.* Boulder, CO, 1999.

Kinnard, Douglas. *The War Managers: American Generals Reflect on Vietnam.* Wayne, NJ, 1985.

Lehrack Otto J. *No Shining Armor: The Marines at War in Vietnam: An Oral History.* Law-rence, KS, 1992.

Maurer, Harry. *Strange Ground: An Oral History of Americans in Vietnam, 1945–1975.* New York, 1989.

McNamara, Robert S. *In Retrospect: The Tragedy and Lessons of Vietnam.* New York, 1995.

Nichols, John B. *On Yankee Station: The Naval Air War over Vietnam.* Annapolis, MD, 1987.

Westmoreland, William C. *A Soldier Reports.* Garden City, NY, 1976.

Appy, William G. *Working Class War: American Combat Soldiers and Vietnam.* Chapel Hill, NC, 1993.

Barrett, David M. *Uncertain Warriors: Lyndon Johnson and His Vietnam Advisers.* Lawrence, KS, 1993.

Bergerud, Eric M. *The Dynamics of Defeat: The Vietnam War in Hau Nghia Province.* Boul-der, CO, 1991.

———. *Red Thunder, Tropic Lightning: The World of a Combat Division in Vietnam.* Boulder, CO, 1993.

Capps, Walter (ed.). *A Vietnam Reader.* London and New York, 1991.

Chinnery, Philip D. *Vietnam: The Helicopter War.* Annapolis, MD, 1991.

Furgurson, E. B. *Westmoreland: The Inevitable General.* Boston, 1968.

Higgins, Marguerite. *Our Vietnam Nightmare.* New York, 1965.

Hooper, Edwin Bickford. *The United States Navy and the Vietnam Conflict.* Washington, DC, 1976.

Kinnard, Douglas. *The Certain Trumpet: Maxwell Taylor and the American Experience in Vietnam.* Washington, DC, 1991.

Kolko, Gabriel. *Anatomy of a War.* New York, 1985.

Lehrack Otto J. *No Shining Armor: The Marines at War in Vietnam: An Oral History.* Law-rence, KS, 1992.

Marshall, S.L.A. *Ambush and Bird: Two Vietnam Battle Narratives.* Garden City, NY, 1982.

———. *Battles in the Monsoon: Campaigning in the Central Highlands, Vietnam, Summer 1966.* New York, 1967.

Pimlott, John. *Vietnam: The Decisive Battles.* New York, 1990.

Sarkesian, Sam Charles. *Unconventional Conflicts in a New Security Era: Lessons from Mal-aya and Vietnam.* Westport, CT, 1993.

Schulzinger, Robert D. *A Time for War: The United States and Vietnam, 1941–1975.* New York, 1997.

Shapley, Deborah. *Promise and Power: The Life and Times of Robert McNamara.* Boston, 1992.

Showalter, Dennis E. (ed.). *An American Dilemma: Vietnam, 1964–1973.* Chicago, 1993.

Spector, Ronald H. *After Tet: The Bloodiest Year in Vietnam.* New York and Toronto, 1993.

Turley, William S. *The Second Indochina War: A Short Political and Military History, 1954–1975.* Boulder, CO and London, 1986.

Wintle, Justin. *Romancing Vietnam: Inside the Boat Country.* New York, 1991.

Vo Nguyen Giap (1911–   )

Giap [Vo, Nguyen Giap]. "Big Victory, Great Task": North Viet-Nam's Minister of Defense Assesses the Course of the War. Intro. by David Schoenbrun. New York, 1968.

———. The Military Art of People's War. Trans. and ed. by Russell Stetler, with some official North Vietnamese government translation. New York, 1970.

———. People's War, People's Army: The Viet Cong Insurrection Manual for Underdeveloped Countries. Intro. and biography by Roger Hilsman and Bernard Fall. New York, 1962.

———. Unforgettable Months and Years. Trans. by Mai Van Elliott. Ithaca, NY, 1975.

———, with Van Tien Dung. How We Won the War. Philadelphia, 1976.

———

Billings-Yun, Melanie. The Decision against War: Eisenhower and Dien Bien Phu, 1954. New York, 1988.

Currey, Cecil B. Victory at Any Cost: The Genius of Viet Nam's Gen. Vo Nguyen Giap. Washington, DC, and London, 1997.

Henderson, William Darryl. Why the Vietcong Fought: A Study of Motivation and Control in a Modern Army in Combat. Westport, CT, 1979.

MacDonald Peter. Giap: The Victor in Vietnam. New York, 1993.

Maclear, Michael. The Ten Thousand Day War: Vietnam, 1945–1975. New York, 1982.

O'Neill, Robert John. The Strategy of General Giap since 1964. Canberra, 1969.

Snepp, Frank. Decent Interval: An Insider's Account of Saigon's Indecent End. New York, 1977.

Spector, Ronald H. After Tet: The Bloodiest Year in Vietnam. New York and Toronto, 1993.

Thayer, Carlyle A. War by Other Means: National Liberation and Revolution in Viet-Nam 1954–60. London and New York, 1991.

Warner, Denis A. Certain Victory: How Hanoi Won the War. Kansas City, KS, 1978.

Young, Marilyn Blatt. The Vietnam Wars, 1945–1990. New York, 1991.

Zhang, Shu Guang. Mao's Military Romanticism: China and the Korean War, 1950–1953. Lawrence, KS, 1965.

Harold G. Moore (1924–   )

Moore, Harold G., and Joseph L. Galloway. We Were Soldiers Once . . . and Young: Ia Drang, the Battle That Changed the War in Vietnam. New York, 1992.

———

Davidson, Phillip B., Lt. Gen. Secrets of the Vietnam War. Oxford and New York, 1990.

———. Vietnam at War: The History, 1946–1975. Oxford and New York, 1991.

Scholarly Resources. Study of Strategic Lessons Learned in Vietnam, 1945–1975. SR Microfilm. Wilmington DE, 1991.

Westmoreland, William C., Gen. Report of the Chief of Staff of the United States Army, 1 July 1968 to 30 June 1972. Washington, DC, 1977.

———

Marshall, S.L.A. *The Fields of Bamboo: Dong Tre, Trung Luong, and Hoa Hoi: Three Battles Just Beyond the South China Sea.* New York,1971. [1st Air Cavalry Division, Vietnam, 1961–75.]

Pimlott, John. *Vietnam: The Decisive Battles.* New York, 1990.

Summers, Harry G., Col. *On Strategy: A Critical Analysis of the Vietnam War.* Novato, CA, 1982.

———. *On Strategy: The Vietnam War in Context.* Carlisle Barracks, PA, 1981.

Falklands War

Arthur, Max. *Above All, Courage: The Falklands Front Line, First-Hand Accounts.* London, 1985.

Beadle, Jeffrey C. *The Light Blue Lanyard: Fifty Years with 40 Commando Royal Marines.* Worcester, 1992.

Bishop, Patrick. *The Winter War, the Falklands.* London and New York, 1982.

Cordesman, Anthony H. and Abraham R. Wagner. *The Lessons of Modern War.* Vol. III: *The Afghan and Falklands Conflicts.* Boulder, CO, 1990.

Freedman, Lawrence. *Britain and the Falklands War.* Oxford and New York, 1988.

———. *Signals of War: The Falklands Conflict of 1982.* Princeton, NJ, 1991.

Hastings, Max, and Simon Jenkins. *The Battle for the Falklands.* London, 1983.

Kitson, Linda. *The Falklands War: A Visual Diary.* London, 1982.

Middlebrook, Martin. *The Fight for the Malvinas: The Argentine Forces in the Falklands War.* New York, 1989.

Perrett, Bryan. *Weapons of the Falklands Conflict.* London and New York, 1982.

Pimlott, John. *British Military Operations, 1945–1984.* New York, 1984.

Reginald, R. *Tempest in a Teapot: The Falkland Islands War.* San Bernardino, CA, 1983.

Nicholas F. "Nick" Vaux (1936–   )

Vaux, Nicholas F. "Nick," Major General, RM. *Take That Hill: Royal Marines in the Falklands War.* New York and London, 1986. Pub. in the United Kingdom as *March to the South Atlantic: 42 Commando in the Falklands Campaign.* London, 1987.

———

Thompson, Julian, Gen., RM. *No Picnic: 3 Commando Brigade in the South Atlantic, 1982.* London and New York, 1985.

Woodward, Sandy, Admiral, with Patrick Robinson. *One Hundred Days: The Memoirs of the Falklands Battle Group Commander.* Annapolis, MD, 1992.

Gulf War

Allen, Thomas B. *CNN War in the Gulf.* Atlanta, GA and Danbury, CT, 1991.

———. *War in the Gulf.* Atlanta, GA and Kansas City, MO, 1991.

Bin, Alberto. *Desert Storm: A Forgotten War.* Westport, CT, 1998.

Bulloch, John and Harvey Morris. *Saddam's War: The Origins of the Kuwait Conflict and the International Response*. London, 1991.

Cornum, Rhonda. *She Went to War: The Rhonda Cornum Story*. Novato, CA, 1993.

Desert Storm: The War in the Persian Gulf. By the editors of Time Magazine; ed. by Otto Friedrich. Boston, 1991.

Dunnigan, James F., and Austin Bay. *From Shield to Storm: High-Tech Weapons . . . Strategy, and Coalition Warfare in the Persian Gulf*. New York, 1991.

Dunnigan, James F., and Raymond Macedonia. *Getting It Right: American Military Reforms after Vietnam to the Persian Gulf. . . .* New York, 1993.

Eagle in the Desert: Looking Back on U.S. Involvement in the Persian Gulf War. [No author or editor given.] Westport, CT, 1996.

Freedman, Lawrence, and Efriam Karsh. *The Gulf Conflict, 1990–1991: Diplomacy and War in the New World Order*. Princeton, NJ, 1992.

Gordon, Michael R. *The Generals' War: The Inside Story of the Conflict in the Gulf*. Boston, 1995.

Hutchison, Kevin Don. *Operation Desert Shield/Desert Storm: Chronology and Fact Book*. Westport, CT, 1995.

Keaney, Thomas A. *Revolution in Warfare? Air Power in the Persian Gulf*. Annapolis, MD, 1995.

Kelly, Michael. *Martyrs-Day: Chronicle of A Small War*. New York, 1993.

Lambeth, Benjamin S. *Learning from the Persian Gulf War*. Santa Monica, CA, 1993.

Mazarr, Michael J. *Desert Storm: The Gulf War and What We Learned*. Boulder, CO, 1993.

Pokrant, Marvin. *Desert Shield at Sea: What the Navy Really Did*. Westport, CT, 1999.

Record, Jeffrey. *Hollow Victory: A Contrary View of the Gulf War*. Washington, DC, 1993.

Reynolds, Richard T. *Heart of the Storm: The Genesis of the Air Campaign against Iraq*. Maxwell AFB, AL, 1995.

Sarkesian, Sam Charles. *Soldiers, Society, and National Security*. Boulder, CO, 1995.

Schofield, Richard. *Kuwait and Iraq: Historical Claims and Territorial Disputes*. London, 1991.

Smith, Graham (ed.). *Weapons of the Gulf War*. Doug Richardson, consultant. New York and London, 1991.

Smith, Jean E. *George Bush's War*. Fort Worth, TX, 1992.

Summers, Harry G., Jr. [Col., USA, ret.]. *On Strategy II: A Critical Analysis of the Gulf War*. New York, 1992.

Wyatt, Thomas C., and Reuven Gal (eds.). *Legitimacy and Commitment in the Military*. Westport, CT, 1990.

Yetiv, Steven A. *The Persian Gulf Crisis*. Westport, CT, 1997.

Norman Schwarzkopf (1934–   )

Schwarzkopf, H. Norman (with Peter Petre). *The Autuobiography: It Doesn't Take a Hero*. New York, 1992.

Bin Sultan, Khaled. *Desert Warrior: A Personal View of the Gulf War by the Joint [Arab] Forces Commander*. New York, 1995.

Brown, Ronald J. *With Marine Forces Afloat in Desert Shield and Desert Storm*. Washington, DC, 1998.

Moore, Molly. *A Woman at War: Storming Kuwait with the U.S. Marines*. New York and Toronto, 1993.

Pagonis, William G. *Moving Mountains: Lessons in Leadership and Logistics from the Gulf War*. Boston, 1992.

Powell, Colin. *My American Journey*. New York, 1995.

Swain, Richard M. *Lucky War: Third Army in Desert Storm*. Fort Leavenworth, KS, 1997.

United States General Accounting Office. *National Guard: Reported Readiness of Combat Brigades . . . Persian Gulf War*. Washington, DC, 1998.

————. *Women in the Military: Deployment in the Persian Gulf War: Report to the Secretary of Defense*. Washington, DC, 1993.

U.S. Army Center of Military History. *The Whirlwind War: The United States Army in Operations Desert Shield and Desert Storm*. Washington, DC, 1995.

Vernon, Alex. *The Eyes of Orion: Five Tank Lieutenants in the Persian Gulf War*. Kent, OH, 1999.

Cohen, Roger, and Claudio Gatti. *In the Eye of the Storm: The Life of General H. Norman Schwarzkopf*. New York, 1991.

Friedman, Norman. *Desert Victory: The War for Kuwait*. Annapolis, 1991.

————. *The US Maritime Strategy*. London and New York, 1988.

Kitfield, James. *Prodigal Soldiers: How the Generation of Officers Born of Vietnam Revolutionized the American Style of War*. New York, 1995.

General References and Bibliographies
Atlas for the Wars of Napoleon

Atlas for the American Civil War. Wayne, NJ, 1986. *Atlas for the Second World War: Europe and the Mediterranean*. Wayne, NJ, 1986. *Atlas for the Second World War: Asia and the Pacific*. Wayne, NJ, 1985. In *West Point Military History Series*. Ed. by Thomas E. Griess.

Caldwell, Ronald J. *The Era of Napoleon: A Bibliography of the History of Western Civilization, 1799–1815*. 2 vols. New York, 1990.

Dictionary of Military History. Ed. by André Corvisier. English edition revised by John Childs. Trans. by Chris Turner. Oxford, 1994.

Duiker, William J. *Historical Dictionary of Vietnam*. Lanham, MD, 1998.

Esposito, Vincent J., Col. (ed.). *West Point Atlas of American Wars*. 2 vols.: *1775–1900*; *1900–1953*. New York, 1959.

Matray, James I. *Historical Dictionary . . . Korean War*. New York, 1991.

McPherson, James M. (ed.). *Atlas of the Civil War*. New York, 1994.

Olson, James S. (ed.). *Dictionary of the Vietnam War*. New York, 1988.

Ross, Steven T. *Historical Dictionary of the Wars of the French Revolution*. Lanham, MD, 1998.

Schwartz, Richard A. *Encyclopedia of the Persian Gulf War*. Jefferson, NC, 1998.

Showalter, Dennis E. *German Military History, 1648–1982: A Critical Bibliography.* New York, 1984.

Summers, Harry G. *Korean War Almanac.* New York, 1990.

———. *Vietnam War Almanac.* New York, 1985.

Tucker, Spencer C. (ed.). *Encyclopedia of the Vietnam War: A Political, Social, and Military History.* Santa Barbara, CA, 1998.